The Fall of the Western Roman Empire

The Fall of the Western Roman Empire

An Archaeological and Historical Perspective

Neil Christie

BLOOMSBURY ACADEMIC

First published in 2011 by

Bloomsbury Academic

An imprint of Bloomsbury Publishing Plc
36 Soho Square, London W1D 3QY, UK
and
175 Fifth Avenue, New York, NY 10010, USA

CIP records for this book are available from the British Library and the Library of Congress.

ISBN 978-1-84966-337-3 (hardback)
ISBN 978-0-34075-966-0 (paperback)
ISBN 978-1-84966-031-0 (ebook)

This book is produced using paper that is made from wood grown in managed, sustainable forests. It is natural, renewable and recyclable. The logging and manufacturing processes conform to the environmental regulations of the country of origin.

Cover image: Jorge Lomonaco/TrekEarth
Cover design: Jim Weaver

www.bloomsburyacademic.com

Contents

Contents

Illustrations

List of Illustrations

Maps

Preface and Acknowledgements

> Whereas the highest aim and function of history is to record events with a minimum of subjectivity and in the light of truth, the details of chronology, intruding irrelevantly like uncalled witnesses, are of no help in this.

The fifth-century pagan Greek historian Eunapius of Sardis offers here an intriguing approach to recounting and presenting the history of the later Roman Empire (his book running from *c.* AD 360 to 404). Tempting though it is to skim over the whens and whys and to look just at the whats, that route is not one open to the modern critical scholar as depth and detail are sought to clarify, interpret and explain. Or at least that can be one excuse for me to try to cover up the fact that this is a book which has been far too long in its gestation, researching, writing, ruminating, finishing and then re-editing – the constant woes of an academic! Scarily, en route to completion, of course, the field has become busy with other, generally much thicker, publications, certainly making this book less unique and more one of many. However, I hope the combining of history and archaeology will offer a different dimension and a wider narrative, drawing in people and places far more than straight history-led tomes.

It is worth noting some recent inspiration to help me through these last, drawn-out phases: in particular, re-reading and, in some cases, first readings of some works by H.G. Wells (1866–1946) have made me think much of 'might have beens'. Wells wrote of the future (e.g. *The War of the Worlds*, published in 1898), but he was also very much a scholar of the past (e.g. *The Outline of History* in 1920), a commentator of the present (such as via *Tono-Bungay*, 1909) and even mixing all together, most notably in *The Shape of Things to Come* (1933). Of note here is his *The War in the Air* (1908), a semi-futuristic novel, recognising fears prior to First World War (and increased by traumas then, as reflected in Wells' later, revised Preface) of the potential collapse of world peace and economies as a result of invasions by airships first from Germany across the Atlantic and from Asia across both Pacific and across Asia and Europe. He compares this collapse with an ancient one (ch. 8, section 1):

> But while the collapse of the previous great civilisation, that of Rome, had been a matter of centuries, had been a thing of phase and phase like the ageing and dying of a man, this, like his killing by railway or motor-car, was one swift, conclusive smashing and an end.

His descriptions of the social, economic, moral, political and religious break-downs as warfare spread and embedded itself and as communications shrivelled are striking. His vivid images of people coping or not (and Wells was very much someone who wrote about people) with food shortages, loss of clean water supplies, disease and plague, breakdowns in industry and technology, mob violence, the rise and fall of local power groups and so on are ones that must have been played out also in many parts of many provinces and in many towns as Roman rule faltered and fragmented in the fifth-century West. We will see in this book how far Wells' image of a slow lingering death for Rome is accurate or whether the 'man' he envisioned was one who suffered and survived injuries, major strokes, patches of good health, disease, shortsightedness, dubious friends and mounting enemies, all before a sudden – if not unexpected – demise.

But thanks likewise go to living inspirations and supporters of my cause: first, I can note the nags from fellow staff, colleagues and students at Leicester especially, plus from colleagues further afield, and suited prompts by the publishers – who have themselves changed with time!); readers of chapters, sections, drafts or simply ideas, plus providers of photographs, include Andrea Augenti, Patty Baker, Pauline Carroll, Tamar Hodos, David Mattingly, Andrew Merrills, Andrew Poulter and Gavin Speed; Debbie Miles-Williams patiently and promptly produced the line drawings (sorry I took so long using them!), and Lou Hannan was always around to provide much needed email support. All advice was welcomed, though there's no guarantee I have remembered or incorporated it all! My brother Ian has always pushed for a 'decline' book told from the archaeological perspective, and I hope he finds this a satisfactory treatment. At Bloomsbury thanks go to Fiona Cairns and Lee Ann Tutton, plus others in the production line, and to the full six anonymous referees for their time, thoughts and recommendations for trimming and bolstering of text! I must also thank Brian Turner at the Ancient World Mapping Center for producing the fine main map of the Western Empire.

Finally, my family continues to cope with the semi-hidden piles of books and articles at home, my red pen scribbles and constant depletion of garibaldi biscuits and of tea supplies – even the dog Alfie seems to sigh when I go fetch another cup of tea to keep the eyes open, but no doubt Jane, Helen, Suzanne and Andrew will be relieved to see that their names are back in print again.

Map of the Western Roman Empire *c.* AD 400

Source: Map © 2010, Ancient World Mapping Center (www.unc.edu/awmc). Used with permission.

S **xx**

QUADI **x**
V.NDIANS

SUEBI **xx**

Barbaricum

Vandals
Marcomanni
Regensburg

Heruls

Augsburg   Lorch   Carnuntum
Noricum   Aquincum
Teurnia   Gorsium
Virunum

Raetia

Aquileia
Brescia
Venice
Verona
Po

PANNONIA

Sirmium

Ravenna   Dalmatia
Pesaro   Split

Pisa

ITALY

Tiber

Rome
Nola
Naples   Brindisi

Sicily
Catania
Carthage   Syracuse

El Djem

Lepcis Magna

Sarmatians

ALANS **x**
HUNS **x**

GREUTHUNGI
OSTROGOTHS

TERVENGI **x**

VISIGOTHS **xx**

Constantinople

Athens

EASTERN ROMAN
EMPIRE

Cyrene

0   250   500   750 Kilometers
0   150   300   450 Miles

x = G 239
xx = K Map 8
pp xxiv - xxv

Introduction:
Questioning Decline in the
Late Roman West

This is now the 60th year since the cruel and savage people of the Vandal race set foot on the territory of wretched Africa. They made an easy passage across the straits, because the vast and broad sea becomes narrow between Spain and Africa, which are separated by only 12 miles ... Finding a province which was at peace and enjoying quiet, the whole land beautiful and flowering on all sides, they set to work on it with their wicked forces, laying it waste by devastation and bringing everything to ruin with fire and murders. They did not even spare the fruit-bearing orchards, in case people who had hidden in the caves of mountains or steep places or any remote areas would be able to eat the foods produced by them after they had passed ... In particular, they gave vent to their wicked ferocity with great strength against the churches and basilicas of the saints, cemeteries and monasteries, so that they burned houses of prayer with fires greater than those they used against the cities and all the towns ... In some buildings, namely great houses and homes ... they smashed the roofs in pieces and levelled the beautiful walls to the ground, so that the former beauty of the towns cannot be deduced from what they look like now.

Thus Victor of Vita (*History*, Book 1, chs 1–4), a Catholic priest in Carthage and later bishop of the see of Vita in the North African province of Byzacena, writing in *c.* AD 484, describes the transition from Roman to Vandal rule. His history is a bitter testimony to the evils perpetrated after half a century of Vandal rule. Victor is bitter particularly for the pains heaped on the orthodox Roman faith: these Vandals and their allies, the Alans, were mainly heretical Arian Christians, and the Arians had sought to gain supremacy, dethroning many Catholic bishops, exiling their clergy and supporters, and encouraging persecution. But Victor was still alive, he remained a Catholic, he held a see and Vandal Africa maintained much of the urban, bureaucratic and economic machinery of late Roman Africa. In this light, Victor disproportionately magnified the griefs caused by the Vandals – though griefs there undoubtedly were, plus exiles, robbings and martyrdoms – to glorify the struggles of the orthodox 'natives'. In reality there had been religious struggles under Rome over heresies, and the Orthodox Church here was long used to troubles – if never on the same scale as under the Vandals. Victor wanted recognition of the turmoils of his fellow Christians: but he could no longer turn to Rome since that city was no longer 'Roman', and his texts were directed at Constantinople, head of the Eastern (but sole surviving) Roman Empire. However, reconquest of North Africa was only achieved by the Byzantines or East Romans in the 530s after Justinian had become emperor.

Other, independent evidence needs considering in discussing the veracity of Victor of Vita's claims of a brutal Vandal regime. Do the towns, ports, villas, rubbish pits and cemeteries of fifth-century North Africa reveal destructions, depopulations and an impoverished economy? Did the transition to Vandal rule in the 430s mark a dramatic downturn in the nature of Roman settlement and in material culture, and was a new, Germanic character superimposed on the provincials? Excavations in towns such as Carthage, Iol Caesarea and Leptiminus; field surveys in their hinterlands and elsewhere; analysis of church remains; and studies of coins and ceramics all combine to inform us (perhaps more accurately) of the levels of material change and transition. For example, Victor of Vita (Book 1, chs 8 and 9) reports the following:

> And there are very many cities with few or no inhabitants, for after these events the ones which survive lie desolate; for example, here at Carthage they [the Vandals] utterly destroyed the odeon, the theatre, the temple of Memoria and what people used to call the *Via Caelestis*. To speak only of the most noteworthy things, in their tyrannical presumption they delivered over to their religion the basilica of the Ancestors where the bodies of the saints Perpetua and Felicitas are buried, the basilica of Celerina and the Scillitani, and others which they had not destroyed.

The image is dramatic. But how does the archaeology compare?[1] The site of Carthage in modern Tunisia has benefited from large-scale international projects, supporting UNESCO's call in 1972 to save and recover the city's long heritage. Projects since the mid-1970s have examined various areas and monuments within and outside the old urban space as well as elucidating the defensive sequence. Most importantly for our purposes, many vital data have been retrieved on the late Roman, Vandal and Byzantine epochs. The picture revealed is, as might be expected, varied. Although the later sequences at the odeon and theatre mentioned by Victor are not known, the Temple of the Memoria has been unearthed as a circular, commemorative Christian funerary structure: documented by contemporaries as active *c*. AD 400, the excavators showed that the Vandal occupation did mark its destruction, with some portions given over to poor housing (it was, however, restored under the Byzantines a century later). Similarly, a Byzantine double-apsed, five-aisled complex with baptistery and chapel was found to overlie and incorporate materials and walls from an earlier (presumed cathedral) church and nearby private structures, all abandoned and demolished in the fifth century. This may well be an instance of deliberate slighting of a Catholic focus.

In contrast, there are good examples of continuity – of people in terms of cemeteries and rubbish deposits and of buildings and churches. Thus, in the same zone as the presumed cathedral, a fine palace-house with new mosaics of *c*. AD 400 as well as contemporary (pagan/classical) sculptures remained in use into the Byzantine period and even gained additional mosaics in the porticoes in the Vandal period. To the north-west, at the 'Villa of the Baths', its thermal establishment had plenty of coins to show usage from *c*. AD 390 to 600. Despite the fact that the famous circular port of Carthage silted up in the fifth century, the main commercial port continued, and imports in the city and exports across the Mediterranean signify much trade traffic. Meanwhile, more recent excavations at Bir Ftouha in Carthage's northern suburbs have explored a pilgrimage complex, whose main unit was a five-aisled basilica church of 60 m × 35 m, with a 5-m-wide apse containing three carefully positioned tombs, undoubtedly those of martyrs or saints or else housing the bodies of privileged persons (e.g. abbots). An ambulatory behind the apse connected to an annex; mosaics (part robbed in early excavations) adorned the floors and perhaps even some tomb covers. Chronologically, the basilica runs from c. AD 450 to 520; the annex and mosaics belong to the early to mid-sixth century, with much of the marble architectural material Byzantine in date (i.e. post 533). In sum, the site not only was active in the Vandal period but was also built then; the subsequent Byzantine phase provided elaborations, enhancing its pilgrimage status, probably by reinvesting income generated by the pilgrim traffic.

This is not to say that Victor wrongly blamed the Vandals for massive urban destruction, but to state that archaeology currently paints a far less bleak image. Archaeology is not an exact science, of course, and a complex such as Bir Ftouha may, with fuller excavation, reveal evidence for burning or some sign that it was in fact an Arian foundation, re-dedicated after Byzantine reconquest. Victor had an agenda and he naturally modified some 'facts': thus, while he attributes the destruction of the *Via Caelestis* to the Vandals, other texts show earlier damages. In particular, the aptly named Quodvultdeus ('what God wishes'), bishop of Carthage for the earliest phase of Vandal occupation (AD 438–50s), although he does record how 'the hand of the Vandals has now destroyed the Sacred Way without leaving any reminder of it', also recounts how the vast, 'long-closed' pagan temple of Caelestis, infested by thickets and snakes, had been razed to the ground by Christians in c.420 – thus prompting the decay of both zone and roadway. In effect the Vandals merely completed the task. Without the text and pleading of Victor of Vita, one might struggle to identify any political and military takeover of Carthage and North Africa; after all, most houses, baths, churches, farms, coins and trade do continue, and burials persist in extramural cemeteries.

This is just one example to bear in mind as this study of the late Empire begins. Much of the archaeology is relatively new and was not available to such major scholars of the Roman and Byzantine Empires as Gibbon, Mommsen, Bury, Stein or Jones, who first framed and explored Rome's Decline and Fall. In the absence of clear material evidence, it is easy to give full credence to the words of contemporary generals, statesmen, bishops or monks, even if we recognise that all carry their own explicit or implicit messages and goals. For example, a Christian annalist or 'apologist' like Orosius, whose hardly subtle *Seven Books of History against the Pagans*, compiled in 417–18, rails against the evil past and its wars, plagues, floods and miseries prompted by paganism and claims that better times had come with God as the Empire's guide: 'countless wars have been stilled, many usurpers destroyed, and most savage tribes

3

checked, confined, incorporated, or annihilated with little bloodshed, with no real struggle, and almost without loss' (VII, 43). Orosius is ignoring, of course, traumas inflicted in a fully Christian era such as the loss of Britain, the Rhine and with Vandals and Visigoths on the prowl inside the frontiers; he even views some positives in Alaric's sack of Rome such as the security of the churches and God's protection of these shrines via their saints.[2] These sources can at times deal with the mundane, but in general they condense the past and point to loss, rupture, change, problems and concerns, which add up to form a wider image of decline of culture, security and Romanitas. Does the archaeology offer a much different perspective? Does studying walls built to defend a Roman town bring us closer to how town councils, citizens and State operated? Can the occupation and defensive sequence at a frontier fort or the building history of a church demonstrate more the processes of change across the time span? This volume targets a balanced view between text/history and material/archaeology – neither to cancel each other out nor to favour one over the other but to show how archaeology provides its own eyes to observe and discuss this period of significant political reworking of Europe and the Mediterranean. How clear and how tangible the material evidence is will emerge as we examine diverse facets of the late Roman West.

The chronological coverage runs from the third to the sixth centuries AD, spanning in turn near fatal anarchy and civil war, the onset of barbarian raids, Christian acceptance and pagan decay, more civil war and larger-scale barbarian assaults and movements, and a progressive fragmentation in the fifth century of the Western Roman Empire – but with the East Empire surviving and indeed prospering after Rome's 'Fall'. Arguably, as Chapter 1 of this book will show, the troubles hit the Western Empire most, and although the East had its fair share of northern problems, notably with Gothic and Hunnic assaults, raids, intrigues and takeovers, this Empire was wealthier, with a more populous and deeper rooted urbanism, and with generally more civilised neighbours – that is, the Persians/Parthians/Sassanians – who fought war in more orderly terms; the East could soak up and deflect her enemies more effectively, and change within its confines was less substantial. Thus, as the Western Empire begins to fragment in the fifth century, we see towns, landscapes and elites struggling, whereas many contemporary towns in the East show growth and maintained elite participation. Indeed, town wall building in the East began in serious fashion only from the end of the fifth century, two centuries after various centres in Gaul had become fortified.

It is important to stress that the 'late Empire' examined here is no short period of rapid blows which brought Rome down: it is a long 200–300 year time span which saw varied modes and levels of conflict, renewal, adaptation as well as ordinary living; change happened everywhere, but at differing times, rates and depths, and this change is documented to varying degrees, with some areas such as Britain largely devoid of coherent text. Yet literary outputs in Spain, Gaul and Italy show the fourth century as highly active, while archaeologies of trade, urbanism and landscape similarly show that despite the wars so often highlighted, farming, living and producing continued without major disruption in many provinces. Indeed, Roman Britain in the third century and the first half of the fourth century did very well for itself in terms of agricultural output, rural estates and mosaic production, even if urban monumental expressions of this period are relatively few. Throughout the fourth century, however, wider politico-military events did impact across all the provinces, and expressions of these changes are becoming more evident or better understood through archaeology. Older analyses of the final centuries of Rome in the West are ones dominated by barbarians and the efforts of the emperors to hold the tide of 'others' at bay; they play down the Empire's internal rebellions and usurpations, and largely ignore the actual centres of power and population and the material expressions of defence and change. Newer studies are much more aware of the need to explore material responses on the ground.

Questions therefore to be asked include the following: What are the historical sequences of the last centuries of Roman rule in the West? Where were the main impacts inside and outside and how did the State and the provinces respond? Is the picture one of increasing militarisation? Are both the fourth and fifth centuries periods of high insecurity on battered frontiers and in threatened provinces? To what degree do the economy and the landscape reflect an Empire in transition? Was the loss of Roman rule the moment at which decline appeared or accelerated, or was a decline evident long before? What sequences occur on the frontiers, in the armies, in the towns? Are the settlements of the fifth century dramatically different from those of the early Empire? How does Christianity impact on the Empire – was its intrusion supportive and did it offer cohesion? How did the Church express itself in town and country, and how far did this overturn older displays of Roman culture? In sum, what can we chart of the 'Decline and Fall' in the Roman West? While this book is designed to highlight the archaeology, documentary evidence will be flagged throughout to show where the archaeology can and cannot contribute; Chapter 1 in this book is necessarily more strongly history oriented to frame the evolving political, military and demographic contexts explored in other chapters, but archaeological inputs will also be noted here.

The late Roman period has become a topical one in the past decade especially, avoiding the older approach of gloomy postscripts or short, sweeping over-views and offering detailed, critical analyses of a fuller raft of sources: there is now an array of scholarly books taking either a purely historical focus or blending in some elements of archaeology – prominent are works by Averil Cameron, Peter Heather, Guy Halsall, Matthew Innes, Michael Kulikowski, Wolf Liebeschuetz, Stephen Mitchell, Bryan Ward-Perkins and Chris Wickham, who are all far better placed than me to interrogate the documentary sources especially. Halsall in particular has interrogated text and material to strong effect, and his *Barbarian Migrations and the Roman West, 376–568* (Halsall 2007) provides authoritative coverage beyond the period I am covering here. As important are the revised volumes (XIII and XIV) of the *Cambridge Ancient*

History and the first of the *New Cambridge Medieval History*, each full of excellent summary analyses of periods, peoples, culture, administration, religion, military and so on and with substantial bibliographies.[3] Furthermore, many more late antique and early medieval works are being translated and made available for historical and archaeological consumption.[4]

An important trend has been to see Rome's decay in the West over a longer span of time: much more is nowadays discussed in the context of 'Late Antiquity', extending from the third to seventh centuries in the Mediterranean especially, recognising that towns, Church, trade, coinage, art and so on persisted on many levels, if undergoing processes of transformation en route. The very vocabulary used to address this period is more guarded or at least far less clear-cut and pessimistic: few scholars now use the labels 'Collapse' and 'Decline and Fall' (although Ward-Perkins deliberately and provocatively uses these words in his title, and Heather's popular works – like this one – still draw on the long-established Gibbonian phrase to grab attention) and opt increasingly for more open terms such as 'transition', 'change', 'continuity and discontinuity' and 'transformation'.[5] Much impetus came from the influential 1990s European Science Foundation–funded programme of workshops, conferences and publications on the theme *The Transformation of the Roman World*, exploring the period AD 400–900 through a strongly interdisciplinary approach, combining the expertise and debates of an array of established and younger historians, archaeologists, art historians, architectural historians and numismatists.[6] These discussions and analyses have all contributed to overhauling and expanding what had previously been a poorly studied and understood period, weak in both textual and archaeological survivals, and prompting new programmes of research and fieldwork. To a degree, however, as some historians have identified, this image of extended 'transformation' can at times gloss over the fact that the fourth to sixth centuries did witness some brutal and very bloody episodes, major dislocations of people and fierce power struggles, and that discontinuities were as strong as continuities.

As noted, archaeologists are much involved in this rethinking of the late Roman, late antique and early medieval period. Their role should indeed be prominent in uncovering the changes in lifestyles, buildings, spaces, landscapes and economies across the time span, and in giving clearer images to the different provincial sequences and to the new peoples and barbarians that begin to take to the stage.[7] New finds, excavations, surveys and analyses provide the data for such reconstructions, and ever more effort is meanwhile focused on enhancing techniques for observing and recording the (sometimes fleeting) traces of late Roman to medieval activity in town and country, in active or abandoned sites, either from research-driven projects or through rescue/developer-led archaeology and for refining chronologies of the material culture and debris recovered. At the same time, we can also draw upon standing archaeology as tangible guides to the period: churches and town walls especially are notable survivals in various Roman provinces, sometimes altered and expanded but still giving clear expression of the changing late Roman world.

Particular note can go to the conference publication series *Late Antique Archaeology* where valuable themes are being explored, including warfare, technology and, equally importantly, theory and method, and proper East–West communication is being encouraged.[8] Archaeology is also at the forefront of key syntheses for specific countries/provinces, notably North Africa, Italy, Spain, Switzerland and the Danube zone.[9] In these, and throughout scholarship into Late Antiquity, towns and urbanism and their fates and fortunes are dominant themes, questioning the old view of an eclipse of classical urban life, exploring urban roles in the new barbarian kingdoms and contrasting trajectories between Eastern and Western Empires.[10] Individual site-based analyses have shown themselves to be equally valuable in charting how blanket discussions of urban change or loss are not always viable.[11]

Objects, buildings, bodies and art further have been central to a spate of important museum exhibitions (many being suitably migratory) with related catalogues; recent notable exhibitions in Italy, for example, include ones on Milan, Ravenna, Rome, the Goths, the Vandals and the Lombards.[12] A very prominent international venture was *Rome and the Barbarians. The Birth of a New World* (2008), a combined effort by Italian, German and French museums and institutions (chiefly in Venice, Rome and Bonn), with objects gathered from a host of public and private collections. At 700 (large) pages long, beautifully illustrated (including maps), the catalogue features an extensive range of short and longer commentaries and analyses by experts of themes and objects in the late Roman and barbarian world – states, peoples, invasions, art, culture, weapons, religion and death; the whole reveals the mass of material available for study but, as importantly, identifies the value of studying a time frame (in this instance *c.* AD 200–900) which is marked by the emergence of a whole 'new world' or sets of worlds in the breakup of Roman control. My own book in no way matches the latter publication for scale, weight, images and for the assemblage of scholarship, but hopefully it will offer some useful archaeological insights into what remains a period of major change and ongoing fascination.

1

The Fall of the Late Roman West: Contexts of Change, AD 200–500

INTRODUCTION

Although writing nearly four centuries before the fall of Rome, the great Roman historian Tacitus provides an apt starting point for a historical overview of the later Empire. One of his principal works is *Germania*, which, drawing on lost works by Pliny among other sources, offers a unique ethnographic and part-historical analysis of the peoples Rome had encountered, fought with or heard of across the firmly established Rhine and Danube frontiers.[1] Tacitus orders and classifies some of the bewildering array of names, framing many as allies or as enemies and providing rough geographical ordering of these; he speaks also of more distant peoples, such as the Gutones, Rugii and Suinones and others by the northern seas (the Baltic). He outlines aspects such as numbers, reliability and ferocity of these peoples and gives some idea of how stable or mobile certain of the groups were. Rome's creation of frontiers and her economic clout seem in fact to have prompted the formation of some of these tribal identities, with the Empire keen to treat with coherent groups and their leaders[2]; frequently, such mediation was encouraged via financial or even military support from the Roman authorities, thereby tying the tribal heads to Rome. Occasionally, Rome imposed or recommended rulers or chiefs to help support trade links or to create buffers over the frontiers, as with the Batavi, who, Tacitus (*Germania*, ch. 29) reports,

> still retain an honourable privilege in token of their ancient alliance with us. They are not subjected to the indignity of tribute or ground down by the tax-gatherer. Free from imposts and special levies, and reserved for employment in battle, they are like weapons and armour – 'only to be used in war'. We exercise the same suzerainty over the Mattiaci; for the greatness of Rome has spread the awe of her Empire even beyond the Rhine and the old frontiers. In geographical position they are on the German side, in heart and soul they are with us.

Tacitus particularly recognises how some power struggles had aided the Empire by keeping threats away, although he states (*Germania*, ch. 33) anxieties too:

> The Bructeri were defeated and annihilated by a coalition of neighbouring tribes. Perhaps they were hated for their domineering pride; or it may have been the lure of booty, or some special favour accorded us by the gods. We were even permitted to witness the battle. More than 60,000 were killed ... Long, I pray, may foreign nations persist, if not in loving us, at least in hating one another; for destiny is driving our Empire upon its appointed path, and fortune can bestow on us no better gift than discord among our foes.

Rome was playing a complex game on the frontiers, but in Tacitus' day the imperial authorities had the stronger hand and plenty of soldiery and money to back it up. The coins, pottery, bronze and silver work, and wine found in the 'Barbaricum' over the frontiers certainly signify the wide audience responding to and feeding off Rome. A constancy of this feeding enabled stability, but the fear expressed by Tacitus was that some of these peoples (both named and unknown) might want to change the rules or to have much more of the materials on offer.

Below we chart the first serious changes to this balance towards the end of the second century AD. This will provide a valuable background to the more serious conflicts that wracked the Empire across the third century and which led to the creation of a much changed political and military entity ('Map of the Western Roman Empire *c.* AD 400', p. xii). From there the key events, names and peoples of the fourth and fifth centuries will be discussed to identify how the Roman Empire in the West adapted and mutated; these provide the historical context for assessing in other chapters the forms and fortunes of frontiers, towns, lands and populations in the last centuries of Roman rule.

THE MARCOMANNIC WARS

If the reign of Antoninus Pius is widely viewed as one of the most pacific and prosperous of the Empire, that of Marcus Aurelius (161–80) witnessed a maelstrom of military problems as war against Parthia first broke out and soldiery were transferred eastwards from both Rhine and Danube provinces to re-establish stability, only then for the northern defences to be assailed in AD 166 by sudden incursions by two tribes, the Marcomanni and Quadi. These tribes boldly penetrated into north-east Italy, destroying the town of Oderzo and laying siege to the commercial hub of Aquileia at the head of the Adriatic. How many raids were involved here, what their exact targets were, and the scale of the forces are unclear, but still in 170 they were causing severe problems in Pannonia which the Romans could little check.[3] The documentary sources are frustratingly scanty for this and later episodes, but there is sufficient epigraphic (tombstones, formal dedications, tile stamps) evidence to reveal some of the major Roman responses: the raising of three new Italic legions; creating a defensive barrier, labelled the *Praetentura Italiae et Alpium*, based around forts in the Julian Alps region; a subsequent reinforcement of the Danube frontier (*limes*) with legionary forts at Albing and Regensburg; plus counteroffensives into Marcomannic territories in AD 171–2 especially.[4] Marcus Aurelius was fully involved, basing himself at the key fort of Carnuntum, at the threshold to Quadi territory: in 169 he met Quadic embassies from these, brokering a treaty with them and securing the release, once peace was formalised and payments made, of a full 63,000 captives. Marcus' military campaigns otherwise centred on the Marcomanni, perhaps even with the aim of carving out a new province.

Here we can flag the essential input of archaeology. First, there are finds of *militaria* or Roman military dress items, such as brooches and belt fittings found north of Carnuntum and along the March Valley, sometimes in destroyed Germanic settlements. Some *militaria* should denote Roman troop advances – and losses – but others might represent Germans on the Roman side, equipped with Roman military dress. As support for the latter, the spectacular royal or princely chamber tomb at Mušov merits comment[5]: located *c.*80 km north of the Danube in southern Bohemia, the likely focus of the Marcomannic territory, the chamber contained at least two male burials and a possible female inhumation, with a mass of accompanying grave goods. Although the tomb had been robbed in antiquity, numerous scattered and broken fragments of some of the less valuable artefacts remained: these comprised a mix of Germanic and imported Roman goods, the latter including bronze, silver, glass and ceramic bowls, cups and lamps; there were eight pairs of silver inlaid spurs, plus shield decorations, lances and arrows, and dress fittings. The most recent objects date the tomb to *c.* AD 170, and thus tightly to the war period. The Roman materials could show the deceased as members of a pro-Roman royal family, either newly elevated (but rapidly dead) or members of the tribe that had supported the Roman cause. How long he/they celebrated the Roman victory is unknown. As importantly, the tomb can be linked to a Roman takeover of the Marcomannic royal hill fort of Mušov-Burgstall, just 1.5 km distant, reutilised as a temporary Roman military headquarters for the Tenth Legion from Vindobona in AD 172 and 177.[6] Another Roman fortress lay at nearby Neurissen in whose defensive ditch were discovered remains of 33 individuals, interpreted by the excavators as executed Marcomannic prisoners. That Burgstall formed the launch pad for Roman campaigns in central *Marcomannia* is indicated by the presence of at least 10 'marching camps' to both south and north and at least 2-km-long blocking ditch between the Thaya and Jihlava Valleys.[7]

On the Roman frontier itself, structural reactions during and after the wars required vast logistical input. The construction of the 382-km-long earth bank and ditch from the Rhine to Lorch and that of the 166-km stonewall forming the Raetian section of the *limes* from Lorch to the Danube remains insecurely dated, but these mammoth projects were probably direct responses to the incursions. Given their scale, the estimate is for 15 years of building activity.[8]

The reasons for the Marcomannic and Quadic incursions are disputed: Were they opportunist, observing a weakened Roman frontier, perhaps debilitated by the 'Antonine plague' in AD 165, and charging in for plunder? Why venture into Italy? Surely they would have expected vicious retributions from Rome for such an act? Were the attacks prompted by internal troubles – individual power struggles and war groups seeking glory and prizes? Or was there some external threat on these, such as new, northerly groups of barbarians creating tension on their territories? While no new powers exploit the zone after the wars (both peoples continue to be attested here until the fifth century), it is notable that the Marcomanni–Quadi attacks came shortly after a less successful raid against the Danube – repulsed by Roman frontier forces – by a claimed 6,000 Langobards and Obii at the very end of AD 166 (Cassius Dio, 72.1). The Langobards (or Lombards) are previously attested by Tacitus as located by the mouth of the Elbe and so their presence on the Danube is confusing, but might well suggest roving mercenaries, seeking glory and exploits to take home; at the same time, they signify something unstable and aggressive in the more northerly tracts of *Germania*. The later *Historia Augusta* (Marcus Aurelius, 14.1) refers to Marcomanni and Victuali provoking the war because of distant threats and a desire for lands inside the Empire.[9] East European archaeologists and historians in fact place the arrival of the Vandals and Sarmatians in the areas of modern east Hungary and Slovakia to the mid-second century AD, thus just prior to the Marcomannic Wars; riding equipment from burials in these zones points to highly mobile warrior groups who may well have been pressurising westerly groups such as the Quadi.[10]

The claim that some of these protagonists sought settlement on Roman soil is striking: in fact, Marcus Aurelius settled some of the defeated groups in the Danubian provinces, to be drawn upon for military support. Others were settled near Ravenna in north Italy, presumably to colonise the marshy land near the Po, but this experiment backfired since Cassius Dio (72.11) reports that some of these rebelled and even briefly took control of the town. This episode may be atypical: the lack of visibility of nearly all the resettled groups (such as a claimed 5,500 Sarmatians/Iazyges transferred as auxiliary soldiers to Britain in AD 175) should indicate that these did merge satisfactorily with the Romanised populations.[11]

A final, essential issue regards trade between Rome and her neighbours after these wars. Previously the frontier zones had formed gateways of interaction with lands beyond: archaeological finds from burials and settlements demonstrate how Roman ceramics, metalwork, glass, wine and coins were traded well beyond the frontiers, certainly beyond the immediate bordering groups, as far as Denmark and the Baltic. Such assemblages are generally interpreted as denoting tribal chiefs or nobility benefiting from and displaying ties with Rome, either via trade or gift exchange, and using these goods to enhance their status.[12] Did Roman material still cross the Danube frontier after AD 172? Or was there a break in the flow of goods on which so many of the 'alliances' and bonds of allegiance (even within tribes) in the 'Barbaricum' probably depended? Interestingly, for the old Marcomannic territory, imports do resume; probably the Roman authorities wanted something of the former *status quo* to be renewed to reassure both local provincial populations and friendlier peoples over the frontier. But Cassius Dio (72.15) suggests a more cautious policy prevailed:

> When the Marcomanni sent envoys to him, Marcus [Aurelius], in view of the fact that they had fulfilled all the conditions imposed upon them, albeit grudgingly and reluctantly, restored to them one-half of the neutral zone along their frontier, so that they might settle to within a distance of five miles from the Danube; and he established the places and the days for their trading together (for these had not been previously fixed) and exchanged hostages with them.

Roman ceramics on transdanubian soil peak in the third century under the Severans, but by c. AD 250, problems had set in, with production disrupted badly by insecurities in Gaul (see below); while some later third- and even fourth-century finds are attested (such as imports from North Africa), these may represent no more than 'sporadic' exchanges and in no way match the healthy commerce of the second century.[13] Did this damaged flow of goods weaken ties between Rome and her barbarian allies and other groups beyond? The southward push by groups in the Marcomannic Wars made these aware of the rich pickings across the frontiers: the sources stress how towns and farms were robbed and much booty gathered. In the modified northern world of the late second century, individual martial strength perhaps became the new mode of power display. Cassius Dio suggests money was now a key demand by the enemy groups – either to help Rome, to withdraw or to stay neutral; as yet there is no clear archaeological proof of a fuller influx of coin over the frontiers, perhaps because much was melted down for reuse for jewellery.

Spectacular 'lake offerings' much further north in Denmark, and especially in Jutland, offer other insights. Best explored are the deposits of military equipment and feasting debris recovered at Illerup Ådal, featuring no less than 15,000 weapons (Figure 1.1). These cover episodes from the first to the late fifth century AD, but with the most prominent relating to a conflict in around AD 200, with local forces victorious over invaders deriving from present-day Norway and western Sweden.[14] There are numerous swords, baldrics, sheath fittings and belt elements whose Roman origins are shown by workshop stamps, design and manufacturing technique, and occasional symbols of gods, war or victory. The stamps were even imitated by a more local armourer, one Wagnico, presumably tied to the court of one or more Nordic chiefs and maybe even an arms dealer with ties to Rome. Potentially, the Nordic sword owners had gained these as booty from raids, perhaps in service with southerly Germanic tribes; but more likely the Roman weapons denote an elite-directed trade, whose scale might signify a formal import to tribal groups right on the fringes of the known world, but who presumably could serve a distant function to Rome, such as in raiding other groups perceived as future threats. The evidence certainly identifies a growing power centred on

Figure 1.1 Illerup Ådal, Jutland. Excavation image of some of the sacrificial weapons cast into the lake and denoting spoil from Nordic forces defeated in c. AD 200 (photo courtesy of Prof. Ilkjær, Moesgård Museum and www.illerup.dk)

the island of East Zealand[15]: its burial ground at Himlingøje features 13 rich burials which include amongst their furnishings Roman imports (bronze, glass) and gold jewellery. This may be the focal point to a dynastic group, with branches of control and allegiances across southern Scandinavia and the Baltic. Did some East Zealand warriors participate in the Marcomannic Wars – maybe fighting for, rather than against, Rome, and obtaining rewards which boosted this south Scandinavian power? Perhaps the Illerup deposits signify East Zealand attacks north to quell Nordic enemies, with the booty brought back to Jutland. If so, was Rome playing games in the Scandinavian arena, supporting East Zealand's elite yet supplying also groups in Norway to try and destabilise this new south Scandinavian unity? The irony is that the Roman swords failed to bring victory to the Nordic warriors, but then victory would have meant that the Illerup sacrificial deposit would not have happened and archaeologists would have been deprived of this valuable insight into otherwise undocumented Rome–Scandinavia interactions.

This discussion of the Marcomannic Wars period and some of the related archaeology hopefully reveals how a complex net of contacts existed between Rome and the tribes over the northern frontiers. Some contacts were secured through trade and alliances, but others were more shadowy. Arguably it was a fine balance: disruptions within and without could easily upset this and prompt change. For the Marcomannic and Quadic assaults, these were known Germanic powers with whom Rome could treat; it would be much harder where threats came from further afield, although the East Zealand and Jutland archaeologies show how Rome was aware of some of these more distant players. The above discussion also highlighted key issues that would dog Rome for the next three centuries and play major roles in Rome's decline: (i) aggressive enemies on multiple fronts; (ii) the displacement of non-Roman groups, many seeking security within Roman confines; (iii) Rome's responses – aggressive, diplomatic, concessionary; (iv) damage to the frontier provinces and their populations; (v) damage to the frontier defences; (vi) demands on the Roman military; (vii) internal threats (such as succession problems); (viii) communications and logistics – responding to threats and supporting the military; and (ix) maintaining order (over the frontiers, on the frontiers, inside the frontiers). The old stability had been punctured; subsequent events were to fracture this even more seriously.

THE THIRD-CENTURY CRISIS

Marcus Aurelius' successor Commodus had no intention to annex *Marcomannia* or *Sarmatia*; he instead secured affairs through consolidation of the *limites*. His preference was the city of Rome and its opportunities for display, although his rule here was 'weak, capricious and despotic' and he built up enemies rapidly, eventually culminating in his assassination. Internal power struggles erupted, with the authority of the professional bodyguards, the Praetorian Guard, holding sway, offering the throne to bidders – the senator Julianus duly purchased power, paying 25,000 sesterces to each of the soldiers, but he only lasted a few months. The potential power of the military was then exploited by generals in Britain, Pannonia and Syria, feeding a 4-year civil war from AD 193, which drew soldiers and attention away from the frontiers, although fortunately for Rome, such gaps were not fatal. By the time Septimius Severus finally gained control (after subduing multiple internal and external threats), the Empire was in a fragile state; however, firm rule ensured order was restored and the economy slowly recovered. Severus also encouraged many a town to undertake a new phase of public building or renewal, as evident in Britain and Dacia, and Severus expended much effort and State grants on the North African provinces – his homeland.[16] His successors Caracalla and Heliogabalus showed few abilities and the dynasty ended with the murder in 235 of Severus Alexander in Mainz on the Rhine frontier – this was the first time since Hadrian that an emperor had visited that zone (he had been trying to broker a peace deal to avoid armed conflict).

The Severan demise set in motion what is generally labelled the 'Third-Century Crisis': over the period *c.* AD 235–85, Rome's Empire was internally and externally shaken and battered and countless short-lived emperors and usurpers fought for and against the Empire, variously fighting barbarians or utilising the same to help in their own struggles (Map 1.1); the State's finances were crippled as vast funds were required to pay and equip armies, bribe enemies, restore or extend fortifications; and landscapes in the frontier regions especially were rendered highly insecure, seriously affecting farming and trade. The picture painted by the texts is fairly bleak, inevitably concentrating on the northern and eastern frontiers, and ignoring territories such as Britain, Spain and North Africa which in fact largely avoided military upheavals.[17] But what must be stressed is that blame does not lie fully in the lap of the 'barbarians',[18] since Roman sources record just as many traumas caused through innumerable civil wars. Events, names, dates and impacts are multiple and are impossible to convey easily. Instead, here we can exploit the words of

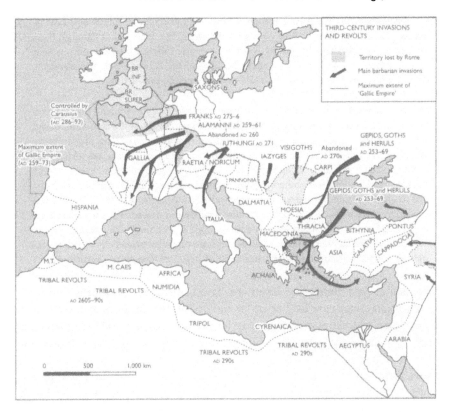

Map 1.1   Map of the main third-century revolts and barbarian incursions in the Empire

Eutropius, a 'Right Honourable Secretary of State for General Petitions', whose *Breviarium* or *Abbreviated History of Rome*, although not admired among modern scholars, was highly popular in the Middle Ages, offering a no-frills summary in 10 short books of 1,118 years of Roman history up to AD 369. Eutropius rattles through names of third-century emperors, usurpers, enemies and battles, pausing to cast occasional judgement. Here we quote from his Book IX for the period AD 245–70, to gain a flavour of the upheavals:

Ch. 4: After these Decius, who was born at Budalia in lower Pannonia, assumed power. He suppressed a civil war which had been fomented in Gaul, and made his son Caesar. He built a bath at Rome. When he and his son had ruled for two years both were killed in barbarian territory. They were enrolled among the gods.

Ch. 5: Subsequently Gallus Hostilianus and Volusianus, the son of Gallus, were chosen emperors. Under them Aemilianus rebelled in Moesia. When both had set out to crush him, they were killed at Interamna without completing two years in power. They achieved nothing at all remarkable. Their reign was notable only for the plague, diseases and afflictions. ...

Ch. 7: Consequently Licinius Valerian, who was serving in Raetia and Noricum, was made emperor by the army and subsequently Augustus. Gallienus too was acclaimed Caesar by the Senate at Rome. Their reign was ruinous and almost fatal to Roman authority, whether through the misfortune of the emperors or through their indolence. The Germans advanced as far as Ravenna. Valerian, while waging war in Mesopotamia, was overcome by Sapor, the king of the Persians, was subsequently captured, and grew old in ignominious servitude among the Parthians.

Ch. 8: Gallienus, although he had been made Augustus as quite a young man, at first governed the Empire successfully, afterwards appropriately, but at the end disastrously. For, as a young man he achieved a great deal with vigour in Gaul and Illyricum. At Mursa he killed Ingenuus, who had seized the purple, and Trebellianus. For a long time he was peaceful and calm, but subsequently, after abandoning himself to every kind of debauchery, he relaxed the reins of government with cowardly inaction and despair. The Alamanni devastated the Gauls and penetrated Italy. Dacia, which had been added beyond the Danube by Trajan, was lost at that time. Greece, Macedonia, Pontus and Asia were devastated by the Goths. Pannonia was ravaged by the Sarmatians and Quadi, the Germans penetrated the Spanish provinces and stormed the renowned city of Tarragona, and the Parthians occupied Mesopotamia and had begun to claim Syria for themselves.

From such abrupt summaries, historians have easily come to perceive the third century as an era of near fatal crisis for the Roman Empire: internal revolts particularly tore at Rome and at provinces, with different armies seeking their own puppet emperors; barbarian incursions almost seem incidental, and Eutropius indeed barely comments on their impact, duration and scale. Yet, for long, coin hoards, datable on the basis of the most recent coin issue, have been used to plot the direction of barbarian invasions and raids, and rarely are they associated with internal rebellions by Roman generals and troops.[19] At the very least, the wide distribution of coin hoards signifies a high state of insecurity across many provinces. A problem lies in having few hoards where context, contents and composition can be fully scrutinised to show whether they relate to panic measures during or in advance of raids, whether hidden under a floor, in a field and so on. One invaluable hoard, found in 1741 at Lunnern near Zurich, comprising gold jewellery plus (since lost) silver coins, had been hidden in a recess in a house wall; its non-recovery points strongly to the owners either being killed or carried off.[20]

Where destructions of sites are recognised archaeologically, as at the presumed *mansio* or road station at Le Thovey, Faverges (ancient Casuaria) near Geneva, whose bathhouse and other structures were 'apparently put to the torch by a band of roving Alaman raiders in the year 270',[21] we must be cautious in claiming that these destructions were not accidental – especially in a bathhouse with fires, kilns and stockpiles of wood for heating. But if a consistent range of evidence emerges – such as collapsed and burnt buildings, abandoned rooms, rebuilding over such layers which have been levelled, bodies, broken possessions – across a number of buildings in a given site or across a number of towns and farms, then attribution of a destruction to external foes is possible; but in the confusion of the third century, some assaults may relate to the evils of civil war. For Roman Germany, destruction deposits are evident at Xanten and Augst; the assaults prompted rapid construction of urban citadels at a variety of centres including Augst where the new defended space enclosed just 3 ha. More dramatic are the remains of slaughtered civilians thrown into ditches and wells at Speyer, Pforzheim and Harting; at the latter, a rural site, 'ritual execution' by Alamanni may account for the bodies of a family group who were apparently tortured, scalped before their skulls were crushed and their bodies thrown into a well.[22] Retrieval of such evidence is rare (often because citizens could clean up debris, bodies would be buried), thus obscuring what might well have been widespread instances of massacre, rape, enslavement, looting and burning.

Of major interest is the 'Victory Altar' discovered in 1992 in Augsburg, capital of the Raetian province.[23] Dating to the reign of Postumus (whose name was later chiselled out when his rule was damned) and specifically to AD 260/1, it first shows that Postumus' 'Gallic Empire' – he had created a rival power centred on Gaul – at least briefly extended beyond the provinces of Gaul, Germany, Spain and Britain to infiltrate the Danube region and thus threaten the other emperor in Italy; second, it indicates that alongside civil war the Raetian governor and army had to cope with incursions by 'barbarian peoples', namely the Iouthungi, 'otherwise known as Semnones'. The inscription records how victory meant 'many thousands' of Italian captives were restored, indicating that these barbarians were retreating from Italy where the rightful Emperor Gallienus had managed to defeat them in late 259; that Gallienus had not pursued them might suggest that his victory was not wholly successful. Finally, the altar records that people from the Raetian capital also fought the Iouthungi, implying hastily enrolled civilian militia to aid Augsburg's defence.

When major conflicts with the Goths occurred, Rome was fortunate to find resourceful soldier-emperors like Claudius II (Gothicus) and Aurelian – only for the former to die (atypically a natural, but premature death) after 2 years and the latter through treachery. Aurelian pursued a tough approach to retain power, condemning various nobles to death, as likewise the mint workers in Rome who had been debasing the coinage: 'he was ferocious and bloodthirsty and a rather necessary emperor in some respects' (Eutropius, ch. 14). Aurelian was the emperor who girded Rome with new walls and who formally quit Dacia and resettled its inhabitants; he also tried to root out the worst elements in the armies. His death, and the rapid assassinations of two successors, showed Rome needed a yet stronger person at the helm. Probus (276–82) was one such person, who defeated various usurpers, between times ordering a first phase of restorations at sites damaged across the previous generation (though archaeology suggests most renewal on the frontiers came after Probus).[24]

Beyond rival Romans, who were the enemies now emerging in the West? New names, different from those recorded by Tacitus and for the Marcomannic Wars, appear: Alamanni, Franks, Saxons and Iouthungi. Had these been tribes lurking beyond the Marcomanni and Quadi? We are of course largely dependent on Roman documentary sources, many much later than the events described, which simplify events by, for example, merging enemies together, while often exaggerating sizes of enemy forces or of Roman victory. At the same time, numerous smaller raids, local border attacks, civil insurrections and provincial troubles were left undocumented and even archaeology will not help clarify who did what and why.[25] Eutropius speaks of the Alamanni as defeated by Gallienus in 260 after their attacks on Gaul and Italy (IX.8), and yet, as the noted 'Victory Altar' from Augsburg shows, locals saw this same enemy as the Semnones or Iouthungi. Do the two names mask one main group and a subordinate one or were the names fluid? Quite probably 'The Romans understood, and helped to construct, the name [Alamanni] as meaning "all men" or "collective contingent" ... By the late third century, the Romans ignored the specific names of the Iouthungi and other groups, lumping them all together as the Alamanni'.[26] Rome thus recognised under this tribal banner name all manner of Germanic warrior groups forming and periodically raiding, with a suitable array of diverse kings amongst these. Comparable is the emergence of the 'Franks' in this same century, with a first contemporary reference in 289. The Franks had been centred on the Rhine frontier, where, as Tacitus identified, in the first century AD a high number of tribal groups proliferated; the 'Franks' seemingly forged components of these into a more effective force to threaten Gaul, Germany and Britain.[27] That these new groups were coalescing into significant powers is also shown through excavation of a number of 'central places', presumed royal bases, such as the Glauberg, 5 km east of the Wetterau *limes* of the Agri Decumates, in Alamannic territory; further south, the Gelbe Burg (near Dittenheim) with massive ramparts; and near Urach, the Runder Berg featuring a triple fortified enclosure.[28] For each, occupation is attested from the fourth century, peaking in the fifth; some occupation, perhaps as refuges or as rallying points, may have begun during the third century.

It is worth stressing here the debates active between both historians and archaeologists regarding the origins, nature and identities of not just these new third-century barbarian power groups, but also earlier tribes and peoples as listed and described by authorities such as Tacitus, and the larger powers which afflicted Rome in the fourth and fifth centuries. Many scholars question how far we should read any ethnic cohesion into these and what symbols, if any, bonded groups together. What made the Alamanni a lasting whole? How soon, if at all, were the varied internal confederate and ethnic identities lost within this? How was the new identity expressed? How might such identities evolve with time and space? What material traces of such identities or ethnicities exist? We can recognise, as noted, settlement power bases emerging in zones attached to names such as the Franks and Alamanni, and these give substance to the image of larger forces becoming stabilised and controlling bigger manpower resources. Burials and related dress items and weaponry may be partial guides too, although there is a recognised need for caution in trying to track movements of actual peoples through such artefacts. As discussed above, Roman goods percolated far beyond her frontiers and tell us less about the Romans than about the various 'customers' receiving these goods. Potentially, however, diminished movement of Roman materials to these tribes or peoples prompted diverse, more internal expressions of identity, much less oriented to the Roman world. But much more archaeology and interpretation are required to clarify all these. Certainly, however, more developed archaeologies of the earlier Germanic peoples are emerging, with greater emphasis on settlements and economies, to let these groups have their own voice.[29]

Comparably, less dramatic changes can be observed in African provinces: back in the AD 170s, Moors (Mauri) caused problems in the western regions and had dared to cross the Gibraltar Straits to attack sites in southern Spain; in c. AD 200 Septimius Severus' forces crushed 'warlike tribes' in Tripolitania, where a range of military installations – forts, blocking walls, guarded roads – attest the need to deal with scattered, mobile tribal groups. But from the mid-third century, confederacies of tribes began to make a mark in Tripolitania: sources refer to the Arzuges and the Laguatan who, like the Alamanni far to the north, persisted well into the sixth century, seeking booty, tribute and recognition.[30] Were these African tribal forces also responding to a weakened Roman State and a reduced Roman military presence? Recent studies argue that on this rather alien desert frontier, Rome tried alternative ways to protect the wealthy economy of the coastal African cities and their hinterlands (rich in olives especially): the first reference to the Arzuges coincides closely with the naming of a new military district, the *regio limitis Tripolitanae*, in the AD 240s, and the likelihood is that Rome helped organise communities on the provincial fringes, at the interface between the fertile north and the desert south and its fluid tribes; these groups were encouraged to settle and to work for Rome, receiving benefits in terms of pay, regular trade links and markets, and even access to regional Roman architects. By the mid-fourth century, the pre-desert zone has many elaborate stone-built keep-like central farm buildings, labelled *gsur* (singular *gasr*) or 'fortified farms', which oversaw elaborate field and water systems. Potentially by this date these communities and their varied clans were attached to such lands and the *gsur* and related funerary complexes reflect localised stability and investment. The tomb artwork and inscriptions denote a merging of local and Roman – for example, a native adoption of Roman names such as Flavius and Iulius, and of military designations, notably tribune. Roman North Africa lacked large numbers of regular troops, and this accommodation with native groups was a valuable route by which to 'soak up' some of these niggling border troubles.[31] It would be these fringe groups that coped best with the later decay of Roman authority to the north, and many persisted well into the Vandal period (see Chapter 8 in this book).

Overall, the physical damages of the military traumas of AD 230–80 were felt most keenly in the Empire's northern provinces and along their frontiers: numerous forts and towns required rebuilding or restorations; indeed, for some regions, the late third century witnessed a redefinition of towns through construction of defensive circuit walls. For Gaul especially, archaeological data indicate a massive urban wall building programme active from the 270s and 280s stretching from the provinces of *Belgica II* in the north (e.g. Senlis, Beauvais) to the west in *Lugdunensis III* (Nantes, Rennes) and in the south in Aquitanica II (Bordeaux, Poitiers) (see Chapter 3 in this book).[32]

Away from these more exposed zones, however, although some realignment and redesign occur – such as in the progressive adoption of urban defensive architecture – towns did recover in the early fourth century, the rural landscape remained busy and indeed featured bigger and more opulent elite estates, and economic activities picked up well. Thus contrasts exist between settlement patterns of the frontier regions of Raetia, Noricum and Pannonia (scattered and less developed) and their inner provincial zones (busier and with more display): the temptation is to view the frontier landscapes as scarred and thus uninviting, with landowners transferring to more secure zones. There were still demands on the frontier lands of course, and fields must have been tilled to help supply the army, but the investment for this probably came from elsewhere. At the same time the land had lost farmers – fled, killed or captured – hence the State's settlement of allied barbarian groups or defeated enemies in the frontier regions to work the land. Pinpointing such colonists and interrogating the farming landscape are important tasks, but not far developed, although studies in northern Gaul have started to show how more Roman farms than anticipated continued, if with occasional breaks, into late Roman and even into Frankish times.[33] Overall, therefore, while the third century should be viewed as one of crisis, it was not catastrophic and despite severe losses and damages inflicted, the body of the Empire was patched up and would soon show new vitality;[34] nonetheless, numerous mental, social and economic scars persisted and a new type of Empire was needed to renew Roman power.

STATE REVIVAL AND REALIGNMENT: INTO THE LATE EMPIRE

Not all of the old Empire survived, since two territories were quitted ('Map of the Western Roman Empire c. AD 400', p. xii): Dacia in AD 271 and before that the territory known as the Agri Decumates in 260. Dacia was the more substantial but more logical loss and needs to be viewed in context. Its annexation under Trajan, famously depicted on his Column in Rome and on the victory monument at Adamklissi, had been Rome's last major military advance, bringing sizeable metal resources under Roman control. In part the province (divided into three units and heavily settled by colonists) formed an advance bulwark of the Danube frontier or *limes*, but increasing demands on Roman manpower made Dacia a logistical burden; perhaps 60,000 soldiers were stationed here in c. AD 200. The zone had been damaged by raids since the 240s, and Gallienus withdrew some of its legionary forces, merging them with his field army; gaps in the coin sequences suggest imperial control badly faltered in the 260s. Under Aurelian, probably in 271, an evacuation was undertaken and the frontier line officially withdrawn to the Danube which formed the northern border to a vastly shrunken province, later divided into Dacia Ripensis and Dacia Mediterranea.[35] Frontier demands were thereby dramatically eased, although some Roman presence persisted across the river, where Aurelian shortly settled groups of Carpi – an intriguing move given that these had previously tried forcibly to enter old Dacia.[36]

To the west, the Agri Decumates were delineated by the *limes* extending east of the Rhine to the Main, Neckar and thence Danube rivers, thus forming the north-eastern part of *Germania Superior* and a northern section of Raetia provinces. Sources suggest that incursions of Alamanni and Iouthungi caused its abandonment at the start of the 260s, but deposits in frontier forts point to a systematic and ordered evacuation of both troops and administrators, not a disorderly flight.[37] To the west, in the Neckar–Wetterau zones, many, but not all, Roman farms and villas were certainly quitted, some prior to 260.[38] As noted above, the Augsburg Victory altar of AD 261 meanwhile points to Postumus, emperor of the breakaway 'Gallic Empire', controlling this part of Raetia; quite feasibly he withdrew troops and people from the Agri Decumates to bolster his own forces.[39] The whole Rhine–Danube territory was in upheaval: raids combined with rival claimants to Gallienus' throne (such as Ingenuus and Regalian, each of whom might have drawn soldiers from the *limes*) created a chaotic landscape into which Germanic groups might have settled. There is even the possibility that one of the Roman rulers negotiated this handover to gain German armed support – after all, Gallienus and Postumus both used Alamanni as mercenaries, even when other Alamanni were busy raiding Roman lands.[40]

These were very troubled times, but it is important to recognise that the 250s–70s did throw up some able soldier-emperors, most notably Aurelian. It is useful to record the titles accorded to him during his 5-year reign (270–5), as they give insights into imperial messages and popular reception.[41] Some titles, to be displayed on statuary, public and honorific inscriptions and notices, and, more widely, on coins, are standard ones: *perpetuus imperator* ('perpetual emperor'), *invictus* ('unconquerable') or *pater patriae* ('father of the state'), but Aurelian also gains the overblown superlatives *victoriosissimus* and *pacatissimus* ('super victorious' and 'most peace-bringing'). Innovative was *restitutor orbis* ('world restorer'), used especially on his coinage for Empire-wide advertisement, while inscriptions call him also 'restorer of people', of land, time, army, liberty, the East and the Gallic provinces. There might be some desperation here, but they do reflect the desire to bring order out of the chaos. Honorific victory names, meanwhile, identify external dangers countered: thus, an inscription set up in Rome in 274 hails him as Germanicus Maximus ('the greatest conqueror of the Germans', following victory over the Iouthungi in 271), Gothicus Maximus (defeating the Goths in 271 in the Balkans), Carpicus Maximus (victory over the Carpi in 273) and Parthicus Maximus (campaigns against Palmyra and Queen Zenobia who were aided by the Parthians). There are also claims for labels linked to Britannia and Armenia, probably provincial acknowledgements of Aurelian's authority rather than any real military venture.

Aurelian made it to Rome at the start of his fifth year of rule to celebrate a formal 'triumph' of his victories.[42] This featured a procession of captured treasures, nobility and other prisoners, ranging from Queen Zenobia of Palmyra to the usurper Tetricus, some Amazonian women and hostages from the Goths, Alans, Roxolani, Franks, Vandals, Arabs and Indians. Subsequent celebrations included gladiatorial combats and hunts (these featuring giraffes, tigers, elephants and elks), chariot races and mock sea battles in the stadia and circus. While the format of the triumph and the array of honorific titles were in keeping with those of emperors of old, few had occurred since the early third century, and with emperors, usurpers and others busy fighting elsewhere, often against fellow Romans, one must assume that the imperial 'aura' must have been much damaged, and the divinity of the emperors was surely questioned, especially given the short lives of so many rulers and aspirants. Aurelian's triumph and titles were as much efforts to restore that aura and reassure Rome.[43] Stability as much as anything was crucial, and while Aurelian had ability and targets, his assassination in 275 halted these. It was only in the 280s, with the firm, extended rule of Diocletian and his fellow Tetrarchs, that a lasting stability was imposed; not surprisingly, this phase also marks a notable realignment of power and display.[44]

Diocletian's roots matched recent predecessors in terms of disposing of competitors and seeking troop loyalties from East to West. Deriving from near Sirmium, Diocletian had fought for Aurelian and then for the Emperor Carus in campaigns in Persia; his key appointments were loyal fellow 'northern' veterans: Maximian, elevated to share the Empire in 286, and the Caesars (heir apparents, but active with commands in West and East), Galerius and Constantius, appointed from 293. Formal investitures, marriage bonds, joint edicts and combined statuary flagged the merging of the parts of the Empire into a working whole overseen by these four senior and junior rulers – the Tetrarchs. The gods were additional guides: on statuary, coinage, inscriptions, in poems (the formal panegyrics, orations honouring imperial visits), the four rulers are supported by selected ancient deities: 'By their deeds the emperors had proved that they were truly the descendants of Iuppiter and Hercules, or rather, had been chosen by these gods to be their descendants without denial of their human descent ... Similarly, the Caesars Galerius and Constantius were related by marriage to the Augusti but were also related to them as Iovius and Herculius'.[45] This association was further exhibited in adoptive names, in naming army units after the favoured gods, and occasionally in names given to cities refounded by the Tetrarchs – such as Gorsium in Pannonia, the focus of a major rebuilding programme under Diocletian, who renamed it *Herculia*.[46] The pagan gods' support had repercussions, of course, and acts of persecution against Christians reached their peak between AD 280 and 305; arguably, these reflect Tetrarchic moves against disorder and potential insurgence: failures to worship the State's deities and its highest representatives were dangerous acts in a period of cautious, yet insistent rebuilding.

The Tetrarchy was an experiment in power sharing, distributing the burden of senior control and reinforcing that control at a lower level by provincial restructuring ('Map of the Western Roman Empire *c*. AD 400', p. xii). Spain, for example, saw an expansion of the existing three (Augustan) provinces

(Lusitania, Baetica, Hispania Citerior) into six, with Citerior split into three more manageable units (*Tarraconensis*, with Tarragona as capital; Carthaginiensis, centred on Cartagena and embracing the Balearic Islands; and Gallaecia, with governor's seat at Braga), plus the small African province of *Mauretania Tingitana* opposite the Straits of Gibraltar.[47] These six provinces were grouped as a diocese and overall administered by a *vicarius*, based at the capital of *Lusitania*, Merida. Civilian and military powers were now divided, and mobile army units (*comitatenses*) were installed in mainland Spain and in *Tingitana*, overseen by counts. This division of powers and troops and tighter regional control (small provinces enabled better tax collection and easier provision of supplies to the army, plus less scope for individual governors to seek prominence) worked well for Spain, which empowered no usurpers and remained productive economically. Some later commentators viewed Diocletian's efforts in less favourable light, claiming overexploitation of farmers and lands to feed the increased numbers of soldiers, and a multiplicity of officialdom hounding townspeople, but, arguably, the Empire required a forcible tightening of its belt to help restore stability. Reforms also covered trade and food, with the well-known Maximum Price Edict of AD 301 designed to curb wild fluctuations in costs for commodities, services and even wages through fixing upper limits for these.[48] Although logical in scope, it caused major headaches and was soon repealed. More sensible were reforms and improvements to the silver and gold coinage, enabling monetary stabilisation and a return to wide trading. That markets functioned on all social levels is seen by the flow of lower-value coins; their increasingly diminishing size means that these coins have become common archaeological finds on late Roman sites.[49]

A full treasury enabled the Diocletianic overhaul to be augmented by structural displays in towns and on frontiers.[50] Emphasis lay in new capitals: in the East at Nicomedia and Antioch and in the West at Sirmium, Milan and Trier – all the latter three, noticeably, set nearer the northern frontiers. The shift of the main imperial court from Rome to Milan in AD 284 is especially striking, putting the emperor in much closer contact with the major Alpine roadways communicating to Dalmatia, Pannonia, Noricum, Raetia, Germania and Gaul; the Po Valley formed a major point of supply for the mobile armies in this central zone, and we will see later how various towns of the region were charged with weapon and equipment production, part of a network of factories in frontier provincial zones. Rome was not neglected though, as it hosted triumphal and anniversary processions and games for the Tetrarchs, and the vast Baths of Diocletian were a majestic imperial offering.

It is worth observing the architecture of imperial power *c.* AD 300, as fundamental new statements were being made through this. As noted, different capitals were being created – not *ex novo*, since most were pre-existing cities – through the construction or major re-elaboration of palaces and related structures. At Milan, Aquileia and Sirmium, these palace complexes occupied up to a fifth of the urban space, nestling near major gates and beside circuses (thus arenas of display), replicating Rome's Palatine Hill and Circus Maximus. (Immediately outside of Rome, off the *via Appia*, the Emperor Maxentius' villa incorporated its own racetrack.)[51] But these emperors also created distinctive walled rural retreats, notably Mogorjelo (near the coast of southern Dalmatia), along with huge, but more traditional villa sites like Parndorf (Pannonia) – all near but not on the river frontiers.[52] Best known is the retirement home of Diocletian (Diocletian taking the unprecedented move of stepping down from the throne) at Split-Spalato on the Dalmatian coast.[53] This was a vast private complex of 216 m × 180 m, enclosing 9.5 acres (Figure 1.2). Although since plundered for much of its marble work, continuity of site usage has been key to its overall survival: it was a bishop's seat from the mid-seventh century, a fairly well-established medieval town, and the palace was still core to Split in the early twentieth century, housing over 3,000 inhabitants. Most prominent was the site's military aspect, with 2.10-m-thick and up to 14-m-high walls, three landward gates provided with octagonal flanking towers, and square corner and interval towers; a passage gave access to a quayside on the south, seaward flank whose curtain wall had a more decorative aspect, comprising galleried loggias – an architectural trend evident in other elite palace-villas. A simple, fort-style internal arrangement of N–S and W–E streets and inner wall lane gave access to the palace structures, mostly two-storeyed in height, and many fronted by colonnades and arcades; in the south half a main peristyle led to private apartments, a mausoleum and a temple precinct; two bath suites are also known. Barracks and guest quarters probably occupied the northern zone. Previous commentators viewed Split's architecture as symbolic of growing court ceremony, with developed and controlled spaces, but the preference now is to view the complex as largely functional and in keeping with Diocletian's retirement quest. Nonetheless, the private spaces respond to new architectural currents and even in retirement formalised meeting and eating spaces would have been present (e.g. the sea views from the south, galleried side); scale and décor were more than adequate reflection of the status of the retired Augustus, and these became notable prompts for emulation.

Equally striking is Gamzigrad in eastern Serbia (in Dacia Ripensis from the late third century), equated with *Romulianum* or *Romuliana*, the fortress retreat of Galerius and his place of birth.[54] Its first phase (AD 311) resembled Split, with polygonal gate towers and square interval and corner towers, and enclosing two temples (one dedicated to Cybele, and a massive one probably to Hercules and the emperors), a palace of 50 m × 50 m with mosaic floors, reception and dining spaces, and baths. A powerful outer curtain wall 3.65-m-thick, featuring projecting polygonal towers, was later added; a second palace complex and possible granary probably also relate to this likely mid-fourth century phase. (Then or slightly later, by contrast, part of Diocletian's Split residence had been converted into a State textile factory.) A final important facet of many of these imperial retreats is the provision of monumental tombs: Galerius and his family were provided for by two

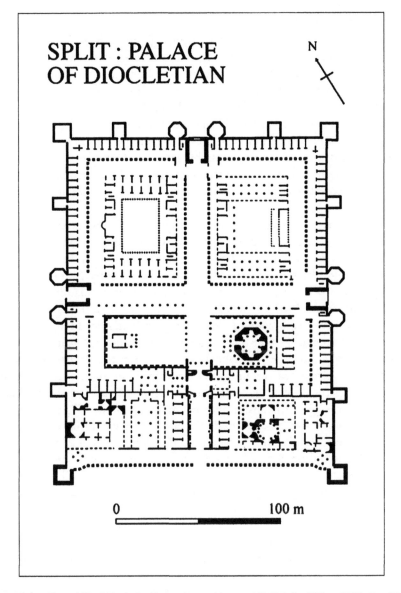

Figure 1.2 Plan of Diocletian's fortified retirement home at Split (after Wilkes 1993: Fig. 13)

circular mausolea located approximately 1 km east of Gamzigrad; at Split, an octagonal mausoleum for Diocletian lay in an enclosure within the palace walls; it was later converted into a cathedral. Burial here rather than in the proper capitals might indicate an attachment to the Balkan homeland by these soldier-emperors; at the same time, the mausolea stand as dynastic statements.[55] Strength, security and authority are thus embodied in these palace-fortresses: together they symbolise the redesigned Empire of the earliest fourth century.

CONSTANTINE'S EMPIRE

Constantine's rise and reign disrupted many of the foundations laid by the Tetrarchs: he emerged as a virtual usurper to the recognised emperor while in York and battled his way past other Romans to Italy; he aimed to reunify the Empire under a single rule, and yet later split the Empire permanently through foundation of a New Rome at Constantinople; his leaning to Christianity posed a further threat to the old order of Rome, her traditions and religions; and his own rule was tainted by family disputes and even murder. But his reign was stable, in part due to successful Tetrarchic measures to restore security on the frontiers, in the armies and within the provinces, and due also to his military and political expertise and, as importantly, his extended tenure of the imperial purple.

Constantine's right to accession was well crafted: while his father Constantius had been part of Diocletian's gang of four, Constantine forged a link with Maximian who had come out of retirement to bring order in the wake of succession issues; both before and after Constantine's entry into Rome, panegyrics proclaimed his descent from the revered Emperor Claudius Gothicus and stressed favour of the goddess Roma; his early coinage thus shows Roma, as well as Sol Invictus, drawing links thereby with another highly respected predecessor, Aurelian. Victory over Maxentius was hailed as a manifestation of rightful accession and the re-establishment of order: the Christian historian Eusebius duly blackened certain memories to brighten the status of the first Christian emperor, claiming Maxentius undertook various abominations, pagan and worse, prior to Constantine's triumphant *adventus*.[56] (If Constantine had lost at the Milvian Bridge, no doubt panegyrics would have proclaimed Maxentius the just ruler and Constantine the tyrant, but if Maxentius had triumphed, the unique set of imperial insignia comprising sceptres, processional spears and silks, recently recovered near the Palatine Hill, would have been lost to archaeologists).[57] Victory saw Constantine allied with Licinius who jointly promulgated the Edict of Toleration to release the shackles on Christians; yet court poets and Christian authors happily spoiled Licinius' image when Constantine turned on him. Constantine's acceptance of Christianity has been generally viewed as recognition of the weight of adherents in Rome and of potential Empire-wide support; alternatively, it was a propagandistic move to counter tensions caused by the very recent persecutions of Christians in Rome especially and to reassure elites with Christian leanings. Certainly, his legislation rapidly gave favours and lands to the emerging Church, though alongside this, Constantine still sponsored traditional building programmes and festivities, showing a diplomatically open policy which enabled new and old parties to coexist.[58]

Much can be gleaned from the magnificent Arch of Constantine (Figure 1.3), erected near the Colosseum and by the entrances to both Forum and Palatine in AD 315 by the Senate and People of Rome in honour of the emperor's *decennalia* or 10th anniversary (dated from his acclamation in York).[59] Its dedicatory inscription proclaims: 'By the inspiration of the divinity and by the nobility

Figure 1.3 Arch of Constantine: above the archway is the extended Constantinian frieze of the siege of Verona/Susa; above this are roundels of Hadrianic date depicting sacrifices for a hunt

of his own mind, with his army he avenged the republic by a just war at one and the same time both from the tyrant and from all his faction. To the liberator of the city and the establisher of peace'. One frieze even depicts victory over fellow Romans in the siege of a northern city (most probably Susa or else Verona). Unlike the victory monuments of the earlier Empire, this arch glorified internal (but 'just') contests and conquests.

Most images on the Arch are noteworthy: instead of the protector gods of the Tetrarchs, Constantine uses, in two sizeable circular panels on the narrow sides of the Arch, *Luna* and *Sol* (moon and sun), associated with sculpted scenes depicting the departure from Milan (an existing capital) and the entry to Rome (the Eternal capital), respectively. Images of conflict on one face of the Arch – such as the noted city siege plus the Milvian Bridge battle – are countered by civilian scenes on the other, where Constantine addresses the populace in the Forum, distributing gifts. These long sculptured friezes, featuring squat figures comparable to the Tetrarchic imagery, contrast strongly with a series of eight large rectangular panels on the top register of the Arch, each 3-m high, containing fine reliefs of, for example, the emperor addressing soldiery or receiving prisoners. These panels are then flanked by large freestanding 'barbarian' or 'Dacian' figures whose presences seem out of place with the theme identified by the inscription. On the flanks, also on the top tier, are large scenes of battles and triumph. In the middle tier of the arch's main faces are set large circular reliefs, 2 m in diameter, depicting sacrifices and hunting scenes. These larger sculptures in fact derive from monuments erected by or in honour of Trajan (battle panels and Dacians – possibly originally on the forum of Trajan), Hadrian (roundels – perhaps from an arch on the same spot, reworked by Constantine's architects?) and Marcus Aurelius (Emperor and troop scenes – sculptures perhaps taken from an arch erected by Commodus). Their prominence indicates more than simple, rapid recycling of past material and should be interpreted as a deliberate relating of Constantine with the glorious past of the second century AD: the military prowess of Trajan, the security and elegance of Hadrian, and the wisdom and strength of Marcus Aurelius. Nonetheless, well-crafted busts of a contemporary and handsome Constantine replaced the earlier imperial heads, presumably as an explicit identification of how he embodied the virtues of these illustrious predecessors – although how contemporaries 'read' the sculptures and whether they even noticed the borrowings or the replacement heads is not known. Interestingly, even if no overt Christian symbols are on display (in fact two roundels show pagan sacrifices or offerings at altars), connections could be made and certainly Eusebius later viewed the imagery of Maxentius' troops drowning in the Tiber as recalling the Egyptian soldiers being swallowed up by the Red Sea, with Constantine thus emulating the feat of Moses.[60] Similarly, the inscription's reference to 'the inspiration of the divinity' is vague and could be recognition of Constantine leaning to one God rather than the long-favoured raft of pagan gods. All told, the Arch of Constantine inspires a complex vision of continuity, change, renewal and new security. At the same time, however, spoliation of old temples, a monument recording victory over other Romans, an ambiguity of beliefs, and new heads for old could have been viewed as an uncertain, insecure and unfocused effort, sending out muddled messages.

Constantine, however, was focused enough to push for supremacy. The messy events of AD 310–13 had resulted in just two Augusti: Constantine in the West and Licinius in the East, but this power sharing was terminated in 323/4 when Constantine twice attacked Licinius, triumphing at Chrysopolis.[61] Rapidly afterwards, construction began of a new, Eastern capital at the site of an existing town, Byzantion, re-dedicated as 'Constantinopolis nova Roma' on 11 May 330. Constantine spent most of his time in 'new Rome' from 330 till his death in 337, also siting his mausoleum here. Unlike Diocletian's Split, Constantinople was an active seat of power and massive growth ensued to impose all the trappings of court and power, with Senate, palaces, walls, hippodrome and even imported statuary to create an air of antiquity. It was not a wholly Christian city, however, since new pagan temples were built to accompany pre-existing shrines.[62] Various other capitals witnessed investment, including the Western seats of Trier, Arles and, most probably, York; coins show how Arles gained the label Constantina; and the provincial seat of Tarraco in Spain features statues and dedications to Constantine and his sons.[63]

Such efforts could only have been undertaken in a context of political and economic stability, and in this Constantine was aided by the Tetrarchic legacy of tightened provincial and frontier control. This was fortunate as Constantine's campaigns against fellow Romans, notably Licinius, cost much in terms of manpower and money; later authors like Zosimus even blamed Constantine for severely weakening the Roman frontiers through the withdrawal of troops for these internal campaigns.[64] Certainly, some external threats were present and retaliatory expeditions first against and then with the Sarmatians across the Danube were sizeable efforts: larger Sarmatian groups had been displaced by movements of Goths further east; Roman tactics turned to supporting Sarmatian resistance against these Goths, formalised by treaties, military support (and equipment), aid in constructing a massive earthwork border and in settlement of various Sarmatian groups. In 334, a reputed 300,000 'free' Sarmatians were accepted onto Roman soil and distributed as families amongst the Balkan provinces, in north Italy and even Britain; these newcomers were to farm the land and were liable for conscription (see Chapter 2 in this book).

Constantine sought a dynasty: his sons (noticeably bonded by name – Constantine, Constantius and Constans) were all Caesars, but initially they, unlike in the Tetrarchy, had no independent powers or bases. Although recognised as heirs and made visible in both West and East in statuary, inscriptions and coins, succession was marked by vicious bloodletting in the imperial household, whereby relatives of Constantine's stepmother were removed, including Julius Constantius, half-brother of Constantine and father of the future pagan emperor, Julian, who was exiled with his brother Gallus; also murdered were the Caesars Dalmatius and Hannibalianus. Constantine's son Constantius probably spearheaded this purge, and then orchestrated acclamations across the Empire by the army to secure his recognition and that of his two brothers.[65] Rule between brothers was no recipe for success: Constantine II was killed when invading Constans' territory in Italy in 340; a coup led by Magnentius in Rome saw Constans' end in 350 – a death avenged by Constantius who defeated the usurper in Gaul in 353.[66] Heirless, Constantius made Gallus, brother to Julian, Caesar in the West in 351, only to execute him in 354; incautiously he elevated Julian as replacement, to deal especially with frontier troubles in Germany whilst he squared up to the Persians. Nonetheless, each gained successes in the field and across the borders, sometimes working in unison, as against the Alamanni, and this brought enough stability to enable Constantius to visit Rome in AD 357 to celebrate the 20th anniversary of his accession.[67] However, he was pulled back to reality by new conflicts with Sarmatians and Quadi in Pannonia and Moesia. Ammianus Marcellinus (Book 17.12–13; 19.11) provides an excellent guide to troubles, describing semi-independent enemy groups operating as well as the Limigantes (these are either former Sarmatian slaves, or else a dependant and subjugated tribe). After victory, Constantius allocated to the 'Free Sarmatians' a pro-Roman king, whereas some of the defeated groups were accommodated by Constantius' generals and governors on Roman soil. One scary incident in 359, however, saw some rebellious Limigantes assailing Constantius' makeshift field court at Acimincum, forcing the emperor to flee, but with his troops swiftly dispatching these upstarts.

Sizeable victories against Franks and Alamanni, and notably victory at Strasbourg in 357 against the forces of seven Alamannic kings ('35,000 men drawn from various peoples, some of whom served as mercenaries and the rest in accordance with pacts of mutual assistance'), prompted Julian's troops to proclaim him emperor in AD 360 (Ammianus Marcellinus, 16.1; 20.4–5). Julian had managed to rid Gaul of varied warbands which had damaged cities and populations, and he pushed across the Rhine against some of the intruders, including the Attuarian Franks and Alamanni.[68] Constantius died in 361 en route to quell Julian, leaving the Empire in the hands of an intelligent character, but one who professed to paganism.

From Ammianus Marcellinus especially, we can observe how the decade AD 350–60 encapsulates much of the changed Empire: shifted capitals; State and imperial insecurity; constant demands on troops, generals and emperors on the northern and eastern frontiers; varied treaties with non-Roman groups; enemy raids into Roman lands; barbarian troops in Roman ranks; Roman generals of barbarian origin (such as Silvanus, a Frank, who, as commander of the Roman infantry in Gaul, attempted a usurpation in 355); barbarian groups settled on Roman soil; towns suffering siege and capture; lands and fields plundered and damaged; and high taxation demands. Contemporary laws and Christian texts meanwhile reveal army recruitment concerns and civic disturbances, plus dissension, debate and doctrinal disputes in the young Church.[69] While other chapters will examine how far the physical and material evidence support this image of a changing and damaged world, here we can stress that the texts overall point to various efforts by Rome's military emperors to resist and respond, but in the face of mounting hardships.

NEW CONFLICTS AND NEW RESPONSES: AD 350–95

Despite Julian's efforts to shift back both northern and eastern enemies, the 360s and 370s were to witness more of the same, and indeed an escalation of the stakes in the central-northern provinces of the Western Empire, due chiefly to Roman internal political power struggles. In clear contrast with the early Empire, where fair internal stability enabled provision of a focused army and a secure network of treaties, alliances and trade agreements with varied tribes and groups in the 'Barbaricum' whether to north or south, the mid- and later fourth-century Empire had emperors looking as much over their shoulders as in front, and generating little or no scope for stability across the frontiers. The trade that had enabled Roman–barbarian communication and which had fostered massive economic growth had all but fallen away. Gifts – of objects but especially of gold or coin – became the principal vehicles for obtaining security and allies, but the apparent multiplicity of kings in tribes and confederacies such as the Alamanni and Franks meant a growing demand for such tribute; delays in receipt, rejections of quantity or quality, and competition within groups could all result in irruptions across the frontiers into Roman lands to grab alternatives. Thus,

The Alamanni violated the German frontier. The reason for their exceptional hostility was that the envoys whom they sent to Roman headquarters to receive the regular gifts that they had come to expect were fobbed off with smaller and cheaper presents, which they thought unworthy of them and threw away in a rage. After rough handling by Ursatius, Master of the Offices, a cruel and passionate man, they went home with an exaggerated account of the matter and roused their savage countrymen to revenge the insulting treatment they had received. (Ammianus Marcellinus, Book 26.5, for AD 364)

Arguably the bulk of these raids were for booty still, as during the turbulent third century, but Rome's ability to strike back was hampered; in most cases, Rome was only responding to assaults and then plugging gaps, meaning that damage was always being inflicted. The impact on the frontier provinces is not fully understood in terms of their Romanised populations, but the ready settlement of barbarian groups on Roman soil (see Chapter 3 in this book) is a clear enough statement of a need to fill voids – of farmers scared and put to flight, killed or taken captive, or forced to move away from the frontier or closer to or even inside forts for security. Ammianus Marcellinus' narrative speaks often of abandoned forts on the frontier zones, and a lack of troops surely forced the flight of many local farmers. Importing barbarian settlers to farm and defend was thus a logical-sounding tactic, but, in time, these requests for lands escalated and extended far beyond the frontier territories.

Ammianus Marcellinus details struggles along various frontiers, with towns like Cologne constantly under siege, fort-towns like Carnuntum barely functioning, and new watchtowers and fortlets being installed to plug gaps. Julian's campaigns against Alamanni and Franks in Gaul, often on Roman soil, are most revealing: cancelling out rebellious fellow Roman generals, undertaking expensive diplomatic exchanges, securing hostages, maintaining troop loyalty and numbers through local recruitment and incorporation of Germans as auxiliaries, and restoring Roman communities. The main imperial names for the 360s and 370s are Valentinian and Valens. Ammianus Marcellinus (30.7–9) readily praises Valentinian, Augustus for nearly 12 years:

He strongly reinforced the army and fortified the high ground on both banks of the Rhine with strong-points and forts, so that no assault on our territory could be launched unobserved … He treated the provincials indulgently and everywhere lightened the burden of tribute. He met a longstanding need by building towns and fortifying frontiers. He was admirably strict in enforcing military discipline … [but he] often turned a deaf ear to the complaints brought against [superior officers]. This led to disturbances in Britain, disaster in Africa, and devastation in Illyricum.

Inscriptions and archaeology substantiate the claim of extensive renewal along parts of the frontiers and in their hinterlands – such as rebuilding a timber bridge across the Maas and establishing defences at Ägerten on Lake Biel. Even if some forts were reduced in size, overall the works imply increased manpower needs to support a tighter and thicker set of *limites*. Works even extended onto enemy soil: Ammianus Marcellinus notes how Quadic incursions against Pannonia in 372 were prompted by new Roman forts north of the

Danube. Such 'bridgeheads' formed advance defences to key points of penetration, at crossings and bridges, and had been applied previously in the fourth century – for example, Contra Aquincum opposite Budapest, at Deutz opposite Cologne and Zasel opposite Mainz.[70] The provision of towers for advance warning and the increased use of river patrol boats were further logical defensive measures.

The main threats came from Alamanni, Franks, Sarmatians and Goths. Indications of enemy numbers are rare or unreliable, but the data from Ammianus Marcellinus signify compact raids which flared occasionally into more substantial assaults, making adequate responses difficult to achieve. These threats were not always coordinated affairs (thus the scale of the so-called 'Barbarian Conspiracy' threatening Britain in AD 367 is much disputed – see Chapter 2 in this book), but events well beyond the frontiers in the 360s and early 370s were to prompt more concerted and sizeable inroads of non-Roman groups which would mark the first movement of these *within* the Empire. Ammianus Marcellinus recounts how 'The seed-bed and origin of all this destruction and of the various calamities inflicted by the wrath of Mars, which raged everywhere with unusual fury ... [are] the people of the Huns, who are ... quite abnormally savage ... with squat bodies, strong limbs, and thick necks, and are so prodigiously ugly and bent that they might be two-legged animals'; a race of wild horsemen, so skilled with the use of the bow, fickle and rapid, 'under no restraint from religion or superstition'. The Huns had pushed westwards and southwards from the Asian steppes and had overwhelmed the territory of the Alans (Iranian nomads) gathered by the River Don and Lake Azov bordering the Black Sea. These Huns then assailed lands held by the Greuthungi Goths (later the Ostrogoths) between the Dnieper and Dniester rivers, and the Tervingian Goths (later Visigoths) gathered near the Lower Danube and Black Sea. Hunnic–Alan forces advanced despite some Gothic successes and despite efforts by the Tervingians to create a rampart defence (probably revamping a pre-existing Roman earthwork defence, the *limes transalutanus*). These defences only checked the advance and Gothic forces needed to fall back further. Although Ammianus Marcellinus implies a vast, rapid flood of Huns, modern scholarship argues for a more prolonged and progressive build-up of threats – possibly from different Hunnic groups – against both Alans and then Gothic tribes, the identities of these latter perhaps being reinforced on account of these new pressures.[71] Similarly, the next stages may have been more drawn out than Ammianus Marcellinus (31.3–4) suggests:

> Weakened by the lack of necessities of life the greater part of the people abandoned Athanaric and looked for a dwelling far from all knowledge of the barbarians [Huns]. After much debate where to settle they fixed upon Thrace as the most eligible refuge ... So led by Alavivus, the Thervingi spread themselves over the bank of the Danube, and sent agents to Valens, humbly begging to be admitted to his dominions, and promising that they would live quietly and supply him with auxiliaries if the need arose.

This move by displaced groups (Eunapius claims 200,000 people) was not due to imminent Hunnic takeover, since the latter shifted eastwards and did not reappear on the Danube for some time. Rome's reception of these refugee Goths on the river was necessarily complex. Such huge numbers (generally accepted by modern commentators) were problematic: even if Rome saw these as potentially invaluable resources for army reinforcement (the Emperor Valens swiftly recruited some Goths for the East) and for farming debilitated frontier lands, not all were accepted for immediate relocation on Roman soil, since it appears that the Tervingi alone were allowed over the Danube in late Spring 376 – the Greuthungi clearly remained by the river, suggesting a second phase of relocation was envisaged by the Roman authorities. Ammianus Marcellinus conveys some sense of the confusion and logistics of ferrying the Gothic groups over the river and allocating food and land, with the Romans struggling to cope – in between apparent extortion of the weakened Goths by some Roman military in search of cheap slaves.

Despite this, no revolt immediately ensued; some time elapsed before the Tervingi were escorted south-eastwards towards the governor's seat at Marcianopolis in Moesia where they were to be divided up and allocated their plots of land. However, new mistreatment, including the murder of a Tervingian chief, saw open rebellion and the defeat of the accompanying Roman troops in early AD 377. The Greuthungi then crossed the Danube led by Alatheus and Saphrac; they probably joined forces with the Tervingi, reinforced by Taifali and Alan mercenaries as well as local miners and slaves: 'What had begun as a controlled migration of a limited group of Tervingi had thus snowballed into an avalanche of rebels loosely united around the original Gothic core'.[72] Fritigern is designated as having been the overlord in this 'rebel' force, but he no doubt struggled to control its many self-styled chiefs or kings, many of whom ranged far and wide to plunder and secure food. The speed of the Roman response is unclear, but new troops were brought in, holding many rebels at bay; bruising encounters saw a Roman withdrawal, leading to further damage on the landscapes and towns of Scythia, Moesia and Thrace by the Gothic groups, and including a march on Constantinople in early 378. Valens, cancelling preparations for campaigns against Persia, advanced into Thrace, calling on his Western colleague, Gratian, to supply reinforcements. According to Ammianus Marcellinus, Gratian was distracted by a significant incursion across the Rhine by the Alamannic Lentienses.[73] Without wanting to delay further, and rejecting more than one offer to parley from Fritigern, Valens engaged the Gothic horde in battle about 8 miles from Adrianople on 9 August, heading a force of about 20,000 troops. Perhaps the Romans were misinformed on the size of the enemy, perhaps they were overconfident, but in the battle they failed to contain the enemy forces, leading to their rout as well as the death of Valens. Surviving Roman troops fled back to Adrianople, which bravely resisted assaults by the Gothic forces. Ammianus Marcellinus (31.16.7) reports one notable incident in the wake of the events at Adrianople:

> At that time, Julius, who commanded beyond the Taurus, distinguished himself by a swift and salutary deed. Learning of the disasters in Thrace, he sent secret orders to those in charge of the Goths who had been transferred earlier to Asia, and dispersed in various cities and fortresses. These commanders were all Romans, an unusual thing at the present time. The Goths were to be collected quite unsuspecting outside the walls in the expectation of receiving the pay that they had been promised, and at a given signal all put to death on one and the same day. This wise plan was carried out without fuss or delay, and the provinces of the East saved from serious danger.

Ammianus Marcellinus here firmly identifies two things: an excessive build-up of non-Roman forces on Roman soil and a growing use of non-Roman commanders; he also contrasts the higher security of the East with a fragmenting Western Empire and a Balkan zone full of potential threat. He is in line with the military strategist, Vegetius, who composed in *c.* AD 390 an Epitome to identify ways to revive Rome's military strengths and quality. But both go against imperial policy manifested most strongly under the Eastern emperor, Theodosius I ('the Great', 379–95): Theodosius could, by AD 382, contain the Gothic threats within the Balkan–Danube zones, but his key means was to employ vast numbers of these newcomers within his army ranks (see Chapter 2 in this book). Theodosius' strong arm (combined with pay and honours) was sufficient to control the Gothic auxiliaries and their chiefs, although we have no real idea of how well controlled these were after battle, while quartered/billeted, and when required to work the land. Problems did exist: Theodosius was first required to recognise a Gothic confederacy's rights to settle and thus control much of eastern Pannonia in AD 380; the other, less amenable Goths (predominantly Visigoths), through a treaty formulated in October 382, were assigned lands in Dacia and Thrace as a group and were exempt from taxation, even receiving a yearly payment – meaning these were effectively independent and in charge of the frontier line to the north.[74] The tribute payment was exceptional in being paid to groups settled on Roman soil as opposed to settled outside the frontiers, and was a sign of future troubles.[75]

Despite Theodosius' efforts, internal wars again flared in the West to debilitate and fragment its armed forces: Zosimus (*Nea Historia*, IV, 35–58) records campaigns by Magnus Maximus (a usurper elevated in Britain) against Gratian in 383 (Gratian was then murdered by his troops at Cologne) and against the forces of the young Valentinian II (elevated at Carnuntum) in the Alps and in north-east Italy before being defeated by Theodosius' large Roman and Gothic army in 388. Italy saw further disruption in 392–4 when Theodosius fought the usurper Eugenius (a teacher of rhetoric) and his Frankish General Arbogast (the real reins of power), with a latest victory against fellow Romans gained beside the River Isonzo in the Julian Alps.[76] In the late fourth century in both West and East, with armies featuring often sizeable groups of non-Romans, the presence of Romanised Germanic or other commanders was not unusual. Ammianus Marcellinus' noted reference to the purge of Goths in the East *c*.378 under the initiative of Julius was in fact via 'commanders [who] were all Romans, an unusual thing at the present time'.

In the East after AD 410, this reliance on non-Roman officers was heavily reduced, but the situation in the West could not be reversed.[77]

ROME AND THE WEST IN THE LAST CENTURY OF ROMAN RULE (AD 395–476)

Defeat near Adrianople was perceived by Ammianus Marcellinus as calamitous for the Roman State, and many modern authors similarly parade it as a disaster on the scale of the loss of Varus' troops in the Teutoburg Forest in the early first century AD.[78] But circumstances were quite different. Varus' defeat came during Rome's attempted expansion and annexation north of the Rhine, thus within German lands; although it stunted military efforts here and reinforced Tiberius' decision later to withhold further advances, Rome's armies otherwise remained powerful and contained any threats. Valens' debacle, by contrast, was on Roman soil, in a fragile landscape long scarred by conflict and already reliant on non-Roman arms and labour to maintain it; although the threat from the Gothic groups was halted, it came at a significant cost in terms of recognising a Gothic confederacy on Roman soil, settled more on their terms rather than Roman and receiving tribute; Rome may have benefited in terms of being able to draw upon these Goths as manpower, but to many authorities – ancient and modern – this was the start of an over-reliance which backfired. A largely independent body of non-Romans now existed within the frontiers and virtually controlled sections of those frontiers. Events of the late fourth and early fifth centuries would reveal the fragility of this arrangement.

Indeed, the late fifth-century Greek historian Zosimus (*Nea Historia*, IV, 59), looking back on the fortunes of Rome in the very early fifth century, paints an extremely bleak image: 'The Roman Empire has been gradually diminished and become a home for barbarians, or has been reduced to such a depopulated state that the places where the cities used to be cannot be recognised'. A contrast comes in the verses of Claudian, whose consular panegyrics basically glorify the contemporary Theodosius' destruction of fellow Romans, and then, in his verses for Honorius, Western emperor from 395, he glosses over an Empire barely holding itself together and elevates small gains and victories into magnificent triumphs. Claudian helps record the breakdown in relations between Rome and the Visigoths in the later 390s, renewed Gothic aggressive movements in the Balkans and marches into northern Italy to wrest new concessions from the imperial court. Three main figures emerge: an indecisive Honorius, lurking in his capitals; his Generalissimo Stilicho, one of Theodosius' military elite, with Vandal roots, but fully Romanised and even wedded to the imperial court – first Theodosius' and then Honorius'; and on the Visigothic side, a royal overlord, Alaric. The conflict across 399–408 was in reality fought out between Stilicho and Alaric, with Alaric's efforts focused on achieving territory and imperial military command; these efforts included war, sieges, assault of Rome and creation of a usurper (Map 1.2). The decade witnessed also the transfer of the imperial court from the strong but exposed city of Milan to the coastal base of Ravenna. Furthermore, it saw a dramatic acceleration of decay in the Western imperial fabric – in Britain, Gaul and Spain – adding to the paper-thin control in Noricum and Pannonia. Even cushioned Africa showed the strain. The fifth-century historian Olympiodorus concisely reports: 'The Western parts of the Empire were in confusion'.[79]

Alaric and the Visigoths

The Gothic settlement in what still counted as Roman Pannonia, Moesia and Dacia and their relative independence under strong chiefs worked against both Western and Eastern Empires. The emergent figure of Alaric was key: he orchestrated incursion into Macedonia and Greece and used the discord between Eastern and Western courts to extract money and other support from each, including military appointments; indeed, his status of *magister militum* effectively put him in charge of all the Western armies and the State arms factories – almost displacing Stilicho who, naturally, did not countenance power sharing. Stilicho meanwhile had to face a short-lived revolt in 397–8 by the count of Africa, Gildo, who transferred his provinces to Eastern control and stopped grain fleets feeding Rome. Later (mainly Eastern) sources painted Stilicho as ineffectual against Alaric (matching a weak and ineffectual emperor in Honorius), perhaps even colluding with the Visigothic king, but this downplays Alaric's tactical nous, army and the highly stretched Roman resources and soldiery.[80] Armies clashed on a couple of occasions, notably at Pollenzo in northern Italy in AD 402 (duly praised in a contemporary panegyric by Claudian as a stunning Roman victory but in reality a stalemate), and Stilicho did well, without Eastern aid, to keep the Visigoths at bay. He bolstered his army numbers – partly as barbarian mercenaries amongst his forces appear to have proven unreliable in early encounters with Alaric – by thinning out frontier forces, notably along the Rhine and in Britain, and by recruiting more Huns; at the same time, he probably reinforced Italy's defences through additional watchtowers, strategic forts and by repairs or extensions to towns walls (see Chapter 3 in this book). Archaeological finds help pinpoint some of these transferred troops: thus, for the northern Adige Valley in central-northern Italy (the Trentino), items of military dress (approximately 70 artefacts, deriving often from burials, from 30 locations, chiefly fixed-plate, chip-carved belt buckles, or with punched or perforated decoration) show likely defended sites, including the Pomarolo necropolis at Servis, set on a high, isolated terrace overlooking the River Adige, where the finds suggest a military station, perhaps comprising Germanic federates, overseeing a strategic Alpine route. Intriguingly, the perforated buckle plaques have roots in British and northern Gallic contexts, and the fixed-plate and chip-carved buckles best relate to Upper Danube and Rhenish soldiery. Here, perhaps, are material traces of troops withdrawn from Britain, Gaul and Germany, and stationed across Alpine Italy in a reactive policy of heightened security and entrenchment.[81]

Despite reinforcements, Stilicho failed to counter the shock of another invasion, from a new protagonist, Radagaisus, whose Pannonian Gothic (Ostrogothic) force, perhaps numbering 60,000 men, invaded the peninsula,

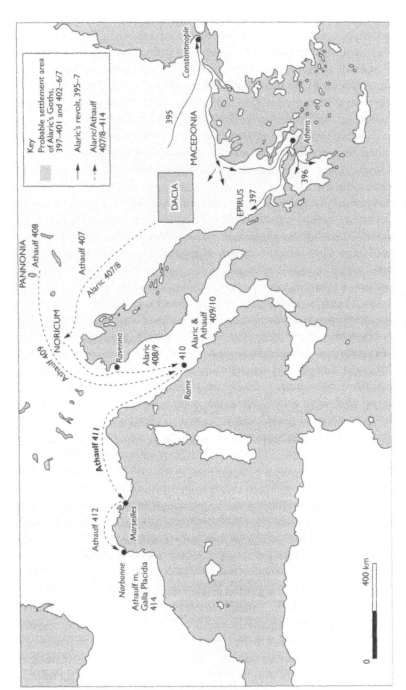

Map 1.2 Visigothic military campaigns and movements between AD 397 and 414 (after Heather 1996: Fig. 5.2)

ranging at will in the north in late 405 before a dispersal of Radagaisus' allied units and a failed siege of Florence enabled the Romans to defeat and capture the leader. Huge numbers of the enemy were drafted immediately by Stilicho (estimates run up to 30,000); others were sold off as slaves, apparently glutting the market at Rome. Possibly, conflict now flared openly with the Eastern court and Stilicho may even have planned an assault on Epirus province, otherwise a foothold for the East against Italy; to do so Stilicho seemingly reached agreement with Alaric, offering official military appointment, moneys and supplies to help move against Epirus. However, the collapse of the Rhine frontier at the end of 406 scuppered these plans, leaving (an unpaid?) Alaric in Epirus.[82] Constantinople then declared Stilicho a public enemy, the claim being that he was plotting against Honorius to put his son Eucherius on the throne. In 408 Honorius ordered Stilicho's arrest and execution: Olympiodorus (frs 5 and 7) reports that '[t]he troops broke out in revolt and slaughtered the prefects of Italy and the Gauls, the generals and other chief palatine ministers. Stilicho himself was killed by the soldiery at Ravenna'. The families of his German bodyguard were slaughtered, prompting other barbarian troops (probably those enrolled from Radagaisus' defeated forces) to flee to Alaric.

These events left Italy horribly exposed. Perhaps unsurprisingly, despite the treaty, appointments and gifts, Alaric, joined by other Goths from Pannonia, moved on Rome and besieged it in 408, 'lining the banks of the Tiber with many of his barbarians to prevent the conveyance of food to those in the city from Portus. Since, after the siege had gone on for a long time, famine and pestilence were ravaging the city and many slaves, especially those of barbarian origin, were deserting to Alaric ... [Alaric] received many gifts from the inhabitants, and for a while he lifted the siege since the Romans promised to persuade the emperor to make peace with him'.[83] According to Zosimus, the gifts comprised 5,000 lb of gold, 30,000 lb of silver, 4,000 silk tunics, 3,000 scarlet-dyed skins and 3,000 lb of pepper. Alaric demanded both of the Western military commands, moneys and grain. Although he reduced these to control of the provinces of Noricum, he undoubtedly envisaged a Gothic protectorate to Rome.[84] As Honorius dallied, perhaps in hope of Eastern armed support, Alaric returned to blockade Rome in 409, forcing acceptance there of a new emperor, Attalus, who was naturally more compliant to granting the required concessions. News of the arrival of some Eastern soldiery may have forced Alaric into actually capturing Rome and holding the Eternal City to ransom. Possibly through treachery – the sixth-century historian Procopius (III.ii, 27) put blame on the noblewoman Proba, but no doubt others wanted to save their skins – the gates were breached on 24 August 410 and Alaric's troops thundered in. We know little of the aggression against the residents, but human loss must have occurred; otherwise Alaric allowed his followers to ransack freely Roman houses and nobility. Emotive are the words of St Jerome which relay the shock of Alaric's desecrations:

A dreadful rumour came from the West. Rome had been besieged and its citizens had been forced to buy their lives with gold. Then, thus despoiled, they had been besieged again so as to lose not their substance only but their lives. My voice sticks in my throat, and, as I dictate, sobs choke my utterance. The City which had taken the whole world was itself taken; nay more – famine was beforehand with the sword, and but few citizens were left to be made captives. In their frenzy the starving people had recourse to hideous food; and tore each other limb from limb that they might have flesh to eat.

Later, he adds: 'The brightest light of all lands is put out; the head of the Roman Empire is cut off. To speak more correctly, the whole world perished in one City'.[85]

Alaric in 410 represents clearly a much changed world, with barbarians imposing themselves inside the Empire, even if still aiming to work with this – after all, Alaric did not set himself up in Rome, choosing instead to withdraw after a week, still negotiating. He died not long after the sack, but his burial site and its treasure beneath the Busento River remain undiscovered. The rest of Rome's stolen booty formed the core to the Visigothic royal treasure which was deposited in Carcassonne in south-west France (and later brought to Ravenna by the Ostrogothic King Theoderic but subsequently returned to the Visigoths).[86] Many captives were also taken, including Honorius' sister Galla Placidia who, on Alaric's death, was taken by his successor Athaulf in marriage as they elected next to move to southern Gaul, after flirting with the idea of sailing to Africa.[87] Soon after this Athaulf was assassinated; circumstances then saw a different policy whereby the Visigoths made a treaty with Honorius, handing over Galla Placidia and Attalus, and in return gaining supplies of grain and a chunk of southern Gaul to settle (see below).

A Fragmenting West

More traumatic events were meanwhile occurring elsewhere in the West, which can be pieced together from near contemporary and later sources such as Olympiodorus, Eunapius, Priscus and Zosimus. Most significant was the irruption of confederated barbarian forces (a claimed 100,000) across a frozen River Rhine on New Year's Eve of 406 (unless 405) in the area of Mainz: Vandals, Sueves and Alans broke through a *limes* weakened by Stilicho's withdrawal of troops, and penetrated deep into Germany and Gaul.[88] The timing is not certain, but perhaps in the wake of these incursions, the Roman General Constantine claimed the imperial purple in Britain in 406/7 and moved his troops across the Channel to restore order and counter the ineffective rule of Honorius; he established himself in Trier and made rapid gains (against Romans and barbarians), extending his control into Spain by 407,[89] dispatching there his son Constans and General Gerontius, putting down claimants and a peasant force in Lusitania. Successes here and disasters in Italy meant that Honorius accepted Constantine III as a colleague. But soon after, Gerontius rebelled and installed his own rival emperor, Maximus. To counter Constantine, he called upon the Vandals, Sueves and Alans, then settled somewhere in northern Gaul, to join his cause. In response, Constantine 'sent his General Edobich across the Rhine to obtain reinforcements from the Franks and Alamanni and entrusted to his own son Constans the defence of Vienne and other cities of the region' (Olympiodorus, fr. 17). Vandals and Sueves ransacked Aquitaine; Gerontius defeated Constans; Honorius' forces then defeated Gerontius near Arles; Constantine was executed en route to Italy; and in between such Roman civil conflicts, the Vandals, Sueves and Alans pushed southwards and in October 409 'captured many forts and cities of Spain and Gaul together with the officials of the usurper' (Olympiodorus, fr. 17).

The absence of any adequate Roman defence meant the Vandals overran what had been, till then, a healthy and secure peninsula.[90] Despite reverses against a joint Roman–Gothic force, the Siling Vandals and Alans took control of much of southern Spain, centred on the provinces of Baetica and Carthaginiensis (including the Balearic Islands), and the Sueves and Asding Vandals occupied north-western Spain and Gallaecia province. Maximus somehow continued as a nominal emperor in Tarraconensis province before withdrawing to Africa in 412. The mid-fifth-century historian Hydatius, a Spanish bishop, fills many of the gaps in charting this annexation of Hispania, although his emphasis is Gallaecia.[91] How the division of settlement was undertaken and how far it was negotiated with residual Roman urban authorities such as bishops is unknown – perhaps the groups were aware of Roman practice of Germanic settlement elsewhere and had briefly been allocated spaces under Constantine III in northern Gaul. But there then followed counter-efforts from Roman Italy: the Visigoths (now under Athaulf) had been given southern France as a new base of settlement, but mistreatment and failures to supply food to his people made Athaulf rebel in 414 and raise against his own emperor, Attalus (he of AD 409–10 fame in Rome), at Narbonne. Honorius' General and new Co-emperor Constantius III pushed Athaulf westwards into Spain, where he was accommodated at Barcelona, earlier vacated by Maximus. Potentially this was a new, formal resettlement of the Goths since, despite initial good contact with the Vandals, Athaulf's successor Wallia was then charged by Honorius with ridding Spain of the Vandals and Alans.[92]

The apparent ease with which the Vandals were cleared made the Roman court draw back the Visigoths and settle them in 418 in lower Aquitania – the Garonne Valley area including Bordeaux, still a prosperous area for the Gallo-Roman aristocracy. This elite initially can have been none too pleased with the barbarian imposition but in time sorted a working relationship, with noble Visigoths seeking to emulate this south-western Gallic elite lifestyle.[93] It is unclear whether the Goths were receiving any paid tribute, and their King Wallia unusually lacks any Roman military position. However, the removal of a Visigothic threat in Spain enabled the Asding Vandals under King Gunderic to reassert themselves, by 421 regaining the southern territories of Baetica – facing the North African province of Mauretania.[94]

Just as Spain became paralysed by the Vandal–Alan–Suevic invasion, Roman Britain rejected its Roman officials as part of a latest rebellion. Constantine's elevation in 407 had in fact followed two other short-lived efforts. Were these rebellions in response to the shock of the overrunning of Gaul and a threat to the Channel ports and defences? Do they reflect distrust that Honorius and the Italian government would bring help – after all, troops had already been deflected eastwards by Stilicho – and a search for a local solution? With Constantine III's shift to Gaul and his possible neglect of Britain through removing even more soldiery, the farthest northern province perhaps felt over exposed. Some authors argue for a rejection of Rome in 409 – but a rejection by whom? Romano-British towns were struggling; wealth still existed, as evident from hoards, but the decision-makers are barely perceptible otherwise. Honorius is recorded as writing to the *civitates* of Britain suggesting they look to their own defence: Is this acknowledging a temporary independence, but stressing Rome was still aware of their presence? Zosimus, writing a century later, states that 'the inhabitants of Britain and some of the Celtic tribes ... threw off Roman rule and lived independently without further submission to Roman laws ... [And] all Armorica [Brittany] and the other provinces of Gaul followed the British example and freed themselves in the same way, expelling their Roman governors and setting up their own administrators as best they could'.[95] Potentially, Britain and Armorica sought Frankish and Saxon mercenaries to aid their defence, settling these in the coastal zones. But how were these to be paid, since official Roman coin in both areas dried up at the start of the fifth century barring a few gold issues extending into the second decade? As Gildas outlines a century later, those Angles and Saxons settled as federates in the east of Britain by the Chief King Vortigern in *c.*428 rebelled within a decade due to inadequate supplies and lands, sending the old province into further upheaval as new non-Romans began to enter.[96]

Disruption and confusion can be charted through coin and metal hoards in Britain between AD 390 and 410, although not all deposits are necessarily responses to insecurity. One major discovery is the substantial Hoxne hoard (Suffolk, eastern England), hidden probably in contemporary plough-land in a large wooden chest and in smaller caskets.[97] All told, as well as silver spoons and elements of tableware, the hoard contained a full 14,865 coins (569 of gold and 14,205 of silver), the latest being silver issues of the usurper Constantine III of 407/8. The bulk of the gold *solidi* are of AD 394–405, and mints centre on Trier, Lyons and Arles, but include Milan, Ravenna and Rome. Was it the portable fortune of a wealthy villa owner or that of a noble official from a military centre? Was it a hoard taken and hidden to avoid the latest usurper's demands for money for funding an expedition and paying troops? The hoard's value certainly belies the view of Britain on the eve of Roman withdrawal as impoverished, although there is no certainty that the wealth was built up in this country. Or perhaps this was a theft, the wealth stolen by the owner's bodyguard and buried in a temporary hideaway? Whatever scenario holds true, both location and wealth were lost (as well, perhaps, as the lives of those who undertook the hoarding), just as Rome's hold on Britain was being severed.

Events in distant North Africa are crucial as they herald future problems in the south Mediterranean. As described above, a principal means employed by Alaric to subdue Rome was to blockade both port and canals, depriving Rome of essential external goods (though we should not doubt the presence of stores within the City, these were probably seriously depleted in the build-up to Rome's fall – movements of Visigothic plus Roman troops cannot have enabled adequate sowing and harvesting of crops in various districts of Italy, and certainly the law codes attest to failures of some regions to meet *annona* demands in this period). Shortages and stockpiling had already been provoked when Gildo had turned against Stilicho and shifted the African provinces to Eastern Roman control, only for Stilicho to dispatch Gildo's brother Mascezel to defeat him in 398 and so restore Rome's grain supply lines. Rome's reliance on Africa since the third century for grain and oil for what remained a vast population (perhaps still half a million in AD 400) must have been made to look delicate by the actions of Gildo and more so by Alaric's blockade. Little wonder that Rome's citizens were scared into elevating usurpers to treat with Alaric when Honorius failed to bring aid. While African loyalty was for a time retained, the provinces here suffered problems too, since the *magister militum* Boniface had to defeat various barbarian raids: in Tripolitania and Cyrenaica, for example, the Asturiani and Laguatan tribes and confederacies had long proved niggling thorns in the provincial sides, undertaking assaults in the 360s, 370s and 400s, even besieging coastal sites, with patchy Roman responses, due chiefly to minimal manpower resources (money and status had been the main means to keep the tribes in check and to use these themselves as border guards).[98]

Carving out New Kingdoms

Even if control over northern provinces such as Britain, Germany, Pannonia and Moesia had been badly damaged, the State remained aware of each and strained to retain some influence, since the territories could still provide buffers to the Empire. The 430s, however, mark more acute losses of control in the West as Rome's policy of barbarian settlement began to unravel as too many of the power groups displayed independence in action and space. Key is the case of North Africa and the Vandals. As seen, in the 420s Boniface governed as count of Africa, but when he fell out of favour with Rome and the Empress Galla Placidia, regent for the young Valentinian III (made Augustus at 6 years old in 425 following Honorius' long-awaited demise), Boniface refused to be recalled, prompting two military expeditionary forces against him. To Boniface is sometimes ascribed an invitation in 429 to the Vandals to cross from Spain to support his ambitions and to help defend Africa, with a division of territories; this claim is made by sixth-century sources and not by fifth-century texts, however, and the preference is to see a Vandal crossing in the wake of internal Roman disorders.[99] The fact that Boniface subsequently shifted to Italy and was made generalissimo to counter the power of Aetius makes no sense if he had sided with the Vandals. We know Boniface had employed federates, but these were Visigoths, who were still in Africa when the Vandals arrived and were defenders at the besieged Hippo Regius.[100] The Vandals may have been pushed out of Spain by Suevic pressure, as well as by continuing Roman-Visigothic efforts to restore the province (General Castinus came close to victory in 422). Vandal raids had certainly occurred against Mauretania previously and they will have been aware of the limited Roman military presence overall, especially in the western territories. Victor of Vita argues for a total figure of 80,000 Vandals and Alans (with families and followers) moving across the Gibraltar Straits; the figure sounds plausible, and perhaps incorporated newcomers gathered in Spain.[101] Oddly, we hear nothing of Boniface countering the Vandal inroads, and numerous coastal and inland towns fell rapidly, only a few showing significant resistance. However, in 435 a formal treaty was signed which allotted the westerly African provinces to the Vandals, who were required to perform as federates, be paid and supplied, in return for ensuring continued food exports to Rome.

The Vandals soon realised their upper hand and they exploited it ruthlessly in 439 by capturing the focal city of Carthage, capturing also its fleet and using this then to assail Sicily. Both Western and Eastern Empires raised forces and ships in response, but sizeable Hunnic incursions in the north meant that this enterprise was cancelled and by 442 Aetius and Valentinian III were forced to recognise Vandal possession across North Africa from Tingitana to Byzacena; Tripolitania remained on the fringes, neglected by Romans and Vandals alike even when ceded formally to the latter in 455.[102] The Vandals partitioned up the lands (elite, State and Church-owned) amongst their nobility and soldiery, in doing so forcing the flight of some elites, exiling others and persecuting members of the Catholic Church. But most land was still largely farmed by Roman provincials and these still paid taxes; many of the Roman nobility continue also to be attested. The Vandal kingdom was urban-centred, implying continuity of activity in these – if with documented conflict against resident Catholic Christian groups.[103]

Rome had lost Africa, even if the Vandals maintained the old trade routes and the economies of the hinterland – since they too needed food and funds. Their command of a fleet was perhaps surprisingly rapid and must indicate the inherited Roman *annona* fleet – grain supply ships, smaller merchant vessels, plus swifter, companion military naval vessels – and personnel. More surprising are the Vandal naval victories, these perhaps due more to Roman failures than superior Vandal skills.[104] By the 460s the Vandals controlled the islands of Corsica, Sardinia, Malta, the Balearics and, crucially, Sicily. These Vandal maritime conquests effectively blockaded Rome and broke the fragile economic imperial unity of the western Mediterranean.[105] Vandal raids even hit mainland Greece and, more consistently, southern and western coastal Italy, forcing emergency defensive responses here (see Chapter 3 in this book). Their impact is attested in the Roman law codes, either in terms of moans from provincials about inabilities to pay taxes and loss of livelihoods, or in references to locals being asked to be vigilant, to bear arms if needed, to help save the State.[106] The historian Priscus (fr. 39) summarises Vandal tactics thus:

> [Geiseric] did not readily attack the cities which the Italians had garrisoned, but seized the places in which there was no adequate force, laid them waste and enslaved them. The Italians were unable to bring help to all the points at which the Vandals could land, being hampered by the numbers of their enemies and by their lack of a fleet. The latter they sought from the Eastern Romans but did not receive it because of the treaty which they had with the Vandals. Because of the division of the Empire this fact resulted in great harm for the Western Romans.

A major tactical change saw Rome itself targeted, and what is most shocking is the ease and speed of occupation by King Geiseric's forces in 455. Priscus forms a chief guide, reporting how in that year, Rome was in disorder after the assassination of Valentinian III, with open conflict for replacements, with one Petronius Maximus prevailing 'through his distribution of money' and taking Valentinian's widow, Eudoxia, as his wife. However, 'Geiseric, the ruler of the Vandals, heard of the death of Aetius and Valentinian and concluded that the time was right for an attack on Italy, since the peace treaty [of 442] had been dissolved by the deaths of those who had made it with him and the new emperor did not command an estimable force' (fr. 30). Procopius later reported the rumour that Eudoxia summoned Geiseric to counter this assault on her family (her daughter Eudocia had been betrothed to Geiseric's son Hunirix in 442, but Maximus had married her to his own son).[107] Maximus was killed as he tried to flee Rome: 'the crowd fell upon his body, tore it to pieces and with shouts of triumph paraded the limbs about on a pole.' Amidst the confusion, Geiseric's army entered Rome, seemingly unopposed, and set to work on 2 weeks' systematic robbing.

The vandalism of 455 appears greater than that of 410, since the Catholic churches of Rome were also ready targets, even if the pope made strong representations to curb robbing. Oddly, however, archaeologically, events are harder to trace than in the wake of the Visigothic assault, and the emphasis perhaps lay strongest on amassing moneys, metals and slaves as opposed to the burning down of buildings. Certainly, some of the key treasures were human: 'when he had despoiled the city of everything, he returned to Africa taking with him the same Eudoxia and her two daughters' (Priscus, fr. 30.3). Victor of Vita's *History of the Vandal Persecution* (c. AD 484) (Book 1, chs 24–5) expands:

> Geiseric ... took into captivity the wealth of many kings, as well as people ... When the throng of captives reached the shore of Africa, the Vandals and Moors divided the huge mass of people into groups. Husbands were separated from wives and children from their parents, in accordance with the custom of barbarians ... [Bishop Deogratias of Carthage] busied himself immediately: he sold all the gold and silver vessels used in worship and freed the freeborn people from being slaves of the barbarians.

A new Western emperor, Majorian (457–61), struggled hard to regain something of the dwindling West, with Generals Aegidius stemming Visigothic and Frankish expansions in Gaul, and Nepotianus and the Visigoths assailing unruly Sueves in north-west Spain, while he himself marched through Gaul to Spain to Cartagena to attempt a naval assault on Vandal Africa, preparing 300 vessels, only to be betrayed, allowing the Vandals to fall upon the assembled Roman naval forces. A treaty was then forced on Majorian which gave full recognition to the Vandal kingdom; his assassination the next year duly saw a renewal of raids by Vandals and Moors against Italy and Sicily.[108]

What of Spain, vacated by these successful Vandals? For the northern regions of this province at least, and for southern Gaul, the Chronicle of Hydatius charts the failing power of Rome.[109] While Hydatius recognised the traumas of the first two decades of the fifth century from Vandal, Alan and Suevic incursions and Roman civil wars, he observed this more in terms of Roman dynastic upheavals, with Rome struggling to reassert her expected control; the major use of Visigothic federates in campaigns and their allocation of lands in Aquitaine were simply part of this imperial policy. However, his accounts for the 430s onwards denote a changing picture: increasingly the Goths in south-west Gaul pursue an independent line, negotiating with the Sueves in Gallaecia and even establishing marriage alliances (as in 449); receiving Roman refugees (including in 444 Sebastian, son-in-law of Boniface); and campaigning against the Sueves, with their own counts and dukes dispatched by kings such as Theoderic. Some Roman names appear, but these seem to be local Romans entering the Gothic military rather than imperial commanders working along-side Visigoths. In 455 the Visigothic court helped elevate the Gallo-Roman nobleman Avitus to the imperial throne; and in 456–7, perhaps without impe-rial sanction (since their favoured Avitus had been deposed), they mounted an invasion of Spain. In the 460s, Ricimer was the Western generalissimo oversee-ing imperial changeovers and he was in fact related to the Gothic royal dynasty. All told, there is a blurring here, with elements of imperial acknowl-edgement and legitimisation (could they do much else?) of a Gothic kingdom, but with the Visigoths taking tasks into their own hands, if in Roman guise – such as supporting Rome against the Huns in 451 and creating some kind of naval force to counter coastal raids by Saxons and Heruls, but choosing their own Roman military officials to serve with them. These Goths were creating a protectorate over western Spain, as reflected in numerous embassies and gifts to the Suevic court from 458. To the Spanish Bishop–Historian Hydatius, southern Gaul was indeed 'Gothic', not Roman, by c.460; Visigothic expansion northwards to and beyond the Loire was not in Rome's name, since they removed here Majorian's General Aegidius in 465. Further north, the Franks were consolidating lands and gains in Gaul, and in 472 the Visigoths turned their attention instead to conquering northern Spain.[110]

Visigothic pressures greatly disrupted the Suevic kingdom, and the impres-sion given by Hydatius for the 450s and 460s is of different and competing war-leaders, who failed to hold onto lands gained south of Gallaecia and who caused damage within their own kingdom, such as in 460 when many of the provincial Roman population of the town of Lugo were slaughtered. Most probably, a single monarchy was restored to work with the growing Visigothic powers, and in fact only in 584 was Gallaecia fully absorbed into the Visigothic kingdom.[111] The broad outline of Visigothic annexation of Spain is understood, with the figure of King Euric being central. If much was already in virtual Visigothic control in the south through the efforts of King Theoderic I, the siding of the Roman Emperor Anthemius (467–72) with the Sueves prompted Euric (466–84) to launch attacks from Gaul against both Sueves and Hispano-Romans in Lusitania and Tarraconensis, culminating in the capture of Tarraco by 475. The leader of the latter campaign was Vincentius, 'duke of the Spains', seemingly another Gallo-Roman working for the new power in this part of the former Western Roman world. Mopping-up exercises continued under Euric's son, Alaric II (484–507), although his death saw Visigothic holds north of the Pyrenees lost to the Franks.[112]

Aetius and the Huns

What of the Huns and their impact on the Empire? As observed, the Gothic build-up on the Danube in the 370s was provoked initially by an expansion of this hitherto little known eastern people into the Black Sea region, and later the Carpathian zone. The cohesion of the Huns in this period is not clear, but the Roman courts, notably the Eastern one, soon exploited these for mercenaries, recognising the value of their horse and archery skills: Stilicho, for example, utilised them against Alaric; he also had a bodyguard of Huns. One key episode comes in 423–4 when, after Honorius' death, the Eastern court tried to restore the Theodosian line in the West in the figure of Valentinian and his mother Galla Placidia. This meant overthrowing the new ruler John, and so a sizeable army was sent to Italy under Ardabur, master of both branches of the military, his son Aspar and Candidianus. The latter captured many cities in Italy including the capital, Ravenna, and removed John; Ardabur was captured, while Aspar faced Aetius, one of John's subordinate commanders, who led a claimed 60,000 Hunnic mercenaries. Aetius then negotiated with the regent Galla Placidia and was appointed count, only then dispatching his Huns home.[113] By 423 the Huns were established in the Carpathians and were recognised by Rome (i.e. provided with tribute payments – probably from both East and West courts); to whom exactly these subsidies went is not clear, but probably a variety of different Hunnic chiefs were capitalising on Roman willingness to pay for peace and troops.

Following defeat by Boniface in 432, Aetius fled to the Hunnic court, where he had in fact been a formal hostage in the 410s. He then used more Hunnic troops to force his reinstatement as generalissimo in 433, removing Boniface's son-in-law Sebastian. Aetius' military efforts centred heavily on Gaul, viewing this fragmented province as crucial to Italian defence, and campaigns were made against Visigoths and Franks; in addition, in the early 440s he ordered the settlement of the federate Burgundians (heavily defeated by the general in the 430s and also by the Huns) in Sapaudia (centred on Geneva), presumably as a defensive tool.[114] Aetius did not, however, divert troops back to either Spain or Britain – indeed, he seemingly failed to respond to a request for assistance from the British in 446. He may have prepared efforts to counter the Vandals, but nothing came of these. However, the commander may have contributed to the formation of a unitary ruling power amongst the Huns: we hear first of King Roua (or Ruga) in the early 430s, and then from c.434 the Hunnic armies were controlled by Roua's nephews Bleda and Attila, who maintained the policy of gaining moneys from the West for troops and gold subsidies from the East for peace, prompted by occasional incursions of the Balkans, as in 441 and 447, by when Attila had murdered his brother and gained sole power. Attila led his forces over the Balkans and into Greece, capturing over 70 towns and extorting moneys en route; but he did not assail Constantinople, despite elite flights from there.[115] In 450/1, Attila went westwards and southwards, perhaps at the instigation of the Vandal King Geiseric, wishing for the Visigoths' demise. In 451 Attila's forces crossed the Rhine, sacked Metz, Trier, Cologne and other sites before pushing to central Gaul and the Loire, plundering land and further towns. Aetius allied with his main enemies, the Visigoths, to counter this threat and it was in fact a strongly Visigothic army that managed to defeat Attila's combined Hunnic, Ostrogothic, Alan and Frankish force near Chalons, in the 'Catalaunian Plains'.[116] The Visigothic King Theodoric I fell in battle, but his troops rallied round Thorismund. Attila's battered forces retreated, leaving the bulk of their booty behind.

Attila looked for vengeance by turning attention in 452 to Italy, leading a substantial confederate army here, sacking Aquileia, occupying Milan and holding other cities to ransom. Aetius, now without Hunnic mercenaries and without Visigothic allies, could not intervene on any significant scale, despite the availability of nearby Burgundian federates; instead he apparently recommended that Valentinian III flee and establish a new capital in Gaul. Remarkably, Rome was spared, seemingly by the intervention of the pope: emulating a predecessor in the time of Alaric, Pope Leo met Attila on the banks of the Mincio River, not far from Milan, and successfully 'delivered the whole of Italy from the peril of the enemy'[117] – though scholars suggest that Attila's army was suffering from disease and was ready to withdraw anyway. We should assume a major financial offering accompanied Leo's embassy as well as promises of more, but these details have been hidden in the papal glory. More probable is a report made by the Spanish historian Hydatius that the Eastern Emperor Marcian had boldly sent an army under another General Aetius to strike at the Hunnic base over the Danube; perhaps Leo informed Attila of the counter offensive and a withdrawal was swiftly implemented by the king to ensure the maintained loyalty of his subject peoples. Whatever the explanation, relief came, enhanced within a year by the news of the death of the Hun overlord (from a burst blood vessel on his latest wedding night). Internal feuding then saw major disruption amongst the Hunnic powers: Ostrogoths, Gepids, Heruls, Sciri and other subject groups broke away and many (but not the Goths) even combined under the leadership of the Gepid king to defeat the Hunnic core at the River Nedao in Pannonia 454. In the same year, Aetius was killed, personally, by Valentinian III, who suffered assassination himself the following year at the hands of two of Aetius' former Hun bodyguards.[118]

As Eugippius records at the start of his *Life of St Severin* in the early sixth century, 'At the time of the death of Attila, king of the Huns, confusion reigned in the two Pannonias and the other borderlands of the Danube'. The dispersal of and battles between the ex-Hunnic subjects must have been bloody and confusing indeed, but these largely escape the notice of contemporary historians; it is noticeable, however, that their identities had been maintained (if remodelled, since archaeology shows some of the people occupying territories later defined as Gepid and Herul adopting Hunnic-style attributes, including decorative artificial skull deformation), implying that they had been kept as coherent tribute subject groups and with their elites emulating their Hun superiors in appearance. Rapidly, though, certain groups began either to offer their services to the Empire, or to seek to impose themselves in Roman lands, or both — notably the emergent Ostrogoths. Indeed, already in 455/6, Goths were granted new lands in Pannonia by Marcian to counter the Western usurper Avitus — though whether these lands were still perceived as 'Roman' in any real sense is unclear and quite possibly these Goths had already been settled in the zone by the Huns and Marcian was simply recognising their control here. Our picture is somewhat distorted by the sixth-century Gothic historian Jordanes who focused strongly on the eventually supreme Ostrogothic clan, the Amals, and neglects the presence and status of other known Gothic groups in the northern frontier zones, such as the federate Goths in Thrace, who would come into direct conflict with the Amals in Pannonia, but eventually united with these to form the Ostrogoths. And he also ignores the bitter factional fighting within the Amals.

Jordanes overall claims three groupings settled in former Pannonia, overseen by Kings/Chiefs Valamir, Vidimer and Thiudimer.[119] Of these, Vidimer moved his group onto Spain in 473 and Valamir, succeeded by Thiudimer and his son Theoderic, moved to Thrace to pester the Eastern court once more. Here they came into conflict with the Thracian federate Goths, who revolted under their leader Theoderic Strabo in 471. The Pannonian Goths moved into Macedonia in 473 and demanded and received lands. Civil war at Constantinople from 476 then brought both Gothic groups into conflict, with the Pannonians, under their Theoderic, siding temporarily with Zeno. Only in 484 were matters clarified after Strabo's death, the murder of his uncles and son, and the merging of Thracian with Pannonian Goths. Eventually, Ostrogothic unity and increasing pressures on Constantinople would prompt Zeno to push Theoderic westwards in 488/9 to occupy Italy.[120]

The Final Demise of Western Roman Rule

One of the last main Roman–German generalissimos and power-brokers in the Western Empire was Ricimer (or Richomer), whose 15-year period of domination saw a further and final dilution of the position of the Western emperor.[121] Identified as an Arian Christian, son of a Sueve, related via his mother with the Visigothic King Wallia and with links to the Burgundian court, Ricimer had served with Aetius, and distinguished himself subsequently in 456 in repelling a Vandal attack on Sicily and chasing and defeating the remnants of their fleet off Corsica; he then assisted in the deposition of Avitus and the elevation of Majorian. Ricimer's power was such that, despite Majorian's campaigns in Gaul, following the emperor's failed naval assault on the Vandals (defeated in Spain at Cartagena even before departure), the generalissimo arrested and then executed Majorian in 461 before electing a more malleable emperor, senator Libius Severus (461–5). This move was not approved in the Eastern court by Leo I nor indeed by some of Ricimer's own generals, notably Aegidius, who set up (seemingly in union with the Salian Franks of north Gaul who perhaps viewed him as a *rex*) an independent Roman space in the remnants of western Gaul north of the Loire; this persisted under his son Syagrius until 486 when Clovis defeated him at his capital, Soissons, to give impetus to Frankish independence.[122]

Meanwhile, Severus' death allowed Leo I to recommend a replacement, Anthemius, accepted by Ricimer partly due to Leo's agreement to undertake a major expedition against the Vandals, who remained Italy's constant aggressor. Victory could have been a platform for revival in the West, but it was not to be: the fleet's failure in the wake of a surprise Vandal attack was followed by civil war in Italy and continued Vandal raids. When Anthemius was finally defeated, Ricimer's resources were so depleted that he had to make a lasting treaty with the Vandals, accepting Geiseric's nomination as emperor of another senator, Anicius Olybrius – brother-in-law to Geiseric's son Hunirix. Effectively, the Vandals gained a stake in the Western Empire's governance, just as the Visigoths had briefly done with their choice Avitus in the 450s. Like Avitus, Olybrius was not on the throne long enough to make any difference, and he and Ricimer both died (peculiarly, of natural causes) in 472.

The new kingmaker, the Burgundian Prince Gundobad, briefly installed his Emperor Glycerius before returning to Burgundian territory to stake his claim for the throne there – implying that that throne meant far more than events and nominal emperors in Italy. As Heather states, 'The centre no longer controlled anything anyone wanted. In consequence, the late 460s and 470s saw one group after another coming to the realization that the Western Empire was no longer a prize worth fighting for ... after hundreds of years of existence, the Roman State in Western Europe was now an anachronism'.[123] The Eastern court recognised it too, as indicated in their conclusion of a permanent peace treaty with Vandal Africa in 474 and in the bare recognition of the next claimant to the throne in Ravenna, Julius Nepos, elected by his army in Dalmatia. Nepos lasted a year before the current 'order' of things was restored: the Italian general Orestes removed Nepos and made his own son Romulus emperor; within a year he too was gone, unable to meet the troops' excessive demands. Orestes also fell from his pedestal and a lesser commander, Odoacer (or Odovacer), of claimed Scirian descent, son of a former king, murdered him and retired Romulus to a fine villa at the promontory of Pizzofalcone near Naples in September 476 – with the generous annual pension of 6,000 gold *solidi*. Odoacer looked not eastwards but westwards for his future, and chose to make Italy his own kingdom rather than use an empty Western imperial shadow. But like other kings in the now Germanic West, he wanted Roman recognition and so, as a parting shot, Romulus was made to send envoys to the Emperor Zeno in Constantinople, 'proposing that there was no need of a divided rule and that one, shared Emperor was sufficient for both territories. They [the Italians] said, moreover, that they had chosen Odoacer, a man of military and political experience to safeguard their own affairs and that Zeno should confer upon him the rank of patrician and entrust him with the government of Italy'.[124] As with the rulers in Visigothic Spain, Vandal Africa and Burgundia, Odoacer maintained Roman institutions and law, issued Roman style coinage (although he did issue – for local consumption – lesser issues with his own image) and contributed to urban and Church upkeep; he undertook diplomatic embassies with neighbours to secure recognition, and he stabilised his frontiers (though this included withdrawing 'Romans' from Noricum, still nominally under Italian rule, in the 480s, and ceding a final chunk of Gaul to the Visigoths).

Ironically, the formal end of Roman rule in Italy brought unexpected scope for recovery: Odoacer engineered an agreement with the Vandals that they withdrew from Sicily in return for an annual tribute payment – Rome's grainhouse was thus restored as were some of the lands of the State, Church and many an extant Senate. Like the population of Rome, now dwindled from a million to perhaps just 100,000, a much reduced and more economically challenged world surrounded the people of late fifth-century Italy and it would need time for recovery to fully manifest itself. In fact, by AD 500, much of the former Roman West, though dissected up, had largely settled down: old provinces for the most part now existed as kingdoms, and in these, old Roman populations and cities largely persisted, if altered and damaged; new powers now dominated, but these utilised remnants of Roman urban administration and religious organisation. Conflict could still flare in these new kingdoms (especially those in the old northern provinces), but without the wide instabilities brought by feuding emperors and meddling generals and their manoeuvres with the barbarian groups, and with scope for communication between kingdoms, a semblance of stability came back to much of the West. But what types of settlements did Rome's successors inherit? The following chapters will explore how and in what ways the towns, landscapes, defences, religion and people of the Western Roman Empire physically evolved across the period AD 250–500: how far can we trace through the archaeology the decline, losses, continuities or transformations of places and spaces?

2

Defending the Late Roman West:
I. Armies, Commanders and Enemies

INTRODUCTION

This done, Probus set out with a huge army for the provinces of Gaul, which since the death of Postumus had all been in turmoil, and after the murder of Aurelian had been seized by the Germans. There, moreover, he fought battles so great and successful that he took back from the barbarians 60 most famous towns (*civitates*) of Gaul, besides all the booty, by which the Germans ... were puffed up with glory. And whereas they were wandering at large on our bank, or indeed through all the country of Gaul, Probus, after slaying about 400,000 who had seized upon Roman soil, drove all the rest back beyond the river Neckar.

(*Scriptores Historiae Augustae*, Probus, xiii, 5–7, for AD 277)

It is Our constant care to provide for the welfare of the human race; for we make provision day and night that all persons who live under Our sway shall be defended by the protection of arms from the attack of the enemy and shall possess unrestricted leisure and security in time of peace.

(*Novels of Marcian*, 2.1, issued in Constantinople, Oct. 11, AD 450, to the Praetorian Prefect Palladius)

These quotes reveal much about the later Roman Empire: in the first, Probus strives to recover a province and its cities from the devastations of Germanic invaders while fighting also against rebellious Roman troops who select and deselect emperors at great pace; in the second, the rhetoric of the emperor recognises the need to reassure a harassed citizen body of their future security. This latter statement comes in the mid-fifth century, at a time when the African provinces had been lost to Vandals (who had commenced vicious raids against Sicily and Italy and would soon briefly occupy Rome itself), Spain had largely become Visigothic, Gaul was again in turmoil, Attila's Empire had only just fragmented and the northern frontiers along both Rhine and Danube were barely functioning. Leisure, security and peace must, to many provincials, have by then seemed ancient memories. Of course, it is easy to take quotes from late Roman sources who are condensing events into restricted narratives and who thereby present images of near constant woe and conflict. Such words clearly hide, for many regions and cities, periods of relative security wherein barbarians and crop failures played no or only a distant part. But by AD 400 we are dealing with an Empire radically different from that of the first century, and changes are perhaps most prominent in the nature of the army, its commanders, its placements and its strategies. This fact was recognised – after all, education saw 'classical' historians such as Livy, Caesar and Tacitus as required reading, their accounts replete with images of famed generals, campaigns against vast enemies, superior Roman training and tactics, pride in serving in the Roman ranks and, above all, victories and conquests. The names of many of the enemies had changed, but not dramatically so: Franks, Goths and Alamanni may have emerged in the third century, but these remained to most Romans simply as Germani, while in the East and in Africa, Persians and Berbers persisted. More significantly the scale and extent of external pressures were greater, and the internal military abilities seemingly weaker. Nonetheless, Rome, as ever, worked to adapt to counter external (and internal) pressures, and, as we shall see in this and the following chapters, both the army and the Empire's modes of defence evolved accordingly. But did they collapse or decay at speed as is often presumed?

A contemporary voice regarding the loss of quality of Rome's military past was Vegetius, a wealthy court official, well placed to access the emperor's ear; he was also a successful horse breeder on his Spanish estates, which may have gained him extra credits at a period when chariot racing was in high regard. The safety of his horse-breeding operations might have been a prompt in compiling his *Epitoma Rei Militaris* or *Epitome of Military Science*, in c. AD 390, perhaps presented to Emperor Theodosius I when attending the Western court at Milan. The *Epitome* is composed of four 'books', and details the state of the current Roman army, views on how the earlier Roman army prospered, old and new tactics for infantry and cavalry, and potential ways of reviving the Romanness and efficiency of the military.

Thus the *Epitome*'s Book 1, ch. 1 lays out the need for careful recruitment, selection and training, with an implicit criticism of the 'alien' forces increasingly being called upon and employed for Rome; Vegetius highlights 'the principles which the builders of the Roman Empire long ago observed' and stresses how 'scientific knowledge of warfare nurtures courage in battle. A small force which is highly trained in the conflicts of war is more apt to victory: a raw and untrained horde is always exposed to slaughter'. The problem is that 'a sense of security born of long peace has diverted mankind partly to the enjoyment of private leisure, partly to civilian careers. Thus attention to military training [has been] consigned long since to oblivion' (ch. 28). Romans are less willing to serve, and yet 'it costs less to train one's own men in arms than to hire foreign mercenaries'. The shock of recent conflicts, notably the disastrous battle of Adrianople (AD 378), had prompted panic across the Empire; Vegetius' text was a plea for immediate strategic rethinking. The emphases are clear: closer control over recruitment and preference for the trained might of Roman soldiers; enhanced discipline and field tactics; wider availability of siege weaponry (offensive and defensive) and training in these; and greater attention to urban defence and supply. Vegetius does not find fault with the whole of the current Roman army: notably he praises (as a horse breeder himself) the cavalry (III – Epilogue) and the river patrol boats, 'which guard outposts on the Danube with daily watches [and whose] increased use has discovered a more advanced science for them than ancient theory had to show' (IV.46).

Book IV is especially telling, for although Vegetius considers the seas as pacified (IV.31) – was he unaware of raids on the North Sea and Channel coasts? – his discussion on city walls, towers, gates, counter-siege weaponry, and on materials to store in case of siege, recognises an Empire under threat and a situation in which townspeople cannot rely purely on the army and on secure distant frontiers:

> Both the recommendations of the authors of arts of war for attacking and defending cities and what the experience of recent emergencies has discovered, I have summarised for the public benefit, as I believe, making the point again and again that the most thorough precautions should be taken against shortage of drinking-water or food arising at any time since such troubles cannot be ameliorated by any stratagem. Therefore, all the more should be stockpiled within walls, in proportion to the length of the blockage that is known to be within the capability of the besiegers.

Vegetius was not a lone voice: in *c.* AD 370 the 'Anonymous' treatise *De Rebus Bellicis* was presented to Valentinian and Valens, bemoaning faults in the army and advocating a heavy defensive cordon, as well as some ingenious machines of defence and offence to help regain tactical superiority in the field:

> Above all it must be recognised that wild nations are pressing upon the Roman Empire and howling about it everywhere, and treacherous barbarians, with the cover of natural places, are assailing every frontier ... An unbroken chain of forts will best assure the protection of these frontiers, on the plan that they should be built at intervals of one mile, with a solid wall and very strong towers (De Rebus Bell. 20).

As Chapter 3 in this book will show, Valentinian's reorganisation of the Rhine and Danube did witness an array of new fortifications, particularly watchtowers, to plug gaps. However, we have no proof that the 'Anonymous' author's proposed cattle-powered warboats were ever test-driven or even employed to save Rome!

ARMIES AND COMMANDS

While Vegetius and 'Anonymous' both register concern at lapses in training, direction and abilities, the very survival of the Empire into the late fourth century demonstrates Rome's military staying power. The traumas of the third century had certainly forced changes. In conflicts against Persians in the East, against confederated forces of Franks and Alamanni in the north, and against fellow Romans, both legions and auxiliaries had suffered losses, struggled to meet and respond to often widely scattered threats, notably swift raids (on land, horse and by sea), faced problems of supply, and also dealt with town sieges. As mobility and speed of response became increasingly vital to counteract extended depredations of Roman soil (including via civil conflict), cavalry units might well have gained more prominence, drawing from varied military traditions – such as the mounted armoured archers from the East, the wily Moorish horsemen or Scythian mercenaries – and a diverse infantry emerged. Old command structures faltered and experienced soldiers gained troop commands instead of the traditional appointments made by the Senate; martial ability in turn secured army loyalty and for a sizeable chunk of the latter third century, soldiery and generals from the Danubian provinces rose to prominence – including the throne (the Balkans then remaining a core recruitment zone). Finally, to this same period of confusion belongs not just tactical retreat from territory (Dacia, Agri Decumates) but efforts to reinforce both frontiers and towns.

Consolidation of these emergency measures came with the accession of Diocletian, whose extended rule (284–305) forged a more workable Empire and army. His reign saw a division of Empire, a sharing of power and commands, and promoted a more secure line of frontiers. Whereas, at the start of the third century 33 legions were in service (compared to 28 under Augustus), 60 were documented for AD 300, although these were not of the same manpower strength as early imperial legions. The practice that evolved after AD 250 of peeling off detachments of legions for specific campaigns may have meant that many of the new units formalised in the late third and early fourth centuries were in the order of 500–1,000 men. Nonetheless, all told, including the auxiliary troops (allies, federate forces), Rome's military certainly continued to exceed half-a-million men.[1] However, roles and formats were much different, with cavalry gaining a more formalised role in the field armies or the *comitatus* – troops accompanying the emperor – to which might periodically be added detachments from legionary troops stationed on or near the frontiers. The *comitatus* or mobile armies were strengthened under Constantine, who utilised auxiliary units of Moors and, especially, Germani in his Rhine campaigns and against Maxentius outside Rome: brigades such as the Cornuti ('horned men') or Bracchiati ('armlet wearers') were the ferocious advance or shock troops at the Milvian Bridge; such units became commonplace in the field armies. Units' names provide some idea of location and origin (Roman or non-Roman, legionary or auxiliary, province or campaign), although others are simply numbered (e.g. 'the Sixth'). The indications are therefore of a wider scattering, with some units and soldiery highly mobile: Aurelius Gaius of the Tetrarchic period, for example, is attested as having served across most of the Empire's eastern provinces and frontiers, plus spells in Spain, Mauretania and then across the Danube; he had first signed up with the 'Legio I Italica', but was then in other legionary field detachments such as the 'I Iovia' of Scythia and 'VIII Augusta' of Germany, whose remit clearly ranged far more widely than their names suggest. New units such as the *Lanciarii* and *Mattiarii* (skilled throwers of lances and lead-weighted darts, respectively) indicate efforts to create specialist shock-units, as used by Julian against the Persians.

The *comitatus* armies (or *comitatenses*) were not all commanded by the emperor in person, but were at 'his disposal' and were often joined by him – particularly since the new breed of emperors from the mid-third century tended to be much more battle-experienced and enemy-aware than second-century emperors; sharing the field traumas of the army was important in maintaining troop loyalty and thus power. The Tetrarchic practice of naming new units after their favoured gods – such as the Ioviani, Herculiani and Martenses – is relevant here. Below the emperor came the praetorian prefect who oversaw both recruitment and logistical supply. Command was effected through two high military officials: the *magistri militum* (Masters of Soldiery), comprising the *magister peditum* (Master of Infantry) and *magister equitum* (Master of Cavalry) – these were occasionally combined as a single command in the later fourth century and commonly combined in the fifth century (see below). There emerged more regional armies with their own *magistri*, but responsible to either the Western or Eastern emperor. These forces did not necessarily have a fixed base attached to the imperial capital; rather, when not active, they were billeted in various towns close to the court or regional capital particularly nearer the frontier regions. Infantry still predominated over cavalry units, with the foot soldiery probably in units of 500–1,000 men compared to 300–500 for the cavalry.

While counts commanded detachments of the *comitatus*, a provincial duke or *dux* tended the *limitanei*, strung out along the frontiers in legionary forts, lesser forts and watchtowers. The impact on numbers must have been strongest at the frontiers as it was from these legions that the specialist and field units were drawn. Significantly, the frontier forces were considered secondary to the mobile army in role and status; after all, their dispersed numbers weakened cohesion and their restricted base-unit size may even have prevented any real engagement with a forceful enemy. Observation duties, policing, river boat or desert patrols, road control and maintenance were the key duties, but with horse detachments available for (relatively rapid) communication to ducal headquarters and beyond. The *limitanei* effectively registered a Roman military presence in a given zone, indicated a defensive readiness, and provided local order and security. Their names often took on a geographical or fort title, such as the *Divitenses*, derived from the fortified bridgehead of Divitia on the Rhine near Cologne, but originally comprising the *legio II Italica*; close by were the *Tungrecani*, a garrison centred on Tongres. Such localisation of troops could be beneficial in terms of providing a strong bond to place and territory and its defence, and also in terms of recruitment; but it may at the same time have required tighter control of training to ensure the garrisons did not go 'soft'. Instructive is the example of Flavius Abinnaeus, commander of a cavalry unit (the *ala V Praelectorum*) at Dionysias in Egypt in the 340s, whose duties are illustrated via surviving papyri. As well as dealing with his own soldiers' bouts of drunken behaviour and occasional theft, and loaning nets to a clergyman to help keep gazelles away from crops, Abinnaeus' main concerns were receiving appeals from the victims of animal thefts or burglaries. Northern province-based unit commanders undoubtedly faced far tougher tasks.

But there was investment still in the *limitanei*, in maintaining food and equipment supply, tower building, fort repair, and, on the northern frontiers, in the riverine defences through fuller provision of swift boats to observe, guard, ferry or respond, plus fortified harbours and bridgeheads. As well as references to fleet commands in the *Notitia* (some centred on lakes such as Como and Maggiore in north Italy), for AD 420 we hear of the provision of patrol craft for the eastern Danubian provinces: a total of 100 vessels (90 new, 10 repaired) on the Moesia border and 125 for the Scythian border (110 new), with new 'fully equipped' craft to be added each year so that 'restoration of the entire number of craft decreed shall be speedily completed within seven years'. The new craft was for use in conflicts and expeditions, whereas the older vessels were for supply and transport, though no doubt commandeered for military duties if required.[2]

BARBARIANS AND THE ROMAN ARMY

Besides the politico-military narrative of Ammianus Marcellinus, much of our knowledge of late Roman military organisation and troop deployment derives from the early fifth-century *Notitia Dignitatum*.[3] The *Notitia* lists the divisions of commands for East and West, enumerates the generals' subordinates and provincial commanders and forces, and generally provides units' station names; en route the *Notitia* (or at least its fifteenth-century copies) provides vignettes illustrating the major offices with schematic fortifications for dukes and counts (such as the count of the Saxon Shore for Britain – see Chapter 3 in this book); weaponry and letters/scrolls of appointment to represent the commanders; shield designs; plus lists and images of treasuries, mints and arms factories (Figure 2.1) – all illuminating the bulky military personnel and State machinery linked to maintaining and serving Rome's armed forces.

The *Notitia* thus yields valuable official information on the militarised landscapes of the Empire (see Chapter 3 in this book) and, equally importantly, on the strong presence of non-Roman subject, allied and federate forces on Roman soil. In Italy, for example, all 15 prefects or commanders of Sarmatian *gentiles* or peoples are listed, who probably represent captured prisoners-of-war settled across the Empire, in theory on vacant or uncultivated land and who performed military or other service when called upon by the prefects. Most of these Sarmatians were settled in the first half of the fourth century, but since Rome was allied with the Sarmatians for a time, not all of these need be seen as ex-prisoners. Their settlement could be dispersed over a region, but for the majority specific urban sites are recorded, such as for the *Praefectus Sarmatarum gentilium*, *Patavio* (Pavia) or *Taurinis* (Turin), implying that these non-Romans worked land close to those towns or within their territory, probably based in village communities. Relevant place names are recorded into the Middle Ages and a few still survive to suggest villages or lands linked to their old tribal name. For Italy these Sarmatian prefects cover much of the Po valley, extending across to Bologna, thus indicating a strategic source of both production and protection (after a generation or two no doubt these groups felt tied to their lands); strikingly, this settlement focus corresponds to the virtual 'heartland' of imperial Italy, servicing the capitals of first Milan and then Ravenna. For northern Gaul, Sarmatians are documented near sites like Paris, Langres and Reims.

Insignia uiri illustris magistri officiorum

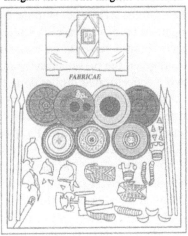

Figure 2.1   Image from the *Notitia Dignitatum Occidentalis* depicting military items produced by the Roman state workshops (*fabricae*) and showing varied shield designs (adapted from image at www.pvv.ntnu.no/~halsteis/notitia.htm)

Prisoners-of-war settled on Roman soil might also be designated as *laeti*, while defeated enemies could supply men for the Roman army as part of a treaty as *tributarii*, or *dediticii*, but the distinctions between these labels are not altogether clear. *Deditio* is the term used across the imperial period for a treaty whereby an enemy or ally accepts or even seeks submission to the Roman State, prompted either through defeat by Rome or the threat of such, or through external pressures. Some of these new subjects then appear inside the Empire, given land to cultivate and required to provide recruits when summoned. As in the aftermath of the Marcomannic Wars in the 170s, such resettlement had a long pedigree and was not peculiar to the late Empire, although the scale and nature of such 'submissions' may have changed significantly from the later third century when warfare along the Rhine and Danube zones displaced many 'lesser' or more fragile tribal groups.[4]

Ammianus Marcellinus (17.13) recounts Roman treatment of the Sarmatians and their rebellious ex-slaves (labelled Limigantes), with the latter eventually defeated in AD 358 and settled elsewhere. The words he gives Constantius are interesting: 'We have forced the Limigantes to move to far distant regions, where they can no longer constitute a threat to our people, and spared the lives of the greater number. As for the Free Sarmatians, we have placed them under the rule of Zizais, who we believe will be devoted and loyal'. Advantages won were fourfold: the emperor gained the label *Sarmaticus*; punishment was inflicted on 'guilty brigands'; captured booty was (re)gained; and the prisoners and subjects formed a new manpower resource for Rome. The mass of Gothic peoples (four tribes), Alans and others who gathered on the Danube in 376 had requested *deditio* and settlement within the Empire to avoid the threat of the Huns. Even after Adrianople the basic request remained largely unaltered, although a weakened Rome then allowed settlement more on Gothic terms: for example, the Gothic, Alan and Hunnic forces of Alatheus and Saphrac most probably gained lands in Pannonia which they had just raided; they may even have been allowed to settle en masse and not be dispersed. At the same time, however, given the presumed substantial Hunnic threat, the Romans may have wanted a concentrated buffer along the Danube.

By contrast, in 370, Alamannic prisoners taken by the *magister equitum* Theodosius were dispatched to Italy 'where they received fertile cantons, and now live as our subjects on the banks of the Po' (Ammianus Marcellinus, 28.5.15). Here Rome dictated settlement, presumably in groups of predetermined size. An edict of 409 in the *Codex Theodosianus* (*CT*) clarifies the process of integration of former enemies: regarding a group of Sciri prisoners, the edict refers to them as *coloni* or farmers, since their role is primarily to till the soil and revive land productivity; indeed, although required to pay taxes, they did not need to provide recruits to the army for 20 years. The text also states that these prisoners-of-war would be settled away from their former homelands. All told, therefore, the Empire hosted, by *c.* AD 400, a relatively high number of resettled immigrant non-Romans who could aid and support Rome; by implication, however, their presence in key territories denotes Roman problems in manpower, army recruitment and productivity.

Archaeological traces of the presence of *laeti*, *gentiles* or *dediticii* in settlement units of detectable size in the provinces are, however, minimal. Place names may exist in northern Italy to support the documented scattered Sarmatian communities, but distinctive 'sarmatian' finds are lacking. Potentially, these blanks should be expected and simply reveal the integration of these settlers into the wider Roman cultural context: they were living on Roman soil now, working within a Roman economy. Nonetheless, it is hard to imagine that no material record of their past endured, even if only for a generation or two; certainly the *Notitia Dignitatum* registers how a formal, named ethnic identity is maintained for official/military purposes. For northern Gaul, well within the frontier zone, traces of settlements of *laeti* have been claimed based on the presence of distinctive burials, deemed both military and 'Germanic' and featuring weapons, 'military-style' belt fittings and, in female tombs, distinctive brooches (notably trumpet brooches). These burials, associated with Roman sites and placed within older cemeteries, or occasionally forming early burials in longer

Germanic–Frankish cemeteries, date to AD 350–425, peaking *c.* AD 400. Their identification with German *laeti* is drawn both from the 'non-Roman' rite but particularly from their geographical correlation with settlements of such *laeti* documented by the *Notitia* (gathered near Trier, Amiens and Langes). However, more recent arguments argue that most artefacts are of Roman manufacture, that the rite of inhumation was at that time not Germanic, that the documented *laeti* settlements are in origin much older than this archaeology, and that *laeti*, *dediticii* and indeed any Roman citizen not in the army were not permitted to bear arms. Alternatively, they might denote federates settled to aid local defence, but this does not tally with the date of the earlier burials attested. Instead, Halsall postulates that these burials denote local (i.e. native) reactions to Roman power vacuums, when elites in a context of weakened central authority had to fend for themselves – perhaps with armed *laeti* or simply with hired retainers and trained estate workers. The burial rites might therefore represent a restated ethnicity for *laeti* (or their descendants) and their women but in a Romanised context. However, the presence of throwing-axes in some graves could indicate Frankish soldiers being brought in by these semi-independent Gallo-Roman elites to aid in local defence. Alternatively, the burials reveal undocumented settlements of federate Frankish groups by the State as formal defensive assistants (it is noticeable that some 'early Germanic' burial sites such as Vermand, Vron and Abbeville-Homblières continue even into the Frankish period).[5] As with much of the archaeology of the frontier provinces in the fifth century, when cultures become mixed and the texts can only sketch people and movements, varied interpretations are possible.

Vegetius' *Epitome* warns how recruits from over the frontiers were swelling the military ranks and swamping out Roman skills and pride. There was a need for willing recruits, however: the law codes make it clear that it was an ongoing struggle to gain sufficient home-grown recruits, and that desertion levels were relatively high (e.g. *CT* 7.18.1–15).[6] The height requirement for service was reduced; levies were made from landowners as a form of tax (though many provided money instead); and from Diocletian onwards there was enforcement by law that sons, from the age of 16, should follow their fathers as soldiers, with soldiers branded to designate their belonging to the State. The laws suggest, however, that in the fourth century the desire to join up was not high and against this pressure, if bribes to the recruiting officers did not work, then young men even mutilated themselves by cutting off their thumbs (though these were then given some other army-related duty or else faced capital punishment (*CT* 7.13.4–5 and 22.1–2); an alternative (and safer) career route was to become a cleric or monk. Unlike earlier imperial armed forces, the likelihood of frequent campaigning or at least not infrequent field duty on the frontiers and thus a potentially short lifespan was high. The State provided some bonuses: regular pay and payment in kind of clothing, arms and rations; donatives with longer service and from victories; scope for promotion, higher pay and privileges; and flexibility in terms of marrying women local to their station. Furthermore, tombstones at Concordia in north-east Italy record soldiers lasting for up to 35 years' service and 'veterans' of 20 years' or more service obtaining land allotments.

In times of high crisis, appeals for extra levies were made, as in AD 406, to help fill the depleted ranks of Stilicho's armies against Alaric (*CT* 7.13.16–17): going against custom, even slaves were summoned, with a promise of freedom and financial reward; preferred choices were those slaves 'retained in the armed imperial service, and likewise the slaves of federated allies (*foederati*) and of conquered peoples (*dediticii*) since it is evident that they are involved in war also along with their masters'. A like appeal to the 'provincials' states: 'On account of Our imminent necessities, by this edict we summon to military service all men who are aroused by the innate spirit of freedom. Freeborn persons, therefore, who take arms under the auspices of military service for love of peace and of country shall know that they will receive 10 *solidi* each from Our imperial treasury when affairs have been adjusted [i.e. the State saved]' but with three *solidi* offered initially. In these times even people 'hiding under the pretext of religious devotion' are rooted out to serve Rome. An earlier guide is the altar from Augsburg dedicated in AD 261 to commemorate a victory against raiding groups of the Iouthungi and Semnones by the Raetian provincial Governor Genialis, whose army was a mix of official Roman troops, local conscripts and volunteers (*populares*) – the text says victory secured the liberation of many thousands of Romans/ Italians captured by the raiders.[7]

To counter such manpower problems caused by loss in civil and external conflict, the employment and recruitment of non-Romans grew steadily greater. Auxiliary forces had long been employed by Rome, offering diverse fighting skills to standard Roman arms. The integration of *gentiles* and *dediticii* from the earlier fourth century made foreign or barbarian recruits attractive, and there seems to have been sizeable enough bodies of volunteers from various tribes drawn to serve and gain status and, later, land: these came as individuals, groups, detachments from Franks, Alamanni, Sciri, Sarmatians, Marcomanni and Quadi in the north or Moors and Arabs in the south and east, reflecting how many of the 'enemy tribes' were composed of a series of small bodies of men (family, kin or blood-sworn groups) fighting under single names. Such 'barbarian' recruits generally served Rome well, and high-born Germans often held quite high ranks, such as King Vadomar of the Brisigavi, from amongst the Alamanni, who had in fact periodically raided Gallic and Raetian lands between AD 352 and 361, but who was kidnapped in 361 while at a dinner party with the commander of a Roman frontier unit; he was dispatched to Spain, but then between 365 and 371 he was attested as a duke, fighting loyally for Rome in the East.

THE BARBARIAN/ROMANO-GERMAN GENERALS

Vadomar is an example of a high-ranking military official of non-Roman birth, ably serving (probably with fellow Alamanni or Brisigavi) the Empire.

Fourth- and fifth-century texts record the names of many comparable Germanic commanders, whose presence is seen by many modern commentators as indicative of the progressive 'barbarisation' of both army and State and an increasing reliance on 'others' to help fight the Roman cause.[8] Sometimes such commanders are indeed named as 'Frankish' by birth or 'Vandal' in origin, or the son of an Alamannic prince, yet often they had lived most of their working/fighting life on Roman soil and classed themselves as Roman, their commands themselves reflecting their acceptance also as 'Roman'. Elton in particular has argued that the 'barbarisation' case is overstated: while names alone suggest that one in four commanders in the Roman armies and even soldiers was probably non-Roman by the mid-fifth century, this figure had been static for about a century; there was no flood of non-Roman authority – 'being 'barbarian' had no effect on promotion. Where we know of individual careers, barbarians followed the same path as Roman officers: *protector-tribunus-comes-magister militum*'.[9]

Certainly we should be cautious in casting doubt on the loyalty or the perceived 'Romanness' of these 'barbaro-Roman' generals because of their ethnic roots. Two examples can be offered. First, Arbogast: 'a Frank and a man of fiery and barbarous spirit, the son of Baudo who had been appointed Master of the soldiers by the Emperor Gratian. Arbogast, through his warlike prowess, compelled Valentinian [II] to allow him to succeed his father as general. He slew many persons of high standing in the Emperor's council, not merely without the Emperor's knowledge but despite his attempts to prevent it' (Eunapius, IX.58, for AD 387). Yet Arbogast had been appointed by the Eastern Emperor Theodosius I as general and guardian in the West; he continued in the court of the Western usurper/Emperor Eugenius (the claim being that Arbogast selected Eugenius) and fought campaigns against the Franks in 388–90. His slaying of council members, arguably, was not a barbarian trait, but indicative of the route to retain power in this period.

Better known is Stilicho, supreme Roman general in the West during the conflict against Alaric and the Visigoths. Referred to as the son of a Vandal father who had been a Roman cavalry officer, his mother was Roman and Stilicho was brought up in both camp and court and actually married a niece of Theodosius in whose armies he served with distinction; he was even made guardian of Honorius in AD 395 after Eugenius' defeat. Later historians such as Zosimus and Orosius are especially aggressive towards Stilicho, claiming he favoured his 'barbarian' troops and entourage; Orosius describes him as 'count Stilicho, who was sprung from the Vandals, that unwarlike, greedy, treacherous and crafty race' and claims he plotted openly with Alaric and with other tribes and sought to put his pagan son Eucherius on the throne. Yet Stilicho's defeat of the vast invasion force led by Radagaisus in 406 shows a commander fully capable of defeating barbarians, while his commissioned praise poems imply wider recognition of his loyalty: Olympiodorus (fr. 5) stated that Stilicho 'attained greater power than anyone and controlled all men, so to speak, both barbarian and Roman'.[10] However, when Honorius ordered the execution of the scapegoat Stilicho in 408, there was a concerted effort to purge towns in Italy (including Pavia, Milan and Ravenna) of 'barbarians': 'The soldiers quartered in the cities, when told of Stilicho's death, fell upon the barbarian women and children in each city and, as if at a preordained signal, destroyed them and confiscated their property'. Unsurprisingly, this brutal reprisal prompted the flight of surviving barbarian troopers and families (Zosimus, V.33–35 claims 30,000 escaped) towards north to join Alaric – an act no doubt fostering the official claim of Stilicho's disloyalty and collusion with the Goths.

Recognition of these Romano-German generals went well beyond military honours. They were frequently awarded other state ranks to accompany their military appointments, and even if posts such as the consulship were largely honorific by the fifth century, nonetheless they indicate acceptance in the 'old' order and established court circle. When Stilicho's son was awarded the insignia of tribune and *notarius* for AD 396, celebratory ivory diptychs were distributed as gifts to members of the Senates at Rome and Constantinople and to esteemed colleagues: the copy preserved in Monza's Cathedral Museum displays Stilicho and his wife on two panels, framed in niches, Stilicho with spear and shield in his hands and a sword on his flank and with cloak held by a prominent brooch (a form typical of high Roman court officialdom); his wife is accompanied by their young son with a like brooch. More splendid still is the large (42-cm diameter) inscribed silver dish (Figure 2.2) found on the western Italian coast at Orbetello in 1769, commemorating the Generalissimo Ardabur Aspar's appointment as principal consul of the West in AD 434.[11] Aspar was of Alan descent, most probably was an Arian Christian, but was part of a distinguished family: his father and father-in-law (both, significantly, depicted in medallions on the dish) had been generals in the East and consuls there in 427 and 419, respectively. Aspar himself had fought previously in the West to help establish Valentinian III on the throne; as consul he campaigned against the Vandals and he maintained high command through the Hunnic war years. A true veteran of the fifth-century upheavals in the West, he was murdered only in AD 471. The dish shows Aspar seated on a cushioned throne, dressed in consular toga, bearing a sceptre but no weapons. The sceptre has two miniature busts of the reigning emperors, the larger that of the more senior Theodosius. Aspar's son is present (already a praetor and in a toga), but more prominent are two flanking city goddesses (Rome and Constantinople). In the foreground lie prizes for the victors of the games being presided over by Aspar. The imagery thus fully conforms to late Roman power display; even the medallions of his perhaps more barbarian relatives reinforce this, with both in Roman garb and holding consular sceptres with imperial busts.

What of actual 'Roman' generals of the fifth century? Did these avoid reliance on barbarians? Stilicho's replacement was Constantius – assigned identical labels of recognition and authority: *patricius, comes, magister militum*, as well as *reparator* or 'restorer'. Constantius too fought for Rome against both Visigoths and Franks, and likewise sought greater power, gaining marriage to

Figure 2.2 The Ardabur Aspar celebratory dish of AD 434 (photo: Museo Archeologico, Florence – Soprintendenza Archeologica per la Toscana – Firenze. Inv. No. 2588)

the imperial princess and then co-emperorship in 421. But he also employed barbarian allies, and when it came to dealing with the Visigoths, he forged an alliance with them and settled them in Aquitaine rather than forcing their banishment, because he recognised their military potential to Rome in trying to stabilise the Western provinces. More striking was the rise of Aetius, made *magister militum per Gallias* and count in the 420s, and consul in 432. He then came to blows in civil conflict with count Boniface of Africa at Rimini, before fleeing to Pannonia. With Boniface's death Aetius returned in 433 and, aided with sizeable contingents of Huns, he compelled a settlement with the Emperor Valentinian III and his Regent Galla Placidia, whereby he was granted patrician status, made consul again in 437, and was *magister utriusque militum* in 445. He was effectively in charge in the West for some two decades, and when the Britons appealed for aid from Rome in 446/7 it was to Aetius and not the imperial court that the request went. His power was secured mainly via his Hunnic allies and retainers, and he and his lieutenants used substantial numbers of Huns, especially as cavalry shock forces, in campaigns against Burgundians, Franks, Visigoths and Bagaudae in the 430s (though there is no archaeology yet to reveal such Hunnic troopers on Roman soil). Aetius saw to the resettlement of the Burgundians in Sapaudia (Savoy), Visigoths in Spain and Alans in Brittany, maintaining the tactics of reusing defeated enemies to defend and occupy damaged Roman space. Valentinian III eventually arranged Aetius' assassination in 454, only for Aetius' former Hunnic bodyguards to gain revenge in 455. Roman and Romano-German generals were not, arguably, any different in their aims, methods and goals, mostly fighting for Rome if also for their own power; nor did they differ much in their ends.

FEDERATES AND FEDERATE SETTLEMENTS

Linked to the rise of these military supremos is the growing presence and exploitation of federate forces. The term federates or *foederati* comes from *foedus* or treaty. In the fourth century the *foedus* placed a defeated or submitted tribe into subject status, but with tribal organisation largely kept; Rome could request military aid and recruits as part of this treaty – hence, for example, a *numerus* of Alamanni documented in Britain by Ammianus Marcellinus – but Rome also often provided gifts and money back. Employing such *foedera* particularly sought to provide buffers along the frontiers rather than a constant supply of troops. Where regiments were enrolled, they appear largely as separate regiments in the *comitatenses* and commanded by Roman tribunes. Such federates may have retained some ethnic distinctiveness – in dress, weaponry, formation – but as they formed part of the regular army, they would have received Roman pay, supplies and equipment and over time ethnic/tribal characteristics might have become diluted. In Britain, the term *Litus Saxonicum* was previously considered to recall not only the enemy it faced but also some of the Saxon defenders enrolled in regular Roman ranks. While a few finds of likely provenance from the Saxony region are known in Britain for the fourth century, associated with settlements such as Caistor, these are in no way sufficient to indicate anything more than a few handfuls of men now serving Rome yet perhaps still displaying some small part of their ethnic background. More telling are the finds from the sizeable cemetery and fort at Krefeld-Gellep (Roman Gelduba) on the Rhine north of Cologne, where an existing burial ground saw insertion of new grave types with males with weapons and females with Germanic jewellery from c. AD 400 to 25. Most probably, this section of the Rhine *limes* became entrusted to Frankish federates who, even if in nominal service to Rome, were displaying their identity in death. Other federate Franks may be evident at the nearby Köln-Junkersdorf necropolis, active from the 450s till c. AD 700, although the fact that this cemetery was unattached to a Roman fort may signify instead part of the process of Frankish colonisation, unattached to Roman federate politics: Cologne had been taken in 459 and made the seat of a Frankish king. For northern Gaul we can note the substantial cemeteries of 700 burials outside the revamped hill fort of Vermand which included one very prominent burial of c. AD 400 containing weaponry, shield, a possible standard, military dress fittings of silver and gilded manufacture – presumed to denote a Frankish chief but one serving as the site's (or region's) Roman commandant.[12]

A sharp distinction must be drawn between federate forces incorporated in the Roman army and those utilised from the later fourth century on as largely separate, fighting units, combating in their own style and led by their own commanders, and supplied for specific campaigns from allies across the borders. Terminology is imprecise, as these may be called federates, auxiliaries or allies. A significant development in this strategy of allied and barbarian troop employment comes in the years after Adrianople, when the Roman authorities, in defeat, were forced to accommodate perhaps 200,000 barbarians on Roman soil. Whilst on paper these peoples formed *dediticii*, in reality many groups remained as organic wholes to form virtual federate territories. So saying, these people now formed a source of manpower for the debilitated Eastern forces, and Gothic troops fighting under their own chieftains played important roles in campaigns of 388 and 394 by Theodosius I against Western usurpers. For 394, Eunapius (IX.60) records that in command of the army the emperor 'placed the Roman Timasius, the Scythian [Goth] Gainas and the Alan Saul, and he also made Stilicho general, a man who was himself of Scythian descent ; he also summoned many of the Huns of Thrace, who served under their tribal chieftains'. For both victories, in Pannonia and in the Alps, commemoration of the Roman blood spilled and the value of these barbarian forces on the true Roman army's side comes in elaborate court panegyrics by Pacatus and Claudian. Pacatus (32.3–5) especially praises the benefits of this influx of alien warriorship:

> You granted the privileged status of fellow soldiers to the barbarian peoples who promised to give you voluntary service, both to remove from the frontier those forces of dubious loyalty, and to add reinforcements to your army. Attracted by your kindness, all the Scythian nations flocked to you in such great numbers that you seemed to have imposed a levy upon barbarians from which you exempted your subjects There marched under Roman leaders and banners the one-time enemies of Rome, and they followed standards which they had once opposed, and filled with soldiers the cities of Pannonia which they had not long ago emptied by hostile plundering. The Goth, the Hun and the Alan responded to their names and stood watch in their turn.

In fact, after Theodosius, employment of allied federate forces became standard in late Roman campaign armies, especially across the northern provinces where Roman logistics were being continually stretched. (One might note how the viciously anti-pagan historian Orosius, in discussing the 'God-inspired' Emperor Theodosius, omits mention of the heavy use of federate forces, but instead speaks of skilful strategy; he likewise says nothing of the bucketloads of Roman blood shed – ch. 35.)

The frontiers were much affected by these changes in power play, since their damaged landscapes offered themselves as ideal stations for barbarian settlement. The expected role of these newcomers is indicated in Eunapius' comments about Theodosius' settlement of the Goths in the 380s (IX:45): 'The emperor received them and gave them supplies and land in the expectation that they would be an excellent and unyielding bulwark against the Hunnic inroads in that area.' What is not clear from the sources, however, is the extent to which regular Roman soldiers and commanders remained still in charge of both towns and frontier installations. Or were forts and towers fully given over to the allies to man in Roman fashion (with pay and supplies promised)? The law codes are nowhere explicit on this matter, except in one decree to the vicar of Africa, Gaudentius, in AD 409 (CT 7.15.1), which states that the border fortifications and lands (terris limitaneis) should be held by the gentiles, the barbarian tribes 'long ago' entrusted with their defence. If other individuals hold them, they must defend 'with zeal' or return them to the gentiles or hand them over to veterans. These tribes count effectively as regular troops in Roman pay. Where other reference to limitanei is made, it is to 'regular' troops: thus for AD 443, 'tried and trusted' dukes only are in charge of the border zones, with the primary duties of overseeing training, fort repair and river patrols. The border militia are expected to cultivate the adjoining lands (although clearly some had extracted themselves from this burden or sold on such plots – Nov. Th. 24.1). The same edict identifies corrupt officials, informing dukes that they must conduct themselves lawfully, and 'refrain from all extortion of the border militia and of the allied tribes, and prohibit their office staffs from such practice'. Although distinctions are being made between troops and tribes, quite possibly the people who made up each were of the same stock, hence the 'extortion'.

This situation might have been that prevailing in the picture contributed by archaeology for the Pannonian frontier from the 380s (see Chapter 3 in this book). While sketchy in detail, the documentary sources indicate that after Adrianople a Gothic splinter group, under two leaders, pushed into Pannonia and was granted lands there. In various frontier fortifications and most notably in some of the smaller forts and towers from this date a diverse material culture with strong trans-Danubian links can be observed, with particular pottery types being produced at some sites (crudely labelled as 'federate ware', but manufactured in Roman fashion). The conclusion drawn by some archaeologists is that these Goths (probably with other peoples amongst them) were allocated lands by the limes and given the official status of border troops. The presence of Roman coin can be taken to indicate 'regular' pay and the likelihood of Roman officials retaining overall responsibility for the mechanics of defence. Alternative interpretations are that there was no major demographic change, but that Roman soldiery adapted to difficult times by adopting ceramics and other goods produced locally or from craftsmen across the frontier (with such transriverine trade long practised); or that a number of Gothic federates were installed and their preferences for local ceramics took on a more visible role (as discussed for the well-excavated late fifth-century fort complex at Dichin on the Lower Danube).[13]

Almost at the end of the period of formal Roman control on the Danubian frontier of the province of Noricum (AD 460–80), we have the testimony (composed a generation after the events described) of Eugippius regarding the life and works of (Saint) Severinus.[14] The region appears a disturbed, fractured one with a fragile Church presence, infrequent supplies of Roman coin and oil, but with frequent raids by groups of Heruls, Alamanni and Thuringians and also by brigands (the 'scamarae'). The eastern part of the *limes* here, extending from Favianis to Vindobona (Vienna), lay under the control of the Rugii – hence the fort/town of Comagenis 'is very strictly guarded by the barbarians established within, who had entered into a league (*foedus*) with the Romans' (Eugippius, ch. 1). We hear of trading between Noricans and Rugii, and Severinus treats with their king, but the Rugii clearly viewed their presence as dominant; in a context of high insecurity, various of the surviving Noricans evacuated eastwards and 'were amicably established in the towns, and lived in friendly alliance with the Rugii' (ch. 31). The contrast is made with the *actual* Roman frontier seats to the west, on which Eugippius comments: 'so long as the Roman dominion lasted, soldiers were maintained in many towns [forts] at the public expense to guard the *limes*. When this custom ceased, the squadrons of soldiers and the *limes* were blotted out altogether' (see Chapter 8 in this book).

In these frontier territories Rome strove to hold sway and to dabble in local power politics through securing alliances with groups to control or buffer borders, to counteract groups beyond, simply to create breathing space for the Roman provincials and their forces, or to buy over mercenaries. Even in bleak periods of conflict inside the Empire, Roman money went beyond the *limes*, implying frequent embassies with gifts, the scale of which depended closely on the scale of threat. While used as part of the military process in the early Empire, the level of such 'gift' exchanges and transfers of moneys (and probably weaponry) escalated substantially in the late Empire, both in terms of numbers of recipients and value. We have figures from some sources, and evidence of coins reused or melted down for jewellery, but we otherwise simply guess at the drain on imperial and urban coffers in periods of economic strain. Whether this growing process of tribute and gift-giving was overall perceived as a valid tool in terms of saving manpower and the costs of logistics on one front when another front drew more attention can be debated. Ammianus Marcellinus, for example, highlights how in 365 the Alamanni revolted from their treaty partly because of Valentinian I's decision to reduce the size of gifts sent to their court; here the diplomatic gift-giving, important for non-Roman kings to display their strengths and to redistribute wealth to their retainers, was threatened. Even tribute payments did not stem the problems: often raids were simply delayed, or else the barbarian groups claimed payments were either insufficient or not prompt enough. Well documented are payments to the Huns: in AD 430 King Roua gained an annual sum of 350 gold *librae* (lb) in 435 this was doubled; in 443 it became 2,100 lb to Attila; and there was also a one-off subsidy of 6,000 lb to Attila.

The drain on Rome's resources must have been enormous. As noted in Chapter 1 of this book, when Alaric besieged Rome, hostages, food and moneys were demanded; elites had to give up much of their portable wealth (although a fair number of the well-to-do had already withdrawn to Sicilian estates or to Constantinople); one embassy from the city presented Alaric with a mass of gold and silver, plus silk garments and jewels taken from imperial statues. This mammoth set of gifts was mainly to enable the inhabitants of the beleaguered city to get in fresh supplies from the port. Alaric was no doubt astounded at the wealth presented, especially as he had been seeking only 4,000 gold *librae* from Stilicho and Honorius for peace during the campaigns in the north! Further gifts, ransoms and bribes denuded Rome's populace, although there was still more found when Alaric did enter Rome, and even more when Athaulf, his successor, came back a year later. Little wonder that Rome's structural recovery was sluggish after the Gothic withdrawal. For the other sack of Rome in 455, according to the Life of Leo I in the *Liber Pontificalis*, the Vandals extorted silver and gold vessels and other liturgical items from all the city's churches bar the major basilicas. The silverware from St Paul's, St Peter's and the Lateran later were melted down and recast to replace all the lost silver services. Other texts emphasise the massive booty accumulated over 2 weeks of looting, both metal and human, from public, imperial and private contexts, mostly then shipped back to adorn the palace and elites of Vandal Carthage. The implication is that there had been relatively strong recovery from the calamities endured under Alaric, but the losses endured in this second catastrophe impoverished Rome more permanently.[15]

Nonetheless, the tribute/bribe/gift system was one repeatedly employed by Eastern and Western imperial courts, meaning that it was a tried and (pretty) trusted approach in Rome's wider strategy of controlling outsiders, whether friendly or hostile. Threats, embassies, words, gifts, banquets and displays all formed part of the complex ritual of power negotiation, often with secret negotiations going on in the background, as Rome's other method was to create dissension within an enemy by favouring a pro-Roman group (although such 'friendly enemies' might cause as much trouble subsequently). The system continues fully into Byzantine times, as in negotiations with the Avars on the Danube or the Lombards in both Pannonia and then Italy in the second half of the sixth century, with many of their dukes and their followers bought over to serve Byzantium, often fighting fellow Lombards; Byzantine policy also included buying in an 'allied' Frankish incursion against the Lombards in north Italy in the 580s, only for the Franks to start their own pillaging and cause extra woes on residual Byzantine bases.[16]

ALLIES: LANDS AND COMMANDS

Many of these would-be allies could often dictate terms to harassed imperial governments. A notable example in the early AD 470s saw the Eastern Emperor Leo send envoys to parley with the Goths in Thrace, who 'had three demands: first that Theoderic, their leader, should receive the inheritance which Aspar [ex-Roman general] had left him; second that he be allowed to live in Thrace;

third that he receive the generalship of the forces which Aspar had led' (Malchus, fr. 2). When Leo rejected these terms, Theoderic marched on Arcadiopolis and captured it through starvation of the besieged population. A treaty was then forged with these terms: 'That every year the Goths should receive 2000 lb of gold; that Theoderic be appointed general of the two forces attendant upon the Emperor that he be sole ruler of the Goths and that the Emperor should not admit anyone who wished to cross to his territory; that Theoderic should fight with the Emperor against anyone whom the latter ordered, except only the Vandals'. This combination – barbarian forces fighting for Rome (for pay, glory and as part of a treaty arrangement), their leaders being granted (often with little real choice available to the Roman emperors) high military offices, and 'allies' being provided with (or, more usually, carving out) land on which to settle and even being paid to be there – lends itself to an image of fragmenting Roman control over its armed forces and territories. Yet the settling of large federate groups offered a plausible route to stabilising matters and in most cases the 'barbarian' desire was to forge partnerships with Rome or to share in the landed benefits: thus recognition, Roman command, land and coin were sought by Alaric from Honorius in the 400s.

Significantly, the proportions of non-Roman/barbarian generals serving and fighting for Rome remained static across c. AD 340–460. However, against this we can observe that the presence on Roman soil of these largely autonomous if allied forces, whether Visigoths, Ostrogoths or Franks, negated the need for their high elites to seek office directly in the imperial ranks for they could now command their own forces instead and still be in Roman pay. The barbarian settlements in Spain and south-west Gaul are cases in point: in 409, Gerontius, generalissimo to the usurper Constantine III, concluded a treaty with the Vandals and their allies in Spain; the Asding Vandals and the Sueves were then allocated north-west Spain by Gerontius who tried unsuccessfully to expand his own power base into Gaul; Vandals and Sueves were thus provided with land (or tax revenues?) and asked to aid in the defence of the Spanish provinces. To recover the rebellious provinces of Spain and Gaul, Honorius commissioned the Goths under their chief (but also now *magister militum*) Athaulf, to be supported by regular Roman soldiery: these successfully dislodged the Vandals – if only pushing them onto Spain – and reduced the Sueves – though these remained as an enclave in north-west Spain. In 418 the Goths were themselves settled in Aquitania Secunda. This Gothic settlement must have been in line with Gerontius' actions for Vandals and Sueves in Spain, settling federates along the frontiers. We cannot easily determine, however, if in Spain as in Aquitania there was available or uncultivated land: were native farmers evicted, or did warfare in the 410s mean the death of many farmers and the abandonment of lands? Or perhaps landowners paid produce to the new settlers as tax to the army? Whichever the case, Rome had been forced to adapt an older policy of *deditio* to much changed circumstances *within* her provinces. These new powers on Roman soil were difficult to dislodge once established; the tribes recognised this themselves of course and we see how they worked both for and against the central Roman authorities depending on the respective benefits (although the for/against policy might often indicate internal power struggles amongst these barbarian groups).

Such settlements and statements of regional authority should have brought with them distinctive displays of identity by these non-Roman groups on Roman soil, and yet, archaeologically, traces are generally very slight. For example, for the Visigoths, we can merely cite one tomb at Villafontana near Verona of c. AD 400 prior to their settlement in Spain, and even then there are few secure Visigothic cemeteries until the sixth century. In fifth-century Spain, however, there are signs of different Hispano-Roman burial rites coming into play which suggest tension and regional identities. The Burgundians, settled around Worms on the upper Rhine in 413, are known only by name there; their archaeology in *Sapaudia* (southern Switzerland) for the second half of the fifth century is minimal and shows instead a maintained Roman presence if with adaptation to new influences; only from c. AD 500 is anything distinctively 'Burgundian' claimed.[17]

ARMS FACTORIES IN THE WEST

When Alaric was toying with the Roman powers as his Visigoths ranged outwards from Dalmatia at the start of the fifth century, one of his additional demands was for Roman weaponry and military equipment to fit out his men.[18] The king was well aware of the State's factories and stores of *militaria* – shields, arrows, swords, helmets, and so on – which were designed to supply both mobile armies and frontier troops. These State factories or *fabricae* are documented in the *Notitia Dignitatum* and testify Rome's ability to mass produce goods to furnish its armies, but the changed provincial landscapes of the fifth-century West, with increasing barbarian settlements within the Empire and unstable, mobile barbarian groups and federates elsewhere, put these factories under major threat.

Understanding these *fabricae* is important.[19] The *CT* (10.22.4 of AD 398) refers to workers in these State factories being branded, like army recruits. Theodosius II makes their role plain: 'The harsh necessity of war has invented the guild of *fabricenses*, which guards the decrees of the Emperors with a kind of immortality for this guild arms, this guild equips Our army' (*Nov. Th.* 6, of AD 438). The listing in the *Notitia* indicates the bond between army and city, with the cities providing the space and the labour pool to undertake the manufactures. Indeed, the distribution of these factories (or extended 'workshops') reflects the geography of State military expenditure, mobile army presences and, arguably, the 'pressure points' within the Empire.

The *fabricae* were most likely introduced during the Tetrarchy, as part of the process of tighter centralised control and articulation via smaller provinces, and initiated in conjunction with the building and rebuilding campaigns in many urban centres and particularly at the new imperial capitals such as

Milan, Trier and Nicomedia, when spatial reorganisations will have accommodated these complexes. Diocletian's retirement home of Split-Salona also had a weapons factory. Some may have developed from pre-existing workshops (as at the legionary forts of Carnuntum and Lauriacum), and we can also identify some late changes or transfers of *fabricae* linked to weakened military control (see below). Our information from the *Notitia* for the Western Empire appears fuller than for the Eastern for which only weapons factories are recorded (Map 2.1): nonetheless, the distribution of these bases covers a wide belt of strategic territory extending from Syria and the Bosphorus westwards along the Danube, northern Italy and to the English Channel, in touch with (but, significantly, generally withdrawn from) the frontiers themselves. The major imperial capitals of Trier, Milan, Sirmium and Constantinople are fully integrated into this factory belt. In contrast, Spain, North Africa and Egypt are excluded, and Britain was probably supplied largely from Gaul. Specific roles are allocated to the individual *fabricae*, producing weapons or shields and armour, parade gear, clothing (wool and linen) or dyes. Factories tend to cluster, but regional productions are never sited in a single place. For Gaul and Germany, the following distribution emerges, with the imperial centres of Arles and Trier being prominent foci of production and redistribution, each containing also a treasury and mint:

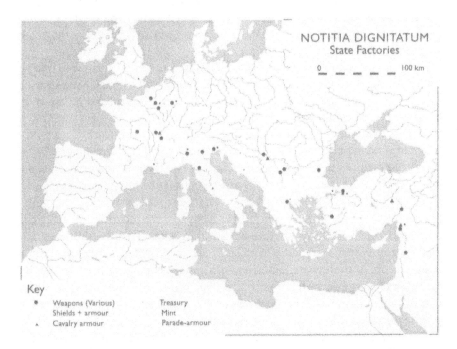

Map 2.1 Distribution of arms and other state factories in the fourth and fifth centuries across the Empire. Note how almost all lie predominantly in frontier provinces (after Randsborg 1991: Figs 52 and 54)

Tournai (woollen cloth); Amiens (swords, shields); Soissons (weapons); Reims (woollen cloth, parade armour, swords); Metz (woollen cloth); Trier (woollen cloth, parade armour, shields, siege artillery); Autun (woollen cloth, shields, cuirasses, cavalry armour, siege artillery); Argenton (weapons); Macon (arrows); Lyons (woollen cloth); Vienne (linen); Viviers (? woollen cloth); Arles (woollen cloth, parade armour); Narbonne (dye), Toulon (dye)

Why the limited production around the Middle Danube frontiers (shield factories at Lauriacum in Noricum and at Carnuntum and Aquincum in Pannonia, and woollen cloth at Iovia (Heténypuszta and Bassiana))? Since only Sirmium is entrusted with wider manufacture (woollen cloth, weapons, shields, saddles), we should assume that other supplies were brought in from north Italy; the rather uncertain control of the territory, especially in the wake of federate Gothic and Sarmatian settlement across the Balkans after Adrianople, may have prompted avoidance of stockpiling arms nearby. Noticeably, even before Adrianople, on the occasion of Valentinian's campaigns against the Quadi in 373, Ammianus describes one seat of weapon manufacture, Carnuntum, as abandoned, implying that manufacture had already ceased here; conceivably Valentinian re-initiated it, hence its listing in the *Notitia*; alternatively, the list was out of date when compiled, but disbanded frontier factory names were not deleted.

What emerge from the *Notitia* are broad distinctions in warfare between East and West, with heavy horse and cavalry armour produced primarily for the Eastern armies, whilst infantry sword and leather armour manufacture, and missile, arrow and bow production, are listed just for the West – peculiar since mounted archers were a commonplace in the East. (There are, however, gaps in the Eastern listings.)

The *fabricae* were thus sited in well-defended towns or fortresses (mostly linked with the *annona* and often with the mobile army), on major communications routes, and with a good labour supply. Imperial control and repair of the roads and of the *cursus publicus* (the imperial courier service) were essential to ensure due supplies from the lands and to the armies. The workshops would have required supplies of raw materials, notably wood for kilns. Logically the State arms factories produced regular supplies as opposed to meeting demands only when required; during more pacific periods, stockpiling must have taken place, unless stocks were transported to frontier zones for redistribution on a regular basis. Unfortunately, no *fabrica* has yet been identified archaeologically and so we cannot say whether work was in covered halls or in spaces akin to small individual workshops. Similarly, we are not clear on the manpower requirements of these State factories, with estimates ranging from 200 to 500 men for each. At Concordia in northern Italy, however, numerous tombstones at least testify to some of the workers and the hierarchy of organisation.[20] The *Notitia* identifies the *fabricae* as overseen by the *magister officiorum*, with subordinate *subadiuvae fabricarum* of high rank and seniority, and below these, grades of clerks. The organisation of the actual workers (*fabricenses*) is less well known, but military-style labels are applied to recorded staff, notably the manager or *praepositus* (although Ammianus Marcellinus refers to tribunes as the directors) and lesser officers labelled *primicerius* and *senator*. Presumably there was internal promotion, and even transfers from armed service to these factories, such as by veterans. Epitaphs of *fabricenses* at Concordia relate chiefly to these internal ranks but include some ordinary workers and minor office heads – enough to show that all could afford a decent burial and memorial stone. Indeed, despite branding as State workers and despite service being hereditary, the *fabricenses* were not slaves (unlike workers in the mints and textile factories) but skilled and valuable craftsmen, with certain advantages: they were enrolled in guilds; they had the same privileges as soldiers or government clerks, being exempt from compulsory public service and having immunity from billeting of troops; there was probably also a fixed length of service. We hear little of desertion but we do hear of decurions trying to get into the *fabricenses* to avoid other onerous duties. One epitaph from Marcianopolis (Thrace) commemorates Flavius Zenis, died aged 50, who served in the army, enrolled in the *fabrica* and worked for 20 years as a *centenarius*, was married for 30 years (i.e. married while still a soldier) and coped with 12 children!

State factories endured in the Eastern Empire into the sixth century, with production necessarily busy in the reign of Justinian I (527–65) whose western reconquests and conflicts against Persia required well-equipped field troops and garrisons. In the West, by contrast, coordinated State manufacturing must have largely ceased by the mid-fifth century as provincial control collapsed and mining likewise faltered. Residual production might nonetheless be expected for Gaul and Italy as the new rulers, who generally maintained Roman urban administration, equally needed weapons to maintain power. Thus, in sixth-century Ostrogothic Italy, Cassiodorus records how the praetorian prefect was in overall charge of the 'arms-makers' or *armifactores*, who are 'fulfilling their customary tasks [to] make arms well and to guard the safety of all'. Quite possibly these factories remained in the same cities attested for fourth-century Italy, although by King Theoderic's day, Concordia was depopulated and no longer suitable; 'royal' cities like Pavia, Ravenna and Milan, each with strong Gothic military presences, may have instead housed these. For seventh-century Rome, excavations at the Crypta Balbi have shown how even smallish workshops were producing good-quality belt sets, buckles, as well as dress items; most probably iron-working and weapon production took place in similar workshops elsewhere in the decayed cityscape.[21]

WEAPONRY AND TACTICS

Rome's military forces remained formidable fighting machines. The ability to survive civil wars, to fend off barbarian intruders, to maintain high levels of recruitment and to preserve vast and diverse frontier lines, all speak of the army's quality training, organisation and durability. Tetrarchic reforms, plus adoption of additional federate and ally forces, reveal an evolution too. Certainly poor leadership, cowardice on the field, failed sieges, lost garrisons and legions are events attested in sources like Ammianus Marcellinus, but this historian also illustrates fully the resilience and strength overall of troops along the Rhine and Danube in the face of turbulent events. Thus, for example, his description (16.12.36–53) of the dramatic combat and victory at Strasbourg in AD 357:

> Missiles were hurled for a short time before the Germans rushed forward with more haste than thought, wielding their weapons in their right hands and throwing themselves upon our squadrons of horse with horrible grinding of their teeth. Our men faced them resolutely, protecting their heads with their shields, thrusting their swords or brandishing their javelins so as to intimidate them with the prospect of death. At the critical point in the battle, when our cavalry were bravely regrouping and the infantry were stoutly protecting their flanks with a wall of overlapping shields, thick clouds of dust arose. The Cornuti and Bracchiati, hardened by long experience of war, intimidated the enemy by their conduct and raised their mighty battle-cry. But the Alamanni, who enter wars enthusiastically, strove even harder, like inspired madmen, to destroy everything in front of them; they were stronger and taller, [but] the Romans had the advantage in discipline from long practice.

Although sounding like front-line reportage, this was not a genuine first-hand vision of the battlefield; nonetheless, Ammianus Marcellinus stresses due Roman order, cohesion and prowess. Vegetius similarly flags those strengths which set the Romans apart from 'the others': building forts, bridges and roads, marching at speed and equipped, and relieving sieges.

The army was also well provided for in terms of logistical support. Granaries were prominent units built within forts, and supply depots were established on many key roads running from provinces interior to frontiers.[22] Certainly, the presence of *fabricae* indicates a standardised production of weaponry and military dress, designed to match the standardised training of the soldiers. Yet our knowledge of late Roman military dress is still fairly limited archaeologically and is drawn as much from sculptural reliefs – tombstones (few exist for the late Empire), sarcophagi, triumphal arches and columns – and other iconographic sources, such as the *Notitia* vignettes, illuminated manuscripts, or rare mosaic illustrations. Much more material evidence of Roman arms in fact comes from outside of the Empire, notably from second- and third-century Danish bog offerings – these weapons either taken as booty from Romans, belonging to soldiery who had served Rome, gained by trade, or even supplied as part of a formal treaty.[23]

Such material evidence, combined with contemporary descriptions of battles, weapons and tactics by historians like Ammianus Marcellinus and Vegetius, suggest little significant change in Roman military provisioning from late Republican times in terms of weaponry, from short sword to lance and javelin, to helmet and shield and body armour; where Vegetius claims that some infantry abandoned body armour or helmets in Gratian's reign, the proof is currently lacking, unless he means those non-Roman troops starting to play a greater role in or alongside Roman armies but equipped with their own weapons and dress (which largely meant no body armour except amongst the elite). Yet the view that Roman weaponry and tactics were static is erroneous, since, as highlighted above, diverse and specialist fighting units like the

Mattiarii come into play, and troops were being drawn from varied provincial and extra-provincial contexts, and being stationed and re-stationed across the Empire, facing diverse opponents and environments. Fighting Berber raiding parties required different tactics to facing seaborne groups in the North Sea regions; and dress varied according to factors like climate, mobility and enemy weaponry.

The archaeology does recognise less uniformity as one progresses into the fifth century, with provincial-oriented differences in dress items such as belt buckles and cloak brooches in particular.[24] These differences may derive from older dress traditions and match evident variations in terms of, say, funerary commemoration – thus, the types of tombstone depictions in Pannonia are quite different from those in Spanish or Tripolitanian works. Influences could be 'pre-Roman' or indigenous or even external: Coulston, for example, has traced how the *draco* standard was introduced into the Roman army by the second century AD and then evolved from a wolf-headed standard to a snake-headed version; each had a free-flowing sinuous body that fluttered and even hissed in the wind, especially when carried by riders, but effective also when waved by the standard-bearers.[25] These may have Dacian or Sarmatian roots, but then became new legionary emblems – perhaps symbols of Rome capturing and then making her own these beasts of war. *Dracones* appear on victory monuments such as the arches of Galerius at Thessaloniki and Constantine at Rome, and sources attest how victory marches, including Constantius II's entry into Rome in the 350s, were accompanied by flowing ranks of such animals; both Julian and Constantius II had associated purple-embroidered *dracones*. The popularity of these standards might in part link to the prominence of Danubian-drawn soldiery from the third century, these perhaps familiar with the Sarmatians and their *dracones*. Furthermore, Sarmatians at times were allies of Rome, with many settled in its territories; their integration inevitably created a fusion of ideas, styles and materials drawn on by Rome.

AN EVOLVING MILITARY BEAST

Rome's military, its operations, organisation and supply were massive, but somehow Rome's Empire did cope with all these demands and continue to deploy and maintain a vast standing or professional army. Changes were necessarily effected to ensure stability internally and externally, and Rome adapted to wider circumstances, notably in terms of employing non-Romans in growing numbers. Use of 'Romano-German' generals was part of this evolution. Things worked, all told: the *limitanei* did allow for a long extension of life to the damaged frontiers; the mobile armies did counter many serious incursions; many efficient generals were produced; and alliances and associated money tributes often held certain tribes at bay or facilitated dealings with future enemies further afield. As Chapter 3 of this book will show, frontiers were being updated; town walls gave new security for populations and administrations; inner defences also offered better advance warnings to provinces.

But there was an increasing militarisation or at least a greater emphasis on the army and its role; emperors too were as much military generals as politicians; and the over-frequent civil wars and usurpations did little to help through diverting troops and logistics away from frontiers, and using up manpower, resources and even provincial support. At the same time, moneys were being squeezed from people and State alike to fund the army and to pay vast annual tributes to not always loyal allies over the frontiers; allied forces within the Empire and *limitanei* had varied loyalties; and insufficient manpower to help defend inner defences and town walls appears evident. While Rome coped in the fourth century, the scale and threats increased dramatically from the end of that century: from Adrianople to Alaric Rome was fighting more in its own backyards and on a level that meant frontiers were breached elsewhere in the West to devastating effect, meaning it became impossible to meet all of these threats over such dispersed fronts. Accordingly, Rome's Western emperors (and their generalissimos) increasingly turned to settlement (some forced, but many granted strategically) of federate bodies. The contrast lies with the Eastern Empire, where enemy penetrations were reduced and the frontiers of the lower Danube and the East remained busy but manageable; a seemingly closer hold over federate and allied forces further limited the power struggles that so wracked the West from the second third of the century. Nonetheless, the military changes enumerated in this chapter became part of the later Roman fabric: the State and army were forced to adapt in the wake of the third-century crises; these reforms were then consolidated and extended; tactics evolved as diverse enemies and conditions emerged. It is easy to see fragmentation and usurpation as well as State aggression towards its citizenry, but the whole clearly functioned on a fairly high and satisfactory level for two centuries until the break-up of the West began in earnest in the earlier fifth century. Life in the inner provinces may have felt relatively secure if slowly different; as Chapter 3 of this book will show, however, life on and near the frontiers may well have grown far less comfortable and, by the fifth century, far less Roman.

3

Defending the Late Roman West:
II. Frontiers, Forts and Towns

INTRODUCTION

Surviving documentary sources rarely discuss the physical characteristics of the defences that the army manned: the forts, fortresses, towers and roads that formed the frontiers which observed enemy movements and protected the hinterlands; the signal stations and fleet bases that monitored the river and coastal borders; and the walls which girded many Roman settlements. Perhaps because these were functional and necessary, few of these works merited more than summary comment in annals, and only the more substantial city defences featured dedicatory honorific inscriptions. Potentially this is an imbalance of survival, since occasional inscriptions for watchtowers on the Danube or for lesser town circuits in Italy exist to indicate a level of pride on the part of the (military) builders; and, arguably, inscriptions recording the name of the emperor whose reign sought to provide such structures should have been common displays over many a formal gateway to fort or town. Instead, for many provinces, archaeology often provides the essential guide to this widespread phenomenon of defence. This chapter, therefore, explores the format and scale of defensive works undertaken in the late Empire: How do such works evolve? How 'scientific' is the military architecture? How systematic were the processes of frontier, intraprovincial and urban defence? Just how safe was the late Roman West?

ROME AND THE FRONTIERS

The frontiers of the Roman Empire were extensive, varied and demanding. These were not all powerful and continuous networks of built walls as might be envisaged on the basis of the standing remains of Hadrian's Wall on the furthest north-westerly confines – after all, just north of this exists the earthen and timber rampart and ditch system of the Antonine 'Wall', denoting a revision to the demarcation of Roman territory. Stone and brick were used for forts and sections of walls on other frontier lines (*limes* – plural *limites*), but earth ramparts and ditches were otherwise employed between, and often not continuously; in North Africa, a solid barrier strung out between desert, mountains and oases was in no way feasible, as recognised also in the borders with Persia. Rome's frontiers varied in terms of context and topography: from river lines to seas, desert and mountain, and to artificial divisions between civilised and uncivilised. Further, they varied in relation to the types of enemy (real or potential) and warfare that Rome sought to counter – from Moorish tribal raids in Mauretania to pirates along the Channel coasts, formal campaigns against the Parthians and occasional massed assaults across the river frontiers by Germanic tribal groupings. The frontiers and their troops were adapted accordingly. Logistically, manpower demands were enormous to patrol effectively these extended *limites* and, as importantly, to maintain them. Rather, tactics were centred on controlling access, by channelling incomers of whatever nature to key or fixed points (Hadrian's Wall is thus punctured at regular points by gates). In periods of stability (as prevailed for much of AD 5–250), such frontier movements were chiefly trading operations – witness the numerous artefacts, notably associated with wine drinking and storage, and dress items found in territories like Belgium, North Germany, Denmark, Scotland and Ireland.[1] Earlier frontier policy was predominantly policing and taxing: taking tolls, checking goods in and out of Roman territory, directing incomers to the right markets, preventing any concerted efforts to rob and pilfer.[2] But the frontier's role was also a visible one, with the presence and solidity of forts, towers and weaponry designed to reinforce the message of Roman control and order. The claim that the north face of Hadrian's Wall was whitewashed to make it stand out on the horizon (except when the Northumbrian mists hung low or snow fell) is noteworthy here.

But inner conflicts and disruptions to trade inside and outside Roman territories easily upset the stability favoured by Rome of the many small and larger tribal groups beyond; socio-economic tensions and the breakdown in the flow of goods needed to maintain power relations saw, from the third century in particular, efforts by some groups to strike out and new power groups emerging.[3] Whilst on paper these disruptive elements should not have damaged a secure frontier, as seen, these were not solid barriers, and punctures were created. Tightened security and limitations on transit could effectively transform the image of these borders from points of negotiation to ones of military control. This does not preclude traffic and trade, but the indications – improperly measured in the zones just over the *limites* – are of a greatly reduced flow of Roman goods outwards. I would argue that for many bordering territories in the third and fourth centuries the former stability was lost and the material expressions of such were reduced; most probably, those who had formerly traded with Rome from outside the frontiers sought to be inside instead. Arguably, therefore, the 'frontiers' of the Empire conform far more to our mental image of an Us/Them barrier from the third century. The many well-documented embassies with related gift-giving show that movement across the *limites* did not slow down, but the nature of exchange altered; Rome increasingly did more to 'cultivate' its external neighbours and use these as 'buffers'. Alongside this came increasing efforts and attention by the emperors to reinforce the frontier lines and create an efficient inward military response system. Thus an edict for AD 443 states how 'Especial care must be bestowed upon the borders, by which the whole State is especially protected' (*Nov. Th.* 24.1). Similarly, the role of frontier provinces is well summarised by Cassiodorus (*Variae* VII, 4) in c.500 for the Ostrogothic kingdom of Italy, which maintained Roman arrangements:

> The provinces of Rhaetia [Austria] are the bars and bolts of Italy, wild and cruel nations camp outside of them, and they, like nets, whence their names, catch the barbarian in their toils and hold him there till the hurled arrow can chastise his mad presumption ... Let your soldiers live on friendly terms with the provincials, avoiding all lawless presumption; and at the same time let them be constantly on their guard against the Barbarians outside. Even bloodshed is often prevented by seasonable vigilance.

The late Empire is when military historians identify the imposition of a system of 'defence in depth': a thickening and then layering of protective components, both structural and human, working inwards from the frontiers, and coming to include a fortification of the Empire's towns. The Empire became 'militarised' and increasingly 'barbarised'.[4] Debate rages over how systematic or coherent this programme of defence was: Can we identify a master plan? Is it right to talk about a 'strategy' or did measures evolve *ad hoc*? Each province and different regions in these saw variable levels of insecurity build from the third century, and some provinces like Spain saw minimal disruption until the fifth century. Archaeology shows an inconsistent picture of reaction, response, preparation and investment in defensive structures. But need this deny an effort of systematic response as well as planning? After all, the Western Roman Empire recovered from the third-century crisis and saw fair economic renewal in the fourth century. Even with elevated threats from outside, the Empire endured many generations after Constantine, indicating its arms, diplomacy and tactics could function well. Below we explore late Roman frontiers and defence: How did frontier installations change and can we observe a 'decline'? What patterns exist with the processes of town fortification? Did the proliferation of walls and soldiery dramatically change the face of the provinces?

WORKING FRONTIERS: TWO CASE STUDIES

We can pursue the tactical evolution of two western frontiers to observe imperial thinking, strategy, support and breakdown. The first, the River Danube frontier in Pannonia (Hungary), is reasonably well documented by text but better by archaeology; the second, Hadrian's Wall, the northern frontier of Roman Britain, largely lacks written testimony but has seen fairly extensive excavation. Overall, in terms of Roman archaeology, frontier studies are the best supported archaeologically, with an extremely long-established

German–Austrian tradition of *limes* excavations for the Rhine and upper Danube borders, along with good Hungarian, Romanian and Bulgarian research for the Danube provinces (where knowledge of the frontier forts far exceeds that of the intraprovincial urban and rural settlement patterns). Much recent work has focused on the Eastern frontiers, whilst studies of the African borders have yet to advance as systematically. In Britain, various studies have been made of the system known as the Saxon Shore since the mid-nineteenth century, with particular focus in the 1960s at sites like Burgh Castle, Richborough, Pevensey and Portchester, and yet with only the latter adequately brought to publication, leaving the sequences of the majority somewhat vague.[5] Arguably, similar problems exist on many of the frontier zones: we can piece together plans and basic chronologies, but often more can be said of origins and floruits than of final phases.

The Limes Pannonicus – The Middle Danube Frontier

The first stages of consolidated military control of the Danube at the northern border of Noricum and the northern and eastern flanks of Pannonia can be placed in the mid-first century AD, with well-spaced timber forts and watchtowers erected, and with most forts containing infantry cohorts and cavalry units or *alae* – these soldiers fairly quickly being locally recruited. For the approximately 200-km stretch of river line for Noricum, the estimate is for about 6,000 men. Forts and soldiery attracted native (and non-Roman) settlers and traders and substantial civilian suburbs (*vici*) grew up in the second century as forts were converted to stone. The 160s marked destructive inroads by Marcomannic warriors which extended into northern Italy, but which chiefly affected Noricum. This revealed the relative fragility of the river defence line against one or more concerted attacks. While Rome recovered and took the fight over the Danube, the frontier was reinforced with a legion established at *Lauriacum*-Lorch and by additional forts.

Third-century upheavals and the Diocletianic and Constantinian reforms saw substantial organisational changes to the Danube *limes*, marked principally by enhanced numbers and mobility (cavalry units and river patrol fleets). From the list of stations and units preserved in the late fourth-century *Notitia Dignitatum*, in Noricum the frontier troops were, in theory, equally balanced along the whole river line, enabling ease of reinforcement when required; the whole to be supported if required by detachments of the mobile army (*comitatenses*). For Pannonia, troops were concentrated in the north, in recognition of the strategic importance of the 'Danube Bend' in the northeastern territory (Pannonia was divided into four new administrative territories, with the Bend the northern and eastern edges of *Valeria*) (Maps 3.1 and 3.2). Here the chief threat was from the Sarmatians, settled in the Central Hungarian Plain, and requiring the installation of additional *limes* watchtowers and forts, as at Visegrád-Sibrik and *Castra ad Herculem*-Pilismarot, both probably built in response to Sarmatian incursions in AD 322, and both comprising hilltop fortifications of irregular plan with mainly U-shaped towers.

At each we see the combination of nature and current artificial military architecture, seeking to maximise protection and enhance the visibility of possible threats. In addition, heavily fortified sites were installed on internal roads as likely supply depots (see below).

A conclusive victory under Constantine against the Sarmatians effected a lasting treaty and some outpost construction on Sarmatian soil. Further, it is argued that the massive earthwork system termed the 'Devil's Dyke', extending up to roughly 500 km and enclosing the core of *Sarmatia*, was a Romano-Sarmatian defensive/territorial rampart, built with Roman engineering support – it would

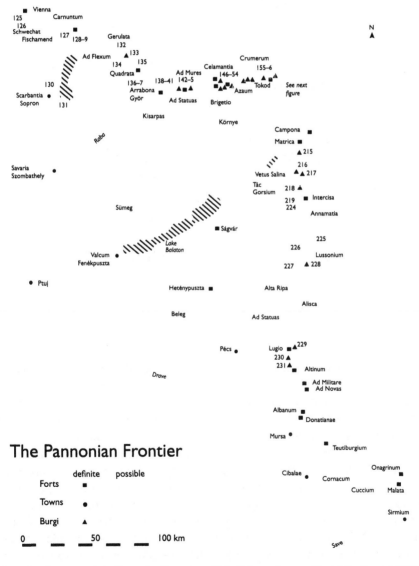

Map 3.1   Pannonia – later Roman frontier system with key interprovince road lines (after Soproni 1985)

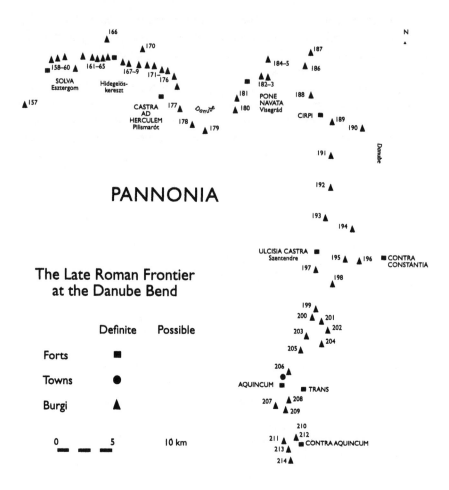

Map 3.2 Pannonia – detail of the frontier arrangements along the 'Danube Bend' sector (after Soproni 1985)

have been impossible to defend wholesale, but potentially would have deflected threats onto more heavily fortified zones. It also seems that Rome was making size-able tribute payments to the Sarmatian royals: up to 45,000 Roman coins of AD 305–61 are known from the Banat zone. The presence of Roman belt sets may signify provision of weapons and dress fittings to these new allies.

The later evidence of the *Notitia Dignitatum* reveals a military make-up on three levels: first, the mobile field army or *comitatenses*, comprising 15,000 troops under the *magister peditum* (infantry generalissimo) for west Illyricum (i.e. Noricum, Pannonia, Dalmatia); second, the specific Pannonian frontier troops, the *limitanei* or *riparienses* which numbered about 20,400, distributed chiefly in the river forts and towers and in certain major towns; third, the river fleets, patrolling not just the Danube, but also the inner Drau and Save rivers; these numbered amongst the *riparienses* to a total of

Map 3.3   Late Roman defences in Britain (after Jones & Mattingly 1990: Map 4.67)

about 5,000. All told, a maximum of 35,000 soldiers is attested for late Roman Pannonia – sizeable forces which required complex logistical support in terms of food, armour, weapons and materials, the mechanics of which are still poorly understood. It is important to remember, however, that the specific Pannonian *limitanei* were strung out in small units across a long frontier, creating a visible but thin line of control; even with advance warning, the ability to assemble larger concentrations of forces must have been problematic – as witnessed in the not infrequent, documented enemy incursions.

One substantial episode came in 356 when the Quadi overran Pannonia, perhaps supported by the Sarmatians. Peace was secured by Constantius II who then saw to a strengthening of the frontier, perhaps even with the creation of extra bridgeheads across the Danube. Further revisions occurred under Valentinian from 364 to 74, dated by coins, ceramics and stamped tiles. This included not only strengthening but also some reductions to forts (e.g. at Carnuntum and at Visegrád, where a large tower over the former gate replaced the former fortress), and possible changes to the series of inner forts and grain depots. One surviving inscription (*CIL* III, 10596) reports a new hilltop fort built at *Solva* in the mid-360s:

> Our masters, the Emperors Caesars Valentinian and Valens, esteemed, great, victorious and harmonious brothers, and ever august, have ordered to be raised from its foundations the walls with towers of this fortress, overseen by the *vir clarissimus* the count Equitius, master of both the cavalry and infantry, and undertaken by Augustinianus, the *vir perfectissimus* (and count of the first rank), duke of the frontier of Valeria, [both men] most dedicated to the divine presence and mercifulness of them [the emperors].

Comparable texts report new *burgi* or watchtowers, several of these excavated and shown to be of the approximate dimensions of 10 m × 10 m or 16 m × 16 m. One of AD 372 at Esztergom in Pannonia also names Equitius, plus Foscanus, commander of the *legio Martiorum*, whose workers built the *burgus* 'Commercium' in 48 days.

Equitius' name is linked to far more dramatic events. We have the detailed narrative of Ammianus Marcellinus, writing in *c*.390, for ensuing traumas; his text is crucial for details of both Roman and enemy strategies in conflicts across the Empire, and in Books 29 and 30 in particular we are told much of the efforts of Valentinian, quelling a whole range of uprisings, revolts, incursions and threats from Saxon pirates against Britain to Moorish chiefs in Africa and Alamanni against Gaul. Whilst viewed as vicious and bloodthirsty, Ammianus Marcellinus says (29.4), 'even his harshest critic cannot find fault with his unfailing shrewdness in matters of state, especially if he bears in mind that it was a greater service to keep the barbarians in check by frontier barriers than to defeat them in battle. To this end, as in Gaul, 'he greatly reinforced the army, and fortified the high ground on both banks of the Rhine with strong points and forts, so that no assault on our territory could be launched unobserved' (30.7). As a show of strength, 'he ordered the erection of a fortress on the further side of the Danube and in the actual territory of the Quadi, which he treated as subject to the authority of Rome' (29.6 – AD 372). The Quadi sent a delegation to complain to General Equitius; however, the prefect of Gaul, Maximinus, then complained that Equitius was dallying over the fort's completion and sent his own son Marcellianus as general to finish the job. The Quadi King Gabinius then formally protested; the King was invited to dinner by Marcellianus, but promptly murdered – 'a most infamous violation of the sacred laws of hospitality' (29.6). The repercussions were vicious:

The news of this outrage at once got abroad, and roused the Quadi and their neighbouring tribes to fury. Mourning the death of their king, they got together and sent out parties to devastate our territory. They crossed the Danube and fell upon the country folk, who were busy with their harvest and had no thought of an enemy. Most of them they killed, and the rest they carried off home together with a large quantity of livestock ... After this the Quadi, together with the Sarmatians, both people addicted to rapine and brigandage, extended their depredations, carrying off men, women and livestock, and gloating over the ashes of burnt farms and the sufferings of the murdered inhabitants.

Raids even extended south to the city of Sirmium, but the Praetorian Prefect Probus stood firm here, after first getting the moats cleared of accumulated rubbish and then 'raising the greater part of the walls, which had been neglected and allowed to decay owing to the long peace'. The Quadi, convinced that Equitius was to blame for their king's assassination, were in pursuit; two legions were sent (in AD 373) to deal with them, but disputes between the two over 'honour and precedence' allowed the Sarmatian forces to attack early and inflict heavy losses. Emperor Valentinian only reached the Danubian trouble-zone in spring 375 from Trier, basing himself first at 'ruinous' Carnuntum to observe the barbarian movements, then receiving Sarmatian envoys suing for peace. A two-pronged attack was then launched against the Quadi, with Valentinian's army crossing at Aquincum and marching 'rapidly forward as far as circumstances allowed, burning the dwellings and massacring regardless of age all whom his sudden onslaught sought still wandering at large'. Returning to Roman soil he headed onto Brigetio as a suitable point for establishing winter-quarters, but 'leaving adequate garrisons for the forts and the camps on his way' and also sending surgeons and medics to attend soldiers stricken by the plague. He rejected wintering at the town of Savaria to the west since that was in a 'weak state' and where one of the town gates had apparently collapsed and been blocked by rubbish. At Brigetio, Quadi envoys were received, 'humbly begging for peace and an amnesty for their past offences, and endeavouring to clear every obstacle from their path by promising to provide recruits and other services to the Roman state' (30.6). But the angry emperor was seized by a (presumed) stroke and died soon afterwards, leaving a new power vacuum.

Ammianus Marcellinus' Book 31 narrative concludes with the build-up of displaced Goths, Alans and varied tribal groups (displaced through Hunnic expansion), who requested security within the Empire, only to be mistreated and mishandled, prompting, in 378, revolt and raiding and culminating in the disastrous battle of Adrianople. The events undoubtedly demanded the (presumed temporary) withdrawal from Pannonia and Noricum of both mobile and limitanean troops. Defeat and the ensuing conflict meant that most of the frontier provinces were seriously undermanned and exposed to the next round of extensive raids. Forts remained, but in a battered state, and archaeology shows a reduced material culture and minimal coin supply; the resolve of the Roman soldiery in these turbulent years must have been horribly shaken.

Further, Pannonia was ravaged by Gothic, Alan and other forces in 378/9; allied *Sarmatia* collapsed, many of its refugees entering the Empire. Rome's solution was to recognise these mixed Gothic forces as federates and to provide lands and commands for them. Most logically these would have been allocated space and duties along the Danube frontier, by then depleted of regular troops; promises of uniform, pay and materials would have helped bond them to these spaces, with their chiefs and leaders conferred with Roman ranks to add an official sheen to the arrangements. Some regular troops may well have endured to monitor the federate set-up, which seems to have functioned adequately – indeed, as seen, federates assisted the Eastern Emperor Theodosius in the civil war against the Western Emperor Maximus in 388.

Stability prevailed into the earliest fifth century, after which Vandal wanderings (401), Visigothic assaults (402) and plundering by the forces of the Goth Radagaisus (405/7) made the interiors of Pannonia and Noricum scarred battlegrounds. The *limes* itself was not the focus of assault in these instances; the threats now lay largely within the Empire, assailed on too many fronts to mount telling resistance. Hunnic pressure was building dramatically in this period, and by 425 the Huns (not under one unified king at this stage) occupied the Great Hungarian Plain and areas north of the Danube, periodically raiding Roman soil. In 433 Roua combined these forces and gained from the Roman General Aetius cession of *Pannonia Prima*; Aetius presumably hoped that these Huns would then lessen their efforts against the Empire. In theory, *Valeria* province at the Danube Bend remained Roman, but this control was as thin as paper and torn up soon after.

Archaeology documents something of this fragmentation of control through excavations, showing shrinkage in the defended area of some forts, plus material culture which indicates a growing non-Roman presence. At the fortress of Visegrád-Sibrik, new pottery types were not associated with the Valentinianic tower, but found with other 'barbarian' handmade vessels in semi-sunken huts in the fort interior. The material is viewed as denoting the appearance and incorporation of federates – that is, allied non-Romans and potentially a mixture of Goths, Huns and Alans – in the latest phase of Roman defence along the Danube. Chronologies and interpretations are necessarily weak in the absence of coins, texts and systematic excavation, but an effort to utilise federates matches available documentation elsewhere in the fourth and fifth centuries. One might ask how far such federate forces viewed themselves as 'Roman' and how far continuing Romans saw these simply as 'barbarians' on Roman soil. Either way it was a delicate balance. There are in fact indications that various Pannonian *castella* continue into the fifth century, although frequently such evidence, forming a site's latest and least substantial phase, is fragmentary and not easy to decipher. Also, there is a tendency to suggest end-dates of *c.*430 and the Hunnic takeover, but not always does this marrying of text and archaeology work. Nonetheless, early fifth-century evidence now derives from various locations along the Pannonian *limes* such as Azaum, Szentendre, Aquincum and Intercisa; later material from Brigetio, Pilismarot-Malompatak and Tokod could signify a local (as opposed to regional) defensive or settlement role extending into periods of Gothic control. Whether any sense of 'frontier' lingered is unknown, although the river continued to divide territories.

Hadrian's Wall

Hadrian's Wall was an impressive feat of military planning and implementation, with interesting modifications to the original plan still visible. In brief, this was a linear cordon, chiefly in stone except for turf and ditch at the western end, where additional lines of earthworks were imposed down the Cumbrian coast to counter possible landings across the Solway. Forts were attached approximately six Roman miles apart, and there were 80 regularly placed mile-fortlets, each divided into two towers or turrets set at intervals of one-third of a Roman mile. A wide ditch lay rearwards to denote the 'military zone' – although the early attraction of village units and farms to the forts shows that this was in no way an exclusion zone. Scattered inscriptions by legionary teams indicate that completion took about 8 years; the creation of the Antonine Wall in c. AD 141/3 would have ensured that military muscle remained in trim. The final abandonment of the Antonine Wall in 163 shows that this wall's shorter length did not make it a more secure border; it required 6,000–7,000 men, compared with 8,000–9,000 for Hadrian's Wall, but the narrow Firth of Forth and the Clyde estuaries allowed for potential outflanking and thus a need for additional forts and watch points south-west and east of the Wall itself (Map 3.3).[6]

While Hadrian's Wall appears a powerful defensive barrier, often perched on strategic high points and acting as a visible deterrent, nonetheless the argument is that the Wall chiefly regulated traffic into (and out of) Roman territory and provided springboards and bases for possible campaign troops. As an investment in labour it also signified a long-term consolidation of position – even though, within two decades, a full-scale northward shift was implemented. The growth of *vici* – civilian communities – outside of some of the larger forts (e.g. Housesteads, Vindolanda, Old Carlisle) meanwhile shows how these stable outposts attracted merchants, farmers and other workers to sites with constant material needs (including wives and subsequent sons for recruits) and with regular pay; these *vici* could be substantial and attain semi-urban status and many see stone temples and shops erected.

The Wall's basic military role was no doubt highlighted on occasions, such as the rather vaguely documented assault of c. AD 180, when, according to Cassius Dio (*History of Rome*, chs 71–7), 'the tribes in the island crossed the wall that separated them from the Roman forts, did a great deal of damage and cut down a general and his troops'. Some contemporary destruction layers have been recognised at Corbridge and Halton Chesters in the central zone of Hadrian's Wall to indicate the focus of attack. The event was vicious enough to warrant appointment of a new governor, Ulpius Marcellinus, to sort matters, presumably via retaliatory attacks. The third century, in general, presents an image of stability for Britain, with no war documented or attested archaeologically between Severus' and Caracalla's campaigns in 208–11 (which saw brief occupation of the forts of Cramond and Carpow on the Forth and Tay, respectively) and those of Constantius Chlorus against the Picts in 306. Indeed, the distribution of Roman materials north of the Wall is fairly strong for both second and third centuries; inscriptions (if fading in number rapidly after the 230s) show fort maintenance and modifications; and excavations show adjoining civilian sites flourishing. Changes may well have come in the late third century, with likely Tetrarchic period upgrading, renewal and reordering at sites like Birdoswald and Housesteads (noticeably coming when *vici* are declining).[7]

A useful guide is the fort of South Shields just 5 km beyond the eastern end of the Wall, now graced by a reconstructed western gateway. Recent excavations have clarified the structural sequences here: the first phase is pre-Hadrian, while the first stone fort relates to the 160s, with a reduced garrison at the end of the second century. Under the Severans, the fort mainly served as a supply base, with a Gallic cohort as resident garrison; this supply role was expanded in the second half of the third century. Fire in *c.* AD 300 prompted rebuildings, including conversion of some of the granaries into barracks; a new regiment or *numerus* of bargemen from Tigris in Syria was then installed – presumably to help patrol the river and coast. The Roman site name of Arbeia probably derives from this 'Arab' community. In the fourth century various modifications occur, and occupation persists into the fifth, when some re-cutting of the defensive ditches is attested. Noticeable is a higher incidence of infant burials in and beside the barracks from the fourth century, perhaps indicating families being housed within the barracks in the later phases of this and other fort sites. Equally interesting is the possible installation of a church in the forecourt of the prefect's house, although its associated structural remains are very fragmentary. The Arbeia data are invaluable for charting change and/or continuity. For the most part we see continuity of usage, if modified, in the later Empire. The bulk of the fourth-century sequence at Arbeia, certainly, lacks startling events – no destruction layers, no vast refortification action – despite the accepted traumatic historical image of the northern frontiers in mid- to late fourth-century Britain. Is this atypical?[8]

We can review one major episode. For long, much weight was put on the 'Barbarian Conspiracy' of AD 367, variously seen as a significant episode of destruction and subsequent defensive reconfiguration in Britain (for towns: reinforcements to defences with deeper ditches, projecting towers, garrisons; for frontiers: reduced stationing, selective abandonment, larger federate and local role). Ammianus Marcellinus' text (Book 27.8) suggests major traumas, and yet there is confusion and vagueness in the short account (odd for an otherwise very coherent historian), notably as regards the multiple sequence of Roman commanders, of attacks and locations, and of the scale of events:

> After setting out from Amiens on a rapid march to Trier, Valentinian was shocked to receive the serious news that a concerted attack by the barbarians had reduced the provinces of Britain to the verge of ruin. Nectaridus, the count of the coastal region,

had been killed, and the General Fullofaudes surprised and cut off ... Finally, in response to the alarming reports which constantly arrived, [count] Theodosius was selected for the task and ordered to proceed to Britain without delay ... Suffice to say that at that time the Picts, of whom there were two tribes, the Dicalydones and Venturiones, together with the warlike people of the Attacotti and the Scots, were roving at large and causing great devastation. In addition, the Franks and Saxons were losing no opportunity of raiding the parts of Gaul nearest to them by land and sea, plundering, burning and putting to death all their prisoners ... From Boulogne Theodosius made a calm crossing to Richborough ... On the arrival of his troops, which consisted of the Batavi and Heruli together with the Jovii and Victores [i.e. joint Roman and federate forces] ... he marched towards the old town of London, since called *Augusta*. Dividing his men into several detachments, he attacked the roving parties of freebooters, who were hampered by the weight of their spoils and driving before them prisoners and cattle. He quickly routed them and wrested from them the plunder which the wretched provincials had lost. He restored everything to its owners except for a small part which he distributed to his exhausted troops, and then entered the town in triumph.

Barbarian prisoners were held and questioned, and there is also reference to Roman deserters granted immunity to return to the ranks. Was this also an internal rebellion? Theodosius then 'asked that Civilis, a man of fiery temper but uncompromising integrity, should be sent to him to govern Britain as pro-prefect. He also asked for the services of Dulcitius, a general distinguished for his military skill'. Theodosius next – in service to 'the defeated and harassed Britons' – carried the initiative into enemy territories (Book 28.3):

He forestalled the barbarians by seizing positions suitable for guerrilla warfare, and imposed no duties on his troops which he himself was not the first to undertake with alacrity ... He routed and put to flight various tribes, whose burning eagerness to attack anything Roman was fanned by a belief that they could do so with impunity ... He restored cities and garrison towns and protected the borders with guard-posts and defence works. The recovery of a province which had fallen into the hands of the enemy was so complete that, to use his own words, it now had a lawful governor.

But how accurate is this account? First, we must note that Ammianus Marcellinus' history was written in the time of Theodosius the Great (379–95), whose father was the discussed Count Theodosius. Understandably, therefore, Ammianus Marcellinus glorifies those achievements and glosses over what might have been messy operations; minimal credit goes to any other generals. Second, we need recognise earlier references from Ammianus Marcellinus, which show a history of threats to the north and west. In AD 360 (Book 20.1), we hear how 'the wild tribes of the Scots and Picts broke their undertaking to keep peace, laid waste the country near the frontier, and caused alarm among the provincials, who were exhausted by the repeated disasters they had already suffered'. Similarly for 364, 'the Picts, Saxons, Scotti and Attacotti were bringing continual misery upon Britain' (26.4) – meaning the frontier zones and exposed coastal zones. We cannot be certain how far raids penetrated and whether the 'misery of the Britons' was more to do with military demands, tax and supply needs on the civil population. Most probably, in line with other provinces in the fourth century, many other would-be emperors arose in Britain, demanding troops and logistics. One significant usurper was Magnus Maximus who, like Constantine III later, took the core of the British troops across the Channel to pursue his ambitions. Many forts in the western Pennines and Wales were possibly quitted in the 380s to accommodate this enterprise; reliance then went on locals and on 'friendly' allies (most of whom needed moneys to keep them content). Furthermore, the repercussions and retributions of such (defeated) rebellions could be hugely detrimental to both property and supporters.

So far the archaeology of Hadrian's Wall does not match these reported po-litico-military vicissitudes. Is Birdoswald, a west-central fort on the Wall, a better guide? The third-century fort here housed an infantry unit, the *cohors I Aelia Dacorum*, but an inscription and the archaeology point to a period of (presumed official) abandonment probably in the 280s, before regeneration in the 300s including restoration of the commandant's house and the bathhouse; the circuit walls saw regular repair, with the final rebuild comprising an earth bank revetted on its exterior by a narrow stone wall. By c.350, however, the granaries had been decommissioned, implying that the garrison's size had been reduced. Nonetheless, the coin sequence extends fully into the later fourth century, if diminishing in frequency; ceramics, meanwhile, attest a more regional supply of pottery (mainly from East Yorkshire) in these latest Roman phases.[9] As at South Shields, therefore, the fourth century features no dramatic episodes: this Wall community evolved without really significant change prior to the end of Roman control.

And yet the written sources do sketch out a much tougher picture for north-ern Roman Britain: for AD 297 a court poet refers to the half-naked warriors of the Picts and Hibernians as the Britons' enemies; in July 305 the Emperor Constantius Chlorus died in York after vicious conflicts with the Picts; Constantine the Great's title Britannicus may record another campaign over the border; and later, Magnus Maximus waged war against invading Picts and Scots. Where are the associated destructions? Perhaps we expect too much of the archaeology. After all, the invaders and raiders probably often bypassed the heavily fortified points to minimise losses. Towns may have been a focus, yet these too were defended. Scale is important here: Do we imagine bands of 300–400 men making concerted assaults, puncturing defences, their scattered patterns preventing coherent defence? Or, as implied in Ammianus Marcellinus' 367 'conspiracy', are sizeable coordinated attacks to be visualised? In truth the evidence for Britain is weak, but the impression provided for Pannonia, if comparable, is of a mixture of these, with periodic larger-scale enemy incur-sions, presumably informed by vicissitudes within the provinces (e.g. troop withdrawals), but largely with speedy run-and-grab raids.

Caution is required, and yet that has not stopped many archaeologists (though fewer recent ones) using documented episodes as pegs on which to hang refortifications, rebuildings, abandonments, destructions and the like.

At the same time, we are not being told everything – niggling, constant raids, brigandage, army desertions and localised crop failures will not have made the 'press', especially for a historian many provinces away, and the 'wearing down' of a frontier district was probably as damaging as the occasional, documented major strike. But we can also observe that many of the army units became progressively local, with families and land attachments to their forts; at forts like Housesteads and Wallsend troop accommodation was, by the mid-fourth century, in modified barracks, less regular in plan, which could point towards family spaces (many of the extramural *vici* do seem defunct in this period).[10] Such (family) attachments may well have helped harden resolve and resilience to defend their places of work/rest. Proving this resilience and continuity is currently very difficult, but the sequences at South Shields and Birdoswald provide some clues: at the latter, the final phases are marked by erection over a granary of a timber hall and other timber buildings close to the west gate, and the excavators suggest these belonged to the frontier troops, either of 'barbarian federate' or local stock, with the hall the seat of the elected leader/commander. As seen for Pannonia, federates worked and fought for Rome but had their own land and thus relative independence; they perhaps maintained their ethnic identities even in a Roman military context, but quite possibly they used Roman nomenclature for their commanders and chiefs. But were these federates interspersed amongst Romano-British troops, and were federates drawn from groups such as the Picts and Scots? Like the archaeology, the reality must be much more complex than the limited textual data we have available on these late Roman soldiers.

EXTENDED AND NEW FRONTIERS

What is often not recognised by scholars is the emergence of a wider net of frontiers in the late Empire, moving inwards to support the external *limites* and at the same time designed to buffer threats which did penetrate the provinces. How ordered and coherent were these additional inner systems of defence? Are they simply symbols of strength or of a crumbling control? Below we examine coastal forts in Britain, Alpine defences and other intraprovincial responses.

Coastal Defence in Later Roman Britain

As Ammianus Marcellinus testifies for Britain, threats did not only come purely across the northern frontier. Already in the early third century, fleet bases emerged at Brancaster by the Wash and Reculver in north-east Kent, complementing likely fortified ports at Oudenburg and Aardenburg across the Channel. While this may perhaps signify an increase in piracy exploiting the busy merchant shipping, by the 270s the problems in these waters revolve around 'barbarian' raids – later sources attribute these to Franks and Saxons, with the former already involved in damaging raids across the Rhine. That these raids affected inland sites too is evident in the growing number of hoards of coin buried between *c.* AD 270 and 285, although other circumstances such as tax avoidance, civil or military disturbances and economic recession might have prompted burial of monetary wealth. Indeed, distribution maps show an even spread, if with concentrations on the south coast. Recall also that political and economic repercussions will have hit Britain in some measure in the light of Britain's allegiance to the Gallic Empire.

A key event for Roman Britain was the usurpation of the province by Carausius in AD 286 (see Eutropius, *Breviarum*, Book IX.21–22). In his official role he had successfully countered serious barbarian maritime raids, using warships launched from fortified bases either side of the Channel; however, he was then accused of failing to give up the booty to the State. His successful usurpation (he was formally recognised) for 7 years was built on possession of a fleet, defended harbours, plus the use of Franks to help control north-west Gaul and the major base of Boulogne. The coastal command outlived Carausius, but much archaeological work has gone into determining its origins and role. The *Notitia Dignitatum* provides a name (the *Litus Saxonicum*) and a commander (the count or *comes*) of a series of fortified sites in southern and eastern Britain, plus continental forts and units under both a *dux tractus Amoricani* and the *dux Belgicae secundae* (these presumably were overseen by the count); the *Notitia* lists also the forts' garrisons (perhaps comprising only a detachment of the whole force) in *c.* AD 400. Its ordering of names indicates a coherent organisation of beach-harbour pairings (Walton Castle-Bradwell; Lympne-Dover; Brancaster-Burgh Castle; Reculver-Richborough; Pevensey-Portchester). Some of these powerful defences survive well today, with the tall circuits and projecting towers of Portchester, Pevensey and Burgh the best known. Coastal erosion means that some forts are lost, part-destroyed or disfigured, but most have seen some archaeological study, Portchester being the best examined, with excavations in the 1960s and 1970s recovering extensive data on Roman, Saxon and Norman epochs (Figure 3.1, Map 3.3).[11]

Carausius may well have overseen the expansion of the former British fleet bases to create a stronger network. There are signs of significant revisions to old forts alongside the creation of new ones from *c.* AD 275: for example, the revised fort at Dover was of quite diverse plan and orientation, and featured regularly spaced, substantial, projecting, semicircular or D-shaped towers, and an external ditch approximately 7.5-m wide. Some forts have double-ditches, U- or horseshoe-shaped towers and inset main gates; most forts are of squared plan (183 m × 187 m for Portchester), except for the large oval design of Pevensey (290 m × 170 m), accommodating itself to a promontory location. Pevensey was long viewed as a later 'plug' to the system of forts due to this irregular design, but 1994 excavations in the castle keep revealed Roman fortress wall foundations set over oak piles driven into the subsoil; dendrochronological analysis established the felling date for the trees providing these piles as between AD 280 and 300, while other construction material included two coins, one of Carausius and another of his successor Allectus. At Portchester too a Carausian coin came from the construction level. The date range is tight and

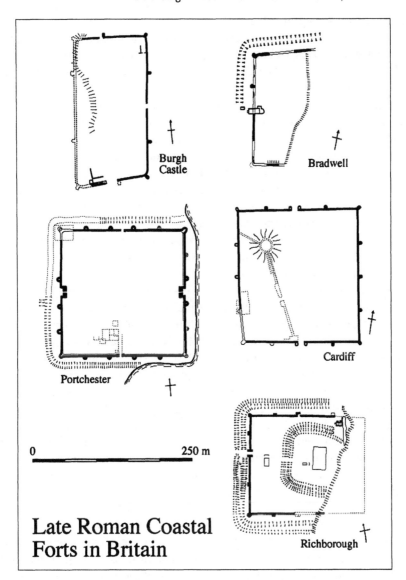

Figure 3.1 Plans of key late Roman coastal and Saxon Shore forts in Britain (after Johnson 1983: Fig. 79)

potentially could signify a Carausian or Allectan entrenchment against continental Roman forces, but most probably we should recognise wider Roman initiation of an overhaul of provision around the Channel to safeguard supplies and then Carausius exploiting and enhancing these to bolster his regime.

The title of the command demonstrates that by the end of the fourth century the enemy threat was constant enough to apply their name – that is, the 'coast[s under threat] of the Saxons'. The designation might also register Saxons settled on those shores as federate forces, as suggested by a limited amount of archaeological evidence from British sites; however, such federates would have been seen as part of the Roman forces on Roman soil and not as a territorial entity. This command is clearly viewed as a frontier (*limes*) or border district (*tractus*). The designation further implies a substantial, not niggling, threat.

All coasts were threatened, however: thus Ammianus Marcellinus' account of AD 367 puts Picts, Attacotti and Scots assailing Britain from the north and probably from Ireland against the Cumbrian coast and Wales. One hoard at Ballinrees in County Derry, Northern Ireland, containing 6 kg of silver ingots and plate and a full 1,701 fourth- to early fifth-century Roman coins, demonstrates that raids went on after Roman rule (as St Patrick would discover). Nor can we discount wider ranging raids across to north-west Gaul and Armorica. For the latter, the *Notitia* lists a duke and a series of troops and forts, of which one, *Grannona*, lies *in litore Saxonico*, this being the most easterly of the bases mentioned; other sites extend west and south into Aquitaine and to Alderney on the Channel Islands. Were these to counter later fourth-century Frankish and Saxon raids, or perhaps pirates from Ireland? Whichever the case, the need for an elongated system of coastal control was growing. Hence fortified sites appear running south from Maryport, Burrow Walls, Ravenglass and Lancaster in north-west England, to Caernarvon, Caer Gybi (Anglesey) and Cardiff in Wales, and with urban reinforcement through projecting towers at Caerwent at least. The picture for the western and south-western Welsh coast is unclear, but as this zone lacked much Roman period settlement, local recourse to former hill forts may instead be envisaged.

While a similarly limited level of Roman urban and higher status rural settlement can be claimed for the east Yorkshire coastal regions, nonetheless here a regular series of military watchtowers was imposed, extending at least from Huntcliff to Filey, but with others suggested (as for Sunderland and Flamborough Head), although coastal erosion has removed some contenders and seriously threatens known sites, notably Scarborough and Huntcliff. These signal stations comprised a tower of about 15 m × 15 m, set in a rectangular enclosure with small projecting corner towers and single narrow entranceway, and a broad outer ditch. Wells and hearths are regular features; at Goldsborough there were signs of production of jet rings. The towers commence in c. AD 360–65, contemporary with the noted scheme of *burgus* construction recorded for the Danube frontier under Valentinian I. An inscription at Ravenscar records the fort's completion by the Commander Iustinianus and the troop Prefect Vindicianus.

Various roles can be assigned: first, to act as a visible deterrent, showing would-be raiders that a military presence was there, through bulk and lighting of a beacon or flare; second, where signalling between sites could occur, messages could be relayed to raise awareness of any threat; third, the towers could have prompted local fleet detachments to set sail and engage; fourth, inland forts like York or Malton would be informed through horse messengers of any threat of landing, and cavalry detachments thus dispatched. Mist or fog would have hindered the functioning of such a system, and single ships of brave raiders might have easily slipped through any defensive net and made a landing. The very provision of these Yorkshire signal stations denotes experience of attacks, perhaps enemies outflanking the more northerly defences. The excavations at Huntcliff in 1911–12 provided what appears to have been dramatic evidence of the bloody end to one such tower: Haverfield described how the skulls and bones of 14 or 15 people – men, women and children – were found in the well, with one skull bearing a deep, lethal, weapon-inflicted cut: 'These bones belonged presumably rather to refugees or to the families of some of the garrison of the fort than to the garrison itself. Whoever they were, they were killed when the fort was stormed and burnt, and their bodies were cast into the ready grave offered by the open well'. The last coins on the site suggest a termination around *c*. AD 400. A similar terrible fate befell Goldsborough to the south-west: three skulls were recovered from the well and in the tower, the bodies of two men were found, plus the skeleton of 'a large and powerful dog, its head against one man's throat, its paws across his shoulders'.[12]

Defending the Heart

Not just on the fringes and borders of the Empire was defence mounted with increasing prominence from the third century: the needs of security percolated fully to its core. The fortification of Rome under Aurelian, in part prompted by the incursions over the Alps by bands of Iouthungi and Alamanni, served to indicate that the new Empire of the late third century was a less safe one, and one needing defensive measures to protect both the outer shell and the innards of a vast territory. The shift of capital to Milan in 284, the creation of additional capitals in seats like Trier and Arles, the mobilisation of field armies, all testify to this reassessment of how security could be better monitored. We might expect, therefore, that much attention went into protecting the home province.

First we can observe the 'north-east corridor' and the passages south and west from Pannonia and Dalmatia. The extensive defensive installations of the Pannonian *limes* have already been discussed, and their relative efficiency in controlling and observing shown. Yet an increasing inability to contain sizeable or multiple incursions saw an extension of defence inwards: thus a series of rectangular, heavily fortified sites was created along roads near the Lake Balaton region. The largest site is Heténypuszta, 500 m × 450 m – bigger than early legionary forts and implying space for up to 5,000 men; these sites contain villa-like structures, granaries, stable blocks and, later, churches. We lack inscriptions or specific documentary references to their roles, although some scholars have identified at least Heténypuszta with one of the forts (Iovia) listed in the *Notitia Dignitatum*. Certainly their plans and defences, plus the sizeable granaries, denote state constructions, quite possibly as supply depots and bases for mobile army troops. Effectively, these forts constituted an inner defensive cordon protecting not only Pannonian lands, but also guarding routes (and thus supply lines) towards (and from) Italy; potentially, they provided springboards for action against invaders and refuge for locals. Problematic, however, are the chronologies of these sites: the name Iovia suggests a Tetrachic origin; the fan-shaped towers on some sites may be Constantinian; the round towers at others may postdate AD 350. If so, similar to Britain's coastal defences, we see a patchwork response, with successive extensions and 'plugging' of gaps. A refortification of inner towns is another element of this process.

Behind this inner cordon, naval units patrolled the Rivers Drau and Save, which provided contact with major urban garrison points at Siscia and Sirmium. Conceivably, small fleets also operated on lakes Fertö and Balaton in a fashion attested for Lake Geneva as well as the Italian northern lakes: rapid boats would have allowed for advance warning to sites at the southern ends of these.

The *Notitia* also identifies a *Comes Italiae* with the designation of the *Tractus Italiae circa Alpes*, implying a military district or command drawn across the Alps. The Alps were not as impenetrable as one might think, as indicated by ready trade and movement over the passes; but the north-eastern corridor, the Julian Alps, is both lower and more broken than the other Alpine ranges, and it was this route that was taken by Quadi and Marcomanni warbands in the AD 160s; in the fifth century it was used by Alaric's Visigoths and by Theoderic's Ostrogoths. The Julian Alps appear at various points in late Roman sources: in Ammianus Marcellinus, for example, as the 'Claustra Alpium Iuliarum', and in Sextus Aurelius Victor as 'Clausae Alpes'. The term *Claustra* denotes a bar, barrier or blocking, and the accompanying image in the *Notitia* depicts a fortified town girded by walls and towers duly barring some of the Alpine slopes. A series of these extended barrier walls is known archaeologically in the mountainous terrain extending north of the Roman town of Tarsatica (Rijeka) towards Emona (Ljubljana) and then running north-westwards; they protect minor routes and deflect traffic to the main roadways which are then guarded by fortified sites. Best recognised are the barriers and forts along the Ljubljana-Ajdovščina (*Castra*) road, and best studied is the defensive arrangement at the fourth-century road station of Ad Pirum (Hrušica), where the walls channel movement through the fortress.[13] The fort itself was articulated in two units, with military finds concentrated in the southern fortified space; the steeper northern enclosure may well have offered refuge space for local farmers and their animals (Map 3.4).

It is striking, however, that references made by contemporary or later historians to the *Claustra* mainly relate to internecine conflict between 'official' Roman emperors and usurpers or former emperors (e.g. Constantius II vs Magnentius in 352; Julian vs Constantius II and the Praetoran Prefect Taurus in AD 361). The eastern Emperor Theodosius, drawn into action twice in these pronounced usurpations, may well have decided that these *Claustra* were a tactical headache, employed far more against fellow Romans than non-Roman threats, and he probably ordered their dismemberment. In his honorific poem *Celebrating the Third Consulship of Honorius* (lines 89–101), Claudian praises

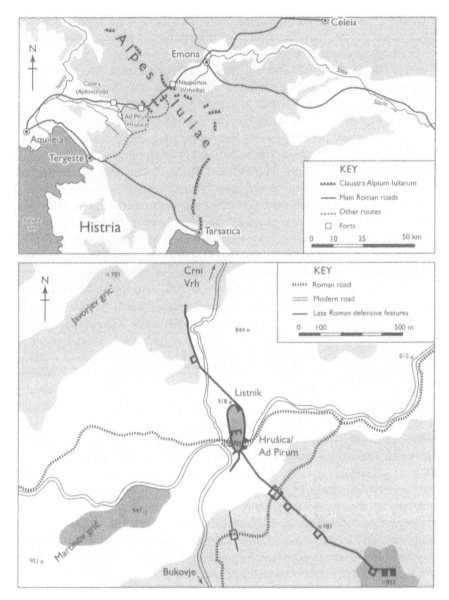

Map 3.4   Top: the defences of the Julian Alps in the fourth century. Bottom: wall and fort articulation at Ad Pirum (after Ulbert 1981: Figs 1 and 7)

Theodosius' work thus: 'Thanks to thee the Alps lay open to our armies, nor did it avail the careful foe to cling to fortified posts. Their ramparts and the trust they put therein, fell; the rocks were torn away and their barriers exposed'. Archaeology supports the image of a rather brutal termination to sites like Hrušica and Lanišce towards the end of the fourth century. However, the decommissioning of the *Claustra Alpium Iuliarum*, almost inevitably, backfired when Alaric's Visigoths broke through to Italy in AD 401/2. Arguably, disbanding the *Claustra* and relying more on a field army simply matched policy closer to the main frontiers. Unfortunately, the mobile army was not good enough to counter Alaric.

Even if the *Claustra* had failed to function in the manner envisaged, this does not mean that an 'Alpine defence' disappeared. The *Notitia* records the *Tractus Italiae circa Alpes* which is suggestive of a wider belt of defensive control, in which the *Claustra* had been just one component. The *Tractus* most probably comprised primarily a city-fort-tower articulation based around the existing network of fortified Alpine and sub-Alpine centres, notably Aosta, Susa, Bellinzona and Trento (Alpine) and Turin, Como, Milan, Verona and Cividale (sub-Alpine). These would have formed the seats of regional control and some held (semi-permanent) detachments of the mobile army. Advance forts and towers would have provided warning to such centres, which then could have mobilised an armed response and taken in refugees; many of these towns are also documented as containing large State granaries, thus enhancing their capability to endure sieges (and support troops and refugees). How coordinated all this was in the first decade of the fifth century as Alaric's forces spilled into north Italy is unknown, but town walls at least offered some hope, and after 410 scope did exist to enhance Italy's defences. Some responses and works must have been ordered by the State and its generals, although in other cases local/town-based responses may have occurred; later we hear of bishops establishing refuges. Archaeology can help, but while certain new defensive works can be recognised, such as fleet bases established on the various northern Italian lakes, with fortifications at sites like Comacina (Lake Como) and Sirmione (Lake Garda), many other late Roman installations have been destroyed through either modern development or imposition of medieval castles (e.g. Bellinzona, Gemona), or simply lie unrecognised as yet.

One region which provides a rough guide to late Roman changes is modern Friuli in north-east Italy, immediately rearwards of the former *Claustra*. Here excavations, place-name study, stray finds, as well as documentary evidence have permitted identification of likely fifth-century fortified and hilltop sites alongside roads leading to/from the key pass routes, plus some lesser forts and watchtowers for advance warning or refuge. Central to the region was the fortified town of Cividale (Forum Iulii), later the seat of a Lombard duke, but probably first seat of a late Roman count with mobile army force. We need not assume large garrisons at the other *castra* and *castella* recorded such as Gemona or Ragogna; these communicated with Cividale, protected locals and provided thorns in the approach of any enemy. The hilltop site of Ibligo-Invillino in the north of the region, excavated in the 1960s and early 1970s, is of particular note: this site overlooks the River Tagliamento and has excellent visibility up- and downstream; the main hill of Colle Santino was where settlement was centred, while the smaller Colle di Zuca hosted a late antique cemeterial church. Colle Santino began as an undefended settlement in the second half of the fourth century, with evidence for glass and iron manufacturing. A first 'military' phase comes in the early fifth century when towers were built to protect the northern approach (erosion has, however, removed any trace of a circuit wall here) and various timber buildings set on drystone footings were erected, some forming workshops. An index of the relative prosperity of this new community is given by the church, nearly 40-m long, featuring good-quality floor mosaics; the church was also rebuilt in c. AD 600. In both late and post-Roman phases, the community appears non-military, but was perhaps charged with 'official' duties when circumstances dictated, providing observation of the valley and pass route, offering space for refugees and presumably for military detachments in periods of conflict.

Quite how many other Invillinos existed is not known, but much effort is now being made by Italian archaeologists to seek late Roman origins for various castle sites; sufficient are postulated to demonstrate that in the last century of Roman control, many new measures, some makeshift, some ordered, were initiated to shore up an increasingly insecure peninsula.[14]

Inner Insecurities

All these actions by the State to protect itself and its provinces progressively impacted on the populations within. While territories like Spain and North Africa saw delayed militarisation, by the early fifth century, all Western provinces, especially frontier ones, were suffering from increased demands for army recruits, supplies and workforces, increased taxation, manpower loss for farms, higher costs for goods, fractured economies, harsher laws, reduced social mobility and fewer slaves. Furthermore, the stationing of detachments of the mobile army in or near urban centres and the scattering of federate barbarian settlements in the landscape created tensions. The laws of the *Codex Theodosianus* (*CT*) offer ample testimony of this: 'It is a ruinous practice that the meadows of Our provincials are being molested and harassed by the soldiers' (7.7.4–5 of AD 415); encampments of troops must not unlawfully claim superstatutory food or money from landholders (7.4.12, AD 364); 'a landholder who has been made poorer [by excessive tax demands] is lost to us, but if he is not overburdened he profits us' (*Nov. Val.* I, 3, AD 450).[15]

Landholders and townsfolk did generally struggle on, but many people fled the net to avoid tax collectors, to flee the army ranks and to escape oppression from rich gentry. Desertion appears fairly commonplace, with soldiers seeking shelter and work on farms or estates, and members of the bodyguard were periodically dispatched to hunt these out: 'persons who desert military camps and turn to depredations or brigandage shall not escape the severity of the State' (7.1.8–15, AD 406). References to groups of bandits are striking: brigands had long been a threat to land travel, but there were greater numbers of social discontents in the later Empire and a wider range of peoples found themselves forced to act to avoid the excessive demands of taxation, conscription and surviving. Symmachus, City Prefect in 383, claimed outlaws outside Rome prevented him reaching his villa (Symmachus, *Ep* . II.22); later, in the aftermath of Visigothic depredations in Italy, Rutilius Namatianus travelled by sea north to his damaged Gallic estates, avoiding roads blocked with rubble and robbers alike.[16] Most prominent in this context are the so-called Bacaudae or Bagaudae, who appear periodically in the sources as organised forces or virtual armies of bandits, slaves, peasants and deserters who seriously damaged areas of later third- and fifth-century Gaul. Salvian tells us that the oppressed amongst the curial, lesser gentry classes (the ones most put upon in towns for tax and tasks) were also drawn into the Bacaudae. By the fifth century, Bacaudae seems synonymous with any group of bandits, and they are deemed a worry for State and provincials alike. How constant, disruptive and coherent such groups were is unclear, although the historian Eunapius, for the 360s, tells of large bands led by one Charietto (III.18); 60 years earlier, under Emperor Maximian, extended efforts were needed to deal with these Bacaudae and their two leaders (labelled 'usurpers'). Similar operations took place in northern Spain in the 440s, and Rome even asked the Visigoths to mop up the remainder in 454; and in 408, the usurper Constantine's commander, the Hun Sarus, had to hand over his booty to these brigands in order to gain passage over the Alps.[17] Some modern commentators see in the Bacaudic uprisings both separatist movements and peasant revolts; others identify 'self-help' groups, let down by the State and forced to defend themselves, aggrieved at failures on the part of the central government in distant Italy to protect them from civil conflicts (non-local Roman troops coming in and disrupting and exploiting), federate aggression (e.g. Visigoths as 'official' settlers but settled without local agreement or accommodation) and the like. They observe how these groups generally lay on fringe or neglected zones, as might be claimed for north-west Gaul (i.e. Armorica), and, arguably, much of Britain in the late fourth and early fifth centuries.[18] However, in Roman State eyes, such groups and their leaders, even if trying to remain Roman, were rebels and effectively local usurpers, especially if taking in army deserters. Furthermore, they threatened to take away much needed revenue and supplies from the central and provincial authorities.[19]

Rich landowners similarly feared for their properties and may either have paid tribute or sought to defend themselves. Relevant is a law of AD 403 (*CT* 18.13–14) giving the right to provincials 'in defence of the common peace ... to administer public vengeance against public brigands and deserters from military service', whereas other laws ban private individuals from possessing their own private soldiery. Possible later fourth- and fifth-century federate burials in north Gaul might denote such unofficial soldiery or recourse to localised display in periods of major instability; indeed, finds of silver, imitation, imperial coinage from this region suggest alternative militarised elites seeking to restore some economic stability.[20]

Only in what were perceived as true crises (probably when the home province was directly under threat) did the State relax laws on private weaponry – and this usually in circumstances in which the citizen body had likely already chosen to defend themselves. One clear case relates to the imminent assault on the coasts of Italy by the Vandals in 440, as reported in an edict issued at Ravenna by Valentinian III and Theodosius II to the Roman people (*Nov. Val.* 9.1):

Geiseric, the enemy of Our Empire, is reported to have led forth from the port of Carthage a large fleet, whose sudden excursion and fortuitous depredation must be feared by all shores. Although the solicitude of Our Clemency is stationing garrisons throughout various places and the army of the most invincible emperor Theodosius, Our father, will soon approach, and although We trust that the Most Excellent Patrician, Our Aetius, will soon be here with a large band and the Most Illustrious Master of Soldiers, Sigisvuldus, does not cease to organise guards of soldiers and federated allies for the cities and shores, nevertheless, because it is not sufficiently certain, under summertime opportunities for navigation, to what shore the ships of the enemy can come, We admonish each and all by this edict that, with confidence in the Roman strength and the courage with which they ought to defend their own, with their own men against the enemy, if the occasion should so demand, they should use those weapons which they can, but they shall preserve the public discipline and the moderation of free birth unimpaired. Thus they shall guard Our provinces and their own fortunes with faithful harmony and with joined shields.

We can only guess at the panic when messages of potential attacks were distributed – families packing belongings and heading away from the coast to hilltop hideaways, joining long lines of refugees; boats of all sizes heading north looking for other havens; military contingents muscling in to shore up defences in towns on the front line or else marching off to more secure stations; portable wealth being bundled up or buried; looters breaking into properties quitted; other citizens and landowners looking to their own weapons and other tools to help defend walls, communities, properties, households, perhaps having sent away their womenfolk and children; slaves running away from owners. Archaeologies of such episodes are rare bar abandoned coin hoards and show little of the fears and traumas that overwhelmed groups and individuals. Presumably hope was put in the State army arriving to protect, but no guarantee existed; and, as seen, in Gaul and Spain at least, communities perhaps felt forced to find their own routes to secure their lands and lives.

The outbreak of civil unrest as a result of State failures is relevant too. Cities in the East in Late Antiquity suffered often quite violent protests and riots, on occasion caused by disputes over circus factions or developing from interfactional conflicts. Urban violence was probably a commonplace in the larger population nuclei and is well attested in both Rome and Ravenna in the sixth to ninth centuries. Disputes over Church elections were one point of contention, although clashes between groups and districts, perhaps in the wake of thefts, judicial injustices and the like, were perhaps more regular.[21] For the most part, however, urban violence was something provoked by more human concerns, notably breakdowns in food supply. Supplies often fluctuated in Rome where reliance went far beyond the immediate urban hinterland, requiring regular grain, oil and wine shipments from overseas and regular meat supplies from both central and southern Italy to fill the vast warehouses and distribution points at Portus and within the City.[22] In periods of extended military conflict and civilian hardship, particularly in the fifth century, when farmers would have struggled to plough, plant and harvest, and when external supplies were disrupted, shortages and tension would have arisen with great frequency and prompted riots, robbery and related violence. In the Gothic Wars of the 530s–40s, Rome suffered multiple sieges and blockades and broken water supplies; despite efforts by Church authorities, pilfering and hoarding of the few supplies occurred, and in extended sieges there are references to the eating of horses, dogs and even instances of cannibalism. Rome was exceptional for its size, but most urban centres had grown used to imports to help feed their townsfolk as well as to maintain social distinctions through importing luxury foods and goods. Economic disruptions and damage to landscapes by raids, army/garrison demands, poor harvests and the like could cause significant stress, impacting, for example, on basic nutrition, health and childbirth levels.

Measures to allay some of the recurrent food problems included the creation of State granaries and stores within many of the larger defended cities. For early sixth-century Ostrogothic Italy, letters from King Theoderic record granaries in Verona, Trento, Pavia, Como and Tortona, and one letter (Cassiodorus, Var. X.27) calls for a redistribution of grain to beleaguered provincials at cheap prices. Most probably these granaries date back to the fourth or fifth century and are associated with the placement of garrisons or billeting of mobile army detachments. Noticeably, in later fourth-century edicts dealing with the ruination and restoration of old public buildings, the only new works permitted are stables and storehouses.[23]

HIDING BEHIND WALLS?

Late Roman edicts identify, with increasing concern in the fifth century, the need for fuller communal efforts in times of crisis: landowners to help in repairs to aqueducts; locals to assist in road building and repair; townspeople to help in wall maintenance; farmers to farm, workers to work, and taxes to be paid. While the clergy and many elite families were normally exempt from such public duties, disasters or lack of funds required full input. Indeed, for AD 441, Valentinian III (*Nov. Val.* 10.1) compared the opulence of the past with the 'difficulty' of the present, and stressed how all must work together 'in loyal devotion':

> Must it perhaps be considered contumelious that, contrary to reason, the name of 'sordid' compulsory public services has been invented, whereby there are designated by a vicious appellation the building and repair of military roads, the manufacture of arms, the restoration of walls, the provision of the *annona*, and the rest of the public works through which We achieve the splendour of public defence, without which no success for the greatest affairs results, by whose aid We guard alike the safety and the glory of the Empire, and not to proceed with details, without which services no necessary work can be accomplished?

This quotation identifies strongly another core facet of the late Roman West: the provision, prominence and protection of walls girding towns – symbols of a less secure world and of a diverse urban identity which endured fully into the late Middle Ages. When Vegetius writes towards the end of the fourth century, he implies that all Roman cities are fortified and that the defence of the Empire is undertaken both on the frontiers and within the provinces. The third century had thrown up enough politico-military upheaval to prompt the renewal of town walls and even to force creation of urban citadels. The Tetrarchs used defensive architecture prominently in their capitals and palaces, and this mentality set the seal on developments into the fifth century. But not every town was under threat nor were all regions, and extended periods of stability in the fourth century probably meant reduced pressure on many communities to invest in walls. At the same time, however, the investment in walls in the provincial capitals would have engendered a need in other large centres to show like investment. We do not therefore recognise a blanket programme by the central authorities of town fortification; instead a progressive, downward pattern of urban defence can be identified, starting from the larger capitals and towns in frontier areas as well as sites of deemed strategic value (such as those containing arms factories or on main communications nodes). Such undertakings would have been enormously expensive, but it is unclear how far there was State financial support or whether all funds were expected to come from civic funds; the laws, meanwhile, show that all people were expected to help, whether physically, by giving up land or properties on the line of the new walls, or by contributing materials and moneys.

Perhaps surprisingly given their impressive scale and value, town walls were rarely commemorated by inscriptions or dedications – perhaps because they became an expected component of late Roman town provision in the West.[24] In contrast, in the Eastern Empire, where wall building becomes a norm only in the fifth and sixth centuries, inscriptions and references are much more commonplace, since the epigraphic habit here was luckily much longer-lasting. Laws provide some guide, but often these (rare) cases relate to emergency measures, such as in AD 396 when, in an edict to the praetorian prefect in the East, the provincial governors were asked to call upon the people and senators of each city to 'build new walls or make the old walls stronger, and the expense thereof shall, of course, be arranged in such a way that the tax assessment shall be apportioned according to the ability of each man'. And in 397 it was permitted to use material from demolished temples to help repair roads, bridges, aqueducts and town walls (*CT* 15.1.34 and 36). With the wanderings of Alaric's Visigoths in the Balkans and northern Italy, the prefect of Illyricum, Herculis, called upon compulsory public service 'to aid in the construction of walls and in the transportation and purchase of supplies' to apply to all, in proportion to their landholdings and land tax units (15.1.49 of AD 407). The public/private input is further highlighted when we are informed of the progress of building the Theodosian Walls of Constantinople: *CT* 15.1.15 of AD 413 states that towers were assigned 'to the use of those persons through whose lands this wall was duly erected' and accordingly 'they must annually provide for the repair of the towers at their own expense' – a regulation to be observed in perpetuity.

In Italy's capitals, Ravenna oddly lacks any inscriptions or even secure contemporary text for its circuit walls (these probably started immediately under Honorius and completed only under Valentinian III), whereas Rome preserves dedicatory inscriptions of AD 404 on some of its main gates (that at Porta Tiburtina remains in its original position):

> The Senate and People of Rome to the Imperial Caesars, Our Lords, unconquered leaders, Arcadius and Honorius, victorious and triumphant, eternal emperors, for restoring the walls, gates and towers of the Eternal City, after removing masses of stone debris, at the behest of Stilicho, most distinguished, illustrious count and master of the two armies, to the perpetuation of their name, set up statues. Under the charge of Flavius Macrobius Longinianus, most distinguished, Prefect of the City, dedicated to their Divine Majesties.

The inscriptions and (lost) statues added to a monumentalisation of the strengthened gates and circuit which would have been admired on Honorius' visit that year. The reinforcements of course did not save Rome from Visigothic capture in 410, but still largely stand to show their scale and bulk, as well as efficiency in protecting Rome for many later centuries. Otherwise for Italy, and for many towns in the West, walls are largely undated except through archaeology – whether finds from foundations, repairs, ditch fills, or in terms of typologies of tower or gate forms. Data are insufficient to clarify how long such wall building (and preparation via clearance) took (texts record 8 months for Verona in the 260s but 5 years for Rome), but in comparison with data for medieval wall and cathedral construction, we should expect such projects to have taken up to a decade to complete – if ever they were fully completed.[25]

In the early Empire, town walls denoted status: a colony would generally derive from a foundation of ex-veteran soldiers or from the translation of a legionary fortress into a town, or was a title granted to successful new towns – as for early second-century towns in Gallia Belgica and northern Germany. Such towns exhibited status through elaborate gateways with friezes, statuary and welcoming inscriptions (expenditure on gates was sometimes at the expense of the quality of the rest of the circuit). The third-century Porta Savoia at Susa in the north-west Alps is a fine extant example of gate grandeur, combining functionality and ornamentation. But early gates and walls were laid out often on virgin soil and defined the towns they enclosed. The contrast lies with the middle and late Empire, by when many towns had long since expanded, often overspilling the old walls and ditches; suburban space was also busy with cemeterial and commercial units along and around the roads. When engineers moved in to fortify towns and cities in, say, AD 300, even in places where the new circuit was a reworking of an older curtain, the requirements were quite different. Military architecture in the fourth century put greater emphasis on defensive entrenchment and security of access: walls were thick, a reduced number of gateways operated, tower design was more substantial; and outside lay wide, deep ditches, plus clear ground for 'lines of sight'. To accommodate all such works, much clearance of tombs, houses, workshops, shrines and more was needed. While these operations created materials or *spolia* to be employed in the cores and facing of the new walls, they also had a substantial impact on the local populations, materially in terms of potential loss of property and space, and psychologically. These walls may have given a higher sense of security, but living up close to these walls will have made for dark and perhaps oppressive spaces – although presumably after a decade or so the walls were no longer 'oppressive' but were simply part of the fabric of the town. Furthermore, Western towns that saw fortification in the fourth and fifth centuries often suffered a sizeable spatial reduction, which meant comparatively more disruption to the old urban fabric. Thus in central Portugal, the Augustan *municipium* of Conímbriga was provided with walls 3,000 m in length, but the fortified space shrank to a third of the town's early size in the fourth century – matching the size of the pre-Roman fortified *oppidum*.[26] As discussed below in the case of Gaul, some towns saw public spaces sliced through, omitted or even made into part of the defensive enceinte; archaeology nonetheless generally shows how the new 'suburban' space, once 'urban', remained active, since the more compact walled area was geared to house primarily State officials and stores. In other instances, in parts of Spain, Gaul and Italy, the late Roman centuries often mark a progressive shift back to pre-Roman seats on higher ground, with the lower Roman towns in time being robbed for materials.

Briefly, we need to draw a contrast with the Eastern Empire, where, despite some external and internal threats, the third century did not enforce any spate of town wall building or coastal reinforcement, and even the fourth century saw restricted employment of new urban defences. However, following Constantinople's lead under Theodosius, and undoubtedly fully aware of traumas in the West, the fifth century (extending into the sixth) did witness an urban defensive overhaul.[27] However, extant and excavated walls at Constantinople, Thessaloniki, Amorium and Dyrrachium show a more scientifically advanced approach to town fortifications (such as in the provision of outer walls), suggesting substantial and planned building programmes, supported by greater financial input than is evident in the West. Oddly, except at Thessaloniki, these sizeable works lack corroborative epigraphic evidence, despite the fact that contemporary forts in the Balkans are documented by inscriptions. Later, Procopius devotes a large chunk of *On the Buildings* to Emperor Justinian's funding of new works, and repairs and rebuilding of both military and urban fortifications.

But was urban defence in the West spasmodic or coordinated? Here we assess the sequences in Britain and Gaul.

Town Walls in Later Roman Britain

In Roman Britain, stone gateways occur at various *civitas* (regional) capitals such as Exeter, Verulamium and Cirencester, but these predate earthwork defences.[28] Replacements in stone for earthwork curtains generally appear a third-century event, but are not part of a rushed programme linked to military exigencies; instead, the transition may simply reflect a need to replace eroded banks and ditches. The new works rarely seem rushed, nor do they encircle reduced urban spaces – indeed, at Exeter, unusually, this later wall enclosed twice as much urban space as the early Roman rampart. Some scholars thus see a drawn-out sequence reflecting staggered civic impetus, with only occasional State input (e.g. the visit by Hadrian spurring completion or commencement of public works), and facing no military threat. London seems atypical in lacking an earthen precursor to the stone wall erected at the end of the second century AD; these new walls were probably built as a mark of status for the provincial capital and initiated under Clodius Albinus (193/7); this governor's claim to the imperial purple would have required a suitably powerful-looking capital (Map 3.3).

Towards the end of the third century and then towards the mid-fourth century, external and internal insecurities and pressures combined to enforce a more ostensibly 'military' response in these civilian centres. Key was Britain's involvement in the breakaway Gallic Empire (260–74) and Carausian and Allectan revolts (286–96) and the escalation of seaborne barbarian raids. Occasional visits by emperors such as Constans in the 340s denote moves to tighten security. Lincoln offers a valuable archaeological sequence: modifications to both upper and lower town walls occurred in the late third century and involved heightening and thickening the upper colony walls and broadening its ditch to 25 m in width. Around AD 350, similar measures were implemented in the lower town, at whose western or Park Gate we see reinforcement by projecting flanking towers, built using blocks and decorative stones derived from a sizeable demolished public structure (Figure 3.2). At London, the riverside was finally fortified in the late third century (shown by dendrochronological dating of the oak piles used as foundation supports); this contained *spolia* in both foundations and lower courses, as evident also in the projecting D-shaped bastions added to the land-wall around AD 350.

But not all Romano-British towns were updated or upgraded: Silchester, a 'lost' Roman town now largely under fields and trees, features extensive and very prominent remains of the town walls, surviving in places to nearly 5-m high and built chiefly in flint with slab bonding courses. From the mid-third century this circuit enclosed the town in a distinctive polygonal form. But what is patently missing from the curtain wall is a trace of the addition of later projecting bastions. Potentially, this might signify a shrinking or impoverished urban population which could not afford the bastions, or rather a decision by the regional authorities not to invest in a failing asset. The sequence of occupation as revealed in the ongoing excavations in *Insula IX* of Silchester might refute this idea, however, since there are still signs of life in the old city in the fifth century. Perhaps the walls as they stood were deemed sufficient for protecting the habitation – although clearly Silchester did fail as a city, seeing no medieval revival.[29]

Figure 3.2   The lower town west gate at Lincoln under excavation in the early 1970s, with *spolia* reused in the thickened later Roman circuit and towers (photo courtesy of Michael Jones and the Lincoln Archaeological Trust)

The Later Town Defences of Roman Gaul

For Gallia Belgica (in north Gaul, adjoining the Germania provinces), the second century AD likewise marks a period of wall and formal gate-building linked primarily to status and the granting of colony or municipal rank, but this extended to few towns (Trier, Tongres).[30] Other settlements of urban character, such as Rheims, Metz and Bavai, were not fortified until the later third or early fourth century, and this event, in contrast to Roman Britain, is generally marked (except at the city of Trier) by the erection of a restricted urban enceinte, at the expense of many public monuments, some of which were incorporated into the defences (such as the amphitheatre at Amiens and the baths at Famars). Thus the *civitas* capital of Tongres in *Germania Secunda* was reduced from 136 ha to a defended space of 43 ha; at Amiens, Soissons and Beauvais in Belgica Secunda, the enceintes or *castra* enclosed 9–10 ha only. Despite an assumed correlation with historical events, with known raids and incursions across the Rhine, plus bloody internal power struggles, the wall circuits are well built, in places ornamental, with good facing stones and careful foundations; the reused materials, from demolished public and private edifices, are not automatically indicative of rushed, panic-induced construction. The evidence currently points to a concerted programme of urban entrenchment from *c.* AD 270 to 300 in northern Gaul, with the provision of defensive cores to a series of what could be regarded 'exposed' settlements. The omission of earlier habitation and public zones from the enceintes rarely signified their abandonment; rather, the *castrum* offered a secure base for the administrative bodies and for grain depots, and a military strong point and refuge when occasion demanded.

Paris (Roman Lutetia) is one striking example of this urban reconfiguration. This had, in the second century AD, comprised about 9,000 persons and was articulated around a major thoroughfare crossing the Seine: the urban focus with baths, forum, theatres and main residential and commercial quarters lay on Mont Sainte-Geneviève, with quays alongside the river, while a significant temple and palace, plus additional quays, lay on the narrow Ile de la Cité (9 ha in extent compared with the main urban space of 45 ha); the temple underlies the cathedral of Notre Dame. Yet this island alone was selected for fortification in c. AD 300, perhaps coinciding with major efforts to counter river flooding. These defences redefined the administrative heart of the city and gave heightened security to the palace residents – representatives of the Gallic prefecture, with occasional visits by the governor, and, in the 360s, the wintering base for Julian and Valentinian I (Julian was in fact acclaimed emperor in Paris in March 360). By the 380s the commander of the Seine fleet was probably also resident in Paris. The island further required space for both Episcopal Church and palace; a fifth-century cathedral of St Etienne is also overlain by Notre Dame. While text and excavations show a busy island, signs exist that the old open town remained populated, if contracted to around the (partially fortified?) forum zone.

One site which has seen extended periods of research and rescue excavation is Tours (Roman Caesarodunum), about 200 km south-west of Paris, in *Lugdunensis* III province.[31] Tours was elevated by AD 370 to capital of this province and became an archbishopric in the fifth century. However, its status was not fully reflected in its fortified size, since around the mid-fourth century a very compact citadel town was created in the north-east of the earlier Roman site, covering just 9 ha. Excavations at the château helped date the construction of the walls to c. AD 350, while work elsewhere indicates limited occupational activity occurring in the new suburban spaces. A striking feature at Tours is the inclusion of the amphitheatre as a projection of the *castrum* south wall, with the complex's bulk easier to convert to defended space than to leave outside. Interestingly, the archaeology hints at the amphitheatre acting as a garrison point and refuge during the turbulent conflicts of the Gallic Empire (a scenario perhaps also enacted at Avenches and Senlis); it may then have acted as stores and barracks. The Episcopal Church and residence occupied the citadel's south-western corner, but the popularity in the cult of St Martin at his burial place 800 m to the west saw already from the sixth century the growth of a new monastic and dependent community, and when the main town was refortified in the ninth century, this twinned centre also gained walls.

What of south-west Gaul? Did this more distant region see a delayed process of urban fortification? Three sites can be examined, each with different sources of evidence. First, two *civitas* centres in the Tetrarchic subprovince of Aquitania Secunda are Bordeaux and Périgueux: the former has excellent map and archival records which allow the late Roman circuit to be pinpointed; whereas Périgueux stands out for the survival of various portions of its fine defences.[32] In terms of the space enclosed by their late Roman circuits, there is a sizeable difference, from Bordeaux at 32.5 ha to Périgueux at just 5.5 ha. The first shows some reduction from its earlier imperial space while retaining its basic order; the latter by contrast focuses on higher ground, with dramatic shrinkage from the older town. Circuit design is relatively uniform in the provision of curtain walls of about 4- to 5-m thick and 9- to 12-m high, endowed with projecting semicircular towers, closely spaced (30–65 m apart). At both sites massive quantities of reused material or *spolia*, notably large building blocks, are employed; estimates are of up to 64,000 m³ for Bordeaux and at least 40,000 m³ for the walls of Périgueux. The works of both demolition and building must have been vast, noisy and hugely disruptive: homes, burial areas and some former public spaces would have been sacrificed, such as the forum complex and amphitheatre at Bordeaux; at Périgueux, in contrast, the amphitheatre was incorporated into the urban citadel to play a diverse role. Problematically, construction dates for these circuits cannot be tied down precisely: for Bordeaux, walled-in inscriptions and epitaphs and a rather fortunate old record of a coin of 268–73 from the wall mortar suggest the final quarter of the third century; Périgueux's diverse plan suggests a later date and evidence from the extramural zones points to levelling of these in the first half of the fourth century. That Bordeaux remained the more populous site is attested by the poet Ausonius, who describes his hometown thus (Ausonius, *Ordo*, 20):[33]

> Her goodly walls four-square, raise such lofty towers that their tops pierce the soaring clouds. Within her, one can marvel at streets clearly laid out, at houses regularly plotted out, at spacious boulevards which uphold their name, as also gates facing in direct line the crossways opposite; and, where the channel of its spring-fed stream divides the town, soon as old father Ocean fills it with his flowing tide, so one witnesses a whole sea gliding onward with its fleets.

A third example is Saint-Bertrand-de-Comminges, further south, in Gascony (late Roman *Novempopulana* province), a successor to the Gallo-Roman town of Lugdunum-Convenae. Excavations reveal that the medieval hilltop town (885-m long) was fortified only in *c*. AD 400, at a time when the public monuments of the lower town were being progressively abandoned. The walls were no rushed construction, carefully reusing brick/tile and stone and limited architectural *spolia* (column and decorative fragments).[34] While this fortress city was well established with an Episcopal Church when it was besieged in 585, the lack of circuit towers except on the flank facing the lower town suggest the walls had a symbolic role in the late Empire. Interestingly, the chronology and format at Saint-Bertrand closely follow those at other sites in *Novempopulana* such as Bazas, Lescar and Carcassone. Carcassone's late Roman circuit is the best preserved of these, occupying the low hill of La Cité; these and a ring of outer medieval walls were restored in stunning fashion in the second half of the nineteenth century under the architect Viollet-le-Duc (Figure 3.3).[35]

Conceivably these 'lesser' towns in south-west Gaul came late in the urban defensive sequence. A possible context might be offered from a fragment of

Figure 3.3 Extant and restored section of late Roman walls, towers and postern at the 'upper town' of Carcassone; the curtain is built of good building stone and tile coursing

the history by Olympiodorus: in discussing the revolt of Constantine in Britain and his rapid gains in Gaul (by AD 407), we hear that his son Constans took Spain, defeating a peasant and slave force in Lusitania. He then returned to Constantine in Arles, and 'left some of his own soldiers to garrison the pass into Spain, refusing to entrust this duty to the Spaniards, as was the old custom ... Later this was the cause of the destruction of the Spanish provinces. For when Constantine's power had collapsed, the barbarian peoples (Vandals, Sueves and Alans) regrouped themselves, seized the pass and captured many forts and cities of Spain and Gaul together with the officials of the usurper'. *Novempopulana* province lay central to these events.

Stephen Johnson has argued that the similarities in wall-building forms, materials and details signify the work of specific teams of engineers and architects within regions and provinces such as *Novempopulana*, and are suggestive of both State funds and directives to governors to initiate programmes of urban entrenchment or defensive overhaul. Possible documentary support for this derives from the fourth century, but rather unreliable, *Scriptores Historiae Augustae*, which claims that in the 260s Gallienus sent (presumed) architects to Thrace to help 'repair and fortify the cities *(instaurandis urbibus muniendisque)*' (SHA, *Gallieni Duo*, xiii.6–7). This instance may imply a rushed, emergency renewal and assessment, but such actions may well have set in train subsequent, more considered reviews and programmes of urban defence. But can we discern an overall strategy in town fortification? Were the provincial capitals and subsequently *civitas* capitals the first priorities, with new, strategic centres occasionally favoured over older seats? Was a wider scheme then applied or granted first to the frontier regions such as

Gallia Belgica and Thrace? How then to explain 'delayed' programmes as suggested for *Novempopulana*, or updating programmes such as additions of bastions in mid-fourth-century Britain? Is this down to recognition of an escalation of threats after *c.*375 and the need for closer inner provincial protection? Might they coincide with where units of the mobile army were stationed? By AD 400 authorisation for walling towns had probably devolved down to provincial governors and dukes, although we lack clear supporting documentary proof. Either way, the relative prosperity of a region would have dictated the scale of measures implemented. The end result was a much changed landscape of urban centres across the whole Western Empire by the earlier fifth century: some retaining their original expanse and with old walls re-commissioned; some shrunken with elements of the old towns dissected, cleared or reused; others elevated and incorporating churches as the new religious and social foci. The next chapter pursues how far other components of these remodelled Roman towns were transformed in the late Empire – how 'Roman' did their interiors still look in the last centuries of rule in the West?

4

Towns and Urban Society in the Late Empire

INTRODUCTION

Archaeological studies in southern Spain have pieced together the life history of an Iberian and Roman township in the former province of Baetica, between Seville and Cordoba. Now a largely open site, with later medieval and modern settlement gathered to the east of the former Roman zone, it has suffered from ploughing, robbing and even metal-detecting work (meaning that few coins were recovered by the excavators). But for the most part, the land lies available for scrutiny by geophysical survey, field-walking and excavation to pinpoint the approximate extent of the townscape, to glean something of the town layout and its contents, to chart its rise and fall, and to assess its prosperity and local impact. The town clearly failed at some point and the lack of standing monuments might indicate a middling settlement of no great prosperity. The town is identified as Celti, named by Pliny the Elder and in late Roman road itineraries, and a centre of adequate status to mint coins and to produce families of sufficient wealth to record their names on epitaphs and to commission good-quality statuary (many of these reused in buildings in the modern village). The local wealth derived chiefly from extensive production and export of olive oil from the fertile Guadalquivir valley; kilns revealed in the town and its environs demonstrate local manufacture of oil amphorae, peaking in the third century AD (one house of that date was even built using fragments of such amphorae!); the local ceramic industry was also involved in producing imitations of imported vessels.[1]

Is Celti a 'typical' Roman urban construct? Or does its very failure make Celti atypical? Should we see in the fate of Celti an approximation of the rise and fall of the Roman West? In other words, does it reveal a progressive take-up of urban living, an identification of local families and a display of wealth in private buildings in the second and third century AD in particular, an associated flourish in the hinterland, to be followed by a decline in textual display in the later Roman centuries, a shrinkage of the active urban space from the fourth, and then zones of decay yet pockets of continuity in the fifth, and with ceramics alone attesting some persistence of human presence at Celti into the seventh century? There is no visible Visigothic presence here to show a take over by new masters; nor is there trace of fires or burning to show a destructive end. Documents refer to a rural church in AD 619 with disputed attachment between Celti and *Regina* – enough to indicate it served local congregations even if these are not visible archaeologically. On the one hand, one might easily see the end of Celti as matched with an end of Rome and her government, with no revival sought by the Visigoths; on the other hand, ceramics and the seventh-century church are elements of continuity, reduced but tangible. Did Celti fail because of its relatively small size or because of its overdependence on the Roman economic market for its prosperity? Or because it lacked strong town walls, prompting its population or at least the wealthier members of that group to move away to more secure seats? Had that move occurred earlier when the local economy first stuttered? Perhaps failure was due to a limited Christian presence, offering no rallying point for the late Roman population? Or perhaps the evidence is too slight, since only a small part of the excavations revealed structural activity of the fifth century; without this one might have argued for general loss in the earliest fifth century coinciding with military upheavals. A similar scale of excavation in the 1970s would probably have failed to recognise the latest ceramics on the site and claimed wholesale abandonment by AD 400. Arguably, since the 1987–92 archaeological investigations were not extensive, potentially a busier late antique area, perhaps with Visigothic-period materials, awaits discovery.

Celti is atypical in being open for archaeological scrutiny: although various Roman urban sites in Hispania (such as Tiermes, Numancia and Segobriga in central Spain and the *municipium* of Conímbriga in central-west Portugal) do lie in what is now countryside,[2] by far the larger proportion of Roman-period towns are built over and largely lost through modern redevelopment and multi-storey building foundations or through late and post-medieval cellaring, which limit space for study to isolated pockets which, again, may hinder reconstruction of accurate images of town prosperity and survival. These, arguably, are towns which did not fail and so reflect Roman to medieval continuities – although proving these continuities archaeologically often remains problematic. Only in the past 20 years has a full appreciation been gained of the material changes that afflicted and impacted on the late Roman and early medieval townscapes and their populations; more systematic excavation techniques and enhanced knowledge of ceramics, technologies and structural data now enable more informed images to be drawn. So saying, disputes endure on meanings and interpretations: How to define 'continuity', whether of town, of people, of mentality, of socio-economic characters? How to define 'decay' and 'change' and when to apply these terms? Where one scholar may see persistence of town life, another may see crude living in what was once a town; a maintained church and a documented bishop need not define an urbanised congregation; likewise the presence of town walls need not denote a healthy and ordered population within.[3]

This chapter will consider the character and make up of Roman towns and then investigate the late antique faces of Roman urbanism to observe levels of physical continuity and change. Chapter 3 of this book highlighted town wall building and assessed how this redefined the urban form. Here we determine more of the evolving fabric of town interiors and peripheries to show that these were in no way static entities. What components of 'classical' urban form and function fell away and why? A spread of examples will be utilised to illustrate these transformations of space and life, and these will set the scene for comparison with the imperial capitals of Italy (Chapter 5 in this book) which are the best documented sites in terms of text, and sometimes in archaeology and survival, but which provide a distorted image since investment in these in both building new and maintaining the old was always high.

LIVING IN TOWNS: THE ROMAN ORDER

Even though the bulk of the population lived and worked in the countryside, towns are synonymous with the Roman Empire. The picture instantly conjured up is of ancient Rome itself, at its peak containing 1 million persons, then as now a melting pot of cultures, merchants, traders, foreign dignitaries, wealthy businessmen, entertainers, prostitutes, beggars and tourists, and a parade ground of religious and administrative buildings of brick and marble, vast public baths and aqueducts, statuary and paved streets. A key aim was to display Rome in all her cities and to encourage the elites and aristocracies of the various provinces to mark their allegiance and belonging to the Empire through seeking office, contributing to urban beautification, monumentalisation and upkeep. Such private patronage of public works – termed euergetism – was core to the creation of a strong Roman urban identity, and was already long evident in the classical and Hellenistic East (and enduring in the Eastern Empire well into the sixth century), it provided the means to administer provinces and articulate Roman trade.[4] Willing elite participation and competitive office-holding also meant that towns often vied for regional and provincial prominence, competing in provision of public edifices and amenities, in honouring the emperors and their families through statues, celebratory games or festivals. Private display was equally a part of this urban participation. In the East, letters between Pliny the Younger, as governor of Bithynia (modern northern Turkey, flanking the Black Sea), and the Emperor Trajan in the early second century give ample testimony of private (whether individual or group) input into public building works in towns such as Nicomedia and Nicaea, with works needing to be 'worthy' and to reflect on individuals, the cities and the emperor.[5]

The Mediterranean Roman world was full of cities whose elites readily and proactively, it seems, participated and enlivened their home or provincial towns and built up their own family's status. Frequently Rome added to pre-existing centres, but sometimes it also relocated sites by imposing a colony or creating a new economic focus gathered at a crossroads, port or river crossing. Encouraging fledgling urban communities was not a straightforward job and depended strongly on their hinterland, economic role and communications networks.

More problematic, of course, was the putting down of urban roots and encouraging growth in new, western and northern provinces such as Pannonia, Germany and Britain, where nucleated administrative, economic and population foci were rare beasts before Rome. Installing an urban package of administrators, colonists, religious heads and the concomitant array of public buildings was a sizeable, costly and lengthy task. In some cases we see a direct evolution from fort, barracks and headquarters to civic colony, houses and forum. An image of a typical Romano-British town in AD 100 would no doubt have featured much building activity, but not on an opulent scale, in more compact spaces and with low budgets; the slabs, veneer, columns of Italian, Greek and Egyptian marbles, so typical of any Mediterranean town and villa, almost never made it to Britain. A modest town in Britain was in fact on a par in size with the Baths of Diocletian in Rome at about 32 acres – but these were worlds apart in terms of opulence and build (and the Baths could host up to 3,000 persons – probably more than the average British urban population). Campaigns in this north-western province most probably stuttered on for decades and probably needed imperial grants and prompts (such as Hadrian's visit) to bring to fruition the proper Roman urban façade.[6] This is not to deny that towns in Britain and in the Danubian provinces did work and did generate taxes and help with administration, but their scale and even material visibility did not match core province displays, especially in the fourth and fifth centuries.

In addition, it is vital to stress how for Roman towns there is no straightforward sequence of growth → elaboration → stability → decay → loss. There are varied phases of urban (as rural) stagnation, dependent not only on external circumstances (i.e. invasions) but also on internal conflict (civil war, political rivalries) and equally on socio-economic fluctuations (changing markets, private hoarding of wealth). North Africa and Spain both see different peaks: arguably, the rise of Spanish emperors such as Trajan and Hadrian in the early second century AD facilitated the rise to prominence of Spanish aristocrats and the dominance of Spanish products in the Roman sea; with the Severan dynasty, North Africa took centre stage in terms of urban growth and embellishment and landed investment; such provincial growth meanwhile weakened the Italian export market and its urban vitality. Local strengths then may have helped counter negative economic trends as stronger regional markets were sought or achieved – as in large-scale production and marketing of local imitations of fineware ceramics.

As observed, the mid- to late third century marks a significant watershed: while the Empire recovers, it is in modified form. Towns and the economy recover too but are also altered or altering: the larger urban centres are fortified; an emphasis on security provokes stricter social control and taxation; office-holding becomes an expensive burden for many and less sought after (something already happening in the second century). As a result, some nobility switch their emphasis away from towns to their own estates and focus production and exchange on these rather than traditional urban markets; villa growth and monumentalisation then contrast with the lacklustre image gained of towns where private euergetism, so vital a force in aggrandising towns in the first and second centuries AD, is weakly registered after the mid-third century except in the larger provincial capitals. Again a contrast must be drawn between East and West: the social burdens and elite changes just noted relate far more to Western provinces, where civil war and barbarian incursions remained more constant than in the East, where private–public munificence was able to persist. But the East also struggled somewhat, and it is dangerous to assume too strong an East–West contrast in the late Roman centuries. On a simplistic level we can observe a dramatic loss in records on stone – whether records of building work, dedications of statues or epitaphs – after the mid-third century, most heavily pronounced in the West. One very well-documented city in the Eastern provinces is Aphrodisias in Asia Minor, where prior to AD 250 roughly 1,500 Roman inscriptions of varied type have so far been recovered, contrasting with about 230 inscriptions for the three centuries following. The Eastern Mediterranean provinces were generally wealthier and their cities bigger than those in the West and are marked also by a stronger urban identity and a longer lasting civic munificence; however, the epigraphic decline at Aphrodisias is striking and, crudely, implies less wealth (or fewer but wealthier elites). At the same time, this epigraphic decline matches a general diminishment in this form of record, and different modes of commemoration (painted especially) may have come into play. As highlighted in Chapter 3 of this book, very few dedicatory inscriptions survive for town walls, even though these were exceptionally costly and important civic ventures ordained by the State/Emperor. Is this purely a coincidence of poor survival or a reflection that inscribed texts were becoming viewed as less vital, with public acclamation of the emperor in markets/fora or in theatre or amphitheatre instead used?[7]

In late Roman Italy, inscriptions by governors or provincial officials become more common than those by private individuals, reflecting how fewer new projects were being started or public structures being invested in by rich members of the local elite; by the fourth century the task was more of repair and restoration, with civic funds and thus State money being employed to meet these needs.[8] Statues to the emperor and governors continued to be set up – no doubt by the governors themselves using civic and State funds rather than their own. Private investment shifted to private residences where there was no real need to document through inscribed text – although some villas had founder's inscriptions and mosaic texts (and the owners engaged in much literary swapping). Arguably also, the scale of urban development in the West diminished after the third century and with it the need to spell out the donors; in the East, works did continue and so therefore do texts, but the range and depth decreased as State involvement increased. Interestingly, when, by c.425, the Church was fully established and its structures started to dominate towns, so inscribed and painted honorary and dedicatory texts reappeared – in both halves of the Empire; private individuals, not just bishops and State, indulged in church building far more in the fifth and sixth centuries and found these a new vehicle for self-display (and piety).[9]

LATE ANTIQUE URBANISM

Much recent research has centred on towns in Late Antiquity, addressing both sides of the Empire and extending discussion fully into the Byzantine-Arab period in the Eastern Mediterranean. This proliferation of research is stimulated especially by improving abilities to date ceramics and to observe physical traces of building use, decay and reuse, but more widely by desires to question the concepts of continuity and decline in the late Empire, with towns a natural focus of attention since many often retain a basic documentary record (of bishops, for example) to suggest some persistence of activity. Questions centre on forms of activity across AD 300–650, population levels, building media, signs of elite input, impacts of economic change, military impositions, wastage, religious changes, burial practices, urban services and attitudes to the past.[10] There is no space here to delve deeply into all these questions – it is better for readers to explore more detailed regional syntheses.[11] Instead, a set of seven short case studies can be offered to highlight the varying as well as shared urban trajectories in the Roman West and to identify something of the character of space and population in these in the fourth and fifth centuries. How much of the old, early imperial, classical fabric continued to be used and maintained? How did defensive entrenchment impact? What were the changes brought by Christianisation? What post-Roman impacts are evident? Discussion will then follow on two specific components of Roman towns, namely baths and entertainment, using these as guides to some of the changes visible across the later Roman West.

Barcino-Barcelona, Spain

Celti introduced this chapter, but it was a failed town – one of a number of towns that existed in the Spanish provinces. Yet numerous other centres there, such as Valencia, Lugo and Tarragona, show continuity – in Tarragona's case with Visigothic churches installed in old Roman spaces such as the theatre (see below), if set close to urban zones that had been abandoned, and at Valencia, excavations at the Almoina east of the old Forum show house survival plus church constructions, followed by sixth-century burials, utilising materials from demolished Roman structures.[12] Another successful town is *Barcino*-Barcelona, which stands out for the survival of sections of its late Roman defensive walls (now cleared of late and post-medieval accretions), erected perhaps towards the mid-fourth century but duplicating the Augustan circuit line and maintained and expanded in the Middle Ages (Figure 4.1). These alone suggest urban resilience, but we can draw also on significant evidence gathered from the recent re-evaluation and full finds analysis of old but extensive excavations at the Plaça del Rei in the city's north-eastern quadrant. This was crucial in recognising the earliest Episcopal complex and its Visigothic successors and expansions – in the same area as the medieval and modern cathedral.[13]

Barcino grew rapidly from its foundation as an Augustan colony *c.*10 BC, exploiting local marine and mineral resources to establish itself as a producer

Figure 4.1 A section of Barcelona's Roman to late Roman and medieval town walls, showing changing building materials, repairs and adaptations (photo: Gavin Speed)

and exporter. Although it may not have reached more than 3,000 urban residents, Barcino provided senators in the second century, and these high elite, along with successful freedmen, duly contributed to the town's monumentalisation, notably in providing public baths, paying for festivals and erecting statues. Statues were still being provided to later third-century emperors in the forum, and this civic space remained active certainly till late in the fourth, since a last attested statue belongs to an ex-proconsul of Asia of *c*. AD 380. By this date the new, distinctive circuit walls defined the old city, and striking features of these are the ready incorporation of *spolia* in the core and the internal face, and with choice reused masonry as part of the external workings. Many pieces of 'spoil' came from the suburban cemeteries – nearly all still active into the later and even post-Roman periods – signifying how the cutting of a wide ditch necessitated clearance of built tombs and shrines. Other materials probably derived from failed public buildings of the intramural space (again victims to the required working space of the wall architects), although it is not easy to identify specific structures.

The forum appears to have been robbed of materials certainly by the time of the Visigothic extensions to the bishop's palace complex, since statue pedestals are reused in this. The Plaça del Rei sequence is exceptional, providing a fascinating window into the insertion and evolution of Episcopal space, commencing from the mid-fourth century (the first attested bishop is Praetextatus in 344). That the first cathedral was squeezed into a busy townscape is suggested from its setting in a zone dominated by industry from the second century – a dye-works, laundry, fish sauce factory, a winery; of these, the latter two were still functioning, the winery with a cellar capacity of 10,000 l, into the fifth century. Quite possibly they came into Church ownership – to bring in income, to supply the Church staff and to assist in Church handouts to the poor. They may even have been donated when the cathedral was first established: certainly the first bishop's palace occupied most of a sizeable and functioning elite *domus* (townhouse), adapting this across time (with a new reception hall, corridors, raised floors – sometimes covering over good-quality mosaic floors), and given that one later fourth-century bishop, Pacian, came from the senatorial aristocracy, it is feasible that the *domus* was actually his. Major reworking and embellishment of the whole zone came in the sixth century, coinciding with when Barcino became a Visigothic royal capital, adding a new bishop's palace, a cruciform church, revised baptistery and a bath suite. All told, Barcino, always a compact city, saw no significant losses but rather blossomed as a town with both Church and Visigothic presences.

London

London had, probably, since the mid-first century AD been the seat of a governor, with his guard based at the Cripplegate fort. From the third century it formed the capital of the southern province of Britannia Superior, and was later honoured as Augusta, overseeing the whole diocese of Britain. Key governors' names are Clodius Albinus for the 190s and Allectus (293–6), both of whom later became usurpers seeking the imperial throne, in the course of which both may have enhanced their capital architecturally. Allectus is linked also to the general Carausius who in the mid-280s himself sought the purple and, to that end, reinforced Britain's coastal defences. These episodes would not have endeared London and Britain to the Empire; the Arras medallion of AD 296 shows the Emperor Constantius with fleet in support arriving at the gates of *Londinium* where a kneeling figure begs forgiveness. Unsurprisingly, the ambitious palace structure identified on St Peter's Hill, dated through analysis of its massive timber foundation piles to spring 294, was left unfinished.

The Arras coin depicts London already defended by high walls. A land-ward wall was constructed between c. AD 190 and 220, perhaps initiated under Albinus and then part-funded and completed under the visiting Emperor Septimius Severus in the early third century. While waterfront terraces were created in the late second century, no riverside wall seems to have been planned at this stage. The date of construction of the Thames-side wall remains unclear, ranging from the mid- to late third century to the mid-fourth. While this added security, it must have made for changes in the way waterborne traffic and goods unloading were organised. The addition of projecting bastions on the landside wall (and a wider outer ditch) should fit a mid-fourth-century date, indicating upgrading of London's defensive capabilities. These walls suggest a population and a town worth defending in the later Roman period. The presence of the governor and diocesan *vicarius*, plus a State Treasury, further suggest an active cityscape, as reinforced by the documented presence in the fourth century of a bishop – his cathedral might relate to a partially excavated, substantial aisled structure on Tower Hill, although this might equally comprise offices linked to the city administration or else a State granary.[14]

But just how bustling a late Roman provincial capital was London?[15] Work at Poultry, adjoining one of the main city west-east roads, and thus an expected commercial focus, shows a busy net of timber houses, bakeries, work-shops (for metal, wood and possibly fulling) by AD 100; the yard of one house was made up wholly of broken millstones or quernstones; others showed less hygienic rubbish dumps and debris. Revisions came during the second century, with some properties not recovering from a fire of c. AD 125, but by the start of the third century stone buildings appear, some with mosaics, wall paintings and heating systems. The roads were renewed as were the side drains, though environmental samples show that the third- and fourth-century street was not all tidy, and some properties and drains were choked with weeds and with evident rubbish and manure dumps. Despite some maintenance, and some crude repair work (including to mosa-ics), by the end of the fourth century the area appears abandoned but with some robbing and clearance of old timber and stone units. Only from the ninth century is habitation, market and road activity witnessed again on the Poultry site. While there is general Roman continuity at 1 Poultry, else-where changes can already be observed in the urban fabric from the later second century: the Huggin Hill bathhouse was by then redundant; glass workshops in the Walbrook were abandoned; by c. AD 300 the forum and basilica had apparently already fallen out of use, the latter systematically levelled, and many of the surrounding streets lay in poor repair; the river-side wall meanwhile contains architectural and decorative elements from a variety of demolished public structures. Furthermore, in many areas of London and, across the river, the 'bridgehead' communities of Southwark (with good evidence here for some well-appointed administrative structures in c. AD 300), layers (sometimes in excess of 1-m thick) of grey 'dark earth' have accumulated in the late Roman period, variously viewed as evidence of 'windblown' soil, midden dumping, imported agricultural soil or decayed timber or brick-earth/clay-based buildings broken up through worm and root action. For long considered in negative fashion to indicate areas of desertion, collapsed buildings and squatter activity at best, in reality most of the explanations indicate continued human activity – that is, houses, cultivation, food debris – but at a level hard to distinguish due to the processes of breaking-up of the associated structures. Maybe these were people living in much more workaday modes, lacking the expected elements of Roman display and order.

Burials certainly indicate a continuing population: thus in Southwark, burials at Great Dover Street extend from c. AD 120 to the late fourth century, late Roman inhumations cut into former settlement space on Southwark Street and a fine fourth-century tombstone to Matrona comes from beneath the medieval city cathedral. For the north cemetery of London (with the Spitalfields area) flanking Ermine Street, nearly 200 third- to fourth-century inhumations are so far known, including a limestone sarcophagus with lead lid finely decorated with scallop shell designs containing a young lady dressed in fine textiles and with bay leaves placed under her head. In the east near Aldgate the majority of some 550 inhumations are later Roman, some perhaps extending into the fifth. There are signs of a number of third- and fourth-century private houses near the waterfront and Pudding Lane areas to show money still flowed in the city, although it seems clear that the majority of the traditional Roman public units such as baths and temples were redundant by the early fourth century and some harbour/port facilities perhaps as early as the 270s. Interestingly, there are indications that the amphitheatre still functioned but perhaps now as a market zone (possibly replacing the decayed forum). London could thus still be seen as a late Roman town of note, with trappings of government and State/military control, but by the early fifth century the former Roman cityscape may well have been a patchwork of active and dead zones, with the latter strongly dominant amongst small settlement nuclei containing a population barely capable of defending its still fine walls. Perhaps by this date new points of settlement and trade were gathering to the west where, not much later, the site of *Lundenwic* would emerge.

Iol Caesarea

Another seat of a Roman procurator was Iol Caesarea (modern Cherchel), the capital of the province of *Mauretania Caesariensis* in North Africa.[16] Iol was largely refounded and rebuilt in the Augustan period under the client King Juba II, who provided a theatre, various temples, an amphitheatre and an aqueduct; its two ports facilitated a bustling trade within the Mediterranean, and this helped in the city's developing monumentalisation in the first two centuries AD, when three sets of baths were added, plus a circus and a town wall. Further urban munificence is registered in the early third century

under the Severans, reflecting also a busy hinterland with high olive oil production; an urban population peak of about 30,000 is proposed for this
epoch. Later imperial Iol Caesarea possessed a strong early Christian community with active bishops, although St Augustine needed to come and preach
during conflicts here in 418; however, while Christian cemeteries are known,
the main churches remain to be properly identified. One documented episode of note for the city's urban innards is the revolt in AD 370–3 of Firmus,
son of an African prince, who used Moorish tribal support to oust Roman
military officials. However, according to Ammianus Marcellinus, by the time
of the forceful reconquest of Iol, much of the city had been burnt down; soldiery stationed there probably assisted in the rebuilding work. Various aristocratic townhouses with good-quality mosaics indicate that a fair revival
had been accomplished by the early fifth century – recall that North Africa
was spared so many of the traumas afflicting the northern provinces in the
third and fourth centuries. But did the monumental heart of the city show
any change?

Systematic excavations in the forum zone undertaken in the late 1970s provide some indications of the latest Roman and post-Roman phases at Iol
Caesarea's old administrative and religious core. The excavation in fact concerned just the north-east corner of the forum, or at least an extension to this,
since the evidence suggested the paving and buildings were laid out probably
in the early third century. A paved piazza was girded by a colonnaded portico
and with podia for the display of statuary; on the east flank was a basilica
about 100-m long. The primary phases of the basilica interior had been
removed. Few data were available for the third- and fourth-century forum,
suggesting stability and order, with the paved areas kept clear of rubbish.
Early in the fifth century, acts of renewal, redesign and change are observed:
although the piazza itself remained largely unaltered, some repaving and
patching of the surface occur, plus cutting of grooves and post holes for a
series of wooden stalls set up to the steps fronting the colonnaded portico
(Figure 4.2). These are identified as market stalls, semi-temporary, for varied
vendors; their presence confirms continuity of the forum's market functions
into the late Roman period, supported also by numerous coin finds found in
gutters and between paving slabs. These coins were predominantly of the
fourth century, but numismatists argue that these formed the bulk of Roman
small change still in the fifth century. Intriguingly, a gap lay between the stalls
on the north side allowing access between columns to the doorway of a new
building on the north-east flank of the forum: its plan, with raised apsidal east
end, indicates a small church of about 20 m × 7 m. Although its interior was
badly disturbed by later activity (including two kilns and a small house plus
various pits), there were traces of the brick-concrete floor and a long wooden
screen opposite the entry – the traces of worn flooring processing towards this
screened area identified this as the location of the altar.

Conceivably contemporary was the refurbishment of the nearby basilica,
marked chiefly by the laying of a new, if not high-quality, black and white

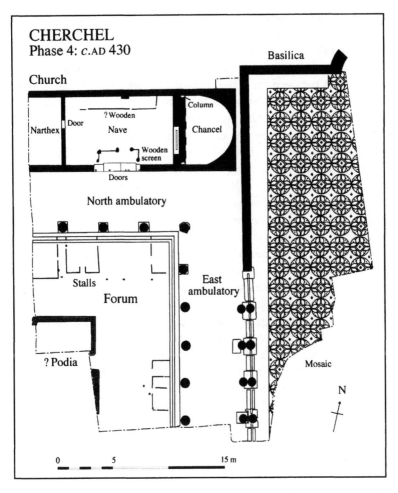

Figure 4.2 Plan of the excavated sector of the forum at Cherchel showing buildings and features of c. AD 430 (after Potter 1995: Fig. 15)

mosaic floor and by the replacement of some of the marble veneer. The excavators also traced much robbing of old features prior to the construction work, plus backfilling of trenches with much burnt material. The latter could have been a vestige of the destructions wrought in the revolt of Firmus; if so, it implies almost a generation passed before the forum zone investigated was restored to some public vigour. Most importantly, however, there was restoration and this included not only administrative and mercantile spaces but also a new religious focus, with a church installed in a core location. The estimated chronology for this construction work is in the 420s, either prior to the Vandal takeover of North Africa or immediately following this; either way, it shows persistence of urban life at Iol Caesarea through the fifth century.

A later conquest, that of the Byzantines or East Romans in AD 533–4, contributed to the final significant changes here, when the church was destroyed by fire and its walls subsequently demolished; the basilica may have suffered a similar fate (some rubble from demolition apparently was left where it had fallen). We should be cautious in linking these documented and archaeological events, since the church fire may well have been accidental – or even the result of conflict between the Arian Vandal and Orthodox Roman Churches – in the later Vandal period. By the early sixth century, the zone may have lost its market, and the basilica no longer performed any administrative function. Even though the zone then lay abandoned and suffered encroachment by clayey hill-wash, towards the end of the sixth century there was brief reoccupation, marked by housing – both timber and rubble-built (including fallen architectural pieces) – and artisanal activity, most notably in the nave of the 'lost' church where both a house and two kilns were inserted.

Few other North African towns have seen comparable systematic excavation work to allow for comparison with the urban sequence identified at Iol Caesarea. The picture that generally emerges, however, is one where new foci gathered around churches, either within the townscape or in the suburbs; rarely do these coincide with the old forum, which in many instances goes out of use as a public (and part-pagan) focus around the end of the fourth century. This occurs even at Carthage where housing, soil and burials slowly covered sections of the old forum; at Sbeitla, where the forum area was 'invaded' by olive oil presses and vats; and at Dougga where statues from the (ruinous?) forum were shifted to the theatre. Clearly, therefore, a new urbanism had emerged at sites like Iol Caesarea by the early fifth century which was heavily dictated by the Church and the economy; this often sidelined the old urban heart and noticeably often meant a failure to maintain older buildings and their functions.

Gorsium Gorsium-Herculia

Next we jump to the Danubian province of Pannonia and the Roman town of Gorsium, halfway between Budapest and Lake Balaton (Map 3.1). The site is an abandoned one and has been the focus of excavations since the 1930s. The remains are extensive but they were much robbed in the Middle Ages when, at the very end of the tenth century, King Stephen I created a capital to the north at Alba Regia, modern Székesfehérvár, and his architects systematically exploited (and in large fashion deliberately redisplayed) stones and sculptures of ancient Gorsium. The Roman town was not stripped bare, however, and circumstances mean that a full image can potentially be drawn of its fortunes from antiquity into the early Middle Ages, observing, most particularly, a significant redesigning of the town in the late Roman period and a tentative occupation by Germanic and Avar groups after Rome.[17]

Gorsium developed from a small first-century AD Roman fort and attendant civilian settlement to the seat of the Imperial Cult and provincial council in the early part of the second century, with the future emperor Hadrian overseeing construction of the temple and its precinct. Sacrificial pits and offerings and statuary linked to the cult and council have been discovered, plus a coin hoard of 3,134 silver *antoniniani*, probably part of the council treasury buried in the riots in AD 258. Public monuments adjoining the compact forum formed the town's heart, and shops and houses fronted onto roads leading to these; a relatively well-to-do population is attested by wall paintings, numerous tombstones and imported materials. Inscriptions record major reconstructions and rededications of both precinct and council house under Septimius Severus after destructions through Sarmatian incursions over 20 years before. The mid-third-century traumas seriously shook Gorsium, leaving the town in ruins and the population that survived living in crude buildings amidst the debris such as inside the roofless granary. When the town was revived at the end of the third century under Diocletian, the past was levelled and built over; new town walls with fan-shaped towers were constructed, and Gorsium was even given a new name, *Herculia*, after the Co-emperor Maximianus Herculius (styling himself after Hercules, while Diocletian took the name *Jovius* after Jupiter: various restored forts and towns in the Danubian provinces were awarded names such as Iovia and Ad Herculem). Effectively, at *Gorsium*-Herculia there is scope for observing what elements constituted a town of the earliest fourth century.

Significantly, the old religious role was discarded and the former precinct remained largely as substantial grass-covered ruins, but with a likely military workshop imposed. The excavators argue that much statuary was removed from the imperial cult precinct to the Danubian fort of Intercisa in *c*. AD 260. The new focus to Herculia was a palace-like structure (60 m × 55 m) combining vestibule, ornamental courtyard, bath suite, stables, living rooms and a large apsed reception hall (Figure 4.3), presumed to have been the seat of the governor of *Valeria* province. The building part-overlay the demolished granary; we should assume a replacement urban granary elsewhere in the townscape, yet to be identified. Immediately to the east are two likely churches, one facing the main street and later provided with a baptismal basin and the second, smaller, over the site of the former council house. Workshops and houses lay in this same zone, whilst a 70-m long porticoed line of shops occupied the opposite side of the road to the palace; well-endowed houses with bath suites, wall paintings and mosaics lay in the suburbs. We lack data regarding entertainment structures or public baths; similarly, evidence for temples is limited, except for a possible early fourth-century cult structure to Jupiter Dolichenus opposite the former precinct. Overall, the town was busy with small-scale manufacturers and traders, presumably with a local economy buoyed by the governor and his court's presence. Herculia was thus still Roman in the sense of public spaces and services (roads, wells, walls, markets, shops) and private structures, cemeteries, material culture and art, but the range of civic expressions was reduced: the palace complex and small churches were the new foci.

All remained active well into the fourth century and to a date around AD 370, despite documented enemy raids and incursions across the Danube;

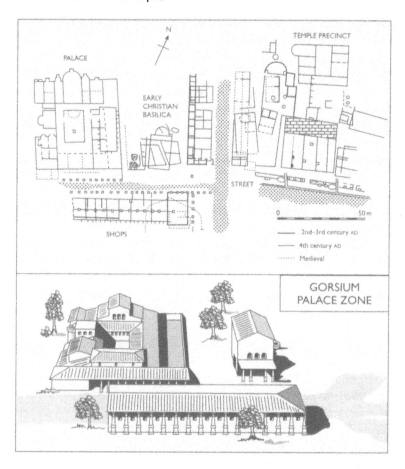

Figure 4.3 Plan and interpretative reconstruction of the fourth-century palace, church, shops and council complex at Gorsium (after Fitz 1980: Figs 2 and 5)

some contraction and revised security measures may have been undertaken after this period, since the extramural villas were quitted, and crude houses within the curtain wall are thought to signify refugees. Burials indicate a full enough population, with the southern cemetery continuing in use into the 430s, although the extension of burials (some claimed as Germanic in character) into some intramural spaces recognises a modified perception of the urban space. Perhaps this act denotes stronger Church influence; indeed, the excavators propose an early fifth-century (final) refurbishment of the main basilica church, probably involving insertion of the baptismal basin. Later shrinkage around this core is evident, with some activity in the *palatium* (the Roman governor and staff no doubt having left in the earlier fifth century) and with Germanic and later seventh- and eighth-century Avar burials representing some final uncertain use of the now rubble-strewn urban area.

A Late Imperial Capital – Trier

By the reign of Claudius, Trier was already viewed as the richest city of the province of Gallia Belgica, its 300 ha early walled space clearly anticipating a big future.[18] Nonetheless, the majority of its typical Roman public structures were perhaps not fully completed until the mid-second century AD, even though, as the seat of the procurator, imperial subsidies must have helped in certain larger building projects, notably the baths (the 'Barbarathermen') and the town walls (with their elaborate northern gateway, the Porta Nigra). Urban wealth was meanwhile depicted also in the many private houses presenting mosaic floors, running from the first into the fourth century AD, and in the prosperous local pottery industry. The late third century, however, marks an even greater upturn in Trier's civic fortunes, when it was selected not just as the capital of the northern Gallic diocese but also as one of the scattered imperial bases and mints of the Tetrarchy. Coinage was minted here from as early as AD 293 and lasted until the 390s. Its status was further enhanced under Constantine the Great, and key imperial visitors included Gratian and Valentinian; the praetorian prefect for the Gauls otherwise provided the highest state presence inside the walls. Trier's selection derived from its position on the Moselle river, close to but strategically withdrawn from the Rhine frontier. We gather much of contemporary local perceptions from the 'list' (*Ordo*) of famous cities put together by Ausonius in the late 380s, who ranks Trier sixth:

> Long has Gaul, mighty in arms, yearned to be praised, and that royal city of the Treveri, which, though full near the Rhine, reposes unalarmed as if in the bosom of deep profound peace, because she clothes and arms the forces of the Empire. Widely her walls stretch forward over a spreading hill; beside her the bounteous Moselle glides past with peaceful stream, carrying the far-brought merchandise of all the races of the Earth.

Besides general renewal (of walls, streets – these relaid in limestone slabs – water supply, forum, theatre, amphitheatre – the latter gaining a new gallery), late third- and fourth-century imperial involvement saw dramatic redesigning of the eastern sector of the cityscape which would have required forceful eviction of various private citizens to secure the space. The principal components of this new imperial zone comprised palace, circus and baths, set close to both walls and amphitheatre (Figure 4.4). Scale was important, and the imperial baths were designed to match the size of the substantial earlier baths while incorporating the most modern architectural forms. Between these and the amphitheatre lay the circus, attributed to Constantine for AD 310 but probably begun some years earlier. Little is known of its format, but its length is estimated at 440 m, and traces of column drums and pedestals imply colonnaded galleries and lines of statuary. It is uncertain on the basis of current archaeological understanding if corridors gave direct access from palace to circus to highlight the link between emperor (and prefect) and games. Best known of the palace constructions is the extant Basilica, an auditorium or audience chamber, originally fitted out with marble veneer and mosaic decoration; this would

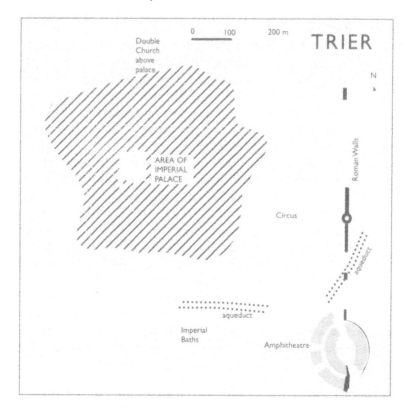

Figure 4.4 Plan of the imperial sector of fourth-century trier (after Wightman 1985: Fig. 40)

have been accessed from formal porticoed passages, halls and gardens to the south. To the north, the cathedral overlies likely private apartments to the palace, indicated by the discovery here of imperial-style portraits (striking for their display of purple cloth and jewellery) which formerly adorned the ceilings. The apartments were demolished to make way for a vast double church (100 m × 200 m) which formed an early Christian precursor to the cathedral; tradition attributes this foundation to Constantine's mother Helena in 326–8, although it may not have been completed until the 370s. A later addition was its baptistery.

A progressive Christianisation of Trier is evident through extramural funerary churches set over the tombs of early bishops, such as Saints Eucharius and Valerius near the south gate. A medieval St Matthias church covers the presumed location, but an inscription refers to a chapel erected by the mid-fifth-century Bishop Cyrillus. Similarly, beside the north gate, the apse of the church of St Maximin overlies the presumed tomb of Bishop Maximinus, marked by a late Roman sarcophagus (with carved biblical scenes) in a funerary vault. A suburban monastic presence is also attested. However, excavations also show that the pagan sanctuary complex of Altbachtal south of the palace zone with its various temples, shrines and theatre, much restored at the end of the third century, remained frequented into the mid-fourth century at least, until it was secularised under Gratian when roads were driven over the temple sites and domestic buildings alone allowed to persist.

As well as the mint and the provincial treasury (locations undetermined), Trier's military links are evident on three levels: first, in the later use of the imperial baths as barracks; second, by local production (attested by the *Notitia Dignitatum* and by Ausonius) of materials and weapons (woollen cloths, shields, parade armour and siege artillery); further, this was the site for a State granary and likely depot point for the *annona* (large warehouses are attested near the river). As a bustling centre, many of the elite selected to reside in suburban villas, although wealthy townhouses with mosaics are also known.

Prosperity and confidence were seriously dented by the events of 406/7 when the Rhine frontier was breached; perhaps even before the then prefect had transferred his seat well to the south, to Arles near the mouth of the Rhone, long involved in Mediterranean trade operations and previously also a stop-off for emperors. Arles' late Roman monumentalisation had come under Constantine (baths and a possible new forum) and Constantius II (restorations), and the transfer of the prefecture led to no new munificence here but more to a busier cityscape with public spaces encroached upon by private dwellings, although the circus, theatre and forum seemingly endured, perhaps even into the sixth century.[19] In contrast, while a sizeable population and some nobility continued at Trier (reflected chiefly in cemeteries and epitaphs), the city's public structures came to be sacrificed for more secular concerns, with both amphitheatre and public baths becoming citadels; undoubtedly, the loss of court/State figures deflated the town's economy, and Trier perhaps became more of a garrison town. The bishops gained extra prominence in these circumstances and provided leadership: although the cathedral was destroyed in the mid-fifth century, rebuilding was swift and the suburban church foci persisted. A century later, Gregory of Tours' *Life of Bishop Nicetius* states that St Eucharius guarded the south gate and St Maximinus, the north; these and the living bishop were the town's protectors from enemy and plague alike.

Falerii Novi – A 'Lost' Roman Town in Italy

As an example of a failed town in Italy, Falerii Novi in south Etruria is a striking site, still girded by tufa-built town walls, in places preserved to 6 m in height, but with an almost empty interior in terms of upstanding remains. Although a colony, dating to the mid-third century BC and replacing a former, upland Iron Age site (*Falerii Veteres*-Civita Castellana), its plan is an irregular triangle of about 750 m × 500 m, its shape dictated by the local topography. This was an aggressive, enforced lowland colonisation, but the archaeology shows that despite some presumed third-century AD investment (the Emperor Gallienus' wife came from here), its Roman urban content had already begun to unravel from the end of that century – in line with a few other sites in the region such as *Forum Novum*-Vescovio, which shrank to small administrative and religious cores in the late Empire and with partial post-Roman afterlives. For Falerii Novi, comprehensive geophysical (magnetometer) surveys of the town innards and some peripheral spaces have been undertaken as part of the wider survey of the Tiber Valley: coverage was 90 per cent of the 31 ha of intramural space; the former Benedictine abbey of Santa Maria di Fálleri and a farm occupy the remainder, and despite the complexities of some of the buried data (reflecting rebuilding, remodelling of space and structures, plus robbing activity), an impressive plot was created of the interior's 73 *insulae*, identifying street lines, house blocks and a variety of major public structures, notably theatre, public baths and forum.[20]

The project also included the plotting of surface materials – building materials, road materials (basalt), marble, ceramic types – to provide a guide to the status of the buried structures (private, public, long- or short-lived etc.) and to offer some chronological sequence (a complex task given farming work, previous archaeological interventions and the difficulty of connecting surface finds with activity below). The surveys indicated that certain areas potentially fell out of use earlier than others: thus, whereas the zone of the central forum appears to have continued to be an active space into the fifth and even sixth centuries, both theatre and south-eastern zones lack clear later Roman evidence. This matches the sequence at Forum Novum about 15 km to the east, with theatre and baths redundant by the fourth century and with church imposed on the forum; despite the shrunken nature of this 'town', it was a bishopric.[21] Excavation on a sizeable scale at Falerii Novi would help determine more closely the processes and sequences of decay. Why did the theatre zone go out of use so early? Did local elites shift south to Rome or simply choose to invest in the land rather than in the town? Who organised the remaining community? Did insecurity fracture the local economy and create problems in terms of supplying Falerii Novi? Did insecurity mean the inhabitants progressively transferred (back) to upland Civita Castellana? Clearly, having good-quality town walls was enough neither to ensure urban survival here nor to prevent urban shrinkage after an early imperial floruit.

ROMAN ENTERTAINMENT AND LEISURE – FATES AND FORTUNES

Core to the modern image of Roman society are the spectacles, violence and luxuries portrayed through film and visible through surviving and restored vast entertainment and leisure structures across the Empire – from the amphitheatre at Silchester to the theatre at Martigny in Switzerland to the imperial baths and cisterns of Dougga. The immensity of these public provisions is not easily appreciated simply through a meander through the stunted streets of Pompeii, nor even through an upward admiration of Rome's Theatre of Marcellus; instead it comes out more strongly through figures on paper and plan when one considers how extensive some of these complexes physically were.[22] Taking Rome as an example (exceptional but symbolic nonetheless), the imperial *thermae* or Baths of Caracalla and Diocletian each cover an area of 120,000 m²; the fifth-century author Olympiodorus stated that those of Diocletian accommodated 3,000 bathers – a figure comparable to the total population of a typical town in Roman Britain. While only a portion of these baths remain fully visible, the *frigidarium* alone serves as the substantial church of Santa Maria degli Angeli, and the Museo Nazionale is incorporated into a sizeable area behind this; moreover, the large modern Piazza della Repubblica overlies part only of the exercise and courtyard zone. Vast quantities of water were required to feed and flush these baths; the mechanics of engineering, building and supply are similarly hard to grasp in a pre-industrial context, even more so if we consider that for Rome the aqueducts and pipes had to supply (according to a Regionary Catalogue of the early fourth century) 1,352 public fountains, 15 *nymphaea*, 11 imperial *thermae*, 856 public baths and 254 reservoirs; private establishments are unlisted. On top of this one can only estimate how many slaves were needed to run, maintain and clean this complex and the other public baths. How much wood was needed to fire the furnaces to heat the floors and hot rooms? Where was such wood stored, how regular and vast was its supply, and from what source did the wood derive? And what of the oils and foods and other goods needed to clean and feed the bathers?[23]

Enduring Cleanliness?

Bathing complexes, both public and private, have long been viewed as core structural ingredients of imperial Roman urbanism, valid even in northern provincial contexts. It rapidly became the case that high social status required ownership of a private bath suite; on most villas by/from the third century, separate bath suites were common features. These were ostentatious displays of resources, not just in terms of use of marble (veneer, flooring, mosaics) but simply to run them; some of the largest public baths in cities like Rome, Trier, Valencia and Carthage required substantial daily running costs, rarely paid back through entry fees where these were taken. Here we explore the evidence for the maintenance of bathing and bathing establishments (and thereby water supply) in the late Roman centuries.

Extant inscriptions of fourth-century date across the Empire reveal that public baths (and their closely associated aqueducts) remained an essential component of Roman town life and that funds were accordingly used to restore these (in mainly larger centres), but predominantly now through the initiative of the provincial governor. Thus laws of AD 374 and 395 announce, 'Lest splendid cities and towns collapse through age, we allot a third of the revenue from public land to the repair of buildings and the heating of baths', and such laws on public works are all addressed to governors. This supports the view that private euergetism was failing, forcing the towns of the later Western Empire to rely mainly on local funds and taxes to aid in maintenance costs. In the wealthy province of Campania, south of Rome, baths were being restored in the late fourth century by governors at Anzio, Terracina and

Puteoli; to the east, one governor in the 350s restored baths in various towns of Samnium province (Saepinum, Allifae, Telesia) after earthquake damage; Rome's prefect, meanwhile, restored the Maritime Baths at Ostia in 375 – to go alongside two other large *thermae* and 12 smaller baths still active at the end of the century.[24]

At Tarraco in Spain, the provincial governor restored the *thermae Montanarum* in the early fourth century but no baths are known for the upper town where, by the end of the century, the main administration and church functions were located. In Trier, the vast second-century Barbarathermen were joined in the late third or early fourth century by new imperial public baths set close to the palace and circus in the city's eastern quarter – all requiring demolition of earlier, generally private structures. Despite the mass of limestone and tile utilised, however, the budget may well have been exceeded and patron interest waned, since there seems no evidence for water pipes being installed or for the furnaces being fired. By the end of the fourth century both sets of baths were being used for barracks or for housing. At Metz, imperial grants under Valentinian I and Valens paid for construction of baths on 'La Citadelle' and for renovation of the aqueduct. Here, too, there was redundancy by AD 400, by when the town as a whole was largely being abandoned. Sometimes loss is explicable through specific causes: thus in Aquitaine, at the prosperous late Roman city of Bordeaux, the public *thermae* on Rue des Frères-Bonie were demolished and levelled *c.* AD 300, most probably due to construction of the late Roman circuit walls, whose south-west corner cut the baths; demolition was necessary to give better defensive visibility, although this did not prevent the suburban build-up in other extramural zones.[25]

In late Roman Britain, at Canterbury both public and private bath units have been shown to have been maintained until the 350s, followed by dumping, industrial usage and flooding; while at Wroxeter the maintenance of the exercise yard and modifications to a reduced public *thermae* perhaps happened as late as the last quarter of the fourth century. The elaborate spa complex at Bath (enclosed along with other structures by a polygonal fourth-century curtain wall) probably persisted into the fifth century, although the evidence of silt and mud deposits indicates periodic flooding (from river and drains) due to a rising water table; late, poor-quality repair work, such as a raising of the floor levels using slabs and stone taken from demolished structures, demonstrates efforts to maintain before dereliction. Perhaps in the sixth century there was deliberate demolition of the reservoir enclosure, and by the eighth century part of the shrine area was used for a cemetery. The Roman town had owed its baths to a natural and constant source, and its waters cancelled the need for a piped supply – hence a longer lifespan to the establishment. However, nature seemingly played a key role in determining the end of the baths.[26]

In sunnier North Africa, by contrast, the fourth century saw a busy round of repair, restoration, extension and even new construction of public baths in many towns, most especially in the more urbanised Zeugitana (*Africa proconsularis*) province.[27] For example, Bulla Regia saw baths constructed near the theatre, in the north-east quarter, and the Julia Memmia *thermae* were enlarged; at Thuburbo Maius both winter and summer baths saw restoration towards the end of the fourth century, repaving occurred in other smaller complexes, and the new Bains du Labyrinthe were established in *c.* AD 300. In Byzacena, Hadrumentum's baths were renewed, and at Sbeitla fountains were set up and the *frigidarium* in the Large Baths restored. Striking are references to the setting-up of statues in baths, most probably in portico, courtyard or exercise spaces, and studies argue that this in part reflects a trend of shifting former public statuary from the forum in particular to these different venues – reflective of a general decay of fora and the possible heightened social role of the *thermae*.

We generally lack coherent data for the continuity of large bathing establishments into the fifth century except for the imperial centres. Clearly their fate goes hand in hand with the supply of sizeable quantities of piped water through aqueducts, and again documentation for aqueduct repair is fair for the fourth century but dries up for the fifth. While this could just reflect the wider decline in use of inscriptions rather than being proof of a failure to maintain the aqueducts, its timing matches the noted downturn in wider urban patronage. For Rome, the city prefect funded repairs to aqueducts in the fourth and fifth centuries, and the Baths of Constantine and those on the Aventine were restored in the first half of the fifth century. Repairs were still overseen in the sixth century by Gothic and Byzantine officials, and in following centuries the popes funded restorations to numerous aqueducts (usually designated as 'long out of use' or 'seriously neglected'), such as the Aqua Traiana, although the primary function of this was to run the mills on the Janiculum Hill. (Excavations in the 1990s in the Via Medici and American Academy identified mill races and gear pits for perhaps flour mills, although these appear to have been redundant around AD 400, after which there seems to have been a dam and run-off perhaps to a private property; presumably, other channels and mills on the Hill continued their State role.)[28]

It would have been harder and much more expensive to restore long-damaged bath buildings than to maintain active ones; long neglect also implies a loss of the basic mechanics of supply (fuel, labour, water) as well as local need/desire. The latter makes us question whether their decay might signify changing public and social perceptions, such as recognition of this as an expensive luxury, expendable in times of economic downturn.[29] Or might decay of this 'traditional' form of Roman culture be linked to the growing or established prominence of the Church and the Christian rejection of conspicuous wealth (marble, mosaic-encrusted interiors and elite visitors with their train of servants) and leisure (slaves, oil, relaxation, public nudity)? After all, the environs of baths, like those of amphitheatres and theatres, tended to be the haunts of booths for prostitutes.

An Eastern example can briefly be drawn to question whether a Christian context might determine a loss of public bathing. *Scythopolis-Nysa* (Bet She'an) formed the provincial capital to the Decapolis in Roman Palestine and derived much wealth through being on a key trade route from Egypt. With Hellenistic roots, it saw much Roman expansion in the second century AD and then much rebuilding after the earthquake of AD 363, with Ablobius 'the Magnificent' as the architect of this revival. The fourth- and fifth-century city boasted at least four public baths, the most prominent being the 'Western Baths', in the city centre adjoining the Odeum and covering at least 8,500 m². These featured numerous heated rooms, open pools, colonnaded porticoes, many ornately decorated with columns, mosaics and marble work; there were also two large latrines. Inscriptions on floors and in mosaics record various renovations and restorations chiefly by governors to these baths. The 'Eastern Baths' probably postdate 363 and were equally well equipped and ornamented, the *frigidarium* featuring niches for holding reused classical statues. Two smaller 'southern Baths' are known, one set between the theatre and amphitheatre in a busy 'late antique' quarter; both venues remained active throughout the fifth century before demolition and reuse of materials in the sixth. What is claimed at Scythopolis, however, is that the fifth century marks alterations to many larger baths, indicating a greater leaning to privacy and away from the public gathering, collective nudity and conspicuous 'open leisure' of earlier times: the large hot and cold rooms tended thus to be reduced in size, and any new baths were much smaller. Cleanliness certainly remained an important civic concern in sixth-century Scythopolis: an inscription of AD 558/9 records that 'Theodore the shepherd [i.e. bishop] allots, renewing them, the baths, to those sick with the very grievous disease of leprosy'. Lepers were a growing concern then, and although banned from using the public baths, the Church offered facilities to tend them.

A generation later in Rome, Pope Gregory the Great stressed that bathing was 'for the needs of the body' and not 'for the titillation of the mind and for sensuous pleasure'. By then the Western Church used water in specific rituals: washing and cleansing feet, especially for pilgrims and the poor, and the ceremonial usage for purifying and for baptising. At the same time, in major towns, bishops and their clergy had the 'luxury' of baths: thus at Ravenna, during the Gothic rule, both the orthodox and Arian clergies had baths, and the orthodox set was rebuilt by Bishop Victor in the 540s, decorating it with marble and mosaics; a recorded inscription states that the city's clergy could bathe in it each week on Tuesday and Friday, free of charge. (Perhaps pilgrims and the poor washed here on the other days?) It was apparently still functioning in the ninth century. Such baths were often attached to Episcopal palaces, as at Geneva and Barcelona. Baths are also attested in various prestigious monastic establishments – such as the papal foundation of San Lorenzo fuori le mura at Rome, built under Hilarius (461–8), comprising two baths, one open to the air, or much later, the royal monastery of Santa Sofia at Benevento for which the Lombard duke Arechis in 774 granted a water pipe and a yearly supply of wood for its hypocausts.[30]

We have very little indication of the size and scale of these baths, although those at Ravenna give the impression of spaciousness and ostentatious display.

Even if 'Roman-style' mass bathing was long gone, pockets of the practice lived on with the elite and the Church. By then, clergy and bishops were generally drawn from the old elite; the Church held the greatest income, and the Church was in charge of maintaining much of the urban infrastructure.[31]

Arena and Circus

Entertainment was equally a measure of an imperial townscape: provision of games and spectacles on a substantial scale was bound up with urban status, and individual high status became tied to the ability to pay for these, in imitation of the emperor's largesse. Rome is exceptional for its mass of related buildings, which made substantial monumental marks on the urban space.[32] Beyond the larger provincial capitals, the provision of such facilities was less excessive; yet their presence symbolised status and *urbanitas*. In Britain, larger towns probably had both theatre and amphitheatre, although few amphitheatres are as yet known outside Wales; indeed, the *colonia* of Lincoln still lacks material evidence for any entertainment buildings. The circus appears largely alien to Romano-British culture even if racing is depicted on a few mosaics and other images; in most instances we might assume races were in open, field settings and with temporary wooden tiered stands, but the recent discovery of a track at Colchester might indicate take-up in the south-east.[33] In Danubian Pannonia, games and entertainment are likewise attested, as at Scabantia-Sopron and Aquincum-Budapest. Even in the East in the second century AD, many cities, especially in Asia Minor, competed against each other to introduce gladiatorial combats to demonstrate their Romanness; most Eastern towns contained theatres and many of these were modified to allow for gladiatorial and animal fights.[34]

The late Empire witnesses significant changes in the public and elite approach to games and entertainment. Mosaics from fourth-century villas such as Piazza Armerina in Sicily demonstrate high elite interest in the circus, with images of the track and of chariot races. Townhouses may be similarly decorated: at Trier, four third- to fourth-century mosaics from different houses, but all located near the circus, show local mosaicists' strong technical knowledge of racing equipment and dress. Other sources are the consular diptychs – pairs of finely carved ivory plaques, presented at the commencement of office, depicting the consul at the games with the office insignia and with a sack of coin to distribute. The diptychs appear to have first been introduced for games at Constantinople; Western examples do not bear images of the games until the second half of the fifth century. Keepsake bronze tokens (*contorniati*) were distributed also at such games (presumably amongst fellow nobility), probably by *praefecti Urbi* such as Symmachus; these run from c. AD 350 to 450, with imagery mainly derived from the circus; such tokens reflect at least aristocratic pride in traditional culture and entertainment.[35] The Piazza Armerina mosaics also include depictions of the capture of wild animals from North Africa (elephants, lions, rhinoceroses and ostriches) to supply contests. Perhaps the villa owner was recording for posterity his major investment of funds for games and was alluding to his African estates and connections.

Texts document the vast sums of money expended in preparation and fulfilment of these consular and praetorian games (normally lasting a week and including combats, circus races and theatrical shows): in AD 400–1 Symmachus paid out 2,000 gold *librae* for his son's games as praetor; Petronus Maximus spent 4,000 in 412; the costs in fact required extended preparation and saving, hence the custom of proposing future praetors or consuls several years in advance! Thus they bore not just costs of putting on games, but burdens of office and mass expectation; unsurprisingly the posts became tied to the highest ranking and richest noble families. There were efforts, though, to curb extravagance, and two Eastern laws of 384 try and set an upper limit to the moneys expended in praetorian games and to prevent any official bar consuls from presenting silk vestments or gold vessels or ivory diptychs as mementoes.

The circus was, of course, mass spectacle, and betting and rivalries and support clubs were rife. We even know of efforts to influence results through burial of curses – papyrus or thin lead sheets placed frequently in tombs, wells or even drains set close to the circus: here, spirits were encouraged to do evil deeds and to stop specific teams from winning. Such curses are known from the third to the sixth century across the central and Eastern Empire, from Rome to Corinth to Carthage and from Beirut to Antioch. One unusual example was found inside a jar with human ashes and bones under a tavern floor on the Quirinal Hill in Rome, directed at a charioteer who must have been residing there. Most revealing is a late fourth-century papyrus from Egypt which involves cat abuse: the text requires a cat to be drowned in a bucket, its corpse then to be stuffed with at least three curses ordering the cat's ghost or spirit to overturn chariots; these were specified on a separate papyrus bound round the cat. The package was then to be buried in the hippodrome or in a human tomb (thereby gaining human spirit support), before the final act of sprinkling the water from the bucket imbued with the cat's dying struggles onto the circus track.[36]

In the later Roman centuries, the provincial and imperial capitals were the focus for patronage of games and races; elsewhere there was a very marked tail-off, tied no doubt to the diminished financial clout of elites outside the capitals. The imperial hand is obvious not only in established metropoleis such as Rome, Milan, Lepcis Magna and Carthage but also in new capitals and retreats such as Trier, Ravenna and Aquileia, with the provision of entertainment structures as adjuncts to palaces. This combination is clearly manifested at the suburban villa of Maxentius at Rome on the *via Appia*, where palace, porticoes, circus and mausoleum form a vast complex. With emperors keen on games, the high elite curried favour through lavish expenditure on these.

In a context of diminished elite input, the expenditure required to stage games of any size – especially where requiring capture, import and housing of wild animals – rapidly fell out of the reach of many towns. While fights between bears and humans or between gladiators could be afforded, these might soon have been deemed luxuries. Once a building like an amphitheatre saw reduced use and maintenance, full redundancy was not a distant future. Theatres might have held a stronger chance of survival, staging plays, acting as the focus for religious festivals and as meeting points for large public assemblies, but these also required maintenance. In the case of Cyrene, there was an apparent relocation of theatrical events to a small temple enclosure after the earthquake of AD 365; much effort was required to adapt the space and yet other, nearby buildings were left ruinous.[37] For Sirmium, Ammianus relates that in 373, when threatened by barbarian attack, the Prefect Probus requisitioned the materials gathered 'some time before to build a theatre' in order to reinforce the dilapidated city walls (29.6.10–11) – signifying a long-delayed construction for this capital.

So when do these entertainments start to fail? For Roman Britain, clear data regarding the final periods of use are still limited. For London,[38] excavations mainly in the 1990s at the Guildhall site offer a very detailed sequence of evolution of the eastern end of the amphitheatre, charting not only its Roman form but also recognising in detail its fate and post-Roman to medieval transformations. It was identified that the amphitheatre's arena and its clever network of timber drains were maintained ill the late third century AD but that across the fourth century water logging and silting clogged up the arena, and the walls decayed. Deposits of animal bones, including whole horse and cattle carcasses, signify a likely official municipal dump and indicate butchers' premises close by. Coin finds suggest that masonry was robbed after AD 350, perhaps to build new town bastions. Subsequently, 'dark earth' overlay the site, potentially denoting ephemeral early medieval timber housing or else simply abandonment. By the tenth century the arena was just a grassy, boggy hollow and was part-used to corral cattle, before buildings started to be imposed from the Norman period. At Silchester-Calleva, two timber-built arena phases preceded the enhancement of the amphitheatre in stone in the first half of the third century AD, though the bulk of the seating for its capacity of about 3,000 persons remained in timber.[39] The costs of timber for the new tiers of seats and of the stone for the arena walls (estimated at about 2,000 cartloads) indicate substantial local urban investment. Nonetheless, this was a fairly simple, functional structure, lacking any of the elaborations found on the Continent, such as underground service chambers. Faunal remains suggest horses featured in performances here, although few finds were securely linked to the usage of the interior; plays, 'hunts' and armed combat may have been the other spectacles offered. No clear signs of fourth-century repairs or maintenance exist.

At Verulamium,[40] a theatre, closely associated with a temple, was constructed in c. 140. Its stage buildings are restored after 345, and there were repairs and modifications to the nearby temple and precinct in the later fourth century. Between the old forum and the theatre, new houses were built and maintained into the fifth century, giving rise to an image of relative stability by c. AD 400, but by then the theatre had become a rubbish dump – revealing an active population but one no longer needful of classical entertainment; presumably, the tomb of the martyr St Alban offered the new focus of congregation.

In Spain,[41] there are at least three instances of circus survival into the late fourth or early fifth century: Toledo, Valencia and Tarraco. The Valencia circus track subsequently became a muddy environment before being colonised by modest houses made up of *spolia* during the second half of the sixth century; the same appears to have occurred at Toledo; at Tarraco, although the amphitheatre was abandoned in the fifth century, references to theatrical games occur still in the early seventh century, implying that part of the circus remained accessible, despite the fact that other parts of the circus were already being used for housing. At the end of the sixth century, a Visigothic basilica church was built in this amphitheatre.

The image of derelict entertainment buildings becoming convenient housing blocks is strongly portrayed by the conversion still largely evident in the amphitheatre at Lucca in Italy, where inhabited houses peer down into the (now cleared) arena space, ideal for parking and market traders.[42] The clutter of houses and the defensive capabilities of an amphitheatre are borne out in a beautiful engraving of the seventeenth century for Arles in France, where towers and houses may well date back to early medieval times.[43] Archaeology has, meanwhile, demonstrated the accretion of houses against the exterior of the circus at Arles occurring as early as the late fourth century but in a controlled fashion and against a building which appears to have continued as a circus and race track into the sixth century. The positioning of ordered (but probably unattractive) housing around an active entertainment structure surely required governor sanction and may relate to an influx of refugees or soldiery. State edicts also hint at some private intrusions into public space; for example, one of AD 398 issued in Constantinople states that private houses and lean-tos against State storehouses will be torn down if they pose a fire risk.

Official texts show a mixture of survivals and losses. For Rome, unsurprisingly, as well as continued animal games at the Colosseum into the 520s (if with long gaps in activity and maintenance in the fifth century), we hear in 510 of the request by the Ostrogothic King Theoderic that the patrician Symmachus, highly regarded for his sensitive private and public building commissions, be entrusted with restoring the theatre of Pompey – restored in c. AD 400 but now 'yielding to the pressure of its vast weight' (Cassiodorus, *Variae*, IV.51). In contrast, the citizens of Catania in Sicily repaired their town walls using blocks of stone fallen from their now ruinous amphitheatre (Cassiodorus, *Variae*, III.49). Noteworthy in this context is an edict of AD 390 issued at Milan and directed to the praetorian prefect of Illyricum and Italy, which states that if restoration work is needed in 'the more renowned cities' and available funds are exhausted, then income from imposts and funds from 'lesser centres' can be obtained instead.

At Catania the entertainment debris contributed to rebuilding official defences. But in a war context, these otherwise solid buildings might become the defences themselves. Thus in the Gothic-Byzantine conflict of the 530–40s in Italy, Procopius describes how the Ostrogoths at Spoleto, unable to use the town defences since they had previously razed these to prevent the Byzantines using the city as a garrison base, blocked up the lower accesses of the amphitheatre and created a powerful stronghold. Indeed, it is noticeable how various amphitheatres – and some circuses – were incorporated within the late Roman urban enceinte, as at Trier or in Dalmatia at Pola, as a part of the northern circuit at Rome (the praetorian camp amphitheatre), in the southern part of Verona's defences or, most strikingly, at Valencia in Spain and at Périgueux in Aquitaine, France, where the amphitheatre forms a vast north-western bulwark to a restricted defensive cordon. Similarly, prominent is the incorporation of the amphitheatre as a central part of the southern city-fortress wall at Tours, with the main road passing through the arena, making this a striking monumental approach and face to the fourth-century town. This incorporation relates to both the bulk of the amphitheatre (i.e. too vast to remove, too easy to be occupied by an enemy force if left outside a circuit) and to its urban bonds – when circuit walls start to be erected from the mid-third century, the arena was generally still active and still therefore a major civic monument. And yet, archaeological evidence at seats such as Tours and Avenches indicates that at many sites amphitheatres had already been decommissioned and converted from the late third century into citadels or grain and supply depots.[44]

Christianity and Games

But did Christianity's presence and later dominance force the closure of such classical entertainment places?[45] Tension must have existed between Church, elites and State, as suggested in the edict of AD 342 (CT 16.10.3) from Constantius II and Constans to Catullinus, prefect of Rome:

> Although every superstition is to be rooted out completely, nevertheless it is Our wish that the temple buildings located outside the city walls should remain untouched and undamaged. For since certain plays, circus spectacles, and competitions have their origin from some of these temples, it is not appropriate to pull them down when they provide the Roman people with performances of traditional entertainments.

Many modern visitors feel both revulsion and fascination for the Roman blood sports – just as people are drawn to watch bull-fighting in Spain and may condemn the cruelty, but the 'sport' continues since it is both tradition and a part (albeit dying) of that culture. Various Romans – pagans, orators, moralists – were hostile in their time to games, though not specifically against the institution. Christian scholars such as Augustine were outspoken in their opposition to bawdy pagan plays in the theatres and to the brutal, bloody games and their impact on the spectators and their morality. Yet such spectacles were so embedded in the life of the capitals that words took a long time to have any effect in these imperial seats. For example, Constantine sent hundreds of captured German Bructeri prisoners to be torn apart in wild animal contests; at the end of the fourth century the highly educated pagan Symmachus, as City Prefect, was highly disappointed that numerous of his condemned Saxon prisoners-of-war had killed themselves in advance of fighting death duels in the arena. In his Confessions (VI.8, 13), Augustine, in the early fifth century, recounts how his young friend Alypius, a trainee lawyer, was seduced unwittingly by the conflicts of the Colosseum: 'He saw the blood and he gulped down savagery ... Without knowing what was happening, he drank in madness, he was delighted with the guilty contest, drunk with the lust of blood. He was no longer the man who had come there but was one of the crowd to which he had come, a true companion of those who had brought him.'

Constantine did issue an edict in AD 326 abolishing gladiatorial displays, dictating that henceforth criminals would be condemned to the imperial mines instead of fighting in games. Clearly the abolition was a rather hollow one and had no effect in provincial capitals at least, and even many lesser towns in Italy continued to host fights during festivals. Augustine's descriptions cited above indicate gladiators still plying their trade in c. 400, despite other legislation between times: in 399 Honorius closed Rome's gladiatorial school; in 404 he ordered the end of all gladiatorial combats, and yet Valentinian III (425–55) at least briefly reinstated them. But for fifth-century Rome, man and animal continued to be pitted against each other, and wild animal shows and fights/hunts (*venationes*) became the main meat of the arena (and circus). Such spectacles are still attested in Rome in the 480s and, as seen, were revived under the Ostrogoths. In Trier, despite the city being sacked on more than one occasion, the citizens yearned for games in the mid-fifth century. In the East, by contrast, after c. AD 400, circus chariot races grew to be the prime spectator sport, rising to dangerous levels in the sixth century in the capital Constantinople.

While one might argue that the decay of amphitheatres and theatres in other locations might be viewed as an earlier breakthrough by Christianity, in reality, the archaeological evidence shows many entertainment structures already well in decay. Traditions of Christian martyrdoms in the Colosseum and in amphitheatres across the Empire in the third and fourth centuries (e.g. the first British Christian martyrs at the Caerleon amphitheatre – Julius and Aaron – and Bishop Fructuosus and his deacons Augurius and Eulogius at Tarragona) must have engendered Christian hatred and association. We may lack secure proof of circuses and arenas as venues for Christian executions; nonetheless these were major points of public assembly and of imperial demonstration, and the memory of these as theatres of death was readily taken up by hagiographers. But overall, the loss of entertainment structures was far more down to hard choices being made by town authorities in terms of where to put money for repairs; games and plays may often have persisted in some cases, but they probably simply became more sporadic ventures played out in open venues.

CHANGES AND CONTINUITIES OF URBAN SPACES

Yet against this progressive Christianisation of urban space (see Chapter 6 in this book), we find reference in the largest cities (and predominantly Rome) to the State's desire to retain something of the Roman heritage, to 'restore those buildings which are said to have fallen into unsightly ruins' or which had suffered 'the ravages of time', and to give precedence to the old over the new. Thus Emperors Honorius and Arcadius (*CT* 15.1.32) inform Eusebius, count of the sacred imperial largesses, that '[i]n order that the splendid cities and towns may not fall into ruins through age, We assign a third part of the income from the land and farms belonging to a municipality to be used for the repair of public works and the heating of baths'. However, as shown in an earlier edict issued by Valentinian and Valens at Milan in 365 to Mamertinus, praetorian prefect (15.1.14, repeated to the vicar of Africa in 15.1.15), problems often emerged:

> We forbid further progress of the presumptuous conduct of judges who, to the ruin of obscure towns, pretend that they are adorning the Metropolitan or other very splendid cities, and thus seek the material of statues, marble works, or columns that they may transfer them. It shall not be allowable to commit such deeds with impunity after the issuance of Our law, especially since We have ordered that no new structures shall be begun before the old ones are restored. If, indeed, any work should be commenced, other municipalities must be spared.

But many structures would have become completely ruinous and cost far too much to rebuild. Accordingly, the State (i.e. local governor or officials) could authorise that their materials be usefully employed elsewhere – the important point being that old public structures had to be shown to be no longer 'in serviceable use' to bring about legal spoliation and demolition.[46] 'Official' victims otherwise included pagan temples, although this only properly comes into effect at the end of the fourth century (thus a law of 397 issued at Milan, but directed at Asterius, count of the East, allows the diversion of material from demolished temples to help repair roads, bridges, aqueducts and walls – *CT* 15.1.36).

Whether such laws against illicit spoliation were effective is unknown. Even if such practice did occur, demolitions meant other structures could be built or enhanced, and public spaces might be cleared of dangerous ruins (and eyesores). Not everyone wanted to live in the past, and rebuilding a theatre or baths might have been rejected if funds and support were not easily (or ever) forthcoming. This is all reflective of urbanism in general: towns are not static and new growth usually comes at the expense of the past – witness any 1950s–60s redevelopment in Britain, cancelling out most residual medieval 'leftovers' but often creating their own 'modern' eyesores. Such losses and changes merely reflect that late Roman towns and populations were different from earlier ones. But they would certainly remain sites with residues of a past still visible – only to be slowly eroded as populations and their needs evolved. The sizeable input of urban archaeology in the past few decades means that we have a strong chance now of properly coming to understand how these sites and populations evolved in and from the late Roman period.

5

Three Capitals of the West: Rome, Milan, Ravenna

INTRODUCTION

In what ways were the third- to fifth-century politico-military and socio-religious vicissitudes manifested in the fabric of the imperial capitals of the late Roman West? By this, the three chief cities of Italy across the five centuries of Roman imperial rule are meant, since although new capitals were imposed at various points of the northern provinces and in the East – from Trier to Nicomedia – the Italian capitals represent the enduring imperial attachment to the home and core province. Thus, here we explore specifically Rome, Milan and Ravenna and chart the contents, plans and changes in their monumental and private zones; discuss their specific roles; and assess overall the levels of 'decline' at each into the fifth century and beyond. Were these still powerful centres of authority and display in the final centuries of Roman rule? How populous were they? How far were military and religious changes imprinted in their plans? What changes were wrought by economic decay?

Sources for each centre are uneven, and significant imbalances exist in terms of the survival of monuments: Ravenna, for example, is best served by church archaeology, art and architecture but lacks evidence for its early imperial past; Rome preserves numerous classical public structures, but many were cleared or excavated before the advent of scientific techniques, thus preventing adequate understanding of their late and post-classical sequences; Milan, as a highly populous modern city, has suffered extensive damage to its underlying archaeology through urban expansion, and often only pockets of data are available to piece together its archaeological histories. Nonetheless, each has seen recent explorations of its late antique and medieval pasts through excavation, systematic archival research, structural analysis and documentary study to draw coherent images of forms and fates. This chapter outlines some of these main results; it will run from early to late capitals, thus commencing with Rome.

ROME: A CAPITAL IN TRANSITION

First among cities, the home of gods, is golden Rome. (Ausonius, *Ordo Urbium Nobilium, c.* AD 389)

Rome was always a showpiece of power and wealth: structures of state, temples to supporting deities, records of victory and expansion, dedicatory altars, statues of the rich and famous, all competed for space and prominence. Successive emperors duly stamped their mark on the City fabric, but always with emphasis on the central core of the Palatine Hill and Forum, and imperial munificence here meant an overcrowding of architectural riches, prompting creation of new forum complexes. Elite participation was also strong, using wealth to gain office, reputation and honour, with buildings and games key to their display. Although documentary sources imply that a vast population was still resident in Rome in the fourth century, the Empire was much changed by then and social, economic, military and imperial crises were duly felt in the Capital too – manifested most strongly first in the erection of the Aurelianic city walls in the 270s and then in a dilution of Rome's role as Milan became imperial capital. As significant was the first imposition of State churches in Rome, challenging the old City religions. But how much else had changed? What levels of continuity existed with the monuments and spaces of the early Empire at Rome, and what losses can be perceived? Did the creation of alternative capitals mean a less substantial and a less imperial Rome? And what of the elites and wider population?[1]

A first guide derives from the description of events in AD 357, when the Emperor Constantius, despite ongoing Alamannic assaults on Gaul and threats on the Danube and from the Persians, headed to Rome to celebrate a victory procession after his defeat of Magnentius in civil war. A near contemporary account of this visit comes from Ammianus Marcellinus who, though disdainfully claiming this emperor 'added nothing to the empire', was keen to recount the astonishment shown by Constantius at the monuments of the Eternal City just as the emperor was keen to astonish its populace with his chariot, standards, retinue and person. We read here the formality of the *adventus* or arrival of an emperor and the expected formalities of State, with Constantius first met at the gate by the senators carrying effigies of their ancestors, then by throngs of citizens of all cultures.[2] 'As soon as he entered Rome, the home of empire and of all perfection, he went to the Rostra and looked with amazement at the Forum, that sublime monument of pristine power; wherever he turned he was dazzled by the concentration of wonderful sights.' He was unsure which struck him most, whether

the buildings of the baths as big as provinces, or the solid mass of stone from Tibur that forms the amphitheatre, with its top almost beyond the reach of human sight, or the Pantheon spread like a self-contained district under its high and lovely dome, or the lofty columns with spiral stairs to platforms which support the statues of former emperors, or the Temple of Rome or the Forum of Peace, the theatre of Pompey or the Odeum or the Stadium, or any of the other sights of the Eternal City.

> But when he came to the Forum of Trajan, a creation which in my view has no
> like under the cope of heaven and which even the gods themselves must agree
> to admire, he stood transfixed with astonishment, surveying the gigantic fabric
> around him; its grandeur defies description and can never again be approached by
> mortal men.

Much sounds like a modern tourist diary and might reflect more Ammianus
Marcellinus' recollections rather than those of the emperor during his (one
and only) month-long stay at Rome; further, we need to note that Ammianus
Marcellinus was no Christian, and unsurprisingly he omits any reference to
Rome's fresh ecclesiastical structures. Certainly, one wonders whether
Constantius, as a strong-minded Arian Christian, really took time to admire
the pagan shrines of the Forum and the Temple of Peace. In fact, it was probably during his visit that the Altar of Victory was removed from its ancient
setting in the Senate House, where senators had formerly cast offerings and
swore loyalty to emperor and Empire.

Ammianus Marcellinus implies that Constantius was amazed at the magnificent scale of ancient Rome (Figure 5.1). But what he does not clearly state
is whether the 'gigantic fabric' was in decay. Arguably it was not, since other
labels such as 'grandeur' and 'beauties' point to a functioning, still highly
impressive heart to the City. Indeed, Rome had seen plenty of substantial
building work in the generation prior to Constantius: foremost in some eyes
were the churches on the fringes – inside and outside the walls – at S. Croce,
St John the Lateran, St Peter's at the Vatican, each preceded by vast clearance
operations; in the city centre, Constantine's architects, builders and slaves
had worked on his Arch, the basilica Nova (of Maxentius), and his public
baths on the Quirinal Hill. Imperial baths were prominent also in the third
century AD: besides those of Diocletian and Caracalla in the south of the City
are the less well-known Baths of Trajan Decius on the Aventine Hill. Texts
indicate that these latter baths were built within Trajan's short reign (249–51)
and were part of a wider programme of work (mainly restoration) – an important proof that the third-century crisis did not halt ongoing monumentalisation of the capital.[3] These fairly modest baths, barely known archaeologically,
can be traced through sculptural and epigraphic finds and particularly
through a ground plan executed by the Renaissance architect Palladio in the
mid-sixteenth century, revealing a complex of 44 m × 70 m (a mere eighth of
the central block only of Caracalla's *thermae*, though still bigger than most
public baths in, for example, Roman Britain). Inscriptions of the fourth and
fifth centuries reveal a senatorial clientele, including the Caeionii Decii family who may have added the Decius name to theirs to add prestige. The inscriptions are on bases for marble statues, set up by/for urban prefects; this
group of seven texts forms one of the largest sets of late antique dedicatory
inscriptions outside of Rome's Forum. They testify to an ongoing desire for
display and memory, and show baths as foci for such. Two other inscriptions
show the Decian baths kept in good order, with repair and redecoration undertaken in 414 (following likely damage caused in the sack by Alaric's

Figure 5.1 The heart of Rome's forum, seen from the Palatine Hill across the courtyard of the Vestal Virgins' temple and quarters to the temple of Antoninus Pius and Faustina. Between runs the *Via Sacra*, along which Constantius II processed in AD 357

Visigoths in 410). Of note also is a possible link with the imperial visitor of AD 357: two of the statues are of Constantius' reign.[4]

But what can be traced of the Visigothic sack of 410, and in what state was Rome after the occupation? First, given that Olympiodorus indicates that St Peter's church avoided destruction, it seems probable that most other churches were left undamaged structurally. However, the precious metals that adorned these – liturgical vessels, candelabra, gifts to the saints – did largely fall victim to the intruders, since Pope Celestine (AD 422–32) is later recorded as re-equipping the basilica of Julius which had been afflicted by the 'Gothic conflagration' with silver patens, chalices, hand basins, candelabras, crowns and the like; although only in the later 430s did Pope Sistus III replace the silver *fastigium* (an apse screen) in the Lateran basilica which 'had been removed by the barbarians' (the new one weighed in at a mere 1610 lb) (*Lib. Pont.*, Life of Sistus III). A focus would instead have been Rome's old Forum which does feature traces of destruction but also evidence for subsequent repair: the floor of the Basilica Aemilia was covered by destruction deposits, and coins were burnt into the paving; its porticoed façade was re-erected only in c.420. While neither the Basilica Julia nor the Temple of Peace saw restoration after the event, renewal did occur at the Senate House, signifying the need to resume the operations of the traditional seat of authority.[5]

Perhaps most affected were the houses or *domus* of the wealthy elite, clustered on the hills of the city.[6] Many properties clearly fell vacant as a result, although some may have been quitted in advance, with aristocrats transferring perhaps to the more settled provinces of Africa and the East; Alaric's presence in north Italy, the upheavals and food shortages in Rome itself were more than excuses for those with means (and other homes) to move out. Indeed, at the start of the fifth century, a hugely wealthy couple, Melania and Pinianus, part of the growing Christian elite, sold off all their properties and possessions in Rome and in various provinces and used the proceeds to help the poor and fund churches, monasteries and shrines. Their sumptuous house on the Caelian Hill was not actually sold off before Alaric's sieges of the City, and we hear even of attempts to confiscate the couple's wealth to help pay off the Visigoths. They had already managed to depart and head to Jerusalem, however, and left intermediaries to continue with wider property sales — which did occur, even in areas like Aquitaine and Spain, despite Vandal movements.[7] Other owners perhaps just fled, and we can assume confiscations by the State or Church, such as on the Caelian, dominated in the fourth century by the *domus* of the Symmachi and Valerii families, and that of Gaudentius (*vicarius Africae* of 409). Pinianus and Melania had owned the Valerii *domus*; fire damage in AD 410 meant subsequently only part was utilised for domestic use, while another portion became a *xenodochium* or pilgrim hostel. Significant structural decay also hit the houses of Symmachus and Gaudentius, but perhaps only later, after Vandal sacks.[8] A sign of inheritance or purchase of land by the Church is indicated by the foundation close by of the church of Santo Stefano Rotondo. Elite spaces on the Aventine Hill saw revival post-410, as indicated at the baths of Trajan Decius, although the house of Marcella was not rebuilt after 410; while on the Esquiline, the well-known Esquiline Treasure — on display in the British Museum — comprising up to 61 silver pieces, was probably buried by a member of the Turcii household in the grounds of their property during Alaric's sieges. The Treasure comprises wedding gifts and prized dining pieces, including plates and a casket with nuptial motifs, and images of Attis and Cybele — but with the inscription on the wedding casket of Proiecta of undoubted Christian form. The religion of the owners and the wedding parties is disputed: the Turcii appear still pagan in their leanings into the 370s, whereas Proiecta was daughter of Florus, who was a key figure at Theodosius' Christian court in the East.[9]

In the Vigna Barberini on the north-east slope of the Palatine, a third- and fourth-century *domus* saw shrinkage of space — plus dumping in some rooms of rubbish from nearby workshops dating to AD 350–450.[10] The Palatine Hill was, of course, the imperial residential quarter, and we might assume fair efforts to maintain its visual dignity and ceremonial status across the fifth century: thus repairs are attested in parts of the palace fabric and substructures and on the *Via Sacra*, and the Forum paving appears to have been kept clean. Yet archaeology identifies elsewhere in the Forum unrepaired basilicas, unkempt temples, intrusive industrial activities, plus disuse of certain spaces; occasional burials also appear, such as at the Magna Mater temple complex. Even so, enough was being maintained physically and symbolically, since still in the seventh century a *curator Palatii* is documented, and icons of the Byzantine emperors were sent from Constantinople for display in the Palatine Church of San Cesario. How active the old palaces were after the fifth century, whether for Gothic king or officials, for Byzantine dukes or visiting generals, is unknown; however, by the seventh century authority lay with the popes, whose own palaces lay at both Lateran and Vatican.[11] By then, no doubt, costs of maintenance must have been prohibitive, and only parts of the Palatine saw upkeep. Nonetheless, this same period saw the Church 'colonising' the old seats of power: conversion of the Senate House into the church of S. Adriano, new symbols inserted in the chapel of S. Maria Antiqua and, towards AD 700, even the documented temporary transfer of the papal residence to the Palatine until the pontificate of Zacchary.

Often the image we can reconstruct of change in Rome's urban fabric in the later Empire and beyond is fragmentary and damaged.[12] One prime example is the Colosseum, whose bulk largely ensured its survival, although its partial use for warehousing, housing and even a fortress in the early and full Middle Ages was also important for enabling its physical persistence, despite much pillaging before, during and after its reuses for materials such as marble, travertine, brick, and metal (clamps, fittings). Despite losses and reworkings (as well as the major nineteenth- and twentieth-century restorations which cleared away many pockets of post-Roman stratigraphy), detailed modern analysis of the extant fabric, repairs, sockets (for posts, pegs and tethering hooks), inscriptions, as well as Renaissance and later images, provides a convincing guide to the post-classical fortunes of the complex and its environs.[13] Games are documented as being held as late as the 520s, and repairs documented in the early, middle and late fifth century, at least twice in response to earthquake damage. This was clearly an interrupted continuity and we must identify that, especially in the earlier fifth century, the massive amphitheatre must have often lain redundant, silently awaiting elite and imperial attention and interest (plus supplies of animals, both exotic and mundane). In this same period, however, probably in the face of sieges of Rome by Alaric's Visigoths, burials were made close to the Colosseum, with further interments in the sixth century – even when, it seems, games were still being held inside. By the late sixth century, the Church seemingly laid claim to the defunct Colosseum, since recent studies argue that various of the arcaded spaces were converted for warehousing: Rea argues convincingly for this being a massive granary and distribution point, with the Colosseum a handy station between the barges of the Tiber and the papal stores of the Lateran to the south.

Providing grain to the poor was a major but earlier feature of the so-called Crypta Balbi and specifically of the Porticus Minucia, lying west of the Roman Forum.[14] A changeover to the distribution of free bread in Aurelian's reign perhaps meant a loss of the primary storage function of the Porticus, which appears in decay in the fourth century, along with its central Temple of the Nymphs. To the south stood the Theatre of Balbus with its eastern 'Crypta' (covered corridors). Although the theatre may have been restored as late as

AD 500, the Crypta square had fallen from public use and saw fourth-century housing inserted in the north-west angle, dumping of rubbish in the south and a conversion of the sizeable public latrine into a glass-making workshop. In the fifth century, alongside earthquake damage, we find building materials piled up in the square and the cutting of new paths across the zone and even in the southern portico; this latter road became a permanent fixture, linking the Forum, Campus Martius and Tiber, and so attracted new structures along its course; its surface (containing cartwheel ruts) was renewed and raised on various occasions into the ninth century. In the medieval (as modern) period, the road – Via delle Botteghe Oscure – boasted well-appointed residences, housing merchants, bankers as well as respected crafts. Burials appear in former built or rubble-strewn spaces in the sixth century; an inscription indicating likely restoration of the theatre was reused as a tomb cover. By AD 550, two small churches were present as well as a *xenodochium* or hostel for pilgrims and, again, a food distribution point. That the site had remained mainly imperial property, however, is indicated by an inscription recording the City Prefect Anicius renewing its role as a food distribution point in the 430s.[15] Some workshops for stone-cutting and carving were also established, and are a link with a busy exploitation of marble and stone in the eleventh century, when a lime-burning kiln was inserted into the theatre exedra (the district duly gained the name Calcarario) which, when excavated, still contained column drums, inscriptions, tombstones and architectural pieces awaiting burning.[16] Similar workshops have been recognised elsewhere, exploiting tombs and catacombs for marble and travertine. The Church was presumably the main customer for lime for its buildings and their upkeep.

Such evidence reveals a decay of monumental components of the classical-built fabric of Rome alongside areas of partial redesigning, but with new streets and lanes, housing, ecclesiastical buildings and workshops indicating continued movement, trade, religion, living and welfare. Strikingly, this new, late and post-Roman activity is set amongst a very visible old, which, despite robbing, was a strong, probably fairly ugly and unkempt backdrop. Church and monastic buildings offered newer and tidier foci, themselves attracting both services and housing, but these were scattered within a vast defensive cordon which by AD 550 featured many desolate or sparsely utilised spaces. Indeed, the Ostrogothic Minister Cassiodorus Senator (*Var.* XI, 39) then observed how

> [t]he great size of the population of the city of Rome in former times is clear from the fact that it required the provision of foodstuffs from different regions to supply its needs. ... The vast extent of the walls, the seating capacity of the places of entertainment, the remarkable size of the public baths and the number of watermills, bear witness to the throngs of citizens.

But this same letter identifies the still powerful architecture of Rome a generation or so after Rome's 'Fall': not only are the entertainment structures visible but they are also active (or reactivated) as King Theoderic seeks to be like a Roman emperor, encouraging games, elite participation and renewal. There is even a minister of works documented, charged with looking after Rome's heritage or at least recruiting aristocratic investment to help maintain this: 'It is desirable that the necessary repairs to this forest of walls and population of statues which make up Rome should be in the hands of a learned man who will make the new work harmonise with the old.'[17]

Most scholars posit a dramatic decline in Rome's population in the sixth century, specifically after the Gothic–Byzantine War, when it shrank to perhaps under 50,000. In c. AD 400, Rome, despite a diluted imperial presence, probably still mustered half a million people, but sieges, disease, migration of elites and entourages to the East, and declining childbirth might have seen a reduction to about a quarter million by AD 500 – huge drops in numbers. Yet Rome would have retained a population far in excess of any other city in the West and most of the East too, with the Church acting as a new focus. Nonetheless, that level of reduction was sorely manifested on the ground: reduced housing needs, decay of residences, reduced investment by elites in public structures, progressive redundancy of bathing establishments, breakdowns in other services, diminished demands on and access to food imports and other goods (plus the Vandal conquest of North Africa and the islands trimming the scale of transhipment of goods from south to north or at least damaging the earlier flow of goods and market activity in the Mediterranean). Much is reflected at the City's ports of Ostia and Portus. The former had, by the fourth century, been largely supplanted by Portus and its superior, custom-made spaces for offloading, storage and transport to/from Rome, including use of canals and barges. Ostia for a time became a high-status suburban retreat, but with a city more condensed, with many older houses and warehouses quitted and dismantled for their building materials: stockpiles of columns in former courtyards have been excavated, some marked with the name of the city prefect. It has even been argued that fourth-century renewals of baths, theatre and fountains and an emphasis on restoring housing on the main thoroughfares explicitly aimed to hide rather tatty and largely redundant urban quarters.[18] Although not securely traced, sixth-century Ostia saw dramatic shrinkage and decay. Portus, the focus of a recent major archaeological project, also suffered in the fifth-century Visigothic and Vandal sieges, and warehouses and living spaces began to be abandoned as the town was reduced to a more compact walled area; the archaeology from here and from the massive Tiber-side warehouses in Rome suggests that, perhaps because of external threats, incoming goods tended to be offloaded from sea vessels and taken straight to the City. These data therefore speak of major redefinitions to Rome and her ports, with elements of the old sacrificed to provide for reduced, arguably much more functional urban fabrics in the fifth and sixth centuries.

MILAN: NEW CAPITAL, NEW ROLE

At Milan also are all things wonderful, abundant wealth, countless stately homes, men able, eloquent, and cheerfully disposed; besides, there is the grandeur of the

site enlarged by a double wall, the circus, her people's joy, the massy enclosed theatre
... the temples, the imperial citadels, the wealthy mint and the quarter renowned
under the title of the Baths of Herculeis; her colonnades all adorned with marble
statuary ... all these, as it were, rivals in the vast masses of their workmanship, are
passing grand; nor does the near neighbourhood of Rome abase them. (Ausonius,
Ordo Urbium Nobilium, c. AD 389)

Milan's selection as a new imperial capital in the West in AD 284 was prompted
by a number of factors, chief among which were the raids by barbarian warbands such as the Iouthungi that had penetrated into north Italy in the 260s
and 270s, and Roman recognition that responses to threats had been detrimen-
tally sluggish. As seen, defensive works came into play in the Alps themselves, but more significant was the fortification of strategic towns in the
Alpine and sub-Alpine band. Milan's central position became crucial for communicating across the mountains; at the same time it was cushioned from
direct threat.[19] Fourth-century milestones – more honorific dedications and
records of imperial investment than traffic markers – testify to sizeable attention paid from the later third century to the major road networks whose maintenance was essential for easier passage by Roman troops, supplies and
messengers. The Po plain, meanwhile, was a major source of grain for the army,
some of whose mobile units were stationed here; settlements of defeated or
even allied barbarians such as Sarmatians under Constantine especially are
further indicators of required intense cultivation of these lands; archaeology
duly attests increased land exploitation in the Milan region at least from the
early fourth century. Furthermore, the northern towns featured a series of
arms and supplies factories. More broadly, of course, the elevation of Milan
was in line with the wider Tetrarchic policy of favouring more strategic sites
as imperial seats and as overseers to a diversely articulated Empire.[20]

Milan gained new (brick-built) circuit walls, probably erected in the reign
of Maximianus, which were 4.5 km in total length and featured seven main
gates. On the west flank they incorporated both the new palace and in
particular the circus, whose curved wall formed part of the circuit and was
duly provided with arrow slits. Stretches of city wall have been recorded
in old and new excavations,[21] demonstrating some variation in foundation
construction – notably timber piles beside the Seveso and Vetra watercourses,
overlain by solid foundations incorporating *spolia*. These canalised waterways, presumably utilised as moats, in time caused stability problems for the
circuit, requiring later efforts at embankment. A bridge (at least 30-m long)
was set over the Seveso leading from the Porta Ticinensis in the south-west.
Additional public works included baths and the roadways.

From the mid-fourth century a significant redefinition of Milan was marked
by the imposition of a variety of church and related structures. Certainly from
Constantine's reign, an archbishop was established here: little is known of the
first cathedral church, although its location in the wealthier eastern part of the
city may signify an early statement of a new order. The most significant phase

came in the Episcopacy of Ambrose, when a veritable Christian re-ordering of the city space becomes manifest. But Ambrose's own letters identify that his works were undertaken in a context of conflict, most notably in AD 386 when the bishop had to counter both emperor and the Arian party. In these politico-religious machinations, Ambrose's Episcopal complex formed a key theatre of operations. His references, combined with archaeological data from excavations, enable a good picture to be drawn up of the Christian core of Milan. The cathedral group covered a vast monumental area of about 400 m × 200 m and comprised three distinct blocks: an old core consisting of the first cathedral (basilica vetus) and baptistery and the basilica minor (perhaps a predecessor to the church of ninth-century S. Maria Maggiore underlying the medieval cathedral); the basilica Nova or San Salvatore, with baptistery; and the palace or domus Ambrosii to the east.[22] Ambrose made more explicit the Christian role of Milan, by imposing his ideology on the urban and suburban fabric. Thus, four churches are arranged in a cross pattern on the main routes into the city, whilst also encircling it: San Simpliciano, San Dionigi, the basilica Apostolorum (San Nazzaro) and the basilica Martyrorum (Sant'Ambrogio). With intersecting lines, these cross just west of the central Episcopal complex. Ambrose's focus was the south-eastern approach – that from Rome – duly aggrandised by its redevelopment as a highly ornate colonnaded route and with access probably marked by a substantial triumphal arch – making it quite 'imperial' and secular, with the road lined by statuary, shops and halls. Symbolically sited halfway along this imperial road, on its north side, was the cross-shaped basilica Apostolorum. Two triumphs are recognised: the temporal one represented by the arch and the Christian orthodox one marked by the cross of the church; further, since the plan of the basilica Apostolorum directly imitates that of the Apostoleion in Constantinople, it effectively emphasises Milan's elevated status alongside the Eastern capital. Equality with Rome might then be signified in the routeway being directed at the Eternal City and by Ambrose's translation of relics of Saints Peter and Paul to his basilica. Other relics of note were those of Saints Gervasius and Protasius in Ambrose's new basilica: their well-documented transfer to beneath the altar made these integral to that church, to the community's worship and to the Milanese Church in general. The bishop announced that '[t]hese are the defenders I have obtained for you, holy people, who may benefit all and harm no-one'.[23]

Late Roman Milan is therefore a quite different imperial city to Rome: while imitating Rome in its powerful walls, palace, circus and adjoining mausolea (imperial mausolea with attached basilicas lay to the west at San Vittore (the tomb of Valentinian II) and south at San Lorenzo (Sant'Aquilino)), in contrast the Milanese Church imposed itself in a core central space and increasingly girded the capital. This was more than a city in transition, being more solidly Christian in design through the efforts of Ambrose in particular. Arguably, imperial visitors to Rome from Milan would have been bewildered by the continued visibility and even vitality of pagan structures, whose presence in Milan after the mid-fourth century was probably rapidly cancelled out.

The 1986–98 excavations at the Università Cattolica at Milan produced a more human impression of the new capital. These uncovered over 600 burials of third- to fifth-century date, organised chiefly in presumed family plots. One particular, undisturbed, early third-century tomb containing a young woman in her 20s and dubbed 'The Lady of the Sarcophagus' saw much attention and in-depth scientific analysis of ritual, contents and person.[24] Scrutiny of the many grave finds from the wider cemetery sought to identify how or if Milan's elevation to capital status saw any influx of diverse ethnic groups and to gauge evidence for soldiery and court officials. Certainly, materials such as jewellery and ceramics could denote close links to finds from both the Rhenish and Pannonian frontiers, suggestive of soldiery and families from these frontier zones (perhaps discharged soldiers?); further, 14 elements were found which can be connected with military dress, notably five crossbow brooches and three ring-buckles – although since some of these items were found in female graves other scholars view them as part of the wider imperial court or State civil bureaucratic dress.

Currently, few data exist for detailing how far private space evolved in this epoch and whether Milan features the appearance of many new higher status *domus* residences inside and out of the city (the landscape around, in particular towards and around the lakes, does feature many quality later Roman villas); some new *domus* do appear, often replacing demolished earlier imperial houses, both near the palace and the new cathedral. Housing and shops naturally sprung up near the new processional route in the city's south-east suburbium. Yet signs exist to suggest that the fifth century marked a downturn in urban fortunes, only fully manifested at the end of the fifth century when, for example, in Piazza Missori, beaten soil and rubble formed the road surface, by when the road drain appears redundant and was possibly discharging waste. The city walls may have seen repair or reinforcement around AD 400, robbing materials from the amphitheatre. Churches continued to be built or restored, but some richer houses fell redundant and were robbed out; in various areas building materials became cruder (matching the situation at Rome). Potentially, even that fine porticoed road of Ambrose's Milan was ruinous by AD 500 – however, it would be far more logical to relate its demise to events of the Gothic-Byzantine War of the 530s and 540s.[25] Indeed, Milan suffered tremendously in 539 when the Goths massacred its male population ('not less than 300,000' claims Procopius) and sold the children and women as slaves to the Burgundians as payment for support (Procopius, *Gothic War*, II, xxi). The image is horrendous, and yet Milan did not disappear as a city, remaining a bishopric and becoming a Lombard capital at the end of the century. By then, however, how much of the fourth-century capital's monumentality remained active or despoiled and ruinous is not yet easy to discern.

RAVENNA: A CHRISTIAN CAPITAL

> And a land army cannot approach it [Ravenna] at all; for the river Po, also called the Eridanus, which flows past Ravenna ... and other navigable rivers together with some marshes, encircle it on all sides and so cause the city to be surrounded by water. (Procopius, *Gothic War*, V.i, 17–18)

The shift of capital from AD 402 to Ravenna sets the broader trend for the fifth century and reflects changing realities: Milan, despite its defences, had been revealed to be too exposed; it and other Padane sites and lands had suffered badly in the Stilicho–Alaric conflicts (these forcing many rushed repairs and reinforcements to town defences). Instead, the Emperor Honorius relocated the court to Ravenna on the north-western Adriatic shore, with its adjoining port of Classe offering (relatively) rapid naval communications with (and thereby a means of escape to) the East. The site also featured surrounding marshes and waterways which enhanced the artificial defences (Figure 5.2). Ravenna was in fact a successful and enduring choice, remaining the Italian capital through to the mid-eighth century, and with the excavated finds at Classe attesting extensive and intensive trade contacts from across the Mediterranean well into the seventh century.[26]

The arrival of the imperial court transformed in dramatic fashion what had been a fairly sleepy and small Adriatic town: a third-century BC foundation, renewed under Augustus, endowed with a fine gate (the *Porta Aurea*) under Claudius, early Ravenna was best known for its gladiators, mosquitoes and foul drinking water; it also, briefly, suffered capture by Marcomannic prisoners who had been settled here as farmers in the 170s. Fragments only of the topography

Figure 5.2 A sixteenth-century engraving of Ravenna showing the still extant line of its fifth-century city walls. The first-century BC colony occupied the south-west corner of the late antique city

of this first town (of just 33 ha) have been investigated, although major public monuments remain largely undiscovered; the suburbs featured not only burial grounds but also some well-to-do residences (best known is the villa at the Banca Popolare site). Many of the houses, already ruinous by the early fourth century, perhaps because of the third-century economic upheavals, subsequently were engulfed in the substantial early fifth-century expansion of Ravenna, encompassing a full 166 ha. Much of the content of this city remains uncertain besides the many stunning, extant churches; the positions of the palaces, baths, circus and mint can be sited but details are rare. Only recently have good data emerged on rich townhouses such as that labelled 'House of the Stone Carpets' not far from San Vitale, with its beautifully restored late Roman and Gothic-Byzantine period mosaics.[27] A contrast lies with the evidence from contemporary Classe, where warehouses, wharves, houses and kilns have been excavated (see below) – the contrast part due to the fact that Classe is an abandoned but heavily robbed site with only the splendid church of Sant'Apollinare in Classe flagging its position amid largely open fields. Combined, the data offer much information on life in a city and its port towards and after the close of the Roman West, revealing an almost unique vitality and wealth into the later sixth century.

The period AD 410–40 witnesses various churches built in new Ravenna and its suburbs. Outside the cityscape, Bishop Peter (432–50) built the basilica Petriana at Classe and an official of Honorius' court, Lauricius, oversaw construction of the vast, funerary basilica of San Lorenzo in Caesarea; inside the city, Honorius' reign saw completion of the Cathedral (the basilica Ursiana) located on the eastern flank of the old colony circuit (its related 'orthodox' baptistery, however, belongs to Archbishop Neon around AD 460), and under Valentinian III (424–55) and his mother (initially Regent) Galla Placidia, the churches of San Giovanni Evangelista, Santa Croce and SS Giovanni e Barbaziano were erected. According to tradition, San Giovanni was built following Galla Placidia's safe delivery from a shipwreck en route to establish Valentinian on the throne, and the second built to contain the tomb of her son Theodosius. The now detached 'Mausoleum of Galla Placidia' formed one of a pair of façade chapels to Santa Croce, dedicated to SS Nazario e Celso; the three late Roman sarcophagi in the arms of the cross-shaped chapel are linked to her family, though she herself was buried in Rome. While San Giovanni exhibits much reuse of *spolia*, the scale of the edifice (47 m × 24 m, less its narthex) demonstrates the monumental outlook of the imperial court's building programme. Furthermore, the stunning vault mosaics in the Mausoleum of Galla Placidia and the remnant mosaic and *opus sectile* work of Santa Croce fully testify to the display of wealth and art in the new capital, whose bishop was elevated to the status of archbishop.[28]

The palace complexes of late Roman Ravenna were sited towards the southeast and the centre, although some argue that Santa Croce may have formed the focal point to a palace in the north-west. The central palace is traditionally attributed to the Ostrogothic King Theoderic, being attached to the palatine church of Sant'Apollinare Nuovo and facing onto the main urban highway. However, re-evaluation and re-excavation of the so-called Palace of Theoderic have identified a longer structural evolution to the complex, commencing with an early imperial suburban villa, much expanded in the fourth century, and elaborated upon in the early fifth and then sixth centuries, notably with new dining halls and decorative schemes.[29] Quite possibly, Honorius' or Valentinian's palace occupied this same site, since the grandiose church of San Giovanni Evangelista lies in its proximity.

Major survivals of late antique Ravenna are its brick-built city walls, extant for roughly a third of their 4.5-km length (noticeably the same length as Milan): these may not be as spectacular as Rome's, but they are just as informative in offering insights into Ravenna's urban configuration, defensive capabilities and economic resources. In many places, particularly on the city's western and southern flanks, the raising of the land surface through silting and flood action in post-Roman and medieval times is very evident, with the late Roman battlements visible at the modern ground level, topped by a late medieval heightening. Although it is disputed whether the bricks used in the building of the Ravenna circuit were newly produced or spoil, nonetheless the erection of the defences on difficult ground, requiring deep foundations, including piles, denotes substantial logistical investment. The value of the natural defences is borne out in both the layout of the built circuit which shows very irregular tower spacing and provision and features a series of apparent water-gates, perhaps for canal traffic. The curtain wall may not match the scale of those of Rome or Constantinople (wall thickness was up to 2.4 m; its height was about 9.0 m), but its overall strength is fully reflected in Ravenna being maintained as the seat of government under Kings Odoacer and Theoderic and later under the Byzantine governor generals or exarchs.[30] Interestingly, contemporary with Ravenna's refoundation as Western capital, the defences at Rome and Milan were strengthened, perhaps as a nominal show of respect to these but also in recognition of their heightened exposure to threat now the frontiers had been broken: 'Fear was the architect of that beauteous work ... war put an end to the decay that peace had brought. For fear it was that caused the sudden upspringing of all those towers.'[31]

For Theoderic, communication with the East and with Constantinople was crucial – letters and embassies moved between courts, and craftsmen and materials certainly flowed westwards to feed the massive building programme initiated at Ravenna from the 490s.[32] Access to waterways and the open sea was equally valuable for trade as well as for military support. Excavations at the port of Classe have generated an exciting body of information on the port's growth, evolution and decay, identifying canals, roads, warehouses and industrial and domestic quarters, with a wealth of ceramic and other finds. The evidence points to a first major planning of the site in the fifth century (expanding what had been a much smaller earlier imperial fleet base) and with subsequent sixth-century growth. Commerce flowed in from a variety of Mediterranean markets, particularly to east and south: Palestine, Syria (amphorae for wine and oil, plus glass vessels), the Aegean, Asia Minor, Egypt, North Africa (for oil and fish sauce, plus tablewares and lamps), and with more limited trade via south Italy, Sicily and Spain (see also Chapter 7 in this book). Many exotic items made their way to Ravenna in the fifth century, although survivals of silverware, silks and ivories belong chiefly to the sixth century.[33] This commercial vitality runs fully into the seventh century, although there are signs of a downturn in parts of Classe (as in Ravenna itself) early in that period, when some buildings go out of use, robbing of materials occurs and some burials intrude on the built space.[34] By the eighth century, Classe was in terminal decline and this and the suburb of Caesarea may have been largely abandoned before the Lombard capture of Ravenna in 751.

Note might also be made of the renewal of other urban centres closer to Ravenna, stimulated by the imperial court's presence. Thus Rimini, which had struggled after the third century, when some of its townhouses appear to have fallen out of use (though the town walls seem to have been revamped and repaired in the 270s, incorporating the amphitheatre), witnessed sizeable fifth-century renewal, as shown in excavations in Piazza Ferrari and Palazzo Palloni, continuing into the sixth century, with perhaps an emphasis on the main north-south road leading out across the extant Bridge of Tiberius to the capital; most probably these *domus* belonged to court functionaries or else local elite and wealthy traders selecting to live near rather than in Ravenna.[35]

How busy Ravenna was cannot easily be determined: a recent estimate is for approximately 10,000–15,000 inhabitants in c. AD 500. But we do not know how far ordinary housing and apartments existed inside the walls, and quite probably a higher population total might be expected given the anticipated number of slaves, court functionaries and related staff and Episcopal and other clerical groups, plus soldiers (billeted partly in Ravenna, in its immediate environs as well as in adjoining towns like Rimini), plus a flow of visiting elites. Classe's own population of merchants, navy personnel, shipbuilders, ferrymen, port workers and shopkeepers would easily have matched Ravenna's own total. Arguably, Ravenna's populace would have been less prone to food shortages than Rome's on account of an active hinterland and, especially, the strong maritime links supplying this more manageable capital. Where records of riots and urban violence occur, these tend to relate to disputes over archiepiscopal elections or actions by heavy-handed Byzantine officials in the seventh and eighth centuries, although sieges of the city and port did happen and associated food shortages must have also occurred.[36]

CHARTING POWER CHANGE

We have scanned three capitals of the West and observed three rather diverse developments. The changes in seat of imperial government matched changes in imperial strategy: first, Milan, adopted by the Tetrarchs as a more forward base, still protected by the Alpine range, but in closer if not immediate contact with the main landward supply and communication lines to the northern, notably Danube, frontiers; furthermore, Milan lay central among the north Italian arms factories and depots, suggesting an 'integrated' strategy. Second, Ravenna, later preferred for its seaward communications and secure port as well as for its tighter defensive cordon. In Milan, the imperial signature was marked by the association of palace and circus alongside the city's western circuit walls; mausolea lay close by, and in time the Church colonised substantial internal spaces. This contrasts with Rome whose historic monumental bulk almost overwhelmed the imperial presence, although it is striking that under a Rome-centric emperor like Maxentius, the old capital again resumed prominence with an assemblage of new building works as well as major suburban, imperial constructions (with the distinctive triple grouping of villa-palace, circus and mausolea). Arguably, however, even with Constantine's efforts to redefine the Eternal City through the insertion in both intramural and extramural spaces of sizeable Christian basilicas, the Church's impact was perhaps less visible than in Milan, in part due to the very scale of Rome and its maintained past. In Ravenna's case, the court's arrival created a city which in no way resembled the oldest capital: the former colony and any residual pagan structures were tucked away in a small corner of the new, amplified city in which State units could choose their location and in which an array of splendid ecclesiastical complexes could be erected to define a strongly Christianised centre. Space continued to exist in Ravenna since, when Theoderic's Ostrogothic capital of Italy was also sited here from AD 490, new palace units, chapels, churches and monasteries were created; indeed, the north-east of the town appears a virtual Gothic quarter, with related cemeteries outside the walls (where still stands the Mausoleum of Theoderic).

It may be incorrect to say that Rome became neglected by the emperors and was relegated in status, since even in the arduous 440s the court alternated between old (Rome) and new (Ravenna) capitals; furthermore, both Honorius and Valentinian III had dynastic mausolea in the old capital. However, visits tended to be for set ceremonials and festivals; the Senate remained operative, as did the Bishop of Rome, the mint and the demands of a vast populace. In the preface to *Nov. Val.* 5, of AD 440, Valentinian III duly speaks of 'the city of Rome, which We rightly venerate as the head of Our empire'. The Visigothic, Hunnic and Vandal threats had variable effects on imperial residential strategies, with potential capture of one capital a strong inducement to reside at the other; occasionally, imperial absences did allow for usurpers to emerge at the old capital.[37] Rome retained a pulling power, certainly, and perhaps the final flickers of imperial power and would-be power were inevitably played out more amid the decaying sprawl of the Eternal City. Ostrogothic rule, by contrast, was firmly planted in Ravenna, with greater scope for the structural display of the new authorities and with far less of the past to intrude.

6

Pagans and Christians in the Late Roman West

INTRODUCTION

The late Roman period witnessed another major transition, namely the acceptance and eventual dominance of Christianity. This transition impacted socially, mentally and physically: Roman rule had long been reinforced by the divine favour of a variety of gods; religious structures, art and offerings were commonplace in the first three centuries of the Empire and are well documented through archaeology. But conversion to Christianity created changes within the organisation of the State, in the society, in the articulation of urban space and in the countryside.[1] This chapter considers what changes occurred; how they were manifested in town, country and frontier; how they contributed to a different late Roman world; and how Christianity impacted also on Rome's external enemies. We will see that archaeology plays a growing role in observing and modifying our understanding of the processes of 'Christianisation'.

But first we need to sketch something of the variety of the pre-Christian cults in the Roman West. Roman religion was in fact widely cast: the Empire's extent, security and economic embrace in the first centuries AD facilitated movement of cults from Greece, Egypt and the wider eastern Mediterranean into town and village alike, with merchants and soldiers prominent disseminators. The multiple polytheism enabled cults to reach all ranks of society but with elites seeking out specifics with scope for display, honour and investment. Native deities and practices were generally permitted to persist in the Western provinces, if often undergoing an *interpretatio* or equation/re-identification with recognised Roman or Latin gods, since deities of Nature, war and so on could be recognisably the same; the variety of altars and dedications from sites along and near Hadrian's Wall (notably displayed at the Senhouse Roman Museum at Maryport) offers ample indication of this diversity and interpretation. Indeed, Roman rule enabled much fuller material expression for many such native cults, as represented in the substantial reworking of the spa of Sulis-Minerva at Bath or the sanctuary of Isis Noreia on the Frauenberg near Solva in Noricum.[2]

Although there is diversity (duly reflecting the numerous peoples incorporated by Rome who continued to show their own identities within the provinces), Rome required towns to have at their centre an area for State public cults, while other religious shrines could be accommodated freely within the urban spaces. A valuable guide is Rome's port city, Ostia, where long-term excavations have revealed not just the forum with its State temples, but also diverse religious structures in public as well as private zones, including third-century temples to Mithras incorporated into houses, baths and corporation buildings, as well as fourth- and fifth-century Christian churches and oratories.[3] As an established city, Ostia shows the 'organic' growth of cult points alongside the official deities, but in most Western provinces, towns were new impositions and scope thus exists archaeologically to observe how religious space was ordered from the outset and how native beliefs were accommodated.

Besides some sizeable sanctuary sites, towns were the principal arenas for the larger Roman cult structures and for 'state' deities – symbols of divine supporters of Rome, namely the traditional 'Capitoline triad' of Jupiter, Juno and Minerva, whose temple would be centrally sited, as part of the forum complex. As prominent were shrines to honour the memory of divine past emperors and to pray for the health of the living emperor. Festivals, sacrifices and games were linked to the various State gods and to living and past emperors in commemoration of births, acclamations, victories, marriages and so on. Forts too had shrines, and oaths of allegiance were required as part of the army ritual.

Effectively the transition to a new, single religion was likely to throw into confusion centuries of accumulated tradition, belief and design. So to what degree did these established, non-Christian institutions and structures survive? What were the speed and character of take-up of Christianity in both core and frontier contexts? Did conflict flare between pagan worshipers and Christians? When do pagan temples begin to fail? What types of churches appeared and who built them? And, finally, how well did Christianity bond the fragmenting provinces of the Roman West in the fifth century?

CONFLICT AND LOSS: CHARTING THE FATE OF NON-CHRISTIAN CULTS

Scholars face many problems when attempting to determine the fate of a non-Christian cult in the late Roman West. Too often, 'ends' are assigned to dramatic, documented episodes – incursions by Goths, anti-pagan edicts, deeds of a certain saint or bishop – but, in reality, archaeological dating can rarely be exact, and documentary support is wholly lacking for the majority of low- and middle-ranking towns; even in the largest urban centres, epigraphic or other textual data are slight, offering guidance at most on when structures might have been founded or repaired or indicating when dedications were made; these thus show dates *after which* a structure might have gone out of use, but the intervening length of time might be fairly sizeable. Across the Empire, epigraphic survivals, apart from epitaphs, are minimal after AD 220, matching the peak of elite contributions to urban monumentalisation and upkeep. Texts do occur after this, notably in capitals like Trier, Rome, Ravenna and Carthage (and, more generally, in cities of the Eastern Empire), but for fringe provinces like fourth-century Britain, inscriptions are almost nil.

Otherwise we rely on occasional references by historians, whether Christians such as Eusebius who refers to Christian victories over pagan structures, or non-Christians like Eunapius who bemoans the aggression of the Christians in the 380s and 390s and their destruction of the cult centres at Alexandria, notably the Serapeum, and the wider ruination of the temples under Theodosius.[4] In the East, the orator Libanius of Antioch in AD 386 delivered a forceful denouncement (*Speech*, 30.8) on these and related events, denouncing how monks and other Christian rabble were wantonly destroying various ancient temples:

> [T]hese people, Sire, while the law yet remains in force, hasten to attack the temples with sticks and stones and bars of iron, and in some cases disdaining these, with hands and feet. The utter desolation follows, with the stripping of roofs, demolition of walls, the tearing down of statues and the overthrow of altars, and the priests must either keep quiet or die. ... Such outrages occur even in the cities, but they are most common in the countryside.

Libanius' fears regarding the illegal and unchecked loss of so many classical buildings are mirrored in imperial legal pronouncements regarding closure, access and desecration: the emphasis early on, under Constantine and then Constantius, was on cessation of pagan sacrifices, but not temple closure. Thus, for 342, Emperors Constantius II and Constans inform Catullinus, prefect of Rome, that 'Although every superstition is to be rooted out completely, nevertheless it is Our wish that the temple buildings located outside the city walls should remain untouched and undamaged'.[5] Only in the 350s do the laws require the closure of temples (*CT* 16.10.4 and 6) – something countermanded by the pagan Julian in the early 360s, but reinforced straight after, when there were confiscations of temple and sanctuary revenues. Valentinian (364–75) took a diplomatic approach: 'He made no attempt to fasten his own beliefs on the necks of his subjects, but left the various cults undisturbed as he found them' (Ammianus Marcellinus, 30.9). Far more aggressive were edicts by Theodosius in the 380s and 390s, especially in the Eastern provinces: various edicts were addressed to the praetorian prefect and devout Christian Cynegius, who perhaps personally organised temple destructions in Syria, Mesopotamia and Egypt.[6] In theory, a comprehensive ban on pagan cults was applied in 391 through edicts issued at Milan (*CT* 16.10.10) and in Alexandria – the former directed at the stubborn elite of Rome and the latter focused on a city still boasting a multicultural, polytheistic population:

> No one is to stain themselves with sacrifices, no one is to slaughter harmless sacrificial animals, no one is to enter shrines, no one is to undertake the ritual purification of temples or worship images crafted by human hand – otherwise they will be liable to divine and human penalties.

Yet in the early fifth century, sacrifices were still being banned, and some temples had not been wholly closed or vacated of their 'illicit things'. By then, however, patronage by nobility would have long ceased, and extant temples would have lacked any financial support for maintenance.

Both historians and archaeologists question how far we can see 'pagan' resistance in words and structures. First, it is important to recognise that paganism was a collection of diverse cults and beliefs and not a unified front – even if temples, shrines, images and rites may have been similar in form. It is very unlikely that devotees of varied cults would have clubbed together to counter potential gangs of Christians such as those claimed by Libanius. Elites were the traditional support and funding base for these varied cults, and while some elites – in Rome at least – remained vocal across the fourth century, upholding the values of a polytheistic past, others retreated to villas to avoid the conflict and office burdens, and yet others (in increasing numbers) peeled away to the new faith that was followed by the emperors. Further, it is clear that Christians and non-Christians intermarried and lived in the same household. For Rome we observe how, towards the end of the fourth century, residual pagan nobility were gathering what they could around them, both to cling onto antique tradition and to stress ancestral links to such traditions and cults: evidence comes in the form of long-winded tombstones, such as that of the Senator Praetextus of AD 384/5 (*CIL*, 6.1779), enumerating priesthoods held in various cults, and publicised disputes, notably over the Altar of Victory between the emperor and the pagan City Prefect Symmachus (his tenure showing that being non-Christian did not bar elites form high office).[7]

Accommodating the old in a new world could, at least in Rome, be achieved, and most emperors worked to this target. Hence, although many pagan festival days (i.e. events linked directly to cults) were removed, various ancient festivals persisted, most notably the *Lupercalia*, still celebrated under the Ostrogoths, alongside games viewed as 'amusements' or 'civic entertainments' once shorn of any non-Christian activities.[8] Emperors hesitated in abandoning all traditions, and the late Empire indeed saw new emphasis on circus games in the capitals (although elsewhere, as seen in Chapter 4 of this book, amphitheatres, associated by many with the scenes of martyrdoms, had already largely fallen into disuse). By AD 450, however, bishop, saint and other holy days had become core to Rome's calendar.[9]

To a large degree, Christian acts against pagan cults were heavily dependent on individual bishops and their supporters. Since certain types of edicts appear to have been repeated, one can assume that enforcement was sometimes patchy.[10] Early acts of ransacking (by Christians as, probably, also by straightforward looters) and destruction must have occurred, but in many centres such violence was probably held in check until Theodosius' stricter edicts of the early 390s. In fact, where earlier destruction occurs it appears to have been via bishops and gangs of monks who were keen to make their own mark, ahead of officials forcing closure.

Whereas towns probably lost all active pagan cult spots by the end of the fourth century, in the countryside the processes of Christianisation and depaganisation may well have been more sluggish, where traditions of the land lingered longer. This is at least what our written sources testify: indeed, still in the late sixth century, Pope Gregory I complains to his clergy about pagan practices reported on Church lands in Sicily and Sardinia; missionary bishops and priests battle it out with peasants and woodland cults both in the central Italian Alps in the late fourth century and in the hilly Lunigiana of north-west Italy in the eighth, and budding saints fight residual spirits as on the height of Montecassino in the first half of the sixth century. As these Christian sources aim, necessarily, to identify the struggles of good against evil and the sanctity of a given bishop, abbot or monk, many battles against pagans were undoubtedly more mental and symbolic. Archaeology, of course, can play a significant role in charting the demise of ancient religious foci in both town and country, and in assessing claims of persistence of rural paganism. Below we explore evidence for one major State cult and one archaeologically well-attested popular cult.

The Imperial Cult

The cult of the living and deified emperors was perceived by Rome in the West, in particular, as a means of encouraging unity and loyalty; by indicating powerful protectors and by imposing shrines on towns in prominent settings, the State could reinforce a centralised urban organisation in its territories. Competition by elites and by town administrators to provide and service such cults (elections to the priesthood, contributions of funds to games or related festivals, erection of statues, offerings for upkeep) served also to elevate local and regional status. To take just one example, excavations at the *vicus* of Eburomagus (modern Bram) in south-west Gaul, a pottery-production centre, have produced a fine second-century inscription dedicated to the spirits of the Augusti and of Apollo, set up by magistrates on the occasion of the opening of a new theatre; through this commemoration these magistrates advertised their own participation and that of their young town in provincial power politics.[11] Not always was the State cult welcomed: the half-finished temple of the deified Claudius at Colchester and its barricaded occupants fell victim to Boudicca's uprising in AD 60, when she fought against an alien rule and its new financial burdens.[12]

Using the evidence of inscriptions set up on behalf of the priesthood, the evolution of the imperial cult on both urban and provincial levels in the West can be traced. Briefly, shrines were inserted into existing larger town centres or were made integral to any new foundations (e.g. Pompeii had shrines to Augustus and a temple to Vespasian and the Flavians at the forum); these shrines displayed the busts of the current emperor and family. Best documented are the provincial cult centres, the majority of which lay at the provincial capitals (including Tarraco, Cordoba, Narbonne, Virunum, Savaria), well served by communication systems (to encourage good attendance at specified ceremonies) and featuring the wealthier provincial elites – the targeted contributors to the cult and priesthood. Initially the cult was centred on Rome and Augustus, but subsequently worship of the deified Augustus (and family) was emphasised, requiring a temple complex and display of statuary (such as the collection of busts of Octavian, Agrippa and Augustus' family found at Beziers in south-west Gaul). Later, Vespasian, to secure his new dynasty, modified the whole to centre on Roma, the deified dead and the living emperor; he also instituted a more formalised priesthood. Trajan established cult centres in the Danubian provinces, with greater focus on the living emperor. At many sites, inscriptions linked to the cult priesthoods die out by the AD180s, though some continue until around 230, notably in the north.[13] But after the Severans, texts disappear, meaning that any reconstruction of the fate of the imperial cult centres lies with archaeology. Did the third-century traumas severely damage the status of the emperor and of his cult? Was change forced by the Tetrarchs, whose religious emphasis was on identification of the Augusti with major gods such as Hercules and Jove? Could emperor worship persist beyond the fourth century? After all, proclamations by the mid-fifth century state that only one God was allowed: 'It is certain that the only protection for Us and for Our empire is in the favour of the supernal Divinity, and that for obtaining this favour, the Christian faith and venerable religion especially support Us' (*Nov. Val.* 17.1 to Aetius, *magister utr. militum* – 8 July, 445). Two well-studied sites may offer some guidance.

Tarraco-Tarragona in Spain was a split town, with the older centre based on the upper town and a new colony laid out in the lower; the lower town forum featured an early altar to Augustus, a theatre, a victory arch of Augustan date and the first temple to the deified Augustus from AD 15. Massive redevelopment came under Vespasian, when the upper town became the grandiose stage for the seat of the provincial council and imperial cult centre – the latter containing the temple to Rome and Augustus, the former occupying a lower terrace but featuring space for statues dedicated by the priesthood.[14] Elites competed for the honour of the priesthood and to contribute to Tarraco's monumentalisation. This picture changes by AD 250, by when the theatre was out of use, the priesthood statuary had come to an end and urban activity as a whole reduced; when new work occurred in the fourth century, such as restoration of the amphitheatre or setting up of honorary statues to the emperors (some of their pedestals recut from earlier ones), the effort came from State officials or government grants, implying a removal of elite participation at Tarraco and suggesting more widely a loss of confidence in State and cult. The upper town's council complex was nonetheless maintained since statuary to emperors such as Constantine was provided, but space was made to accommodate a governor's palace or *praetorium*.[15] By the mid-fourth century the lower town was struggling, but only by the mid-fifth century, under Visigothic occupancy, did the upper town suffer, with rubbish dumping and houses in parts of the former provincial council complex, burials in the area of the cult precinct and a likely conversion of the old temple to Rome and Augustus to a church, with adjoining Episcopal palace. Whether any of the new Visigothic elite knew of the site's past history cannot be ascertained, but we might assume that statuary pedestals and their inscriptions at least remained visible to offer hints.

A second example is *Narona* (modern Vid near Metkovic in Croatia), an Augustan colony in Dalmatia, about 20 km from the Adriatic coast.[16] Since only a small village now occupies part of the settlement, much scope exists for systematic, modern examination to trace Narona's Hellenistic to late antique history – although some disturbance and illegal excavations have caused damage, and nineteenth-century antiquarians removed sculptures to museums and private collections. Previous work had identified the forum, town walls, three early Christian basilicas and a baptistery, and fragmented statuary from a presumed temple to Augustus noted on inscriptions. Excavations from 1995 on the west side of the forum revealed a well-preserved cult building which, remarkably, contained the toppled statues and bases from three groups of statuary originally arranged on low walls on three sides of the inner chamber (*cella*), with pedestals for two (lost) silver statues of Venus on the floor against the back wall. All told, 14 large statues – notably one over life-size one of Augustus, three smaller statues and a further base – were recognised, most *in situ*, from a likely ransacking and deliberate slighting of the complex in the fourth century, with the statue heads removed and thrown out of the building.[17] Most of the high-quality statues belong to the first century AD but include a few of second-century date, notably two (missing) Venus statues. Striking is an absence of any later emperors such as the Severans. Potentially, these latter may have been sited in the forum square itself, leaving the temple a shrine for the earliest dynasties only.

When did this ransacking happen? Pottery indicates activity to the end of the fourth century (though was the pottery from offerings or might it be from activity after the temple fell redundant?), followed by deliberate infilling with earth, mortar and rubble from slighted walls; later, in the sixth century, burials cut into these fills. No church was imposed on this pagan edifice – the early Christian basilicas instead lie a few hundred metres away to the south, north and east to serve a new townscape. The excavators claim a violent end, 'probably following Theodosius' edict in the later fourth century or around 400', with Christian victory claimed by removing the imperial heads and toppling the statues into a heap. Christians deemed that 'cult statues were inhabited by maleficent demons who would take vengeance on them for daring to enter into the places where pagan rituals had once brought these demons to life'; only by fully erasing these would the demons be removed. There are many further examples of cult statuary, other art and buildings that reveal vicious assaults on them, presumably by Christians, at various stages in the fourth and early fifth centuries, such as those of Serapis, Isis and Cybele from a sanctuary at Sarsina in Italy which had all been hacked to pieces.[18] In fervent Christian eyes, any past emperor, Augustus included, could be associated with the persecutions; in this regard, their statues were like any other idols which had required sacrifice to honour them. Indeed, Septimius Severus had passed a law that forbad conversion to Christianity, while his successor Caracalla required all to participate in the imperial cult: 'Christians' exclusivist refusal to participate meant that treason and sacrilege overlapped in injurious, insulting defiance of the emperors, the gods, and the state.'[19] The third-century persecutions can be recognised as brutal efforts by the emperors to secure loyalty for stability in troubled times.

Recognition of Christianity under Constantine did not mean cessation of the long-established imperial cult: on his arch at Rome, Constantine links himself to the famous (deified) emperors Trajan, Hadrian and Marcus Aurelius through reuse of sculpture from their temples; as seen, at Tarraco, inscribed pedestals for statues of Constantine, Licinius and the Caesars Constantius and Crispus show commemoration at least till the 330s and with a much later plaque dedicated to the Emperors Leo and Anthemius revealing a (probably discontinuous) display until AD 470 – as honorific (not cult) images. So, would imperial cult temples have seen Christian attacks before the end of the fourth century? Certainly, after the mid-fourth century, laws prevented temple investment, and even if private worship persisted at these, presumably many people would have been scared away from doing so. Finds such as pottery in the latest phases of sites like Narona could relate to ritual activity but could as easily denote non-ritual usage. Nothing archaeological has yet emerged to show renewal of activities in the reign of Julian, but this is such a narrow time span that only contemporary inscriptions might reveal this. Blanket conclusions must be avoided as, undoubtedly, certain shrines fell victim to plundering and desecration at an early date and others suffered later, each dependent wholly on local circumstances.

The Cult of Mithras

From epigraphic data, Alföldy argued that Egyptian and Oriental cults became more prominent in northern provincial townscapes from the second century AD onwards, in part as a response to the 'growing uncertainty of life and deeper religious demands' after the upheavals of the Marcomannic Wars.[20] While the cult of Jupiter Dolichenus gained footholds in both towns and forts here between AD 180 and 270, a much fuller distribution of archaeological evidence is attested for the cult of the Persian god Mithras, whose compact, semi-subterranean temples featured complex rituals of initiation and advancement. Viewed as having a particular take-up amongst the higher military grades and known in fortresses from Hadrian's Wall to the Lower Danube (yet barely known in North Africa), this cult also appears in towns in the third century – Ostia has at least 15 mithraea so far uncovered.[21] Mithraism was later associated with the unconquered Sun (*Sol Invictus*), adopted by Emperor Aurelian in the 270s; the cult was not exclusive, since statuary and objects linked to other deities, notably Bacchus and Silvanus, appear within temples. However, Mithras was never a substantial cult, and while comparisons have been drawn with Christianity in terms of shared aspects of ritual, it was not compatible with the early Church, as summed up in one episode in AD 367 when Gracchus, prefect of Rome, smashed up and burnt down a Mithraic cave to confirm his conversion to Christianity.[22]

Did other mithraea meet similar Christian destruction? Texts are not so helpful: Mithras dedications are strong for third-century Noricum and Pannonia and are present in reasonable numbers in Gaul and the Germanies, but only to the AD240s, and in a smaller number in Britain, the latest of which is of 252, set up at Housesteads on Hadrian's Wall (though for Britain, dedications to the emperor's cult and to Jupiter run into the 280s). Archaeologically, Sauer has considered two evidence types: coins and statuary. The coinage recovered in excavations tends to be in low denominations but was presumably deposited originally as gifts along with higher value coins and items, the assumption being that temple closure witnessed ransacking for precious goods and less valuable coins were largely ignored. If so, the coins could reveal any extended persistence of worship.[23] In the Balkans, at Ptuj (Dalmatia), coins from two of five temples extend to the last decade of the fourth century, as also at Septeuil and Nuits St Georges in central Gaul; at Konjica and at the Mühlthal they may run into the first decade of the fifth. At the Martigny (Switzerland) mithraeum, an altar was presented by Governor Publius Acilius Theodorus in c. AD 300 and floor restoration occurred in c.360. Bronze figures plus at least 1,250 coins (extending to the 390s) were found here, the coins scattered in and above layers relating to the decay of the complex; a pit was later cut and an altar to Jupiter buried in this, perhaps for security by pagans, since two others were later smashed up. In time the walls crumbled and filled the abandoned mithraeum.[24] Frequently, Mithraic altars and other reliefs, where recovered, show evidence of iconoclastic destruction, from hacking with axes, burning or chiselling. Two good examples come from Sarrebourg and Strasbourg-Koenigshoffen, each originally over 3-m high, but each fragmented into a minimum of 300 pieces, with other pieces pulverised, notably the head of Mithras (unless removed for some other formal end).[25]

Along Hadrian's Wall there is a confusing early chronology for Mithraic closures, but weak excavation data make precision difficult. Of four coins from Carrawburgh the latest belonged to the 290s; pottery here and from Housesteads and Rudchester is no later than c. AD300. In direct contrast, however, coins (a full 16,000) from the sacred spring of Coventina's Well, near the Carrawburgh mithraeum, extend into the AD 390s.[26] Later coins come from two mithraea elsewhere in Roman Britain: Caernarfon (also military) and London (Walbrook). Caernarfon was perhaps abandoned following a deliberate fire and smashing of altars in the mid-fourth century; London's temple had the heads of other gods – notably Minerva, Mithras and Serapis – buried around AD 325, but finds related to the cult of Bacchus imply renewed pagan worship by the 340s. Sauer sees various ends: gradual abandonment (loss of revenue and worshippers), formal closure, anxieties about desecration prompting concealment of cult figures and altars, destruction.[27] Destruction and iconoclastic actions are most easily ascribed to Christian fanatics, but looting and desecration might equally represent work by State officials and their teams, searching out and confiscating portable wealth.

For the City of Rome we should likewise not expect a single phase of termination. Thus, while we hear of Gracchus' vandalism in 367 against a Mithraic cave, at the mithraeum at Santa Prisca on the Aventine Hill a systematic filling-in and a sealing of the entrance (perhaps denoting a ritual act of closure) have been set to AD 400.[28] Interestingly, there is a close correspondence in Rome between the sites of former mithraea and early Christian basilicas, attested by excavations beneath, for example, San Clemente, S. Susanna and S. Balbina.[29] Is this simple coincidence or were some early house churches deliberately installed as rivals in the same or nearby apartment blocks as the mithraea?

The nobility, as noted, were core to maintaining the public visibility of cults and their temples. As their wealth base waned from the third century, individual investment perhaps shifted into smaller cults such as Mithras. But once Christianity made its presence felt through imperial acceptance, elite displays of allegiance to cults, especially within an urban context, must have been challenged. In Rome and Ostia those displays to old cults persisted more because of the grip the old elite maintained in the administrative hierarchy, but elsewhere the days of most temples were numbered, their persistence dependent more on lingering noble sentiment and on a weaker Church presence.

Rural Pagan Shrines

Many elites shifted their interests away from towns in the fourth century to invest more in their landed estates. Thus, while towns like Tarragona, London and Paris began to appear rather run down, in the contemporary countryside, many large villas exhibited new architectural and artistic trends, testifying to wealth and even continued traditional beliefs, if with the progressive appearance of Christian motifs in mosaics or in portable artefacts (e.g. bowls, spoons) (see below). But what of the bulk of the rural population? Can archaeology help identify their conversion in the landscape? Frequently, scholars view the landscape in blanket terms by seeing it (in reality 'it' comprised multiple forms of production, interaction, population, exploitation etc.) as socially backward – that is, 'rustic' and resistant to change. Accordingly, when hearing in hagiographic sources of the wanderings of saint-bishops and missionaries into the murky countryside, their battles against enduring pagan worship are too often accepted as real. This totally ignores the fact that the land was owned largely by elites, by the State and, in time, by the Church and that the land was generally worked for those owners and provided for a strongly urban market; the networks of roads enabled good communications with towns and other rural communities.[30] Even if later Roman insecurities saw some of this interdependency broken, most town authorities still oversaw landed production: Church lands were farmed to help feed both clergy and poor, State lands provided for the army and bureaucracy, elite lands provided for villa estates and all landowners produced surplus for taxation purposes. Thus, the countryside should have been equally affected by the first official stirrings of Christianity, but like the towns, progress in terms of converting populations and farmers would have been patchy. What can we see, though, of persisting rural paganism?

For North Africa, Riggs[31] has discussed the goddess Caelestis, the Punic Tanit, who was honoured across many of the provinces in both town and country, in public and private space, with multiple roles, including patron of agricultural production and the 'promiser of rain'. In the landscape, her shrines and temples feature on imperial and private estates, and dedicatory stelae occur in sanctuaries, in the mountains or by water courses. In Tripolitania, her cult was far less prominent (except in the largest towns like Lepcis and Sabratha) than the Libyan god Ammon, whose cult extended into the hinterland and indeed to the desert tribes (in fact, the Laguatan tribal confederacy who fought against Byzantine rule in the 540s remained largely pagan, despite interactions with Christian Romans).[32] The African Church thus faced a native religion deeply rooted in the daily lives of rural workers and landowners, and it needed the vocal Augustine of Hippo, in particular, through sermons and letters, to bring to imperial attention the fact that pagan banquets and idol worship persisted on many rural estates in the early fifth century. These sermons also reveal that landowners took affront at Episcopal interventions and resisted their and their workers' conversion; many perhaps considered their prosperity a reflection of the support of the native gods. Still in 419 the Council of African bishops held at Carthage was petitioning the emperors to order destruction of 'any remaining temples without artistic value together with their idols' in coastal and inland communities.[33]

Key was encouraging the conversions of the landowners. Some were still urban based and the sermons of major bishops such as Ambrose of Milan and Maximus of Turin in the 370s–80s are partly geared to this audience. Indeed, Maximus stressed that *domini* should actively assist the process of rural Christianisation 'because they would be held directly responsible for idolatric practices on their estates'.[34] Analysis of fifth- to seventh-century epitaphs from Turin's region of Piedmont supports the idea of Episcopal evangelisation utilising the road network and with epitaphs of clerics deriving from villages or townships and from likely estate centres – suggestive of churches founded by elites.[35] One key episode documented by Maximus regards villagers in the upland Val di Non region of the Trentino in the north-central Alps violently rejecting three missionary clerics, who tried to halt ongoing pagan rituals and to build a church – only for the wild and barbarous Saturn worshippers to burn them to death using stakes fashioned from the beams of the church. The authorities and Church subsequently forced the locals and their landlords to abandon their old religions; the Church meanwhile ensured the clerics were recognised as martyrs. A comparison comes in the missionary efforts in the Tours region of Gaul, documented by the *Vita Martini* and compiled by the Aquitanian landowner Sulpicius Severus to honour Martin, bishop of Tours (371–97), and recount his feats in both town and country.[36] Sulpicius states that Martin was aided by fellow clergy, monks, locals and soldiery (indicating that he had State backing), who helped pull down Jupiter columns, fell sacred pine trees, demolish shrines and temples and blot out images. Martin occasionally faced angry rustics, but often his saintly demolitions (and rapid church building) inspired locals to seek conversion.

Archaeology indeed supports a first phase of rural church building in this epoch, but with few secure direct replacements of temples, since a good number of these appear abandoned already by the end of the third century – best evident in the west of Gaul, where a lower population density might have accounted for failures to continue to invest, especially after the third-century upheavals (although Goodman observes how the areas closer to the frontier zones show a stronger resilience of pagan cult sites). Based on the comprehensive survey by Fauduet of Romano-Celtic temples, expressing changes in terms of the proportion of such temples active during each century, Goodman shows that 8 per cent of those cult centres active during the first century had been abandoned by its end; during the second century, 19 per cent more were abandoned; during the third, 30 per cent; and in the fourth, 79 per cent. Local economic changes, population densities, elite inputs, perhaps conversion and perhaps loss of confidence can all be taken as factors at play – certainly, currently, instances of direct destruction and transformation of sites by St Martin and fellows do not appear to have been high on the basis of the archaeology.

Text and finds testify, for the full Roman period, numerous rural shrines and temples at significant locations in the landscapes – passes, springs, river mouths and favoured hilltops especially – serving villagers, shepherds, farmers and merchants. In addition to these, farms, villages and hamlets had their own idols and altars – that is, not public ones or ones overseen by or responsible to municipal authorities and not therefore directly subject to law.[37] Potentially, the larger the cult site, the more anti-pagan attraction might have come from budding Christian missionaries, but the archaeological data for damage, loss or abandonment are often ambiguous. In central-northern Italy, for example, the sanctuary of Minerva at Breno in the Val Camonica endured into the fifth century before suffering a serious fire, after which there was looting of materials from fountains, floors, doors and walls. Is this primarily vandalism inflicted by Christians, followed by exploitation of the ruins by locals? Studies of eight sacred and pilgrimage sites, both pagan and Christian, in the Aquileia region have identified how these lay near strong natural features (springs, woods, caves, rivers); while many of the pagan centres were Christianised through chapel, church or monastic foundations, few of these directly overlay the pagan structures. But chronologies of decay and church imposition are unclear without full excavation, and all that can be proven is that the church builders exploited the pagan sites for materials – as at S. Martino alla Beligna, where a large fifth-century martyrial church has flooring containing reused dedications to the Celtic god Belenus (from which the place name Beligna derives) and other deities honoured at the nearby pagan sanctuary.[38]

Conversion was thus progressive rather than rapid, reliant often on targeted missionary work. Reports by Caesarius of Arles and Pope Gregory in Rome on pagan survivals, idols and the continued efforts of holy men and women across the sixth century might indicate a superficial rural Christianisation in places, but this probably had far more to do with hagiographic invention than physical reality.

ELITES, BISHOPS AND THE CHURCH

It is relevant to consider the sequence of conversion of elites since these were the former leaders and principal patrons of the multiple pagan cults and their related festivals. Do we see resistance or delayed conversion only in the larger capitals? Why delay if the emperors were all Christian? And how quickly did elites become bishops and high-ranking clergy? The first Roman Christian historian, Eusebius, naturally claimed rapid Christianisation of the court and officialdom in Constantine's reign, but in reality it was patchy at best, before gaining momentum.[39] The old elites' concerns were logical: seeing temples which they or their ancestors had funded suddenly being closed, or even ransacked, was damaging to their name and memory. Elite wealth and patronage were threatened: the new Church busily favoured the poor and weak and emphasised charity; some nobility after the 330s even gave up their moneys, houses and lands to the Church or used them to fund pilgrimage to the Holy Land or to found monasteries; and other elites sought chastity. Only towards the end of the fourth century were compromises secured, with the Church allowing elites to convert but keep their moneys and lands so long as charity played a role and they funded churches or monasteries. Ambrose of Milan was a major figure in this debate, recognising that elite inclusion was vital for providing both prestige and economic clout to the Church.[40] Subsequently we see members of the established aristocracy begin to fill the ranks of the high clergy, with the fifth century as the main phase of incorporation. Thus, for Gaul, van Dam argues that the 'conversion of the Gallic aristocracy in the fifth century can more properly be seen as the transformation of Christianity in order to conform with existing aristocratic structures of authority and ideologies of prestige'.[41] A key example is Germanus of Auxerre who studied law in Rome, went from administrator to military commander and then to governor, but who in 415 was elected bishop of his home city. His own transformation provided a model for other elites to mull over: Germanus clearly held elevated status, both urban and regional; his legal training aided him in sermons, judging cases, embassy work; his military background helped when asked to visit Britain to help both its Church and people there in the struggle against Pelagianism and against Pictish intruders in 429; and he had wealth from the State and community and used this to build churches and monasteries, which honoured his name. Thus an Episcopal career could be prestigious in one's lifetime and endure beyond that.

This is certainly matched in the case of Paulinus of Nola, recognition of whose pious reputation is reflected in the survival of many of his writings and correspondence connected with him (e.g. with Ausonius).[42] Born in the mid-fourth century and educated at Bordeaux, Paulinus early on was appointed governor of Campania in Italy (perhaps in 379), a wealthy province with well-to-do towns but also featuring important bishoprics and Christian shrines. Civil war prompted Paulinus to return to Gaul and thence Spain, where he married the wealthy Christian Therasia; his brother's murder and the death of his 8-day-old son, however, took him in a new direction and he was ordained a priest by the bishop of Barcelona. Probably in 395 his most important set of decisions was made, as reported by Bishop Ambrose (*Letters* 58, 1–3):

> Paulinus, a member of one of the greatest families in Aquitaine, has sold his possessions and those of his wife, with the intention of bestowing the proceeds on the poor, and, having himself become poor instead of rich, is preparing to bid farewell to his home and country and kindred, in order to serve God more diligently. It is rumoured that he has chosen a retreat in the city of Nola wherein to pass the remainder of his days, away from the tumult of the world. ... What will the nobles say when they hear all this? That a man of such exalted family, such famous ancestry, such brilliant genius, such gift of eloquence, should actually quit the Senate and suffer his noble house to become extinct – this, they will cry, is not to be borne! They themselves shave their heads and eyebrows when they consecrate themselves to Isis; but if a Christian, out of zeal for religion, takes to wearing the dress of a monk, they call it a shameful deed.

Paulinus and his wife sought less Nola in Campania and more the tomb and shrine of St. Felix outside of the town at Cimitile. Although already provided with a basilica, he funded major rebuildings and extensions to the shrine: pilgrim lodgings were added, a monastery and nunnery built, the water supply improved to allow for fountains in front of the new basilica (although some citizens of Nola were concerned that his work might deprive their town of its full water supply). Paulinus may have instigated some of the new buildings when he was the governor; his financing of the extra works from the 390s reflects how he still held property around Nola and how the money gained from the sale of his other properties in Gaul and Spain had been directed here. Extant poems (the *Natalicia*) by Paulinus describe his ornate basilica, with fine wall frescoes to inspire visitors and painted verses on walls and over doorways. Paulinus implies that many of the local peasants followed a very loose religion and saw the shrine as a point of recreation and gathering. Wealthy and famous Christian visitors included Melania the Elder, travelling back from her pilgrimage to the East and bringing a piece of the True Cross – one of many prized relics used to attract pilgrims to Nola-Cimitile; Paulinus' poems (recited at each annual saint's festival day) and his correspondence stress the power of these relics and recount numerous miracles performed by St. Felix. Rich refugees from Rome sheltered for a while in the context of Alaric's assaults on Rome in 409–10; by then installed as bishop of Nola, Paulinus was there when the Visigoths captured the town; he too was imprisoned until sufficient portable wealth was stripped from Nola. He subsequently organised the town's revival (as praised by St. Augustine in *The City of God*), and by the 420s he was probably one of the foremost Italian bishops; Gregory the Great 150 years later ascribed to him the ransoming of prisoners taken by Vandals from Nola in 455 – even though Paulinus died in 431.

Paulinus' verses offer much to archaeologists (and art and architectural historians) exploring earliest Christian church building and patronage. In this case we also gain an idea of how early wealthy converts tend to establish churches more in the rural context, often in fact at or alongside villas (see below), generally from the late fourth century. In the urban context, however, it was the State that embarked on the first phase of church building and elaboration of cemeterial shrines/*martyria* beginning earlier in the fourth century AD. The emperor acted as the provider in the capitals and largest urban centres, especially via showpiece foundations in Rome, Trier, Arles and Carthage. For other centres bishops could access funds to commence building projects (see below). Income was generated chiefly through State-granted lands – with goods and rents directed to the ecclesiastical coffers and stores. For Rome, a key source is the Book of Pontiffs (*Liber Pontificalis*), compiled from the sixth century and containing Episcopal biographies; earlier entries curtly spell out imperial and pontifical generosity in founding and endowing churches. Thus in the *Life of Sylvester* (AD 314–35), Constantine's establishment of major basilicas in Rome and central Italy is detailed, showing St Peter's and St Paul's to be supported by revenue drawn from far-flung properties, including estates in North Africa and even gardens and taverns in Cerataea in the East. The bishop's church at Ostia similarly drew on various sources to fund both edifice and staff to an annual total of 1,118 *solidi*; the consul Gallicanus further contributed materials and properties for an annual value of 869 *solidi*, and a variety of precious metal liturgical items, such as lamps and basins, were presented (very rarely do such items survive to the present day).

With fuller integration of the aristocracy around AD 400, a new, different phase of church building in and around towns emerges (this too late, of course, for a province like Britain). Figures such as Paulinus emerge as patrons to properly 'Christianise' towns, often participating as bishops and high clergy. As Paulinus' texts show, patrons and founders gained much popular credit and recognition, and dedicatory inscriptions – painted, sculpted or in mosaic – were employed in a fashion resembling texts once displayed on temples and baths. In fifth-century Rome an array of intramural churches was installed (some within/from Roman aristocratic houses), suburban churches were expanded and cemeterial shrines gained attention.[43] Similarly, across regions like southern Gaul and eastern Spain, the Episcopal network and related church building, plus wider, elite patronage, are attested consistently in the first half of the fifth century despite documented politico-military upheavals. In some areas there may have been a tardier input by the aristocracy, as Bowden has argued for Epirus Vetus (Albania) province, perhaps delayed because of the military turmoils of the earlier fifth century – although as there was precious little later stability, maybe instability itself was the prompt for such elite devout display.[44]

Bishops were the Church's principal representatives, but they were supported often by sizeable bodies of clergy and monks; these were all exempt from taxes and public duties. As more elites entered the clergy, the problem arose of servicing towns in terms of their secular offices and their funds; while initially the Church authorities had the care first of their congregations, poor, staff, lands and buildings, increasing numbers and increasing income and landed or property donations magnified the administrative burden. Certainly, by the sixth century, bishops combined a variety of offices, managing tasks previously the preserve of governors, prefects and town councils – such as overseeing collection and distribution of food, ensuring water supply, rural land management and even road and town wall maintenance. Signs of this future status and role are evident already with the examples of Paulinus and Martin of Tours; to this can be added the apparently crucial roles played by popes when treating with Alaric, Attila and Geiseric. Effectively the old order was failing and the Church was holding the remnants together; the fact that some bishops gained prominence and even became saints to their local communities meant that a new type of social and urban unity was being forged – although such unity was often localised and rivalries might emerge between Christian communities, as attested for fifth-century Arles and Vienne.[45] Archaeologically, the growing net of churches and monasteries around and then inside towns bear close witness to this extension of authority. Historically, however, we should be somewhat cautious, since we necessarily reconstruct much from hagiography or saints' lives, which are blatantly designed to paint images of effective and charismatic religious leaders. A good example is Eugippius' *Life of St. Severinus*, composed in AD 510 but telling of events in the 460s when Severinus – probably a general, perhaps a bishop – is the rallying figure for remnant Roman troops and peoples along the battered Norican *limes*, organising soldiery, parleying with the enemy, distributing supplies and founding monasteries.[46] Recounting Severinus' multiple Christian and secular acts enabled Eugippius to highlight the importance of the new saint and to enhance his cult's standing (see Chapter 8 in this book).

CHRISTIANISATIONS OF SPACE

Town and Church

Although Paulinus was elected to an active bishopric by *c.* AD 400, not every town gained a bishop from the early decades of Christian acceptance. Indeed, even in Italy, where one might expect rapid investment in the Episcopal framework, progress was somewhat sluggish, and the evolution of the 248 known urban dioceses predating the seventh century is a chronological patchwork. In central Italy, for example, the earliest bishops are documented for AD 313 at Pisa, Siena, Florence and Chiusi, followed by Arezzo, Spoleto and Gubbio in the mid-fourth century, but it is another century before Asti and Luni are attested, and some bishoprics only emerge in the later fifth century (e.g. Spello and Populonia). In the south-east, larger towns form the first bishoprics and other urban centres are likewise equipped by *c.*400. However, some bishoprics and dioceses are documented only through excavation, such as the discovery of a probably first Episcopal church under the Romanesque cathedral of Barletta.[47] Sequences of Episcopal appointment would have related mainly to sites of urban status and population size but did not necessarily link into the presence (or absence) of, for example, martyr burials and shrines.

Excavation of early churches can provide important data on the contemporary wealth of a given centre – through its size, construction, design and internal ornamentation – and chart aspects such as maintenance, expansion, re-elaboration, attraction of burials and insertion of relics. For Italy, important excavations of this type have been undertaken at, for example, Luni, Pesaro and Florence. Some have even identified the presence of pre-church structures (occasionally interpreted as pre-Constantinian house-churches) and cemeterial spaces – with Rome especially well served by such finds. In some cases the very location of an early Christian church is only pinpointed through archaeology (since not all early churches underlie later ones): a recent example is the Episcopal church at Ostia, discovered close to the town's south gate through a combination of air photography, geophysical survey and test trenches. Outside of Italy, excavations of the major Episcopal complexes (comprising churches, palaces, baths, stores) at both Barcelona and Geneva stand out for the wealth of otherwise undocumented data on siting, scale, expansion and change across the late Roman and early medieval periods.[48]

Installation of a bishop denoted the formal creation of a State-linked church. Usually at this stage we trace the start of the process of Christianising intramural urban space. What is then of interest is the placement of churches, whether central or peripheral, and whether choice is dictated by pre-existing foci of worship (e.g. house-churches), by available space or lack of space. Potentially, the more prominent the placement of a cathedral, the more prominent the perceived role of the bishop. Yet a peripheral location – such as for St John the Lateran at Rome or Ostia's noted Episcopal basilica – might be selected on strategic grounds: near to an imperial palace, near to major suburban martyrial burials or on a specific roadway. Or selection might have come through negotiation with Senate/council/elites – in larger cities, the centre in the early fourth century was often still a busy one, and insufficient space might have been engineered to accommodate a church; in other sites, ruinous public spaces might have been cleared to provide space. Another possibility is that a church was sited to exploit or cancel out the (pagan) past: one example is Turin, whose early Christian basilica of S. Salvatore[49] was placed near the town's north-eastern angle, immediately south of the Roman theatre. The archaeologists here argue that the theatre was redundant when the church was built and that the builders made full use of its bricks, tiles, columns and other marble work. Conceivably, local Church leaders had protested viciously against the crude theatrical plays and managed to bring the final curtain down on the complex, with the city authorities then sanctioning both construction of the church and plundering of the old theatre. Alternatively (and more probably), the theatre had closed long before due to lack of funds, and the reuse of space and materials was simply a matter of convenience, not symbolism. A final possibility, having seen how some town centres were becoming run down across the fourth century, is that 'fringe' locations were suited because they avoided dilapidated and dangerous spaces – and perhaps avoided old pagan sites too.

Whatever the location, space and materials were presumably donated or authorised by the civic council and on many occasions must have required some displacement of residents, in terms of houses or shops. At the same time, however, the works provided employment and a new point of urban pride. Rapidly, these churches would have attracted new housing or shops as they became the new social and religious theatres for towns. Accordingly, much research is needed to tackle the issue of Christianisation of towns, to see the levels of redefinition and especially to identify how far the imposition of churches helped bond communities and maintain an urban identity. Alternatively, did the building of churches and the mental and physical rejection of pagan (and 'lost' classical) spaces forge a new urban identity and ideology? And was the reuse of materials (*spolia*) from abandoned pagan or secular structures seen as a 'conquest' by the Church, or was it simply a reuse of a convenient building and decorative resource?[50]

In this context, we might explore the treatment of redundant 'pagan' and 'classical' urban space. In the East, various instances exist of the pagan past being directly blotted out by insertion of churches into cult buildings or over their razed foundations: in Asia Minor, examples include the temple of Aphrodite at Aphrodisias, the temple of Cybele and Augustus at Ankara, and that of Zeus at Aezanis; in Jordan at Jerash, the cathedral of *c.* AD 365 was on the site of a temple of Dionysus. However, such changes came chiefly after the mid-fifth century, with the first churches otherwise focused on suburban cemeteries; when intramural they reused former public, secular buildings instead, whether basilicas, stoas or baths. In lesser towns in Anatolia, at least, it is argued that a strong pagan signature continued to be inscribed on the urban landscapes into the fifth century, and in much of the East, only in the sixth century is a full 'colonisation' of ex-pagan space enacted.[51] In Western provinces, reuse of temple buildings appears much less common, even in the fifth century, or is much delayed: in Rome, conversion of both Pantheon and Senate House occurs only in the early seventh century; in Spain, conversions also seem delayed until the sixth or seventh century (as at Tarragona), although some temples may have been robbed or used for housing prior to this (e.g. Merida); in southern Gaul, two well-known examples of temple-to-church conversion are the Maison Carrée at Nîmes and the temple of Rome, Augustus and Livia near the forum at Vienne, but here too there was probably a long interval between pagan demise and Christian spatial 'conquest'.[52]

Instructive are details surrounding the complex dedicated to Caelestis at Carthage, reported by Bishop Quodvultdeus for the earlier fifth century: 'When it had been closed for a long time and, from neglect, thorny thickets invaded the enclosure, and the Christian inhabitants wanted to claim it for the use of the true religion, the pagan inhabitants clamoured that there were snakes and serpents there to protect the temple. This only aroused the fervour of the Christians all the more and they removed everything with ease and without suffering any harm so as to consecrate the temple to the true celestial king.' Oddly, Quodvultdeus states that the temple (converted but perhaps not kitted out with Christian furnishings?) was subsequently (after a pagan prophecy) razed by the tribune Ursus in c. AD 420. Perhaps pagan spirits lingered and consecration as a church could not be formalised. Alternatively, locals still viewed the cult centre, even if ruinous, as a part of their city space; after all, Caelestis had, for centuries, been the patron goddess of Carthage, and we hear of resistance by local elites and farmers to quitting offerings and festivals linked to their protector. This example demonstrates that pagan monumental structures could continue in ancient townscapes, even in decay; Church authorities accordingly created alternative foci, perhaps with the expectation that, in time, old space could be reclaimed.[53]

What of urban church locations in Gaul? Two examples suffice. First, *Augustodunum*-Autun, whose late antique focus lay beyond the walls to the north-east where three churches are attested: a funerary church precedes the medieval Saint-Pierre-L'Etrier and lies in a cemeterial zone attested in the later sixth century as the burial place for the town's early bishops; to its north-west in the mid-fifth century Bishop Euphronius founded a basilica over the supposed tomb of the third-century martyr Symphorien; later, to the west, a monastery dedicated to the late fourth-century Saint Martin was established. The sole intramural church (St Nazarus) lay in the very south of the walled town, close to the Romanesque cathedral church of St Lazarus. Second, Arles in south Gaul, a major trading centre, saw extensive remodelling in the fourth century, being favoured by Constantine and Constantius II and elevated to the seat of the praetorian prefecture of the Gauls; imperial visits and patronage expanded Arles' monumental repertoire to include new public baths and triumphal arches. Convening the first Church Council here in AD 314 denotes a strong Christian centre, no doubt favoured by imperial financial support. While a logical candidate for the first cathedral is the present-day St Trophime in the town centre near the forum, sixth-century texts instead imply a location in the town's south-eastern angle – a strategic spot on a low hill which enabled the bishop to look both inwards to the secular city centre and outwards and eastwards to the important cemetery of Alyscamps and the tomb of St Genesius.[54] As elites began to participate more from the fifth century, the Christian presence expanded, occupying intramural space more prominently. In later fifth- and sixth-century Arles, Bishops Hilary, Caesarius, Aurelian and Virgilius contributed to this process with many monastic foundations. As Gauthier points out, in the fourth century, the classical ideology of towns persisted, and late Roman pagan authors such as Ammianus and Ausonius could ignore the few scattered churches; however, by the sixth century, churches, monasteries and saints framed and protected the urban spaces and populations; the sanctity and honouring of local bishops, combined with the rise in the importance and movement of relics – some local, some imported – helped reinforce (Christian) urban identities.[55]

Burials clearly became more prominent under Christianity: veneration at martyrs' tombs, belief in the afterlife, care for the deceased and their memory, shrines and basilicas built to honour the dead and their place in heaven all reflected a new ideology. Around Rome, catacombs expanded on new levels and in new galleries and received burials into the sixth century; each had one or more foci, and some gained extra prestige through specific interments, such as at the catacombs of Callixtus featuring tombs of various third-century popes; new burials clearly jostle to be near to these, and we can assume that those with money obtained more prized locations and tombs (such as finely carved sarcophagi or vaulted tombs with wall paintings, plus funerary epitaphs). Churches, endowed by bishop or by local aristocrats, form the above-ground focal point for these subterranean cemeteries and no doubt gave due recognition of donors. For Rome there were also distinctive funerary basilicas, notably the so-called open-air 'circiform' (circus-like) complexes (a major example lies close to the small mausoleum-church of Santa Costanza and the adjoining Sant'Agnese basilica – with its own catacombs), erected to cope with increasing demand for burial near the saints (ad sanctos). Pilgrims to these catacombs and churches are well documented from the later fourth century, with pilgrims seeking burial at one of these when their time arrived; careful planning enabled visitor flow to view holy burial spots in many major catacombs.[56]

Burial ad sanctos is manifested across the Roman West, with 'privileged' tombs gathering near church apses (with saintly remains normally under the altar) and occasionally inside, under the floor or in the atrium or entry hall. Burial space was closely regulated, with bishops, high clergy and elite taking the most favoured plots. At Vienne in Gaul, a busy net of suburban churches existed with burials inside and outside, frequently gathered close to known saintly resting places or to displayed relics: south-east of the town lay the memoria of the two Milanese martyrs Gervasius and Protasius, whose cult was established from the time of St Martin of Tours; Martin had baptised one Foedula, whose epitaph is preserved here. To the west, the church of the Apostles hosted the burials of the bishops of Vienne from the 460s onwards and was probably the Episcopal church from the mid-fourth century. Other cult buildings dedicated to St Stephen, St Laurence and St Blandina lay in the north and were active from the earlier fifth century, also attracting burials ad sanctos. To the second half of the fifth century belongs Bishop Mamertus' funerary basilica of the martyrs Ferreolus and Julian of Brioude (these latter bodies obtained less than legally from Clermont, whose bishop demanded a 'share of patronage' – illustrating how visitors gave gifts to the martyrs and thus church).[57]

In sum, ecclesiastical urban intrusions were initially detached, and the process of Christianisation emerges as dependent mainly on the fuller conversion of the elite urban groups from the fifth century. The transfer of relics to internal points of worship and the burial of bishops and high clergy at these were the first steps in creating intramural burial zones (previously banned).[58] The inward movement of relics was not wholesale, however, and many suburban shrines and cemeteries persist, as evident at Arles and Autun. Questions of status and security may have encouraged the shift, or else it was a natural process associated with the Church's ongoing colonising of old public space and with population shrinkage. By the mid-sixth century, arguably, apart from robbed (or adapted) classical structures, churches and town walls were just about the sole stone- or brick-built complexes. Effectively, they represent the end product of a long process of urban decay and change; towns were, by AD 450, much different, occupying many of the same spaces but serving different audiences and with the Church established as the new city authorities.

Land and Church

In Britain, Gaul and Spain a flourishing of villas and villa culture, manifested in architectural elaborations (reception, dining and presentation spaces) and artistic display, is prominent between c.325 and 375. In particular, mosaic schemes show many elites displaying their secular, ancestral, academic and classical credentials through imagery from mythology, of specific gods, of hunts and circus or gladiatorial events; sculpture was similarly displayed to honour and glorify the past.[59] Arguably, these displays represent a parading of traditional social power and learning and not religious debate. Texts from fourth- and fifth-century Gaul and Spain certainly show villas as seats for correspondence and literary battling and sharing, and the output does indicate that by the early fifth century, the majority of these estate owners are Christians and that many had churches at their villas or on their estates. The status of these villa chapels is hard to ascertain, however. Some were presumably private oratories (as perhaps at Lullingstone in Kent); others had a funerary role (for the estate owner's family and kin), but some examples were grander and served estate populations, being provided with priests and deacons – for example, the biographer for Melania the Younger asserted that she owned numerous estates with over 60 farms and 400 slaves, and held one estate as big as a city which was serviced by numerous craftsmen as well as two bishops. Church Councils tried to regulate such 'private' church building and to set conditions for endowing these with relics, priests and burial rights; that there were criteria laid out for parochial status probably means that some estate churches already acted as virtual parish centres.[60]

Clear indications of the conversion of rural elites come from excavations of the later phases of specific villas.[61] In Spain there is a high incidence of church construction on villa sites; chapels/oratories might occupy rooms in the main residential block, as at Montinho das Laranjeiras and Sao Cucufate; some feature associated burials. However, occasionally scale, form and position might indicate ownership in the hands of the Church (or a monastery), with the complex providing a parish or community role – as sometimes indicated by the presence of a baptistery. In Portugal, at Torre de Palma, the mid-fourth-century church lay 100 m north-west of the villa itself but was sited over the villa's burial ground and a possible shrine; a baptistery was then added in the early fifth century, and later on in the same century, the building attracted up to a hundred burials of Visigothic date.[62] Comparable is San Giusto in northern Apulia, south Italy.[63] The site first featured a middle-ranking early imperial villa with residential, productive and storage/service zones; all was enlarged after AD 350 when the site's wine production also expanded. In the mid-fifth century a nearby church and baptistery were built, the church endowed with rich marble, mosaic and fresco decoration; a narthex communicated to the adjoining large, marble-clad circular baptistery. High-status burials occupied spaces between the buildings. In the first half of the sixth century, a second church was added, whose interior contained over 70 inhumations. Later, after destruction of the first church by fire, the second church became the new focus. Who owned the villa in the fifth and sixth centuries when the churches were imposed: a wealthy private landowner still, the region's procurator governor or even a bishop?

CHRISTIANISING THE FRONTIER PROVINCES – CONVERSIONS IN THE NORTH

What picture can be made for late Roman Christianity beyond the Empire's core? Did Christianity take longer to apply the 'glue' on its frontier territories, and did this damage urban and population survival prospects? If take-up was limited, might that have reflected a weak Episcopal, State and urban presence? Many outer provinces lack solid documentation: saints' lives or hagiographic texts are rare, as are inscriptions; Ammianus Marcellinus, while detailing politico-military affairs, barely notes religion, only occasionally giving notice of bishops and of conflicts; synod or council lists simply register Episcopal presences in the larger population foci. Again, therefore, we must draw strongly on archaeology for assessing Church presences in the Danube region and in Britain.

Noricum

Noricum was split between a southern Alpine zone (*N. Mediterraneum* – the more urbanised province) and a northern frontier zone (*N. Ripense*) (Map 6.1). Despite medieval claims that the evangelists St Mark and St Luke personally blessed the population (specifically at *Lauriacum*-Lorch/Enns), there is no tangible evidence for any Christian presence in the first centuries AD. However, the full selection of State, native and imported Greek and Eastern cults in centres like Carnuntum, *Ovilava*-Wels and *Celeia*-Celje attest the receptiveness of the provincial civilian and military populations, fed in part by the flow of merchants along the Danube and along the 'Amber Road' from the head of the Adriatic.[64] One event reported by the fourth-century Church historian Eusebius relates to Christian soldiers in the Marcomannic–Quadic Wars in the 160s and 170s who, while in enemy lands over the Danube and on the point of defeat to Quadi forces, were saved by 'a thunderbolt [which] drove the enemy to flight and destruction, while rain fell on the army which had called on the Almighty, reviving it when the entire force was on the point of perishing from thirst'.[65] The event is even depicted on the Column of Marcus Aurelius, with the apparition of a Rain god, bearded, with arms outstretched and torrents of rain flowing from his arms and body, washing away the bodies of the enemies, as the Romans protect themselves with their shields.[66]

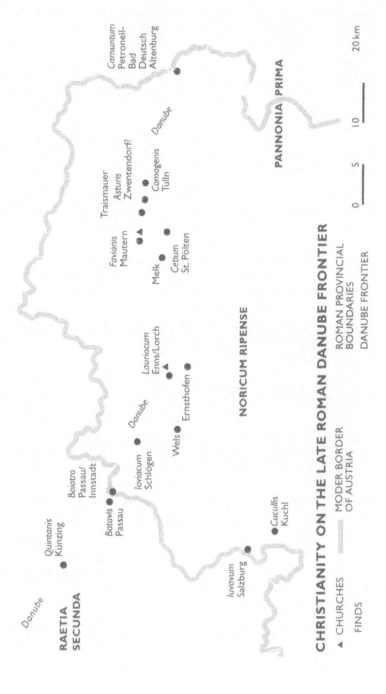

Map 6.1 Christianity along the late Roman Danube frontier – Raetia, Noricum and Pannonia

Only one victim of the Great Persecution under Diocletian is recorded for Noricum, namely Saint Florianus, whose ninth-century *Passio* recounts that in response to the Edicts, 40 Christians were gathered up for interrogation at Lauriacum, plus one Florianus from Cetium, a local civil servant who was probably an ex-soldier since he was recognised by some troopers. Failing to reject their beliefs, the *praeses* Aquilinus threw them all into the dungeons. After being tortured, Florianus was led to the bridge over the River Enns and thrown in with a millstone tied to his neck to drown; at which point the eyes of the man who pushed him fell out. Tradition says Florianus' body was recovered by a noble widow, Valeria, who buried him in her house; her own remains may be those interred in the small box-sarcophagus in the crypt of the church of St Florian; the crypt also contains the culpable millstone. Although this church is not of great antiquity, excavations at St Laurentius church uncovered remains of an early Christian basilica and its early medieval successors. Built around AD 370, this church was damaged by a fire and restored in *c*.450, with the altar zone expanded to include a sunken reliquary. Linked to this is a plain sandstone casket found during remodelling of the later Gothic church's high altar, which contained the long bones (wrapped in a cloth) of 31 individuals, mainly adult males, plus a few animal bones; potentially these bones relate to Florianus' 40 unnamed companion martyrs.[67]

From later fourth-century burials in Enns come finger-rings and lamps with chi-rho Christograms, while for *Olivava*-Wels to the west of Lauriacum mention should be made of the fine, late fourth-century epitaph of one Ursa, set up by her husband, Flavius Ianuarius, a soldier, who tells us that Ursa, a 'faithful Christian', was 38 years old when she died. Strikingly, the epitaph's verses are composed in a classical, pagan sense, implying that Ianuarius was not himself a Christian.[68]

In terms of Norican bishops generally, we are poorly informed: although identified as attendants at the Serdica synod of AD 343, no Norican sees are actually named. Lauriacum may have been the sole frontier see; the other bishoprics probably lay in the southern territory and comprised by *c*.375 Aguntum, Teurnia, Virunum and Celeia. For these we possess good fifth-century evidence: at Celeia, the old capital, an eastern church with good floor mosaics, including donor panels, has been uncovered, while church items are known from the hill of Vipota, 3-km distant, potentially the early medieval refuge site for Celeia. The environs of the replacement provincial capital, Virunum, have seen important excavation work in recent years, in particular at the early Christian pilgrimage centre and late antique refuge of the Hemmaberg,[69] where occupation ran from *c*. AD 400 to 600. The site featured an astonishing array of well-furnished churches (notably a double-church with attached funerary chapel and octagonal baptisterium) and associated pilgrim quarters and cemetery. The late antique provincial focus was, however, Teurnia, ancient Tiburnia, which retained its hilltop site (St Peter in Holz) throughout the Roman epoch. Excavations have identified the first bishop's church and extramural cemeterial church of AD 400, both endowed with mosaics, marble work and wall paintings in the later fifth and sixth centuries; furthermore, the late Roman defensive wall incorporated numerous altar stones and architectural units from demolished pagan temples and shrines from the hill and vicinity. This might well be viewed as a sign of Christian conquest over the pagan cults, but as yet too few data exist to chart when the old cult foci went out of use. Elsewhere, however, for Virunum, some evidence is offered for a late frequenting of the Dolichenum till c.370 and perhaps later at temples to Mars at Lendorf and St Margarethen – these sites seemingly suffering destruction shortly after.[70]

Pannonia

As with Noricum, the assumption is that both soldiery and merchants, each drawn from varied parts of the Empire, were the earliest source for Christian converts in Pannonia. The Diocletianic persecutions provide some proof, with martyrdoms of a number of bishops and priests from the towns of Cibalae, Poetovio, Sirmium and Siscia. Victims at the capital of Sirmium included the Seven Virgins and the Four Crowned Martyrs who comprised a set of (in truth, five) skilled stone cutters (of Persian stock, bar one local) who provided much work for the emperor but who refused a request to carve a statue of Aesclepius and then failed to pray to the gods; their insubordination meant they were thrown into the River Danube alive, locked up inside a lead box. Ten sees are attested for mid-fourth-century Pannonia, with many bishops and Christians adherents of the Arian sect, supported by Constantius II.[71]

Two possible pre-Constantinian house-churches are proposed in the civilian and military centres of Aquincum-Budapest, both set in proximity to house-mithraea; a combination of nearby burials and epitaphs of Christian association (perhaps also indicating Jews), plus lamps and sherds with the chi-rho symbol, forms supporting evidence, although no formal church was subsequently built over these. South of Budapest, at Intercisa-Dunaujváros, pendants, glass vessels and bronze casket-mounts come from burials attributed to Christian soldiery, some of Syrian derivation; a small, apsed building in the civilian zone might be a church. More typical of the relevant finds in Pannonia are the items from Arrabona-Győr, comprising two rings with images of a hand (of God) and a cross, and a clay lamp with the chi-rho symbol.

Basilica-churches, belonging to the mid- to later fourth century, are identified in a small number of sites, mainly away from the river zone, such as the 'inner forts' of Ságvár and Fenékpuszta; both the churches lie near granaries, which might signify clerical supervision of grain collection and distribution from State-owned lands. Gáspár, however, criticises past interpretations of these 'basilicas', arguing that almost no supporting evidence exists to substantiate their Christian roles; more widely, she claims too enthusiastic efforts have been made to identify a coherent Christian presence in Pannonia. She disputes also two claimed Christian basilicas at Gorsium-Tác, yet others are convinced by their date, form and location (near forum and governor's palace), plus paintings and later associated burials. More secure are the remains at the villa of Kékkút and in the town of *Sopianae*-Pécs: at the former, two large basilica buildings without apses were labelled as churches by the excavators, though only one can be securely tied to a house-church, with openwork bricks decorated by chi-rho symbols found at the façade; Pécs, meanwhile, features two painted tombs of the later fourth century, a chapel and, in front of the cathedral, an early Christian mausoleum with 14 burials and at least three sarcophagi on the lower level, plus fine murals including scenes of Adam and Eve and Daniel in the lions' den; the upper level probably was a funerary chapel. These units may have been maintained into the fifth/sixth century and restored in the Carolingian period, when the site was revived as a focus of pilgrimage.[72]

Britain

Like Pannonia, an official Roman presence in Britain after *c.* AD 400 was fragmentary, and in fact, much of the final third of the fourth century saw internal and external disruption. Furthermore, we know this period saw Britain embroiled in heresies and sects, including Priscillianism, but especially Pelagianism (Pelagius, a Briton educated in Rome in the 380s, denied the notion of the Original Sin and of human free will). Missions to counter these came from Archbishop Victricius of Rouen in 396 and Bishop Germanus of Auxerre in 429 – both efforts signifying how even if detached from direct Roman rule, the old province remained attached to Rome's ecclesiastical orbit.[73] Such heresies cannot be traced archaeologically, but excavations and finds can at least show something of the levels and depth of Christian take-up in the late Roman province in both town and country. Interestingly, just three British bishops are recorded attending Church synods on the Continent in the fourth century. These three represented the provincial seats of York, London and Lincoln, and a fourth is to be expected for Cirencester in Britannia Prima; most probably priests acted as Episcopal representatives in other urban and rural contexts. However, the restricted number overall might point to a British Church only partly established prior to the termination of Roman rule.[74]

Just three martyrs are attested for third-century Britain, with two, Saints Aaron and Julius, executed probably in the military amphitheatre at Caerleon. They are noted in Gildas' sixth-century history and later by Bede, claiming 'many others of both sexes throughout the land' had suffered persecution and death.[75] Best known is Saint Alban, martyred at Verulamium in AD 304. His shrine was visited by St Germanus, bishop of Auxerre in Gaul, who came to Britain in 429 to remove heresy; Germanus' visit may have been the prompt for a dissemination of Alban's Life to steer British Christians along the correct path. The tradition recounts how Alban was a pagan who converted after sheltering a Christian priest; Alban took the priest's garb and was tried before the local judge who condemned him to death by decapitation in the arena; en route, the miracles of the stopping of the river and then the appearance of a spring occurred, prompting one executioner to seek God too; the eyes of the reserve executioner, however, fell out after he completed his foul task – matching the fate of Florianus' executioner on the bridge at Lorch in Noricum.[76]

Faulkner has calculated that of known pagan temples in Romano-British towns, out of 24 only 13 appear active still at the start of the fourth century, just 5 by its middle and 2 only by c. AD 375 – figures matching (based on townhouses and sizes) a decline of population.[77] Some pagan persistencies are recognised in the fourth century: in Wales, at Caerwent, a new Romano-British temple was built near the forum in c. AD 330 and remained active to the end of the fourth century; in Cirencester, the Jupiter Column was restored c.360, perhaps during Julian the Apostate's reign; coin deposition at and some repair work to other shrines, urban and rural, notably in the Cotswolds-Severn area of south-west Britain, meanwhile, denote ongoing cult practice into the second half of the fourth century – with later destruction of some sites, notably Uley, c. AD 390–400, ascribed to Christians. In villa mosaics of the zone, a flourish of mythological imagery can be interpreted as displayed elite paganism. At Colchester, the nearby religious complex of Gosbecks (with temples, precincts and theatre) was demolished only after AD 337; the largest of the Romano-Celtic temples at Sheepen, close to the city, appears, on coin evidence, still active near the end of the century.[78]

What of built church structures? A number of urban and rural churches have been claimed – but with disputed levels of evidence for form, function and chronology. The Episcopal sees just noted are not that well served. At York, for example, the massive Norman and medieval Minster overlies the Roman military *principia* and covers the preceding Anglo-Scandinavian ca-thedral cemetery; however, robbing of much Roman masonry for these later church phases has seriously damaged chances of identifying any late Roman ecclesiastical complex here. For London, a substantial basilica-like structure dating to the mid-fourth century is claimed in the south-east corner of the city, although the limited scale of the excavation and the extensive robbing damage mean that plan and character are only partially identifiable, and while some scholars see here the Episcopal church, the postulated dimen-sions, up to 100-m long, seem over-vast for Britain and for a London display-ing few other signs of vitality. Alternatively this basilica was an audience hall, linked to the provincial governor, comparable to the extant edifice at Trier.[79] A further urban church is claimed at Silchester, in the forum *insula*, but there are no supporting artefacts and the claimed date of c. AD 300 is surely too early for an intramural church (and the suggested 'relic' space is also odd, since relics only become 'active' from the late fourth century).[80] Nothing secure is yet known for St Alban's, although a Christian cemetery is attested on the abbey hill and St Germanus' visit testifies to some shrine here.

In fact, the only secure late Roman urban church is that of St Paul-in-the-Bail at Lincoln (Figure 6.1): a likely first church, of just about 12 m x 6 m, it may date to the earlier fourth century (but could be later); it was rebuilt on a slightly larger scale with an apse, probably in the fifth century with burials gathered around and part inside; a possible successor chapel of seventh- to

Figure 6.1 View of the late/sub-Roman church at St Paul-in-the-Bail in Lincoln with robbed-out walling, with apse in foreground (photo courtesy of Michael Jones and the Lincoln Archaeology Trust)

ninth-century date is then postulated. Striking is the preference for construction largely in timber for the churches. While not an imposing edifice, what stands out is its location, within the old forum courtyard of the upper town: this implies a claiming of State land, suggestive of an Episcopal installation.[81] The small size may, at the same time, reflect a shrinking urban population and economy; there will also have been few elites around to contribute much.

Nonetheless, rich Christians are evident from rural contexts: the British landscape witnessed a boom in villa construction and elaboration in the third and fourth centuries, with examples dominant in the south-west. In some, notably Frampton and Hinton St Mary, Christian imagery is inserted into or accompanies a wider repertoire of mosaic designs which include mythological and elaborate geometric works – designed to display more the villa owners' cultural and classical knowledge than solely their religious leanings.[82] A unique survival of wall paintings with Christian images is in Kent, at Lullingstone villa, where a first-floor house-chapel was positioned above what was termed the 'Deep Room', which had first been a nymphaeum linked to the worship of water spirits and later contained sculpture/busts.[83] The house-church, perhaps created *c.* AD 375, featured an anteroom with a painted chi-rho and a main chamber with painted figures – notably standing, praying figures set between columns of an arcaded scene; high-quality excavation and meticulous collection of the plaster were crucial in preserving this exceptional evidence and highlight the likely loss of comparable works elsewhere.

Diverse Christian expressions are registered in Suffolk, notably at Icklingham and its environs, which feature various ritual deposits, some largely Christian in character but with some clear pagan and early 'hoards' too. These deposits comprised buried groups of lead or pewter vessels and tableware, silver spoons, occasional coin hoards (two dating to the time of the Emperor Honorius) and at least four circular/ovoid lead tanks with panel decoration (including the chi-rho symbol), some of which contained iron objects (functional pieces such as hinges, nails and saws). The size of the tanks, about 0.6 m in diameter, argues against a role for baptismal immersion, but they could have served for ritual foot washing or even child baptism. Strikingly, in a 20-mile radius, another four lead tanks and five pewter hoards have been discovered.[84] Were these tanks buried by missionary priests and the 'hoards' by well-to-do local landowners at the conclusion of a specific rite – whether baptism, marriage or funeral? Is this a sign of a pagan or traditional 'ritual' somehow transformed into a Christian design?

What of British military contexts? From AD 312 army units most probably had to show devotion to the Christian God as well as to the emperor, and the insertion of chapels into fixed military bases should thus be expected. Currently, churches are attested at Richborough in the south-east and postulated on Hadrian's Wall at Vindolanda, Birdoswald, South Shields and perhaps Housesteads. Richborough is one of the Saxon Shore forts showing military usage into the early fifth century; a timber church lay in the fort's north-west corner, with a nearby stone-built baptismal font (some Shore forts were later utilised for Anglo-Saxon chapels and monasteries – e.g. Bradwell and Reculver).[85] On the Wall, later fourth-century (presumed) chapels at Vindolanda and South Shields were centrally located (in the *praetorium* courtyard and *principia*, respectively). At Vindolanda, identification is supported by some small finds with Christian indicators and the fifth- or sixth-century tombstone of Brigomaglus – the latter a valuable sign that some forts had lives beyond the end of direct Roman control, perhaps with small chapels forming a religious link with the Roman past (see Chapter 8 in this book).[86]

Arianism Over the Frontier

Brief mention was made above of heresies in late Roman Britain, but one that affected not just the fourth-century Roman State but also the world north of the frontiers, with many later repercussions, was Arianism. The perceived heresy derived from Arius, a priest of Alexandria who placed the Son secondary to the Father. Although exiled after the Nicaea Council, Arius was later restored, and emperors such as Constantius II (340–61) were sympathetic to him. Arianism seemingly took hold strongly in the Danubian provinces, in part due to imperial family roots in the area; although formally condemned in 381 at Constantinople, Arian supporters continued there into the fifth century.[87] More seriously, Constantius II probably sponsored ambitious missionary activity across the frontiers to convert some of the Germanic and other groups, notably the Goths or Tervingi. Ulfila was the lead figure, helping out existing Christians in Gothic lands (former Dacia) and then expanding the Christian message, chiefly through making a Gothic translation of the Bible. But Ulfila was banished from the Goths in c. AD 348, when anti-Roman sentiment was high and Christianity viewed as distinctly Roman – leading to persecutions of Gothic Christians and Christian slaves in the 350s and 370s. In the 370s, the pro-Arian Emperor Valens came to side with Fritigern, rival to the aggressive Athanaric, and when the latter was defeated, Fritigern and his court converted to Christianity – but this came before the condemnation of Arianism in 381. The Goths cited their Christianity when they sought lands on Roman soil in 376 to avoid the growing pressure from Huns, but like other later historians, Eunapius discounted the faith of these newcomers:

> Each tribe had brought along from home its ancestral objects of worship together with their priests and priestesses. ... What they revealed was fiction and sham designed to fool their enemies. They all claimed to be Christians and some of their number they disguised as their bishops. ... They also had with them some of the tribe of so-called 'monks' ... [but] under cover of the deepest secrecy they worshipped the holy objects of their native rites with noble and guileless intent.[88]

Nonetheless, the Christianity, of some at least, of the new powers must have facilitated dialogue: for Gothic Italy and Spain, Burgundian Sapaudia and Frankish Gaul, Arians and Catholics, Germans and Romans managed to live and worship in the same centres. In these territories the strong numeric dominance of the continuing Romanised populations was significant, but a contrast lies with North Africa where Vandals did persecute Catholics (in the 480s–90s especially):

> First of all the tyrant [King Huniric] decreed, in a dreadful command, that no one could hold an office in his palace or carry out public duties without becoming an Arian. There was a great number of these people in these positions who, unconquered in their strength, abandoned temporal office so that they would not lose their faith; afterwards they were cast out of their homes, despoiled of all their possessions and banished to the islands of Sicily and Sardinia. On one occasion he hurriedly issued a decree throughout Africa that the fisc was to claim as its own the possessions of our dead bishops, and that the successor of a dead bishop could not be ordained until he had paid 500 *solidi* to the royal fisc ... He sent bishops, priests, deacons and other members of the Church, to the number of 4,966 to exile in the desert. (Victor of Vita, Book 2, chs 23, 26)

Yet despite all the words, what stands out is the fact that archaeologically we cannot identify Arianism on the ground, in objects, art or buildings: the Ostrogothic churches in Ravenna in c. AD 500 were, after all, built and orna-mented by local (Roman) and Byzantine artisans and workers, and even if some of the Arian liturgy was distinct we cannot trace these in surviving works and images. There are certainly changed iconographies in some church mosaics (e.g. figures and objects being covered by drapes) after the Byzantine takeover, but these changes mainly blotted out images of Goths.[89]

MONKS AND PILGRIMS

Finally, here we outline two significant movements in the late Roman Christian West: monasticism and pilgrimage. According to the documentary sources, each was an attractive route for rich converts, although archaeologically only monasticism had left much of a signature in the landscape, if often masked by later evolutions; for pilgrimage, except for pilgrim flasks and the relics and churches visited (with crypts as later insertions to enable better flow of pilgrims), texts alone currently tell us of hostels (such as the pilgrim districts around the Vatican from the sixth century).[90] All provinces featured monasteries, and as identified above for Gaul, urban and suburban foundations might be established to honour specific saints or relics and to act as new points of devotion; they were less 'retreats' from the secular world as we picture them for the Middle Ages. These could be small or large communities and could vary greatly in their structural expression: exploiting converted houses, units attached to palaces or comprising houses around a church; in the countryside monasteries might be imposed in active, or often, disused villa sites (e.g. Subiaco, San Vincenzo al Vulturno in central Italy) and sometimes with nearby eremitic monk cells and hideaways. Paulinus of Nola established in *c.* AD 400 a community of monks and nuns, accommodated, he reports, in divided space with paintings of holy men and women on the respective sides and with males with distinctive trimmed hair and the nuns with veils. Female monastic groups became fairly commonplace: later sixth- and seventh-century Gaul had many predominantly female 'double monasteries', which had attached – but separate – groups of male monks to help with manual tasks and to provide priests for liturgies; Anglo-Saxon nobility often sent daughters to these Frankish aristocratic nunneries.[91] Although both male and female communities existed in Egypt and Cappadocia early in the fourth century, pilgrims' travelogues to the Holy Land show monks in both landscape (from village to mountainside) and townscape, but with males very much dominant; nonetheless we know of nunneries set up by the Roman noblewomen Paula and Melania in later fourth-century Palestine. For fourth-century Italy, asceticism was a feature amongst wealthy widows, and there was a strong push by bishops such as Ambrose of Milan in recommending young women to pursue chastity; indeed, there were cries that 'the overthrow of marriage would cause the world to perish and the human race to fail, an argument [Ambrose] sought to turn on its head by claiming that the lands where virginity was practised most widely had the largest populations'.[92]

Monks could be highly active in contemporary society. The noted St Martin of Tours, for example, had been a hermit first at Milan, from where he was expelled (showing he was neither hidden nor quiet), then among other hermits on the island of Gallinaria off the Ligurian Riviera, and later at Poitiers in Gaul, till called upon by admirers to set up a monastery. Elected bishop of Tours in 371, he created a further monastery at Marmoutier, which was his launch pad for quasi-military missions to depaganise the landscape around.[93]

Bishops, monks and hermits were combined in the offshore seat of Lérins, east of Marseilles, which hosted ascetics before Abbot Honoratus organised these into a community in *c.* AD 400 and established a training school. This produced many influential monks selected as mainland bishops who founded monasteries in their own urban dioceses.[94] Such monasteries would hold lands, produce crops and contain libraries, and thereby denote a mix of working and religious foci; they were probably fairly well integrated at this stage with towns and the wider Church structure.

Occasional textual survivals offer a window into how the contemporary world was perceived by monks. For earlier fifth-century Gaul, a province disturbed by Vandal and Suevic incursions and subsequent warfare with Visigoths, two poetical sources, Prosper of Aquitaine's *Carmen ad Uxorem* and the *Carmen de Providentia Dei*, are illuminating. In the first, Prosper urges his wife to join him in devoting her life to Christ, since all is collapsing around in the face of warfare, plague and food shortages. The *Carmen de Providentia Dei* shocks readers by enumerating the destruction of churches, beating of bishops, murder of hermits and rape of virgins, alongside observing overgrown fields, deserted courtyards and burnt-out villas; the *Carmen* stresses how salvation lies in spiritual renewal. The elite were, of course, the audience, and so the language and metaphors used relating to villas, estates and palaces were designed to strike strong chords with landowners whose wealth and livelihoods were threatened.[95] Such vicissitudes certainly induced some Gallic elites to head East, either moving with family and portable wealth or else taking the path of pilgrimage.[96]

Helena, mother of Constantine, represents a first imperial pilgrim, visiting and embellishing early Christian sites in the Holy Land and bringing back a first powerful relic, namely the True Cross. By disseminating this (splinters abound as relics in Western churches) and bringing back other relics to Rome (for churches like Santa Croce in Gerusalemme, the Lateran), the city's status was also enhanced, creating additional pilgrim points and, in time, bringing much traffic and revenue.[97] It also prompted other major churches to seek relics.

We can neither pinpoint numbers of pilgrims nor their roots and tactics regarding funds and their own fortunes. Many were certainly once wealthy and had renounced their moneys and lands to become pilgrims, but others clearly returned to their homelands and needed funds to pay for travel, transit, accommodation, food, guides and protection (such as in obtaining official escorts between sites and stopping off in forts). Thus, travelogues such as that of the anonymous 'Bordeaux pilgrim' in 333 or of Egeria (a Spanish nun?) in the 380s show trips were drawn out or even multiple and required gifts and donations to churches, shrines and monasteries visited. In return, pilgrims might gain relics which could add prestige to a recipient church or monastery back home. Other pilgrims saw the Holy Land as an end destination. Alternatively, pious individuals and communities sent alms and gifts to monks in the Holy Land so as to avoid the long travel.

CHRISTIANITY AFFIRMED

By AD 500, the powers and authorities that urban and rural communities looked up to in the old Western provinces were quite different to those of AD 300. The third-century crises had brought fear and panic on various levels, including religion, centred in large measure on the need for loyalty to the State: damage to the image of the emperor and of other major cults was matched by persecutions against Christians who failed to accept the imperial deities. More study is needed to see if certain pagan cults faltered or were rejected and to question why others, such as Mithras, may have been reinforced. Yet, as shown, there is no clear pattern: why, for example, do some of the Mithraic temples along Hadrian's Wall appear to end early in the fourth century, even before Christianity makes a formal appearance? Was pagan cult survival strongest in the largest towns or in the smallest? Did the persecutions have the effect of enticing more to the Christian fold through acts of martyrdom and resistance? The general uncertainties of the fourth century appear matched by the stuttering growth of the early Church, its varied heresies and the oft-repeated and presumably partly ineffectual legislation against pagan rites. But by the fifth century, religious choice was curtailed and elite expressions of church building and charity (and job-hunting), combined with the demise of relict pagan buildings, began to create more rounded Christianised urban and rural landscapes. As seen in Chapter 5 of this book, the capital of Ravenna is one site where this Christian dominance is evident in the array of extant monumental churches.

Fifth-century upheavals did much to enhance the Church and its leaders – papal embassies to enemies, churches spared damage, tales of bishops and monks protecting and feeding populations, saints providing miracles gave a different, mental trust which no longer lay with the emperor and his armies, who did little to secure lands and settlements. One guide to this is the sixth-century *Life of Sainte-Geneviève*, which recounts how the noblewoman Genofeva, in 451, when news of Attila the Hun's invasion over the Rhine reached the city of Paris, reassured its residents that they would not need to barricade themselves up behind the island's ramparts; her prayers, her journey to Troyes to collect grain to alleviate a shortage and various other acts and miracles strengthened the resolve of the Parisian community in these last phases of Roman rule. Genofeva even aided in Paris's peaceful transition to Frankish rule, reputedly dealing with the Frankish King Childeric and later Clovis, perhaps even encouraging the latter's conversion to Catholic Christianity. Key also was her foundation of the church of Saint Denis. Her death in c.502 in her 80s saw a rapid elevation to sainthood and as heavenly guardian of Paris. The acts of such heroines were recorded and embellished to serve as beacons of hope to communities no longer in a Roman world. Indeed, in Genofeva's case, the new Frankish dynasty of Clovis tied itself to her sanctity by dedicating a new church near her tomb in her name and then helped diffuse her cult.[98] Such churches and tombs, sometimes extant, sometimes buried under medieval expansions and rebuildings, can provide the tangible and material links to this transforming of space and society in the late Roman and post-Roman centuries.

7

Communications, Trade and Land

INTRODUCTION

From reading early Church historians or texts such as the *Liber Pontificalis*, and from describing Christian basilicas and their contents, the fourth and fifth centuries could be seen as active, expansive and wealthy: the Church occupied urban and rural spaces, gained patronage from elites and sent missions to the countryside, populating this with chapels, monasteries and even new land-lords. Towns remained across the fourth century points of administration, taxation, redistribution, religion and industry. Army ties to towns increased and, as observed, in the fifth century, billeting and urban garrisons necessitated additional burdens of supply (grain, wine, cloth, wood, metal). Both towns and armies could only function effectively with secure logistics and so required lands and hinterlands that were able to produce and communications systems that facilitated movement and redistribution. All towns had grana-ries, perhaps with larger ones in the late Empire, set inside the defences, per-haps even within converted classical monuments (e.g. the amphitheatre at Tours) – and we have seen fortified grain depots created in frontier provinces like Pannonia and Raetia, signifying State-controlled collection via taxation of food and resources (the *annona*).

Archaeology is crucial for putting flesh on this documentary image of evolv-ing late Roman economics and for showing how towns and State communi-cated, how the landscapes supplied the varied populations and armies, what foods were produced and what objects were traded, and how these systems and products changed in the last centuries of the Roman West. This chapter thus asks the following: how much was damaged by mounting insecurity, heightened taxation and by barbarian raids? Were there failures in farming, trade outputs and communications networks? Did the items of Roman trade and material culture disappear in the fifth century? Previous chapters regis-tered some positives in the trajectories of the Roman State and provinces in the fourth and fifth centuries: most towns continued, the elite utilised and invested in the land (or at least their own villas/estates) across the fourth century, the

Church invested in the landscape and pilgrims and bishops freely travelled by roads and water. Similarly mention has been made of much archaeological evidence for these centuries – coins, ceramics, buildings, boats, bodies, brooches and weapons. What changes and losses occurred and from when?[1]

TRADE AND TRANSPORT I: LAND, MAPS, ROADS

First we can consider communications – vital for framing economic change. Rome's control, unity and, for long periods, stability were articulated principally through sizeable urban centres interlinked by well-made roads and better controlled rivers, and with a secure Mediterranean; all these factors facilitated trade and exchange on a vast scale. Furthermore, provision of a huge army scattered in provinces and along distant borders in particular required efficient production of materials and reliable supply mechanisms for basic commodities such as wine, oil, fish sauce, grain and ceramic lamps. Production on such a scale for 'essentials' enabled cheap prices, ready competition and wide participation in the market (even Cornwall, lacking villas or other Roman structures, had Roman pottery and materials aplenty). Cities and towns with elites and middlemen jostling for prestige, profit and display meanwhile encouraged more specialised productions, craft diversification, extensive trade for precious commodities such as silks and peppers well beyond the Roman borders and also prompted booms in building industries, marked notably by the vast trade in marbles and by architectural and artistic evolutions. Within all this, common coin and credit circulated, providing an apparent economic unity from Carlisle across to Jerusalem. Even if there remained a broad West = Latin, East = Greek divide, learning and language were fluid, and Syrian merchants were as at home in Paris as Spanish metalmongers were on the Black Sea.

Despite all this, personal geographies – knowledge of the world(s) around individuals – were undoubtedly overall small, since for the majority, daylight time was consumed largely in work, if often meaning for many moving between town or farm and fields and to markets. But politicians, the well-to-do, large landowners and especially merchants and soldiers knew of bigger worlds and properly tasted of the cosmopolitan geographies of Rome's Empire. Did these personal geographies expand or shrink in the Late Empire? On one level they expanded for many: new names of enemy barbarians, and allied barbarians, surely made people aware of 'others' beyond Rome; paradoxically, this may have meant a narrowed world whereby war and invasion were threats pressing in, making home seem more exposed to danger. Roman religion had meanwhile also long offered tastes of other cultures, and the wild animals at games revealed distant exotica, but these did not percolate to all provinces and all towns. In the fourth century, as paganism and games waned, the advent of Christianity opened another door for the flow of people and ideas: pilgrimages were made to the East, bishops and entourages moved between synods, monks established themselves in the West, iconographies spread and architectural forms were imitated.

How then did Roman road–river–sea transport systems function and evolve? Our current world of easy travel and instantaneous transmission of information is one wholly alien to the first-century Empire: movement of the spoken and written word over distance under Rome could only be ferried in person and could not, therefore, be swift – although then, unlike now, instantaneity would not have been expected and schedules or likely dates of arrival of goods, troops, messengers, tax demands and so on were the norm. Some speed did exist, notably in the form of the imperial post and government freight system (*cursus publicus*)[2]: this persisted still in the fourth century and exploited the same major highways as the army; this enabled official/State messages, personnel and small materials to be relayed over sizeable distances using relays of horse especially, and pack animals and wagons for materials, based at regular stations. Such animals and other services were initially provided at a set rate by locals, but by the late Empire this was a public duty, and free hospitality and accommodation were expected at the official *mansiones* or *mutationes* (rest stations or stage posts – some with attached bath units) on the highways. State functionaries and professional messengers were employed as well as ranked troopers for army dispatches, and these carried official warrants to allow for use of the *cursus*. In the military context, a more flexible dispatch system was necessary using mounted messengers, presumably supplemented by signalling systems, but this was separate from the *cursus publicus*. The *cursus* operated to allow for the official passage of dignitaries of State – including, from the fourth century, Church elite. But it was also a means of eluding potential capture – such as when the Praetorian Prefect Taurus in AD 361 fled the approaching army of Julian by 'using the quick relays of the public post service to cross the Julian Alps'. The *cursus* continued under Germanic regimes, under Ostrogoths in Italy (see below) and under Vandals in Africa, as shown in AD 483 when King Hunirix dispatched an edict 'by speeding post horses, to the whole of Africa' (Victor of Vita, Book 2, ch. 38).

The maps that existed in the Roman world link to the necessary mobility of State officials and soldiery: paper-route summaries such as contained in the third-century *Itinerarium Antonini* listed stations and distances between these. The late Roman military strategist Vegetius reveals their wider application (III.6), especially when supplemented by up-to-date and local data (i.e. local guides):

> First he [the general] should have itineraries of all regions in which war is being waged written out in the fullest detail, so that he may learn the distances between places by the number of miles and the quality of the roads, and examine short-cuts, by-ways, mountains and rivers, accurately described. Indeed, the more conscientious generals reportedly had itineraries of the provinces in which the emergency occurred not just annotated but illustrated as well, so that they could choose their route when setting out by the visual aspect as well as by mental calculation.

To the State bureaucracy, knowledge of lengths of journeys required in provincial tours, tax gatherings and postings of official notices were invaluable.

The itinerary and related accounts for Theophanes, a member of staff for the prefect of Egypt in the 320s, record routes, mileages and costs incurred (official and personal – for himself plus accompanying staff and slaves), presumably to demonstrate use of the *cursus* in appropriate fashion. Less common were the roll-up 'maps' with schematic imagery of seas, rivers and mountains and with standardised vignettes of towns and stations, such as depicted on the 6.75-m long *Tabula Peutingeriana* (now argued to be of private origin and not a State publication). Such maps undoubtedly existed in the offices of all key major provincial staff – witness how the Peutinger Table's parchment places Rome at the heart of the vast provincial sprawl. Comparable sea itineraries (*períploi*) existed: the fascinating *Periplus of the Erythraean Sea*, composed *c.* AD 100 and revealing Rome's trade links (or rather links by individual Roman traders) with east Africa, Arabia and India, primarily enumerates ports and approaches, while giving a handy checklist of 'best buys' at certain places. Maps and roads were likewise invaluable to the new travellers of the late Roman/antique world – pilgrims.[3]

There were standard routes for supplying goods to troops, but tolls were required on specific routes such as through the Egyptian desert to the marble quarries of Mons Claudianus or Mons Porphyrites. Most ordinary people knew only of their local roads, and 'road itineraries' were alien to them, but we do know of incised stone 'local' route-lists at towns like Tongres and Autun, presumably displayed at gates; where people did venture out on the highways, milestones were posted to inform travellers of the distances yet to traverse; otherwise natural landmarks and known farms were the easier guides. We might think that merchants used all manner of routeways, but often a key port or town on a river artery was the main drop-off point for merchandise, after which local trading networks came into play.

Since trade persists throughout the Roman period, communications and their support systems must likewise have persisted. Roads were key in this infrastructure, and in the *Codex Theodosianus*, edicts in Book 15 on Public Work identify how it was a public duty to help build and repair roads: governors held overall responsibility but made individual towns responsible for maintaining roads within their civic territories; the burden fell also on private landowners across the landscape. The State elite might avoid such burdens, but it is noteworthy that in AD 399, at a time when rapid movement of troops and supplies was vital in Italy, the Emperors Arcadius and Honorius at Milan directed this edict (*CT* 15.3.4) to the Praetorian Prefect Messala: 'It was formerly established that the patrimonies of Illustrious dignitaries should be considered exempt from the construction and repair of roads. But on account of the immense ruin of the highways, it is Our will that all persons, with helpful devotion, shall eagerly desire to hasten to the repair of the public roads.' These were not minor jobs: most main Roman routeways were significant investments, and construction, metalling and repair were costly in time and resources. The survival of many Roman routeways into the medieval period and even in the landscape today demonstrates their general quality. But constant use by heavy wheeled traffic in and out of towns required regular maintenance; not every Roman community had funds, materials or even manpower for this, nor the technical know-how for instances where bridges were broken. Brigands deliberately blocked sections of road to aid their efforts, and sometimes natural damage took much time to be cleared. Thus, when the Poet-Senator Rutilius Namatianus travels in AD 416 from Rome to his battered estates in Gaul, he reports, 'I will travel by water because roads can flood or be littered by slides and falling rocks; Tuscany and the Aurelian Highway have already fallen to the Goths. It is best to trust the sea because the rivers are not bridged and the land has become wild again' (Rut. Nam., *De Reditu Suo*, I. 3942). For sixth-century central Italy, Cassiodorus (*Variae* XII.18) requests repairs to the Via Flaminia, 'furrowed by the action of torrents': the *vir experientissimus* Constantianus is asked to 'join the yawning chasms by the broadest of bridges; clear away the rough woods which choke the sides of the highway; procure the stipulated number of post-horses, and see that they have all the points which are required in good steed; and collect the designated quantities of provisions without plundering the peasants'.

Anxieties regarding control and serviceability of roads appear in the texts of milestones, which gain a new prominence in the fourth century. In the frontier provinces and even in central ones such as Italy and Gaul, instances of these large, monolithic (usually) cylindrical inscribed stones become frequent along the major highways. The route from Verona to Trento across the Resia and Brenner Passes in the Alps into Austria/Raetia, for example, features various milestones of the Tetrarchs and especially of Maxentius of AD 306–12, as well as examples belonging to the reigns of Constantine, Julian, Crispus, Valens and Gratian, and Maximus.[4] These particular routes were for the imperial post and for the mobile armies, moving towards the frontiers or between key provincial urban centres; these were the roads therefore needing most maintenance and were probably the best policed – although as major highways, pickings for thieves and larger bands of brigands would also have been larger. The texts of many of the milestones were far more imperial dedications than distance markers, inscribed in honour of the living and current emperor(s) or highlighting work by local elites and their commitment to restoring/maintaining the roads. Harder to explain are the five late third- and fourth-century 'milestones' from Cornwall in south-western Roman Britain, an area seemingly devoid of military roads and towns: someone/bodies here felt the need to display knowledge of the emperors and to indicate attachment to the distant State; conceivably they were messages on roads leading to/from the important tin sites to maritime tradesmen.

TRADE AND TRANSPORT II: SHIPS, WATERWAYS, PORTS

The vast distribution of items across the Empire reveals a secure control of the Mediterranean, ready urban and port markets (with investment in harbour space, warehouses, dredging etc.), wide-scale manpower commitment (e.g. slaves, port workers, shipping companies), efficient vessels (including substantial sea-going vessels), a security of movement and people eager to make money. Visits to the archaeological sites of Ostia and Portus offer ample guides to this investment of resources, space and technology in trade operations.[5] Roman shipping – from canal boats and barges (with goods transferred at ports from bigger vessels to smaller riverine crafts) to vessels designed to carry cargoes of wine, oil or fish-sauce amphorae (these themselves mass-produced in a format designed for hold-stacking) to huge grain ships owned or financed by the State to ply across the Mediterranean to bring food to Rome and, later, Constantinople (or to bring here and to other cities marbles – such as 140-ton columns cut and transported from the Egyptian desert or more 'locally' from the Carrara quarries of the Italian Riviera or from Proconessus) – are attested by text, graffiti, paintings and especially by excavated wreck sites, which are widespread throughout the Mediterranean. Wreck numbers are strongest for the first three centuries AD, in part due to the visibility of the material culture (big cargoes are more easily identifiable) and a reflection of the greater scale of traffic within the Mediterranean, especially across that time frame.[6]

Analysis of the ceramic evidence from excavated sites meanwhile identifies points of production and distribution of oil, wine and fish-sauce amphorae as well as other ceramic types, helping to chart shifts from, for example, Italian to Spanish to North African markets across the first three centuries AD – again reflecting a busy, 'open' market, with many regions in many provinces contributing to such flow, and signifying high agricultural productivities.[7] Well known is the artificial Monte Testaccio near the Aventine Hill in Rome, located close to the Tiber and the vast State warehouses alongside the river and its wharves: 35-m high and covering 22,000 m², Monte Testaccio comprises millions of fragments of broken amphorae (perhaps around 50 million vessels) of first- to mid-third-century date, indicating dumping not just of broken cargoes but of containers dumped after transfer of liquids or other goods into sacks, skins and barrels for onward transportation. The material has a strong Spanish emphasis – up to 85 per cent of the total derive from Baetica. There is no comparable fourth- to fifth-century dump in terms of scale, but a 'piccolo Testaccio' is claimed downriver of the first, and a possible waste pile is postulated for Monte Citorio, close to Marcus Aurelius' Column. Certainly the scale of importation remained high in these centuries, if with noticeable changes in content and origin: North African, Syrian, Egyptian and Spanish amphorae, tableware and lamps are well attested in Rome (and most other major centres in both West and East), recovered in urban and rural middens; however, for Rome, the emphasis was now North African (for oil) and eastern Mediterranean (for wine). Most likely Baetican production continued apace, but was transported directly to Western sites, stores and troops as part of the *annona* supplies, and more widely as traded goods (as duly registered in urban and fort sites like Trier and Mainz).[8]

Surprisingly, there are strikingly few later Roman cargo wrecks known: in Parker's (1992) survey, of 1,259 likely Roman wrecks, only 54 fourth- and fifth-century sites were recorded. Why the imbalance? Additional late Roman wrecks have since been added, including one secure wreck (the *Isis*) and three likely others, victims of the Skerki Bank reef off north-west Sicily (there were also three likely medieval wrecks here).[9] The *Isis* debris covered about 10 m² and should represent a boat of 15-m length, of shell-first construction, belonging potentially to an independent merchant and not a State-employed grain shipper. Finds comprised just 10 complete amphorae, some cooking wares (including a pot from Pantelleria, an island halfway between Sicily and Carthage), a lamp, millstone and anchors (including spares); the amphorae were a mixture of Tunisian and south Italian (Calabrian), and one from Asia Minor; their interiors showed pitch lining and indicated fish preserves/paste and some oil as the contents. This was either a tradesman moving round the east and south coasts of the Mediterranean or one who plied his small-scale trade between North Africa and south/central Italy only (picking up the Asian amphora at a market in Carthage); the wreck indicates that he was one who braved (perhaps fatally) open/deep sea routes rather than taking the more protected route on the east flank of Sicily. The finds and C14 dating of the timbers reveal a late fourth- or earliest fifth-century shipment – no doubt one of a high number of merchants carrying selected cargoes, perhaps crossing alongside and in the security of larger State vessels.

Of slightly later date are the more recently discovered remains of at least 11 seagoing vessels of 15- to 30-m length in the ancient port of Olbia in north-east Sardinia.[10] While cargoes could not be easily assigned to these boats (some may have just been unloaded, or else various of the sunken goods were salvaged), associated North African manufactured tablewares, lamps and amphorae, plus coins signify a calamitous early fifth-century event, potentially linked to a Vandal assault – either sunk by the aggressors or deliberately sunk by the defenders to block access into the port. Far to the north, of presumed military function, meanwhile, were the fourth-century ships found at Mainz in 1981–82, with Ship 5, dendrochronologically dated to *c.* AD 390, preserving a distinctive warship's prow; all were fast-rowing ships for patrol and engagement along the Rhine, with shallow draughts but with provision of a mast.[11]

These newer discoveries show that many more late Roman wrecks are likely to be found to testify to the continuity of trade, traders and shipping into the fifth century and beyond. Their traffic is, of course, reflected also in ongoing port facilities at Portus, Rome as elsewhere (although for Portus demolition of some former *annona* warehouses from *c.* AD 450 probably signifies transhipment to barges for immediate transfer up the canal and Tiber to Rome).[12] The excavations in Carthage (see *Introduction*) have provided fascinating details on the vitality of the port installations of this late Roman capital.[13] Carthage was famous for its circular port and dry boathouses which formed safe berths for State ships and barges; to the west lay the commercial (or rectangular) port. Carthage had long played an important maritime trade role, but from the fourth century the level of outward trade expanded, in terms of wine, oil and ceramics. In chief this linked into the *annona* and the supply of grain to

Rome (see below). Certainly the start of the fifth century is marked by much reorganisation of space at Carthage's ports, with the commercial one provided with new, large, stone-built warehouses on the west side, with vaulted foundations; to the north of the circular harbour, two-storeyed, porticoed buildings comprising shops, stores, houses and workshops were erected, replacing less well-built earlier units – these new buildings suggestive of bases for small enterprises (notably cloth making) and merchants. This vitality of trading diminishes with the Vandal takeover, primarily with the cessation of North Africa's role as grain supplier to Rome (the new focus becoming Sicily with its large imperial and senatorial estates and Church lands), although it is very evident that ceramics and olive oil remained core exports. The circular port then slips out of use, mainly due to a failure to maintain dredging operations to keep the waterways clear of silt and sand. Nonetheless, the Byzantine takeover from the 530s sees renewal works and a heightening of trade production; the archaeology accordingly shows the larger, open port works continuing into the mid-sixth century at least.

Problems of late Roman maintenance can be observed elsewhere through archaeology. At Olbia in Sardinia, where the ship excavations also found traces of jetties and quays, two port sectors were noted, these divided by a natural land spit: after enforced abandonment of the southern space (at least two wrecks were buried under thick mud) by c. AD 200, the northern quays became favoured, protected by a mole linking the port to the isola Peddona. Some disaster caused the sinking of 11 late Roman ships – perhaps victims of defensive blockade measures – in so doing compromising access to the port; although sixth- to ninth-century material is known in the port debris, where later boats docked is unclear. A second site is the well-excavated Luni (Roman *Luna*) on the north-west coast of Italy. This Republican colony saw major early imperial growth on account of the massive exploitation of the famous (still active) marble quarries of nearby Carrara, with the fine white marble being shipped south and elsewhere in the Mediterranean and beyond – some pieces even making it to London. But growth stalls at Luni in the wider third-century crisis, and reduced private and public munificence across the Empire meant diminishing demand for new cut marble. As a result Luni saw stagnation: the forum is largely redundant as a public space by c. AD 400, part covered by soil, and few buildings are repaired after earthquake damage in the latter fourth century; most significantly, the port slowly silted up and the coast receded (Luni is now some way from the sea). Nonetheless, the land was good enough to support a continuing, more compact urban community and some marble extraction persisted (on a private entrepreneurial, not State, level); Luni even became a bishop's seat from the fifth century, and the archaeology shows revival in the sixth century with good quantities of imported wine, oil and ceramics – but these perhaps more in connection with the presence of a Byzantine garrison and general. How the port and harbour functioned in this phase is unclear.[14]

Similar problems surfaced even in the more secure Eastern Mediterranean provinces, which were central to much of the trade flow in Late Antiquity. To note just two sites in Palestine, first, Tel Dor possessed one of the few natural harbours in the province, supplemented by artificial Roman (and Hellenistic) works and de-silting channels to facilitate shipping and offloading, plus rock-cut boat-bays for shallow-draught boats. But a sea rise in *c*. AD 200 flooded these larger installations, and instead of revising these, shipping reverted to offshore anchorages. Despite this, seven wrecks and 12 recovered anchors of fourth century and later date reveal it continued as a busy port. Second, at *Caesarea Maritima*, massive first-century BC investment (particularly under Herod) created the artificial harbour of *Sebastos*, through sinking barges and caissons with concrete to form moles and breakwaters and spaces for basins, quays, warehouses and promenades. Although there was later silting and tectonic slumping, the harbour still functioned, as shown by finds and ongoing warehouse construction. Only when dredging occurred in the sixth century and repairs were made to the moles did an effective port re-emerge, persisting into the Islamic period.[15]

Were late Roman failures to dredge and counteract silting due to manpower shortages, lack of technical skills or increased river discharge? These cannot yet be easily answered, but fuller geomorphological studies, such as those undertaken in the territory of Luni, will in time aid discussion. What must be recognised, however, is that the solution of offshore anchoraging did not mean a lessening of trade activity; it simply meant that emphasis lay on a system of transshipment which probably had always existed, using small ferries or lighters which could then be beached and offloaded. Another argument is that the size of boats in the later Roman period was reduced (perhaps because of smaller cargoes overall), meaning that more boats could anchor in shallow waters or be beached. Certainly for somewhere like Roman London, the port on the Thames functioned chiefly via barges and smallish seagoing and river vessels, and most other river- and coast-based centres would not have hosted the massive vessels seen arriving at Portus for Rome or at Constantinople. The example of London is also important in showing how archaeology is crucial in documenting the nature and development of waterfronts and related installations and identifying the goods coming in and their sources – all aspects lacking contemporary texts. Such excavations are complex and challenging – especially in centres of constant growth, where Roman works lie buried and disturbed beneath roads and buildings.[16]

FOOD, TRADE AND THE STATE

London's port excavations have shown that although imports continued to arrive into the third and fourth centuries, these became increasingly national and regional rather than international. Numbers of amphorae of oil, wine or fish sauce and ceramic tableware or lamps diminish but do not disappear, suggesting a smaller market – perhaps centred on the civil and military bureaucrats. London came to be served by potting industries based in the Midlands and in Oxfordshire, with (presumably cheaper) goods coming down the Thames. In part this reflects Britain's economic take-off in the third century, being cushioned from the continental traumas, and the industries establishing secure markets in the fourth. Britain is certainly recognised as productive, and Ammianus Marcellinus records grain supplies for troops and towns in Britain, north Gaul and Germany from here. The Rhineland pottery in London, Cirencester as elsewhere might signify shipments returning from such grain dispatches.[17]

One argument is that for the fourth and fifth centuries, partly in response to Tetrarchic changes in terms of provinces and *annona* supply, trade flows became modified. We have noted already how at Rome, the Monte Testaccio debris relates predominantly to Spanish wine and oil inflow to the City, but that after AD 300, Spanish imports drop substantially, with such goods being directed northwards to Gaul, the Rhine and Britain; subsequently for the western Mediterranean, North African products take centre stage – the wine and oil producers profiting from the guaranteed massive flow of goods to Rome in terms of the grain fleet. Further, while the fourth-century witnesses continued penetration of traded goods inland, for the fifth century there is a concentration of coastal and big city trading and importing, with inner sites generally excluded. Major trade for long worked with the *annona* and army supply, but as army units became more localised and supplies were also drawn more locally (hence the arms and cloth factories scattered evenly across the northern provinces), opportunities for movement of long-distance goods diminished. This is not to deny some traders did good business – African olive oil might have become more 'exotic' in, say, Mainz, as a result, but prices would have risen and the market would have shrunk too. Thus we need to be cautious in equating diminishing Mediterranean materials in northern territories with a declining economy – it is more the case of a modified economy, one more regionally determined.

For southern Gaul, with Marseilles as a main source of data, excavated finds show variations in importations: while North African ceramics are well attested, amphorae come from a mix of areas, with Eastern vessels dominant for the late fourth to mid-fifth centuries. Crudely, this might reflect more secure output in the East in this period, although the main disruptions to Gaul and Spain come from the early fifth century onwards. Against this, however, we can note how wine/oil exports from Africa increase from the mid-fifth century – despite this territory now being in Vandal hands. This might in fact reflect a response to new economic needs, whereby Rome had been forced to switch her grain suppliers to Sicily and Sardinia (both regions still busy producing for the City under the popes in the sixth and seventh centuries), and so the Vandal (and remaining African-Roman) elite upped trading efforts in the western Mediterranean (the Vandal raids documented for the 440s and 450s against Sicily, Sardinia and Italy probably preceded this renewed trading effort).[18] Indeed, looking to the materials themselves, studies of Tunisian centres producing African red slip (ARS) ware from the mid-third century into the sixth reveal extensive workshops and complex, but little understood, production and distribution networks.[19] Two key sites are El Mahrine near Carthage and, in central Tunisia, Sidi Marzouk Tounsi, offering data on the ranges and methods of production in terms of firing materials, wasters (discarded, distorted or misfired pieces), kiln structures and clay punches (for the characteristic stamped decorations) (Figure 7.1). The complex at Sidi Marzouk Tounsi covered up to 40 ha and was probably linked to a nearby villa estate and its extensive olive groves – the latter providing cuttings and dried pulp for kiln-firing. The vessels produced here comprised plates and small bowls with varied stamped motifs, including cross-monograms, figures (animals mainly, of Christian connotation, notably doves, fishes) and floral designs. The main period of manufacture of this new decorative repertoire at Sidi Marzouk Tounsi belongs to *c.* AD 440–510/530, that is, the full Vandal period; ready markets lay in Gaul, Italy and Greece.

Crudely, one might state that in the early imperial period, when manpower (and slavery) levels were high, trade was widespread and frontiers were secure, so production and storage of crops (grain, oil, wine etc.) were never major concerns. Most Roman colonies and towns were planted to exploit suited and adequate hinterlands, and to utilise both river and road communications, but a site like Luni with its specialised economic role shows that such towns, strongly dependent on external food supplies, could also prosper. Bad harvests might occur but the Empire and its trade were extensive enough that shortfalls in one area could be compensated for (at due financial cost) from elsewhere; after all, Roman town administrators as well as ordinary householders must have been fully aware of the need to plan and store ahead for winter months, and were aware that harvests vary in quality and quantity from year to year. Despite this, however, our sources suggest recourse generally to reactive emergency measures rather than long-term strategies, with a reliance on private enterprise. In many areas specialised

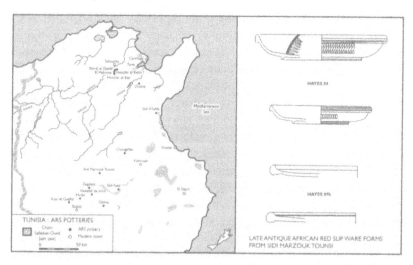

Figure 7.1 Fifth-century ARS production sites in Tunisia and a sample of products (after Mackensen 1998)

production was evident (e.g. for wine and oil); presumably, local municipal attention was turned to ensuring grain supplies were adequate alongside these (but not for an export market). We know less about animals in this context (except for the large flocks of sheep and herds of swine that helped feed Rome); while the bulk was no doubt stocked on farms and common land outside towns, some urban households probably possessed a few animals for their own needs. Communities were, overall, primarily self-sufficient – that is, their local territories provided suitable lands for varied crop and livestock-raising – with roads and water communications to facilitate wider input, such as the movement of transhumant flocks across wide territories for summer pasturage.

In contrast, the capitals were the ones whose hinterlands needed supplementing on substantial scales – especially where high elite and court presences existed. For cities like Milan, perhaps attaining up to 100,000 residents, the Po plain and river were essential supports, but a large population also meant a large market and traders were naturally drawn to these. Far less easy to picture is the scale of operations to maintain Rome and its estimated population of 1 million for the period AD 1–350. Rome's own immediate hinterland has been shown by archaeological survey (notably in the south Etruria region and Tiber Valley to the north and north-east) to be busy with farmers – whether small-scale or large landowners – and with industrial and other economic activities (tufa and travertine quarries, brick and tile production, charcoal burning, tree felling, water management); all were articulated strongly around the main rivers, notably the Tiber, and highways, and there must have been a near continuous flow of goods into, and empty carts and barges out of, Rome.[20] In a much later time span, by AD 800, the popes had established a net of estates around the city to help supply and feed the Church, the poor and the flocks of pilgrims with grain, oil and wine, supplemented by goods from farther-flung estates in Sicily and Sardinia especially. This was sufficient for an urban population then standing at perhaps 75,000, but for the mid-imperial city, Rome's 'hinterland' far outstripped central Italian heartlands and southern Italian estates and their resources: for oil and wine it looked overseas, and wide tracts of the landscapes of eastern Spain (such as the Ager Tarraconensis), coastal North Africa and north Syria must have been given over to specialised mass production to meet Rome's perpetual demands – though with many elite landowners generating fortunes as a result, enabling additional landed and human investment.[21] To give an idea of the scale of operations, estimates point to a minimum figure of 20 l (litres) of oil per person per year in Rome, giving a total of 18,000 metric tons for Rome's 1 million, and for wine (at 100 l per person per year), 100,000 metric tons. With amphorae to add in plus ship sizes, Mattingly and Aldrete propose an absolute minimum of 1,702 shiploads reaching Rome a year, with the truncated sailing year (of about 100 days) requiring 17 ships per day coming to Ostia/Portus; they estimate about 4.5 million amphorae, 4.5 million grain sacks, plus 9 million 'porter-loads'. Understandably, the depots and warehouses in Ostia, Portus and along the Tiber in Rome were vast,[22] and ideally these held extra stores to cope with shortages. The system clearly functioned successfully for a long time, but disruptions to regional production and trade systems could create problems; as observed, the Mediterranean for long remained 'secure' to enable the required flow of goods, but from the early fifth century, Spain and then North Africa became less stable, and the Vandal takeover in the south Mediterranean must have been particularly telling.

Logistics remained vast for feeding Rome even in the 450s when the city population is meant to have been in decline – with some elite transfers (plus entourages) to Constantinople, loss of the court and so on – perhaps trimmed to around 300,000 persons. Even then, its population was unmatched, save for Constantinople, and simply ensuring weekly provision of vegetables and meat from the surrounding countryside would have been a major undertaking. Regarding fresh meat, Rome continued to draw on southern Italy; thus for 452, an edict (*Nov. Val.* 36) to the praetorian prefect (the man responsible for ensuring Rome stayed fed) concerning 'swine collectors, cattle collectors and sheep and goat collectors' and particularly the re-established guild of swine collectors (these centred on the provinces of Lucania, Samnium and Campania) requires the collectors to furnish 100,000 lb of pork and, in total, 3,629,000 lb of meat to Rome for 150 days each year – all implying a vast rearing, feeding and then transportation (on the hoof) programme, organised between different communities, stockholders, landholders and officials. It would have required not only suitable provision and maintenance of woodland and other pasturage but also provision of shepherds, herders, plus policing of these trains of animals en route to Rome.[23] Warfare and military demands could seriously undermine such supply systems and provoke shortages and disease – hence for AD 451 an edict from Valentinian III to the General Aetius (*Nov. Val.* 33) recognises how 'Very recently the most terrible famine raged throughout all Italy and men were forced to sell their children and parents/kin to escape the danger of threatening death'. Disease hit animals too: for example, Paulinus of Nola records locals bringing sick cattle to the shrine of St Felix to ask the saint to cure them, and a Gallo-Roman friend of Paulinus, Endelechius, composed a poem *On the Deaths of the Cattle*, claiming that the sign of the cross applied to the foreheads of one herd protected them from the 'fierce pestilence' that had necessitated the slaughter of many animals.

How regular the grain and wine fleets were in the fifth century is hard to determine: the documented sieges and blockades of Rome by Alaric, the Vandal raids and sack, and wider Vandal activity in the Mediterranean must have meant uncertainties and severe problems in creating adequate stockpiles. The changing system of transshipping materials direct to Rome rather than storing at Portus, borne out in the archaeological evidence at the port, signifies how Rome's authorities tried to avoid potential loss of supplies. What seems evident also, archaeologically, is that Rome's hinterland did not respond well to the changed circumstances – the landscapes of the fifth and sixth centuries are in no way as busy as those of the earlier Empire. Life in the big city was no longer one of potential excesses.[24]

Tensions between East and West and civil conflicts also prompted exclusion orders and even physical blockades of ports. Thus an edict of AD 408 issued at Ravenna in Italy informs us that 'The public enemy Stilicho devised a new and unaccustomed practice, in that he had fortified the shores and harbours by numerous guards so that there should be no access to this part of the Empire for any person from the Eastern Empire. We are disturbed by the injustice of this situation, and in order that the interchange of different commodities may not become too infrequent, We command by this sanction that this pernicious guarding of shores and harbours shall cease and that there shall be free opportunity to come and go' (CT 7.16.1). Distrust and insecurity clearly persisted, since in AD 440 Theodosius and Valentinian call for Greek tradesmen to return to Rome to live and trade there, 'even though dissension and the very great envy of the [non-Greek] shopkeepers rather than the welfare of the venerable city of Rome has removed them from business'; thereby 'abundance may be furnished to the people, and during these critical times [i.e. Vandal threat] the city may be inhabited by a greater multitude' (Nov. Val. 5.1).

The laws also show farmers, landowners and merchants struggling to meet what became increasingly desperate demands from the Italian State authorities. Various edicts report remission of taxes for certain war years or recognise the inability of certain zones to perform effectively: 'The accumulated supplies of the State storehouses [i.e. probably Rome's] shall hope for nothing from these 20 years [AD 407–27]; the chest of the Most August Prefecture shall hope for nothing; Our two treasuries shall hope for nothing' (CT 11.28.16, issued in 433). For central Italy in 418, 'Campania ... shall bear only a ninth part of the past amount of payments to the State, since a very heavy tax assessment of former times burdens her territory, and since that assessment, she has been devastated by the incursion of the enemy [the Visigoths]' (CT 11.28.12). However, even following Vandal incursions of Sicily and Sardinia in 440, Valentinian III's edict to the prefect maximus (Nov. Val. I.2) stresses how some tax must still be forthcoming, since the army must be provided for:

> The remission of tribute which was granted in consideration of the nature of the [Vandal] devastation affords an incentive for renewed devotion. Health cannot be restored when diseases attack, unless the medicine affords its own effectiveness ... The landholders of Sicily, together with the surrounding islands, in consideration of the barbarian devastation, must pay to the fiscal tribute a seventh part of that tax assessment which is contained in the present records.

Such laws centre strongly on the home province, and while we lack details elsewhere, the hardships and demands must have been equally high – with the result in some instances, as seen, of usurpations and break away groups seeking to salvage matters and counter an increasingly oppressive State.

LANDSCAPE CHANGES

But were farmers being forced off the land? Does the landscape falter and do farms and products fall out of use? The law codes imply food resources were still being provided, but with fluctuations and problems increasing in the fifth century. Does the archaeology reflect this documentary image of instability and fear? Is decline a feature of the late Empire generally or solely of the last century of the Roman West? There are certainly many references to devastated and deserted lands, untilled soil, spoiled crops and scared farmers, highlighted especially when sources recount evils perpetrated by enemies (whether barbarian or other Romans) in campaigns, and the imperial edicts stress the pressures of generating surpluses and taxes to feed the State, its armies and its citizens. For long the tendency was to take such claims of *agri deserti* at face value and to recognise cultivated landscapes falling victim, thus reflecting a shrinking rural population and the burden of insecurity. But modern re-evaluations prompt scholars into seeing many of these desertions as tools by landowners to avoid paying taxes; instead of prime agricultural lands, these abandoned spaces are more marginal ones, perhaps upland or reclaimed spaces and pasture, or they are lands which the State is trying to get people to farm to maximise output – they are thus 'uncultivated' rather than 'deserted'.[25] In fact, the texts tend to refer mainly to what were some of the wealthier provinces and regions – such as Byzacena in North Africa and Campania in Italy – where imperial and aristocratic landholdings were prominent. Some larger tracts of land may well have been quitted due to insecurities, but others could have fallen out of use through elites choosing to focus efforts, or else choosing to move away, or even through donating lands to the Church. In the third and fourth centuries the State countered some weaknesses in landscape usage by settling barbarian groups and prisoners of war; to do so around the new capital of Milan seems to speak less of deserted lands and more of a need to up levels of cultivation and productivity in the Po valley to feed the city and court.[26] On the frontiers, such barbarian settlement enabled lands to be cultivated when provincials had grown less secure and had withdrawn (as marked by shrinkage or loss of fort *vici*) – as for Pannonia in the later fourth century. In the fifth century there were, of course, the major added problems of wider barbarian movements, and this impacted especially on some of the larger elite landowners, whose properties we know were dispersed across different provinces – figures such as Melania, Symmachus, Sidonius and Rutilius Namatianus. The loss of Britain, fragmented control in Gaul and Spain and, most damagingly for many senators in Rome, the Vandal occupation of North Africa would have meant estates lost, profits cut, product supply curtailed and control over workers broken. Yet such Roman loss did not mean a cessation of farming in these areas. In North Africa, new Vandal landlords took over but largely maintained existing estates, labour forces, outputs and administration. Thus, comparison between two well-known mosaic images from Carthage – one of a complex villa with country scenes of the late fourth century (that of Dominus Iulius), the other a Vandal-period scene of an aristocrat riding out from his equally well-appointed villa – shows a continuity of elite landed expression.[27]

The documentary pictures – of either desertion or continuity – can now be checked against the archaeological record, which, for rural studies, has grown enormously in the past 30 years especially. A host of summary guides, regional overviews, survey reports and excavations are available to illustrate Roman landscape use and evolution, and to explore late Roman and early medieval rural settlement in both Western and Eastern Empires.[28] Sections above have more than flagged the maintained outputs of exports and thus surpluses of oil, wine, grain, plus ceramics across the final centuries of Roman rule in the West and later; all these testify to both markets and workers/producers and active landscapes. To a large degree the archaeology – primarily field survey data (analysis of material evidence recovered on the surface of fields and sites), combined with targeted villa and farm excavations – reveals at least the rudiments of this rural activity. In particular the archaeology provides good evidence of the densities, scales, distributions and qualities of settlement on the land, although there are imbalances, with an emphasis still centred on the larger rural sites, the villas, and with imprecise understanding of the actual peasant workers (including those living on the villa estates); it is easier to spot stone- or brick-built complexes than timber-built units and harder to trace workers and livelihoods where minimal identifiable pottery is recovered (true for long stretches of the early Middle Ages in many regions).[29]

Equally important is the fact that only careful excavation can recover full sequences of site transformation, as borne out especially in recent detailed studies in Spain, which possesses a rich bank of well-excavated villa sites.[30] Understanding these higher status residences is essential to understanding patterns of land ownership, investment of resources as reflections of landed output, late Roman social and economic changes, and transitions from Roman control.[31] The fabric of such sites – room sizes, designs, mosaics, material culture – and their evolution – such as in the redesigning of space, disuse of sectors, insertions of chapels and burial insertions – also help chart losses of 'Roman' culture. As with late Roman towns, villas are not all alike and each must be understood in context – again something not easily achievable. For late Roman Spain we find changes that mirror other Mediterranean provinces of the West, with resonances also for northern territories: first is the substantial flourishing of many villas in the fourth century, marked often by architectural redesigning, with reception rooms, new bath suites and expanded mosaic schemes and sculpture collections. This villa 'boom' continues in some areas, such as in the fertile and vast plains of Lusitania (and along valleys such as the Ebro and Duero – major sites include La Olmeda and Torre de Palma), into the early fifth century and is seen partly as a 'retreat' of the elite to the countryside to avoid towns and also as a sign of the accumulation of landed wealth into a smaller number of hands.[32] But the pattern is not constant, as some areas see a diminished role for larger villas from the third century in terms of habitation and display, and yet often these persist, becoming chiefly working centres, with insertions related to productive processes (presses, kilns, storage dolia), with indications of specialisations in wine, oil or fish production (e.g. at Torreblanca del Sol the baths were reworked for fish processing). These sites tend to be those on the south and east coasts and should denote economic investments to exploit busy trading demands (State and private) across the third and fourth centuries.

Economic expansions should explain villa expansions in contemporary Britain, although here we might not assume all were native landowners and aristocrats – as noted, records of late fourth-century Mediterranean and Italian senatorial elites owning far-flung properties in Britain, Gaul and Africa reflect how there were beady eyes for profit across the whole Empire; but how often such elites visited each of their estates or actually invested in foreign residential villas is unknown. British villas certainly took on major complexity compared to their precursors and show 'currency' with trends in core provinces: our problem lies, however, in too many of the better known sites like Woodchester, Great Witcombe and Chedworth (all in Gloucestershire – the late Romano-British equivalent of the Spanish Lusitanian plains) having been exposed prior to modern scientific excavation techniques, meaning that their latest phases are poorly understood (although other sites like Frocester Court have seen recent analysis and have far more to say about sequences of decay, conversion and loss).[33]

Very striking is the proliferation of late Roman villas across the Danube and Balkan provinces, notably Pannonia and Moesia, thus in territories presumed most susceptible to barbarian raids. But this was also the zone from which many later third- and fourth-century emperors (and usurpers) were drawn and through which many emperors moved on campaign or on checks of the river frontiers; there are sufficient data to indicate, for example, that certain substantial villa complexes, such as Parndorf near Carnuntum, were either imperial in ownership or held by governors and hosted imperial visits (e.g. by Valentinian I in 375). The larger sites lie near main roads, often in proximity to regional capitals. Mulvin's analysis of the plans and architectural developments of 64 main sites shows the majority originate in the second century, with peaks for a number in the fourth century, but there are also new foundations in both third and fourth centuries.[34] From c. AD 300, apsidal reception and dining rooms, corridors and courtyards define a modified elite villa architecture, presumably matching trends in palace architecture; scattered survivals of mosaics and sculptures are additional components of display – these again all in line with trends in Hispania and in the core Mediterranean zones. A small number offer clear traces of Christian insertions – chapels or larger church buildings, burial areas, even baptisteries – which might relate to the owner's own religion or could denote Episcopal presences, with some villas donated to or inherited by the Church (see Chapter 6 in this book). Often the difficulty is determining when these Christian units appeared and how far they formed part of an active villa: in Pannonian instances like Kékkút the association appears strong, as likewise for seats like Lullingstone in Kent in Britain. In Spain, studies suggest two scenarios, one with the owners inserting chapels or private oratories in the fourth or early fifth centuries (e.g. Fraga), the other (seemingly more common) with a delayed church imposition, sometimes inside villa spaces or adjacent, and sometimes with baptisteries provided (e.g. El Saucedo), suggestive either of parish foundations or monastic presences.[35]

Distinctive for the larger Balkan villas is the use of defensive architecture – sometimes clear in terms of defining enclosure walls with towers or in other cases nominal in terms of turreted corners (these latter perhaps suggesting an architectural trend rather than a military function). As seen in Chapter 1 of this book, two substantial defended villas known to have belonged to retired or active emperors are Split and Gamzigrad (Figure 1.2); quite possibly, the more military-looking sites are imperial – certainly the scale and defensive attributes of Mogorjelo in Dalmatia and Ságvár-Tricciana in Pannonia imply military engineers, and the presence of internal granaries, workshops, possible barracks, along with well-appointed residential complexes might signify specific military roles, such as grain depots, stopover points for governors and troops or for emperors/generals and their bodyguards. Some villas seem to have been taken over directly by the State and converted for military roles – such as on the promontory of Sirmione on Lake Garda (north Italy) as a fleet base in the fifth century and on the island of Brioni Grande in the bay of Dobrinka (Istria-Dalmatia), where villas as retreats continued into the sixth century, with one site, Castrum, being fortified and perhaps converted into a State dye factory in the fifth.[36] Turrets are depicted on villas in a few late Roman (and Vandal) mosaics, and sources for Gaul mention defended and hilltop villas, but we lack a systematic exploration of how far villa society sought to defend itself in the fifth century: enclosures and turrets, plus a large workforce (perhaps even bodyguards), could keep bandits or raiding parties at bay but would not stop determined larger forces; more likely owners would quit these exposed sites, removing portable wealth (we assume rich gold and silver hoards, such as for Hoxne in Suffolk, relate to rich landowners in flight), if with hopes of a return.

Indeed, it seems unusual for archaeologists to trace clear evidence of destructions of villas, although evidence for robbing of materials (perhaps for churches in nearby towns) is a relatively common feature.[37] Many villas, as in Britain, are quitted and progressively decay from the late fourth century; in Spain, as in Italy, after decay (whether in the late fourth, in the fifth or as late as the sixth century), some sites are 'colonised' by burials (e.g. Tinto, Aguilafuente in Spain; Desenzano, Selvicciola in Italy), often a century or more later. Yet burials may sometimes coincide with the latter phases of villa usage. What is key here is to recognise that the burials indicate a set of local inhabitants, either on the same site as the old villa or in its immediate vicinity; these might then denote either the villa owners continuing to reside and work there, sometimes now in timber housing or occasionally in less ruinous spaces within the complex (such maintenance of use is rarely easy to trace when archaeologists are digging only the stubs of walls), or else new farmers being drawn to the site. Exploitation of the past is not unusual – Anglo-Saxon burials often occur in Bronze Age barrows, for example – and may signify people drawn to visible landmarks, even if they comprised a mound of ruins. Incoming Ostrogoths, Visigoths or Franks may well have inherited (forcibly, through sale or through the lack of any resident owner) lands and remnant estate buildings; they may have used these sites but lived in towns, or they may have established their own buildings nearby. We cannot tell without clearer archaeologies, although we can identify that in Ostrogothic Italy, senatorial elites still lived in villas in the south and that the king himself used rural, palatial villa retreats like Galeata and Monte Barro in the north.

More important is to recognise that even if the villas as buildings fell redundant, the working landscape around – fields, pasture, woodland, boundaries and tracks – normally remained active; indeed, pollen analyses in many regions tend to point to no major change in land use (cultivated/uncultivated) after Roman rule, except in terms of a drop from specialisation (e.g. intensive vine or olive cultivation geared to producing surpluses for State and for busy urban consumption) to an emphasis on a more mixed agricultural output serving more compact markets.[38] Specialisation must have persisted in some areas,[39] although documentation for such only really emerges when monastic landowning and outputs become prominent from the eighth century on. What we generally are ignorant of are the more workaday sites, namely the small farms and hamlets that would have existed and continued to exist in the late and post-Roman landscape – hence the value of field survey and ever-improving abilities to recognise and date coarse ware ceramics; tracing these and the new settlement patterns that emerge in the late and post-Roman periods (such as upland or nucleated settlement in Italy)[40] are the route to qualifying how far rural population levels collapsed after Rome or how far the landscape remained populated but visible on a scale far reduced from Roman times. Like the towns and the frontiers we have surveyed, decay and change may have been evident but life did still persist.

8

The Ends of Rome in the West

INTRODUCTION

In what state, then, was the old Western Roman Empire in AD 500? Were towns in full decay, had economies failed, were landscapes empty? Provinces had been lost and transformed into a variety of kingdoms – were these losses detrimental and divisive? Was warfare endemic within and between thes' kingdoms? In other words, are we viewing a Roman corpse being picked over by barbarians, just as Gildas describes for sixth-century England in his *De Excidio*? Chapter 1 of this book identified that this dismemberment was destructive on various levels and yet in no ways total: many of the new kingdoms, for example, largely maintained the overall size of the former Roman provincial territories; almost all of these new kingdoms retained an urban-based administration; most were Christian and used and built churches and monasteries. But, as seen, the new politico-military powers were by far the minority in terms of population grouping, as the majority were 'Roman' in the sense of being the native population continuing and still using Latin, generally still living under Roman law, and practising an Orthodox Christianity – although, as noted in the *Introduction*, some powers like the Vandals used persecution and their otherness to impose authority early on (but probably far less so as time wore on and as populations became integrated).

There are three sorts of 'after Rome' contexts: the first is for provinces quitted by Rome before Rome's formal end in 476 – Britain, Pannonia, Dacia – where Roman influence might continue to exist, but materially may be limited, and aspects of 'Romanitas' such as towns largely fail; the second (again before AD 476) is where Germanic rule took hold in Roman provinces, either with Roman recognition – Burgundia, Suevia, Visigothic Spain – or without – Vandal Africa; the third follows the formal close and loss of Roman control in the West – Noricum, Gaul, Italy. This chapter briefly tracks each of these contexts and considers the relative levels of decay, decline and continuity. Should we, for example, expect a greater level of 'Roman' loss in the first group and better survival in the last? Do towns, therefore, fare worst in those first failures? And how far within the second and third groups was the name of Rome and her past relics integral to the new states that emerged?

SUB- AND POST-ROMAN BRITAIN

What then of Britain, detached and lost from the Empire before Rome's fall in a period of substantial upheaval at the start of the fifth century? The second half of the fourth century saw many a usurper on the island emerge, deflecting supplies away from 'official' Roman troops and adding new burdens to Britain's military needs. Such usurpers had drawn on local loyalties through highlighting how Rome was ignoring the island, but many then damaged Britain through embarking on campaigns for wider rule by crossing to the Continent and removing troops in (generally) lost causes. The last to do so was Constantine (III), whose own rule slowly unravelled as he tried to cope with multiple fronts, including countering Italian forces. Stilicho had already drawn troops away to assist Italy's defence; Constantine had denuded Britain further. One mid-fifth-century source claims that unchecked Saxon assaults in 408 or 410 were the prompt for Britannia to rebel again, but this time to break formally from Rome – or, more probably, from 'Roman control', meaning Constantine's – with an expulsion of Roman (i.e. Constantine's) 'magistrates' as a gesture of separation.[1] No replacement emperor was elected. But who chose to do this, how unified an action was this, and which 'magistrates' were removed? Was it an ejection of officialdom and tax collectors from London only or from other key urban centres? Later sources combine to call the new rulers 'tyrants' – that is, rulers outside of Roman control and, in Roman eyes, illegal. Zosimus reports an official letter from Honorius in 410 (unless earlier), telling the cities to fend for themselves: was this responding to a last attempt by the new British authorities to stay Roman, to get assurance from the centre of the Empire (bypassing Constantine) that they would be looked after if they returned to the fold, or some extra request to both Constantine and Honorius for military aid?

Events on the Continent in any case did not enable efforts (forceful or diplomatic) to restore Roman rule here. Where did power now lie in Britain? Honorius' reply to the 'cities' is taken to show a residual set of urban-based authorities, presumably the provincial centres of the later fourth century, who would have overseen regional defensive points. They seem to have still worked in Roman fashion, including drawing upon barbarian federates or mercenaries to help defend the shores – in the 440s, Vortigern (labelled 'arrogant tyrant' by Gildas in the mid-sixth century), for example, settled Saxons on the eastern shores. We hear of three shiploads of Saxons arriving: 'On the orders of the ill-fated tyrant, they first of all fixed their dreadful claws on the east side of the island, ostensibly to fight for our country, in fact to fight against it', with revolt once 'supplies' became insufficient to 'shut the dog's mouth' (Gildas, ch. 23). We are unclear whether these authorities initially were headed by 'kings' or whether these titles only emerged later amid power struggles, particularly when federates rebelled and Saxon annexations began. Some Church authorities remained too and kept in contact with the Continent, duly gaining a few missionary visits (notably by St Germanus, twice) – these lacking armies and moneys but with clerics and books to help tidy up the Britons' variable Christian leanings. But such missions could not counter the growing secular power divisions.[2] It may not have been total chaos, but with a possible 13 'kingdoms' (many of these compact units in Wales, in particular) established by the sixth century – facing by then an equally fragmented 'Anglo-Saxon' eastern England – there was more chaos than cohesion and a landscape far more Iron Age than Roman.[3] Indeed, Gildas bleakly argues, 'The cities of our land are not populated even now as they once were; right to the present they are deserted, in ruins and unkempt. External wars may have stopped, but not the civil ones ... Britain has kings, but they are tyrants; she has judges, but they are wicked' (Gildas, chs 26–7). Warfare meant that many took flight, some overseas, and others 'trusting their own lives with constant foreboding to the high hills, steep, menacing and fortified, to the densest forests, and to the cliffs of the sea coast' (Gildas, ch. 25). Below we trace some of the sub- and post-Roman archaeology of Britain to gauge the character of life after Rome.

Despite Gildas' words, the early fifth-century British 'government' must have retained the main towns as ostensible foci of control: walls, likely churches/bishops, industry, markets and soldiers were core to these, and rule could only happen if populations were available to listen and work. London potentially had the most to lose after AD 410, with the exile of the governor and *vicarius* as well as some of their entourages. But this capital may have already been struggling if any large-standing garrison had been withdrawn to Gaul (or earlier to Italy), and there must have been major diminishment of state-oriented trading activity via the river. Back in 1935, Mortimer Wheeler imagined some heartbeat in the near corpse of latest Roman London: he pointed to the lack of pagan Saxon sites within a 5- to -10-mile radius to support his view of the incomers avoiding a well-defended sub-Roman enclave. However, new archaeology modifies this picture: Saxon occupation sites are now recognised close by, at Clerkenwell and Tulse Hill, and a few scattered artefacts come from the city core. But work at Poultry and at the amphitheatre/ Guildhall near the heart of Roman London reveals decline from the late fourth century, the former showing some late repairs followed by robbing, but neither then show human activity on any scale again until the ninth century. Currently, therefore, the old space appears almost wholly out of use in the fifth century. Indeed, it is noticeable that when trade and urbanism resurfaced in the seventh century, the focus lay to the west, outside the old Roman confines and between the Strand and Covent Garden (*Lundenwic*); to the south, at Westminster, recent finds at St Martin-in-the-Fields include not only early seventh-century burials but also fifth-century tombs (one sarcophagus contained bones dated to *c.* AD 410), plus a tile kiln last fired in the first half of the fifth century. A different late and post-Roman focus perhaps lay here, exploiting remaining river trade, and later seeing expansion into *Lundenwic*. For old Roman *Londinium*, only from AD 800 is there revival in the form of a *burh* within (but not filling) the defended space; however, the site of St Paul's may signify a church and royal presence from the earlier seventh century.[4]

A contrast lies with other towns in south-east England where gaps in activity are less apparent even if the archaeology is still quite patchy. For example, fourth-century Canterbury shows fairly high levels of occupation, especially in terms of timber houses and shops even if the public facilities of temple, theatre and baths were redundant by *c.* AD 350; shops and industrial workshops continue into the fifth century, in places encroaching upon roads. On the one hand this shows a decline in urban standards, but on the other it implies economic vitality. A silver hoard outside the London Gate, dated to *c.* AD 410, meanwhile reveals some still wealthy residents. Although 'dark earth' deposits are well attested, Canterbury is important for its evidence of later fifth- (unless sixth-) century 'colonisation' by timber (both sunken and post-built) huts cut into abandonment deposits; over 40 are known, with a concentration near the former theatre and public baths; in addition there is a goldsmith's hoard containing a Visigothic coin (*tremissis*) of *c.* AD 480, which may denote that such 'huts' belonged to an elite group. Significantly, early Anglo-Saxon cemeteries lie in the town's immediate vicinity to further indicate a populated town, even if one dominated by ruins. Finally, when St Augustine arrived from Italy via Gaul at the court of the Kentish king in 597 he found a small but active Christian community at Canterbury (one probably promoted by the Frankish Christian queen here), focused on the small church of St Martin.[5]

Similarly, Verulamium features small timber houses with hearths or ovens set over various intramural and some suburban late Roman houses and spaces, although associated material culture to secure them chronologically is minimal. However, there are none of the expected Saxon-style, sunken-featured buildings or early Saxon burials — the nearest is about 20-km distant. Here, too, Mortimer Wheeler suggested a 'sub-Roman enclave'. What we do not know are the transitions from sub-Roman to Saxon rule in such urban sites — aggressive, passive, new overlords rather than population change, flights by the Britons? Nor do we understand the attitudes to the Roman structural remnants, whether avoidance, exploitation for materials or simple acceptance.[6]

Western Britain in the fifth and sixth centuries did not succumb to invading Saxons or Angles but suffered from localised power struggles which seem to have prompted a progressive shift of power foci from towns to hill forts — or at least an investment in these as regional fortresses — with a retention of the old towns as likely Episcopal seats. In these regions the Church was actually fairly strong, evident in the figures of Gildas and, much earlier, St Patrick.[7] Threats also came from Ireland (St Patrick was himself carried off as a slave by Irish raiders in the first half of the fifth century), although there are signs of the use and settlement of Irish federates. New settlement centres include promontory seats like Tintagel, and finds of imported Roman amphorae from these and from some beach or dune sites like Bantham show trade links with the Mediterranean persisting into the mid-sixth century (these perhaps a mix of links for trade in tin, cloth, slaves even, and with supplies of goods to the regional churches); some 'trade' may even be tied to diplomatic gifts, signifying external recognition of the 'tyrants'. Striking are the numerous standing inscribed stones of mid- and late fifth- to seventh-century date, in part commemorative, found across western Britain and especially in Wales, which use Latin, and provide Roman-style titles, including 'Protector' and 'Priest', and other formulae to suggest elite association with the imperial past – even in zones never properly Romanised.[8] Of much value are the excavations at Wroxeter,[9] where minimal medieval and modern overlay has meant that ephemeral post-Roman structures can be recognised – although some have disputed the interpretations of the excavators, in particular regarding questions of chronologies, since the almost non-existent material culture of the sixth century allows no precision on foundations and longevities. The claims are for a post-Roman sequence at the Baths basilica which shows maintenance fully into the fifth century, with stalls and timber and daub houses in both portico and interior towards the end of that century; demolition and levelling in the early sixth century were followed, c. AD 550, by construction of over 35 timber buildings in the space. Selection of this space and the earlier demolition signify careful choices – after all, why not refocus on an alternative, more open area requiring less effort? – and control of that space by a figure of authority, such as a bishop or local magnate/commander. Either way, the data point to continuity of activity within a former Roman town, a suited level of population and some urban authority. At the same time the material poverty in terms of small finds – domestic, dress or other – is clear testament to how far removed these sub- and post-Roman towns were from their Roman antecedents, and how much smaller their economic sphere was.

Archaeology is meanwhile expanding the understanding of the afterlives of people and sites along the once powerful Hadrian's Wall.[10] The slight sources point to various small successor states or 'tyrannies' carving out territories north and south of the Wall, benefiting from the ready presence of forts and soldiery. There may even have been some unified efforts, since by c. AD 450, the Scots had withdrawn to Ireland and the Picts north beyond the Forth, and subsequent raids into the mid-sixth century seem small scale. Boundaries probably fluctuated between groups, but broadly the powers gather along former pre-Roman tribal zones, until the kingdom of Bernicia expands outwards successfully.[11] Some material signs of this earliest phase can be observed: as seen in Chapter 3 of this book, South Shields (Arbeia) remained untouched by destructions or abandonment throughout the fourth century. There was even a timber gate inserted in the early fifth century where the masonry south-west gateway had part tumbled and then its debris cleared. Badly damaged burials of fifth-century date were recovered from the gate area and near the commandant's house; signs of stone robbing occur, and a small number of late or possibly sub-Roman penannular brooches were recovered. But what sort of population existed here? Did they view themselves as soldiers or

Romans? Nineteenth-century excavators argued for unbonded walls linked to a Saxon-period occupation, and for the presence later of a royal vill, but these claims remain to be confirmed through modern archaeology. In the centre of the Wall, at Birdoswald, by the mid-fourth century, the granaries had been decommissioned: one was demolished and quarried out, but the other was converted into a 'hall' with hearth, subsequently replaced by a timber-built successor; lesser sill-built timber buildings were set against the inner face of the curtain wall immediately facing the hall (Figure 8.1). Chronologies are by no means secure, but the structures should take the sequence of occupation at the fort site into the later fifth century at least. The evidence is so far limited to the area close to the western gate of the fort, but the implication is of a fairly busy site in the sub-Roman period. The excavators stress that the evidence for the timber phases is far clearer than that offered at Wroxeter, and they argue for residual frontier troops carving out a local power base, the hall thereby forming the seat of the commander of the force. The fort provided a tangible connection to Rome, but whether any mental allegiance to Rome remained is unknown.

5TH-CENTURY
BIRDOSWALD:
GRANARIES TO HALL

Figure 8.1 Interpretative reconstruction drawing of the fifth-century/sub-Roman period hall at Birdoswald (after Wilmott 1997: Fig. 154)

ST SEVERINUS IN NORICUM

More central to the Empire, Noricum's provinces (*Ripense* and *Mediterraneum*) largely avoided the physical damages of the worst of the politico-military traumas of AD 380–410; yet problems existed in terms of contact with Rome, removal of troops and logistical support. Alaric tried to claim Noricum for his own in 403, stating that the regions no longer paid taxes to Rome anyway. But allegiance persisted, even if regular pay failed to reach the residual troops – a good many of whom would have been federates. A Roman population was detectable in the 480s when it was required to evacuate and move south to Italy under Odoacer, and before this, in the 430s, Aetius came to quell disturbances in the provinces. Archaeological evidence suggests that, even before the fifth century, populations of both urban and rural open sites in southern Noricum were shifting to upland seats, notably around the old capital of Virunum, on the Hemmaburg, Grazer Kogel and Maria Saalerburg; Teurnia took over as the new capital from the early fifth century and was gathered around plateaux, notably the Holzerberg; many studies have occurred on the Lavant, replacing Aguntum, showing usage already from the third century. Good-quality churches and fortifications signify investment in these upland centres in the late Roman period. Such centres were logical responses to an insecure northern frontier and were a sensible use of naturally defensive Alpine positions; they nonetheless remained generally close to Roman roads and would have performed some military duties – as garrison points, storage depots, Church foci and refuges.[12]

Fewer hill forts were employed to this effect further north, where Roman fortresses, defended townships and a few rural seats endured. We are fortunate in possessing a near contemporary source which helps chart the progressive and final break-up of official Roman control in this delicate frontier region, but it also flags the ways in which Roman life was being subsumed under increasing barbarian influence and presences (Map 8.1). The compact but fascinating *Vita Severini*,[13] composed by the Monk Eugippius in *c.*510 but recounting events of *c.*455–88, describes Severinus, in a governor-cum-general role but portrayed effectively as a Holy Man, seeking to stem barbarian inroads by reorganising native settlement along the Danube and, in particular, reviving the many Christian communities of the region. The *Vita* identifies both active and inactive fortifications on the Roman side of the Danube; it mentions stores, religious buildings and market spaces, and it notes something of the provincial population, including priests and monks, and suggests that some wealth was evident – such as in references to a rich widow concealing landed produce and to tribute paid to the Rugii (chs 2, 22). That these communities were worth raiding – for materials, food or just for show – is signified in the many claimed assaults (most probably very small scale) by Heruls, Sueves, Goths, Alamanni and Thuringians (chs 4, 9, 22, 27). Key figures are the Rugii who play a confusing game: Severinus treats with their royalty (chs 6, 22), they host markets (ch. 9), they form a protectorate to at least some of the

Roman sites, yet are also hostile on occasion, notably forcing the inhabitants at Lauriacum, the largest of the Roman sites, to transfer eastwards, to be 'amicably established in the towns and lived in friendly alliance with the Rugi' (ch. 31). In a few places the non-Roman presence was very tangible: thus Comagenis was a town 'very strictly guarded by the barbarians established within, who had entered into a league (*foedus*) with the Romans' (ch. 1). The landscape still functioned to produce crops, fruit and other goods (if with an occasional locust plague), which were stored (presumably in urban granaries) and sold at markets; we hear also of an open market over the river, though the main items for sale comprised Norican provincials captured as slaves (chs 2, 6, 9, 11, 17). The text also implies that farmers resided in the towns.[14] Some external Roman contacts are attested, with goods (notably olive oil) coming downriver from Raetia and with clothing sent from the southern territories (chs 17, 28), but the *Vita* is at pains to point out that military pay was not getting through – something reflected archaeologically in the minimal coin finds at forts for much of the fifth century – and yet still soldiers guarded the territory for Rome. One set of troops from Batavis, however, headed south to get their cash – never to make it (ch. 20). Despite the claims in the *Vita* of minimal troops,[15] constant enemies and recourse to prayers – all designed to magnify the efforts of Severinus, of course – it is evident that some Roman life still functioned and coped, if changing with the times: working relationships with aggressive neighbours, using these to help deflect other threats; barbarian

Map 8.1 The Norican frontier of c. AD 470

federates as troopers and probably farmers; trade locally without dependence on external suppliers; and some maintained command structure.

The archaeology of the sites noted by Eugippius reinforces some of this: ceramics are much more locally derived, very few rural settlements are registered (supporting the idea of farmers residing in towns/forts), coins are almost non-existent, housing is often in drystone or rubble construction, and yet church structures (often compact) are relatively well recognised, showing due investment in what would have been crucial communal focal points and constants for mental security. The *Vita* was, of course, aiming to stress the vital role of the Church and of Severinus' deeds in supporting this, but we should not doubt that faith and belief were strong facts in this troubled era and space. The sixth-century fortunes of these churches and monasteries are hard to trace currently, although given that many saw later, early medieval and medieval reuse and rebuilding, and given place-name survivals, the implication is that some of these fortified sites remained occupied in some form – otherwise why was Lauriacum sacked in 731? This argues against the claimed full evacuation of northern Noricum under Odoacer in 488 and, to some degree, also against Eugippius' record of Severinus' earlier orders to quit certain exposed forts.

NEW POWERS ON LOST BORDERS: BAVARIANS AND MOORS

Although Rugian power dissipated, this same ex-*limes* zone saw a more stable kingdom emerge, gathered indeed around Roman sites, in the form of Bavaria and of the Bajuvars-Bavarians.[16] The focus was the fortress of Regensburg – Castra Regina (whose name alone demonstrates a continuity). Unlike for the Lombards or Goths, no 'History of the Bavarians' was composed, and we rely on archaeology and later texts to identify origins and growth. The first formal references to the people are in the second half of the sixth century, when they are recorded as occupying an area of the Danube east of the Sueves, extending down to Augsburg; by then they appear a coherent enough force to control a named territory, to possess a duke (Garibald), and to be allowed to participate in Frankish and Lombard marriage politics. Only from the late seventh century, however, are Christianity and monasticism established forces, imposing themselves in and around their towns. Burial archaeology indicates that the Bavarians emerged from a complex fusion of diverse Germanic groups, including federate settlers from the mid-fourth century, mainly from across the river or to the west (notably Iouthungi and Alamanni), plus, after AD 400, groups with material links with Bohemia to the north-east, whose presence fairly swiftly extends across the frontier zone and into various forts, notably Regensburg, Straubing and Eining. These too should equate with federates, in Roman pay and uniform – or at least trappings of this (perhaps with the 'officers' and chiefs allocated Roman brooches and titles); they may well have formed some of the soldiery seen by Severinus. At the formal withdrawal of 'Romans' under Odoacer in 488 and after Rugian defeat, a power vacuum may have ensued; subsequent struggles for territorial control would have been arduous, and the emergence of the

'Bavarians' as a dominant force by the mid-sixth century, with a name probably recalling a (real or newly created) link by the new elite with a Bohemian 'homeland', denotes a new order from the chaos. Recognition by Franks, Ostrogoths and Lombards reinforced the name and demonstrates contact with the wider world. Much later, in AD 770, Bishop Arbeo of Friesing called Regensburg 'impregnable in its construction, built of square stone blocks, dominated by high towers and adorned with numerous fountains' – all largely Roman survivals.

Although far removed from Hadrian's Wall, it is useful to observe how different sectors of the Roman *limes* on the Danube formed cores to new power groups (Heruls, Rugii, Lombards, Bavarians). These are larger in scale but not so different from postulated chiefdoms centred on forts like Birdoswald. The river resource was perhaps key to Bavarian success; in Birdoswald's case location may have meant a restricted longevity, lacking the stronger economic security of coast or river like Bamburgh for Bernicia and South Shields for Northumbria. We might even draw comparisons with emergent, independent kingdoms on the opposite side of the old Empire, in the former southern border zones of Mauretania in the fifth and sixth centuries.[17] Numbers and relationships are not fully clear, but they are expressed, initially at least, in a form and with a language of power still heavily reliant on Rome: thus, for AD 508, an inscription (Figure 8.2) records construction of a fort (*castrum*) at Altava for

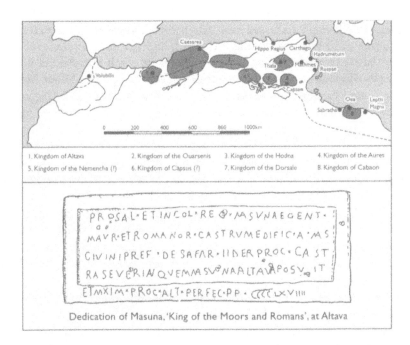

Dedication of Masuna,'King of the Moors and Romans', at Altava

Figure 8.2 The Altava inscription of AD 508 commemorating King Masuna's construction of a *castrum* (after Rushworth 2000: Fig. 6)

King Masuna, head of both the Moors and Romans; the officials listed bear honorific and administrative Roman titles – Maximus as procurator at Altava itself, Masgivinius the prefect at Safar, and Iider, procurator at Castra Severiana; the inscription also bears the date of the province (cccclxviiii). A Romanised population clearly persisted here, with Latin the administrative language; the procurators and prefect perhaps controlled sub-units within the kingdom, based on old, but fortified Roman sites. The kingdom may have later extended its power westwards to Volubilis, where four tombstones of AD 599–655, again in Latin, refer to a *princeps* and a *vice praepositus* and even display a 'royal' Roman past through the name Iulius. Such 'Mauro-Roman' powers were still active when the Arab conquest occurred and as Islamic states were established in the Maghreb in the eighth century. Do we define Masuna's kingdom as a 'successor', that is, *replacing* Rome on the frontier zones in the fifth century? Given that various Moorish tribes and their chiefs had been involved as paid allies before that, and one law of 409 spells out their tasks in frontier control and maintenance, perhaps these federates viewed themselves as maintaining and inheriting Roman government here. Certainly the continued use of forts, titles and epigraphy into the sixth century is highly significant, indicating a desire to preserve that formal, if increasingly distant, link with Rome.

THE OSTROGOTHS IN ITALY

The last example comes from the old heartland of the Empire and West. Chapter 1 of this book discussed how Italy became increasingly exposed in the fifth century and how the fractured frontiers and scattered armies could not prevent barbarians penetrating not only the fertile north but also the Eternal City itself. Other sites suffered in the fifth century – Aquileia, Milan, Verona, Albenga – and the legend of Venice's roots is tied to the flight to the lagoons of mainland townsfolk from Altino, Padua and Concordia in the face of Attila's advances. The expectation is of massive destruction and loss of urban and rural sites, and documentary sources duly relay such devastations. And yet archaeological support is far less forthcoming: some rural sites in the north do disappear, and towns appear at a low ebb (as at Brescia, with previous elite housing succumbing to partitioning, mosaic floors covered up with dirt, and streets poorly tended), but towns are not all depopulated, nor do destruction levels fill the stratigraphies. Rome, certainly traumatised and pillaged of portable wealth, and with various elite *domus* quitted and signs of other decay, shows continued life and even renewal – even the Colosseum is brought back into action after spells of neglect.

Yet the final phase of renewal of the emblematic amphitheatre belongs not to the last vestiges of Roman rule, but rather to the period of Ostrogothic government of Rome and Italy. In the late 480s the Eastern Emperor Zeno negotiated for the Ostrogoths under their King Theoderic (who had been causing numerous problems at Constantinople and in Thrace – Theoderic seeking increased powers for himself and rights and space for his soldiery, Zeno keeping him at bay while holding on to his throne) to head to Italy and wrest control off the tyrant King Odoacer. Zeno promoted this as an imperial venture, with Theoderic to hold and govern Italy as patrician and general, but once established in Italy, Theoderic created a kingdom on a par with powers such as the Vandals and the Visigoths.[18] A long rule and firm alliances with neighbours gave rise to a kingdom of economic and political stability, enabling a residual Roman aristocracy and bureaucracy – and peasantry – to continue without major disruption. Indeed, archaeology and documents (notably the letters by the Senator-Prefect Cassiodorus) show villas active in south Italy especially, with strong wine and oil production evident. At Rome, restorations to the Colosseum (attested by tile stamps, dedicatory epigraphs and even by the names of late fifth-century senators inscribed on marble seating inside)[19] and the holding of games here and at the Circus Maximus, combined with restoration works on theatres, churches, walls and drains, symbolise how Theoderic viewed himself as worthy to do as emperors had done in patronage and display: 'Our care is for the whole Republic, in which, by the power of God, we are striving to bring back all things to their former state; but especially for the City of Rome'.[20]

However, it was the current capital, Ravenna, which received the greatest injections of wealth and personnel in both city and port, much still tangible in surviving architecture, art and amphorae (see Chapter 5 in this book).[21] Siting his capital here was for both strategic reasons – proximity to the kingdom's delicate northern territories, access to naval and commercial communications via Classe – and logistical ones – a relatively small military core, needing to be focused in the north rather than scattered (thus there were other Gothic foci at cities like Verona, Milan and Como, various of which gained new walls or had restorations, and possible new palaces). And Ravenna was also already furnished with fine churches and an imperial palace complex, and was well defended. Potentially, Ravenna featured a demographic/ethnic division of space, with a Gothic emphasis placed in the eastern and north-eastern zone and related cemeterial spaces (gathered near Theoderic's own mausoleum); various Gothic churches arose in the eastern half of the city, including S. Stefano, S. Eusebio, S. Andrea dei Goti and S. Zeno. But integration rather than separation of communities was far more logical, and in reality a number of Gothic-period churches were interspersed in the 'non-Gothic' zones. Certainly, we would expect some division of court, ceremonial and military space, but the palace of Theoderic, to which the stunning church of Sant'Apollinare Nuovo was attached, was very much central to the city plan.[22] Population estimates are variable, the most recent suggesting around 15,000 persons, although this is probably an underestimate. Certainly, it was still much smaller than contemporary Rome.[23] Religious differences existed, however, since the Ostrogoths were predominantly Arian Christian in creed, and thus a separate Arian Episcopal complex was required to service the Gothic court (and no doubt some locals switched to Arianism to merge better with the new rulers). But, unlike in Vandal North Africa, where Victor of Vita claimed a brutally imposed Arian dominance, the Ostrogothic approach was diplomatic: the Ostrogothic Arian cathedral and baptistery are structurally similar to the Orthodox pair in the west of the city and in fact are somewhat smaller in size; no demolitions occurred, and no rededications are known for Orthodox complexes. Some surviving artwork may reveal Arianism (e.g. contrasting modes of depicting Jesus in the Orthodox and Arian baptisteries), but our restricted understanding of Arian theology and iconography means we cannot confirm these.[24]

No doubt Gothic military control stifled any vociferous anti-Arian sentiment; when this was expressed at the end of Theoderic's reign, it met with vicious (if restricted) retribution.[25] The subsequent conflict between Byzantium and the Ostrogoths in Italy from the 530s may then have prompted serious anti-Arian acts by Italians; for Ravenna, churches were rededicated (but not immediately) and some (but not all) of the iconography altered (though this chiefly in terms of removing images of the Gothic court, as apparent on the Palatium mosaic in Sant'Apollinare Nuovo), but there are no archaeological indications of Arian churches being mutilated.

Important for our discussion is the material evidence of continuing high levels of building and external contacts. Theoderic's Ravenna contained many churches, each adorned with mosaics, and almost all exploiting new marble work – that is, not culled from demolished buildings of earlier date; the architectural units (columns, capitals, choir screens, sarcophagi) derive heavily from eastern Mediterranean quarries and stores, and the sculptors and mosaicists were drawn chiefly from Constantinople itself. Letters from the Gothic court duly spell out the admiration for such craftsmen. Again, Theoderic was being 'imperial' in his choices and actions. This also meant that Ostrogothic Italy was a ready market for Eastern products: economic growth is fully reflected in the extensive remains of workshops, stores, kilns, houses, streets, canals and rubbish dumps uncovered at Classe. Extensive imports from across the Mediterranean are attested for the whole Gothic period – best recognised in the warehouse (no. 17) burnt down in c. AD 510 with its stacks of amphorae of varied types, plus tablewares and lamps, with goods predominantly from (Vandal) North Africa (Figure 8.3); deposits elsewhere in Classe show strongest leanings towards wine amphorae from Syria and Palestine; and striking is the use of broken pottery in floor make-ups for buildings and the roadways.[26] Ravenna was not all of Italy, of course, and it is dangerous to argue that economic vitality here was matched elsewhere, but there are signs that other large centres benefited from the peace and stability provided by Theoderic's regime. As noted above, however, the resurfacing of political, religious and even ethnic tensions from the late 520s marked the start of problems which ultimately resulted in long-lasting and highly damaging conflict between Goths and Byzantines.

THE NEW IN THE OLD

The loss of Roman rule manifested itself on various levels, therefore, dependent heavily on context. In Italy and many other Mediterranean contexts,

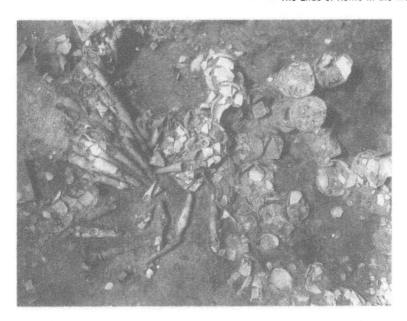

Figure 8.3 Ceramic debris of the early sixth century AD *in situ* in a burnt-down warehouse at the port of Classe, near Ravenna (photo courtesy of A. Augenti, E. Cirelli and Ravenna Soprintendenza)

Roman rule had been long established, its cities and towns densely occupied, its trade and monetary system widely flung and its Church more prominent. The powers that came into these territories recognised these strengths and – willingly for the most part – sought to share and work with the existing (if weakened) power structures. The adoption of Latin, the continuance of Roman law, the issuing of Roman coin types, and the maintenance of city living and the Catholic Church fostered a relatively strong level of continuity. Some changes were forced and created: insertion of an Arian faith as an equal in some kingdoms (Ostrogothic and Visigothic, Lombard) or as principal in others (Vandal), Germanic soldiery as the military core and elite, Germanic elite as landowning equals (or dominant) and acceptance of new figureheads (as depicted on lesser coin denominations). These incomers did not force or reinforce decay: for the most part, in fact, their establishment of kingdoms, largely occupying Roman provincial spaces, and the dialogue that developed between these new kingdoms, fostered a fair stability in Mediterranean society, economy and settlement. The contrast lies with 'fringe' regions, where Roman collapse was marked also by a physical Roman removal and by the withdrawal of troops plus ejection of officials. In these cases a skeleton only of Roman power remained for the new powers. Without the larger imperial State machine, its army, related taxation and logistics, these areas, left to their own devices, were forced to 'cope' as well as they could. In some instances, residual towns, forts and Church provided a basis for display and manipulation of authority, noticeably looking to old Roman labels for legitimacy. Our ability to trace these threads of continuity archaeologically is improving: nonetheless, whereas for

Italy, Spain or Africa it is generally now less problematic to recognise 'continuity' after Rome, problems remain in defining and qualifying this; certainly it is clear that each centre has a different set of evidence to be identified. The task is harder for regions like Britain and Noricum where Roman withdrawal determined a cessation of Roman coin supply, a vast reduction in the importing of goods, and near neglect by the narrators of contemporary history; and these gaps make us still think of these regions as shadowy, their populations and actions less visible, their interactions harder to define. In reality there is much archaeology in these, burials, rural sites and dress, but they are at a different level from that of Rome – less showy and monumental – and therefore too often seen as lesser; arguably, however, such materials give us more chance to explore the people themselves. Archaeology here forms the key tool for 'writing' post-Roman histories.

Conclusions:
An Empire Lost and Transformed

INTRODUCTION

Much ground and many centuries have been covered in the preceding chapters, outlining the historical sequences of names, events and peoples impacting on the third to sixth centuries AD, and charting the ways in which the late Roman Empire in the West responded or sought to respond. More importantly, this volume has explored some of the physical manifestations of these events and their social and economic repercussions in both the core and fringe provinces of the Western Empire, observing material changes to frontiers, towns, landscapes, beliefs and populations. This physical perspective provides, on many levels, a control to the textual guides and a better route to seeing how different being 'Roman' was in the fifth century compared to the second. It has also allowed a better grasp of the speed of change and of loss, although it must be recognised that we are looking back and condensing events and changes in a fashion not so far removed from late Roman annalists like Eutropius, cramming the highlights of a year or a reign into a few bare sentences. But the archaeology, hopefully, reveals that many changes were slow and generational, revealing a progressive evolution and devolution of the Western Empire in the later Roman centuries. From our vantage point we, of course, term these as the 'late' or 'last' centuries of Roman rule; yet contemporaries would not have conceived of such passing of time, but mainly observed ongoing changes to their built spaces, the populations around, the faces and words on the coins, and the prices in the market. This final chapter therefore merely draws together some of the transformations examined, first in terms of the historical stage, and then in terms of the archaeological evidence.

AN HISTORICAL DECLINE AND FALL

It is difficult to argue against the claim that the fifth century witnessed many dramatic upheavals across the whole Roman Empire, first marked by breakdowns in the northern provincial defences, then by Rome chasing enemies within those same territories before they snaked into the Roman core; from the 420s territorial control faltered, in some cases fatally as barbarian groups took full control, in others Rome and the newcomers negotiated on the control. Not all towns and villages saw or suffered in these events; transitions in rule may have been registered but without turbulent change. Political change did not necessarily mean human change, although in larger towns and in forts new governors and orders must have been more visible. The story explored in Chapters 1–3 of this book especially showed how the leaders, generals and soldiers did change with time, often at pace.

It is natural to view the fifth-century events as rushed, confused and catastrophic, with diverse groups emerging as threats, Roman armies failing to respond, usurpers distracting and disrupting the Empire, and barbarian groups variously accepted, settled and exploited with only patchy success for Rome. It is a vastly different image of Empire than that traced for the first century AD when Rome coped with barbarians on and outside the frontiers, when the scale of threats was generally low, and trade kept many an outsider content. Even with the third-century escalation of threats from outside and despite Roman internecine conflict, Rome contained most of the barbarian problem, and by Constantine's reign, Roman imperial order and supremacy were renewed. The frontiers, their forts and the army remained effective and extensive, if with changing emphasis. The progressive reliance on non-Roman troops as part of the terms of settlement of groups on Roman soil was also contained, but the escalation of this barbarian settlement in terms of group size from the fourth century and a failure of Rome to disperse and oversee groups were root causes to the major problems of the fifth century. The retained cohesion of large groups such as the Visigoths – even if their identities might be reformulated through incorporation of new groups or different leaders – worked against Roman supremacy. Pressure elsewhere and conflict between Eastern and Western courts further reduced effective responses, as borne out most clearly in clashes during Alaric's and Attila's ascendancies. An inability to meet the simultaneous threat of Vandals and Sueves in the Rhine zone and these powers' retention of group size and identity forced Rome to accept them as they were – despite efforts to play one off against another (such as Romans and Visigoths against Vandals in Spain). Severe distractions elsewhere were the prime causes for territorial losses, notably the Vandal takeover in Africa and for failures to respond and effect change militarily. Battles were being fought out, and even if Rome did not lose all of these, the pressures were on multiple internal fronts – not like the more distant cross-frontier threats of earlier centuries.

One can observe an intense strain thrown on the imperial coffers in the later fourth and earlier fifth centuries especially, when the need to feed, pay and arm the Roman forces plus allies was substantial and spreading; tribute payments and bribes to non-Roman groups (beyond, on or inside the frontiers) were constant and high, and shocks like the capture of Rome in 410 saw material wealth lost plus the wealthy elite transferring themselves eastwards with their fortunes or else donating moneys to the Church. The loss, between AD 405 and 420, of Britain, the bulk of the German and Danubian frontier lines, and large chunks of Spain dramatically reduced available food supplies, manpower and tax revenues, although much money locally had had to go on wall repair for towns and forts, and equipping and hiring mercenaries. Demands on remaining Roman lands necessarily grew; yet the ability of provincials to pay, work and produce shrank – as reflected in the edicts issued over the fifth century recognising the need to reduce taxes. Rome fought hard to adapt to the shrinkages: the Vandal capture of North Africa saw the massive food support from Africa broken and Rome turned instead to Sicily; its concern then was to vouchsafe this island and internal local supply zones. But coping was more than a major struggle for the shrinking Western Empire in the fifth century, and the struggle was not one that could be easily maintained once Roman provincial forces became separated. Even so, it is remarkable how much energy the government put into trying to deal with usurpers and rebellious Romans as non-Romans carved up lands.

Such rebellions and usurpations, desertions and manpower shortages (through loss in war, to the clergy and monasteries, or flights from the land) reinforced the need for reliance on non-Roman groups for military roles and as manpower for lands inside the Empire. Theodosius I's policy is striking in this regard, and although it functioned, contemporaries voiced concerns. Indeed, a subsequent dilution of imperial power (with weak or short-lived emperors in the West) distracted resources, and defecting and defective officers meant that Rome increasingly failed to control its forces (Roman and non-Roman) over what were becoming ever-widening fronts: uprisings, Germanic movements and demands, civil wars and the Bacaudae were all expressions of this progressive fragmentation of control in the West – a fragmentation which was occurring *within* the Empire, as opposed to occurring just on the fringes and creeping inward. The State's edicts for this time recognise insecurities and anxieties – though we might wonder how many people were reassured by, or even heard, such pronouncements:

> It is Our constant care to provide for the welfare of the human race; for we make provision day and night that all persons who live under Our sway shall be defended by the protection of arms from the attack of the enemy and shall possess unrestricted leisure and security in time of peace. (*Novels of Marcian*, 2.1, issued in Constantinople, 11 Oct., AD 450 to the praetorian prefect, Palladius)

Various scholars view the Huns as final nails in the Western coffin: under Aetius, there was an exceptional reliance on Hunnic mercenaries to counter usurpers, Goths, Bacaudae and others; Attila's switch to independent action deprived Roman generals of this manpower reserve and brought severe new losses in conflict; his armies' vicious expansion and conquests further divided provinces and scattered and reduced troops. The subsequent Hunnic collapse saw major infighting and cancelled out hopes of renewing recruitment on any scale – although the East continued to obtain Hunnic mercenary groups.[1]

Furthermore, as territories were peeled away, so the diminished Western court had far less of a bargaining counter to tempt demanding barbarian kings – money, land and offices had been staple imperial payments, but as scope for each faltered so the incipient kingdoms sought recognition as powers in their own rights, in some instances with the barbarian kings seeing it as their task to select and support their own, short-lived puppet emperors: Avitus by/for the Visigoths, Olybrius by the Vandals and Glycerius by Gundobad of the Burgundians. By the time of the latter pairing, the name of Rome and of the Western Empire meant little to the successor kingdoms; more effort went into seeking alliances and marriage links between each of these than treating with an anonymous emperor in Ravenna lacking military strength. Geiseric put greater value on gaining recognition from the Eastern Empire which did retain authority, wealth, territory and military power; the Vandal king could have chosen to take Rome permanently rather than plunder it, but preferred Carthage as his royal seat.

The Eastern court did on occasion assist the West, as with the joint campaigns against Vandal Africa and Marcian's expeditionary force against the Hunnic realm in 452, but these were inconsistent, and the hostility that normally prevailed between Eastern and Western emperors and generalissimos (and Churches too) largely hindered a working union that might have staved off a final decay. Later policy shows Eastern emperors not willing to throw money at a lost cause, preferring instead to dictate some element of control in the ensuing break-up and rewriting of the West – hence the push of Theoderic's Ostrogoths to reclaim Italy at least nominally as imperial land. One can note, of course, the way that the Germanic kingdoms still looked up to Rome (or rather east to Constantinople and the continuing Roman emperors there), as reflected in the imagery of their higher denomination coin, maintaining the bust of the Eastern Augustus well into the sixth century – this as much for wider trade needs as any political statement.[2] The art and architecture of Theoderic's capital of Ravenna also reflect this leaning to Constantinople. Such works meanwhile attest the fact that by c. AD 500 much of the western Mediterranean had stabilised and could participate economically; indeed, these Mediterranean-oriented kingdoms remained part of a network centred on towns, with fair population levels retained. Less coherent were the former northern provinces, where urbanism and economies faltered – although various Roman fortified sites would later form the backbone to new states.

The Eastern had matched the Western Empire in its use of allied non-Roman forces, mercenaries and federates, as well as its mass of tribute payments, but there was a difference in the threats it faced. Key and powerful was the Parthian–Persian Empire along its long eastern frontier, but this enemy was an old, civilised and equally urbanised superstate, with whom warfare was intermittent but far more negotiable. Northern enemies like the Huns certainly dented the East, but a stronger army, a wealthier base and a more resilient elite prevented a likely breakdown of control on the variety of fronts faced in the West. Distance kept the Vandals at bay, and diplomacy and respect fended off the Ostrogoths. It is beyond the scope of this book to explore what scholars call the 'Byzantine' Empire, which reached its territorial peak in the mid-sixth century, when the generals of Emperor Justinian I reclaimed Vandal Africa, Ostrogothic Italy and a part of Visigothic Spain, and so for a time revived a western half of the (new) Roman Empire. But this was a poor cousin to the fourth-century West, with only a partial input of investment and a different set of priorities. Military and religious structures then dominated, generally compact and with borrowings of materials from the past, as best evident in remains in Byzantine North Africa. Church and army officials oversaw and the secular elite voice was limited: Byzantine Rome was run by the pope, with Senate, prefects and consuls long since past.[3]

Byzantium retained a sizeable hold in the central Mediterranean even after the expansion of the Arabs, but Arab assaults on Syria, Asia Minor and Greece from the 630s saw the East Roman Empire suffer major territorial losses and marked the start of a decay of urban, rural and economic life as had characterised the fifth-century West. Archaeology is contributing hugely to current interest in tracing these seventh-century changes in the East and to observing transitions to Arab rule in regions like Egypt and Syria.[4] The same sorts of questions are being asked here as have been raised for the last centuries of the Roman West: How brutal a transition was there, how rapid a decay of urban life, spaces and amenities, what defences were thrown up and how far were classical and even early Christian monuments sacrificed? What happened to the economy as a result — collapse and chaos? Was late antique rural life overthrown? A few years ago, replies would have been gloomy, and yet archaeological input now enables a clearer image, one that shows trade continuing in the Mediterranean, if reduced; towns were not all reduced to depopulated shells; and economic dialogues between states and rivals existed. While the archaeology cannot always easily guide us on the documented and undoubtedly bloody wars, sieges and reprisals of the Arab–Byzantine conflicts, nonetheless, the defences, houses, food remains, burials and religious buildings will offer us a fuller image of how settlements, communities and individuals lived, worked through, adapted, prayed and died in these periods of major social and political upheaval.

AN ARCHAEOLOGY OF DECLINE?

A final question remains: could we write a narrative of the decline and fall of the Roman West from the archaeology alone? For early fifth-century Britain and Pannonia, the loss of coin, the collapse of a villa economy, the dissolution of town living and monumentality, and absences of imports on any scale would all speak of a retreating or broken superpower. And for each in c. AD 500, diverse burial displays, changed material cultures, localised industries and a minimal register of activity in former urban seats would point to more inward-looking societies, fractured power and new settlers, even if occasional coins and other finds from burials betray contacts with a richer, continental or southern world. In the Mediterranean Western provinces we might say these changes do occur if less acutely at first, but progressively affect both town and country. Yet here we would observe a pronounced urban resilience, since a tangible Church presence would point to a continuity of population and control. However, we must be careful not to let a scattering of churches and monasteries mask significant and evident changes and decays: town living had been much transformed by the mid-fifth century across Italy, Spain and Gaul, and elite signatures in particular diminish, and the classical infrastructures of towns appear largely ruinous. Indeed, the 'ordinary' archaeology of the sixth and seventh centuries is almost an alien world compared to the fourth: limited ceramic production of note, minimal imports, few coins, rubbish deposits around timber houses, tracks winding their way round ruins and sometimes over the former broad Roman streets, and burials scattered in old public spaces or near the islands of church activity. The picture is true even for Classe, port of the Italian capital Ravenna, in the seventh century: various streets here are blocked, many warehouses derelict and robbed, small-scale housing of timber and reused brick inserted into decayed store buildings, canals partly inoperative, and even churches struggling to make repairs.[5] Here, too, scholars, without the aid of documents, would register mere remnants of an old power.

What of the fourth and fifth centuries in the Western Empire? A fourth-century archaeology features the start of many of the aspects of change and redefinition that were fully manifested by c. AD 500: an expansion of defensive measures, a damaged monetary economy and a decay of old urban public structures. These elements would signify a power under stress, taking measures to defend that power, and finding new ways to express authority. Indeed, the growth of fortress-palaces and imperial mausolea and polarisation of wealth – manifested sometimes in large urban houses but more so in villa growth – would be indicators of this modification in power. Furthermore, the imposition of a new religion, with churches occupying suburban and in time intramural space, shows an alternative authority competing and eventually overseeing towns and territories. There could be traced impacts lower down the social scale: reduced or no display of items in burials, a regionalisation of products as imports especially come to focus on the larger cities and ports only, and housing using timber or exploiting robbed materials. The changing systems of disposal of rubbish and the loss of civilised traits like piped water and public baths reflect meanwhile on society adapting to circumstances in towns which became more functional and far less arenas of authority and display.[6] In addition, we might recognise changes in expression: dress, as gleaned from material finds and occasional burial items, such as brooches, buckles and ceramics, might point to identities that became more regional, owing less to the imported varieties of expression and relative sameness that had dominated first- and second-century archaeological contexts.[7] Bones and bodies from burials might themselves help reveal a late Roman world with reduced mobility – far less of the wide movement of peoples (chiefly merchants and soldiers) that characterises the earlier Empire – just as they might tell us far more about the scale of movements of non-Roman groups into the western and northern realms of the old Roman world. Currently, however, there are few such bioarchaeological analyses of late Roman populations, and their potential remains untapped.[8] Until such scientific studies occur and accumulate we will still debate how 'Roman' the old frontiers, provinces and their populations remained, and how they themselves viewed their own identities, whether associated with Rome or not. One might note, for example, how high denomination coins in the sixth-century Visigothic, Frankish and Ostrogothic realms still bore Eastern imperial busts and Latin legends, and the languages of law, history, religion and death continued as Latin.

More fundamentally we need to recognise that archaeological data for late Roman and late antique urban, rural, military and religious sites and their sequences are still accumulating: with interest and debate stimulated and interaction with historical analyses developing, more questions can be asked of the evidence as it emerges and as our abilities to see, read, date and interpret this grow. The archaeology will in time enable clearer stories to be composed of how people lived and worked, reacted and adapted, worshipped and died in town and country across the Empire's changing provinces – we are some way yet from being able to reconstruct lives as we can for first-century Rome and Pompeii.

Yet we have to be careful: archaeology alone cannot write a complete late Roman 'history' as many voids, uncertainties and inconsistencies persist. For Italy, late Roman to medieval urban archaeology is far more advanced in northern than in southern Italy, and Late Antiquity awaits proper scrutiny in Sicily; in the Danube regions, frontier forts are much better understood than villa sites, and ceramic sequences and industries remain insecure; British fifth-century archaeology struggles without secure material pegs to hang theories on. Nonetheless, in each of these and in other instances, work is progressing and scholars and field archaeologists are much more aware of needs and possibilities. For instance, recent field studies on the Balearic Islands are enabling a first coherent image to be drawn of both urban and rural trends and failures, and of processes of Christianisation, thus allowing us to see how far the Mediterranean islands responded to or were affected by events chiefly afflicting the mainland provinces. At the same time, however, there is almost nothing from the evidence uncovered yet to identify Vandal raids or subsequent Byzantine domination on the Balearics: the ceramics might hint at slightly modified trade flows, but without the documentary guides, one might otherwise be unaware of the changes in territorial power. Clearly, therefore, combining where possible all types of evidence (written, built, buried, environmental etc.), questioning each thoroughly and letting all material sources 'speak' are crucial to help construct a fuller and more reliable picture of this long period of Western Roman transformation, decline and fall.

Notes

Introduction: Questioning Decline in the Late Roman West

1. Carthage's archaeology: Ennabli (ed.) 1992; wider survey of late Roman to Arab archaeology in North Africa: Leone 2007; and on Vandals: Berndt and Steinacher (eds) 2008, notably papers by Von Rummel, Schwarcz and Béjaoui. On harbour activity, see Hurst 1994. Palace and royal court at Carthage: Abed and Duval 2000. Pilgrim churches and burials: Stevens 1996; Stevens *et al.* 1998. For historical context of Vandal takeover, see Moorhead 2001: 49–61; papers in Merrills (ed.) 2004; Aillagon (ed.) 2008: 324–36.

2. Orosius' work, style, audience and aims: Ward-Perkins 2005: 21; Innes 2007: 1–2, 20–2.

3. Cameron and Garnsey (eds) 1998; Cameron, Ward-Perkins and Whitby (eds) 2000; Fouracre (ed.) 2005; plus the volumes *Storia di Roma III.1* and *III.2* (both 1993).

4. The Liverpool *Translated Texts for Historians* series makes available known and little-known sources on Frankish Gaul, Visigothic Gaul and Spain (e.g. Mathisen 1999b), Vandal Africa, Justinianic Constantinople, middle Saxon England, the deserts of Sinai and papal Rome (e.g. Barnish 1992 for Cassiodorus and Ostrogothic Italy). Innes 2007 offers various extremely handy bibliographic essays.

5. For 'Collapse' see the now classic essay by Tainter 1988, debating Rome's collapse with those of Minoans, Mayans and others. Tainter successfully draws together (nb. pp. 128–52) numerous older theories and debates, such as those related to manpower losses, landscape decay, monetary collapse, fiscal drains (e.g. Boak 1955) for Rome's Collapse, and yet draws on minimal archaeological evidence.

6. Summary volume: Webster and Brown (eds) 1997. Other key titles: Pohl (ed.) 1997; Hodges and Bowden (eds) 1998; Brogiolo and Ward-Perkins (eds) 1999. Important to flag is the journal *Early Medieval Europe*, active since 1993. New from 2008 is the *Journal of Late Antiquity*, whose first issue included papers such as Ando 2008 revisiting 'Decline and Fall' and debating 'Transformation'.

7. On landscape change, see Christie (ed.) 2004a; and Francovich and Hodges 2003 for central Italy. Ceramics: Saguì (ed.) 1998; Reynolds 2010. Housing: Haug 2003; Lavan, Özgenel and Sarantis 2007a; Bowes 2010. Roman-Barbarian interactions and frontiers: Pohl (ed.) 1997; Pohl *et al.* (eds) 2001; Curta (ed.) 2005b. Social and religious change: Brogiolo and Arnau (ed.) 2007; sections in Webster and Brown (eds) 1997; and forthcoming in *Late Antique Archaeology*.

8. Lavan and Bowden (eds) 2003 and Lavan *et al.* (eds) 2007b. Principal journals comprise *Journal of Roman Archaeology*, *Medieval Archaeology* (and its French and Italian equivalents) and *Germania*.

9. Furger (ed.) 1996; Kulikowski 2004; Christie 2006; Leone 2007; Poulter (ed.) 2007 – with an excellent editorial Introduction.

10. Rich (ed.) 1992; Brogiolo (ed.) 1996; Christie and Loseby (eds) 1996; Gelichi (ed.) 1998; Brogiolo and Ward-Perkins (eds) 1999; Brogiolo *et al.* (eds) 2000; Ripoll and Gurt (eds) 2000; Burns and Eadie (eds) 2001; Lavan (ed.) 2001b; Liebeschuetz 2001a; Saradi 2006 for cities of the Byzantine East in the sixth century; Sami and Speed (eds) 2010.

11. Italy – Naples: Arthur 2002; Brescia: Brogiolo 1999b; Ravenna: Cirelli 2008. Spain – Barcelona: Beltrán De Heredia Bercero 2002; and Tarraco: Keay 1996. Gaul – Tours: Galinié (ed.) 2007. Albania – Butrint: Hodges, Bowden and Lako 2004.

12. For example, Sena Chiesa and Arslan (eds) 1992; Bierbrauer, von Hessen and Arslan (eds) 1994; Ensoli and La Rocca (eds) 2000; Donati and Gentili (eds) 2005; Augenti and Bertelli (eds) 2006.

Chapter 1 The Fall of the Late Roman West: Contexts of Change, AD 200–500

1. Quotes here come from Mattingly's 1948 translation; revised translation in Rives 1999, stressing the *Germania* as an exposition of Tacitus' varied and innovative writing and research skills: 48–56. Potentially it also is pushing the new emperor Trajan to complete Augustus' aim of conquering the Germani.

2. Wells 1999: 117; cf. Brather 2005.

3. Gabler 2002 plots related archaeological evidence, chiefly coin hoards and burnt deposits.

4. Cassius Dio, 71.11, 72.13; Eutropius, 8.13.1. See Birley 1987; Christie 1991; Kerr 1997. A crucial visual guide is the Column of Marcus Aurelius in Rome: Becatti 1957.

5. Rajtár 2002.

6. Tejral 1997; Rajtár 2002: 104–09.

7. Air photography documents other campaign or marching camps: these extend from Engelhartstetten just north of Carnuntum to Olomouc-Slavonín, 200 km away on the Upper March river – Rajtár 2002: 111–19.

8. Creighton and Wilson (eds) 1999: 25–6; Sommer 1999: 187–90.

9. Rajtár 2002: 100–02.

10. Visy (ed.) 2003: 270–1, 278–9, noting scattered cremations with accompanying weapons, belonging to the late second to early fourth century AD. Todd 1992: 26–7 stresses that the culture covers too vast an area to be associated with a single tribal entity. Ammianus Marcellinus later observed the long coexistence and cultural affinities of Quadi and Sarmatians. 'Antonine Plague': Duncan-Jones 1996; Buora 2002a.

11. Cracco Ruggini 1984: 14–17.

12. Tacitus, *Germania*, ch. 15. Exchange and display in Gaul, Germany: Cunliffe 1988; papers in Creighton and Wilson (eds), especially Wigg 1999. Roman finds in Slovakia, Moravia and Lower Austria: Krekovič 1997; Kuzmová 1997 and 2002. Cf. Bursone 2008.

13. Kuzmová 2002.

14. Ilkjær 2002; www.illerup.dk. Analysis of the weaponry: Von Carnap-Bornheim and Ilkjær 2000.

15. Jørgensen 2001; Storgaard 2001a; papers in Storgaard (ed.) 2001b.

16. Britain: Ottaway 1992: 82–95, focussed on York; Dacia: Bogdan Cătăniciu 1981: 48–52; Diaconescu 2004; North Africa: Raven 1993: 132–43; Mattingly 1995: 54, 55, 116–31, notably Lepcis Magna. Overhauling of frontiers: Mattingly 1995: 80–4. Severan dynasty: Birley 1988; Hekster 2008.

17. Witschel 2004 is keen not to overblow the crisis empire-wide. Hekster 2008 for source commentaries.

18. One modern commentator, Herwig Wolfram, crudely claims, 'From 238 the Gothic assaults devastated the eastern provinces of the Roman Empire for more than 40 years' (Wolfram 1988: 13) – implying a constancy of warfare.

19. See plots in Johnson 1983b, for example, Fig. 24, with too ready an association with barbarian waves of assault.

20. Martin-Kilcher, Amrein and Horisberger (eds) 2008.

Notes

21. http://www3.uakron.edu/modlang/thovey.html
22. Carroll 2001: 138.
23. Bakker 1993; Schallmayer (ed.) 1995; summarised by Kuhnen 1997; Carroll 2001: 131–2; Roberto 2008.
24. A remarkable survival is the set of six gilded bronze imperial busts from excavations at the capitolium at Brescia: two are of Septimius Severus; the other pairs are of Probus and Claudius II, their more austere imagery matching their military roots – Morandini 2008.
25. Lee 1993: 133–6 on frontier troubles, questioning how informed Romans and barbarians alike were of troop movements.
26. Carroll 2001: 114; Todd 2001: 70–1 on the varied names for groups comprising the Alamanni, based more on territories or lands settled rather than on personal or familial names.
27. Frankish roots, names, expansions: James 1988: 1–58.
28. Christlein 1978: 42–9; Todd 1992: 71–2, 209–10; Hamerow 2002: 55–80, 106–14; Stuppner 2002: 28–32.
29. On ethnogenesis debates, see papers in Pohl (ed.) 1998; Curta (ed.) 2005b; Noble (ed.) 2006. Clear discussion on this and on identities and ethnicity in Halsall 2007: Chapter 2, plus pp. 14–18, 457–61. New archaeological work: for example, Wells 1999; Wigg 1999; Hamerow 2002; Visy (ed.) 2003: 263–83.
30. Mattingly 1995: 89, 171–8.
31. Mattingly 1995: 194–201, noting the Ghirza and Bir Schedua sites. Mauretanian names and groups: Blackhurst 2004; Rushworth 2004.
32. Survey by Johnson 1983b. Contrast other regions, like Spain, with selective city wall building prior to the mid-fourth century: Kulikowski 2004: 101–9. On building works across the Anarchy period, see Rambaldi 2009.
33. Van Ossel 1992; van Ossel and Ouzoulias 2000.
34. Kulikowski 2004: 67–9 for Spain, arguing against any physical trauma; Witschel 2004.
35. Haynes and Hanson 2004: 15–24. On military presence, see Zahariade 1997. On provincial redesign, see Zahariade 1997: 24; cf. Watson 1999: 8, 157; disputed by Diaconescu 2004.
36. The name of the Carpathian Mountains derives from this people, who might have been allocated the northern, upland spaces of the old province, while the southern spaces apparently remained well-enough occupied for a few towns such as Sarmizegetusa to persist, its amphitheatre later employed as a fortress – Diaconescu 2004: 128–36; signs also exist for late Roman Christian communities.
37. Mackensen 1999: 200–02; Watson 1999: 34.
38. Sommer 1999: 190–1.
39. Mackensen 1999: 200–1; Sommer 1999: 191; Watson 1999: 220.
40. Carroll 2001: 133.
41. Watson 1999: 172–5.
42. Watson 1999: 177–80. Roman triumphs: Beard 2007.
43. On Aurelian's favoured gods, see Watson 1999: 183–98.
44. Overview in Cameron 1993a: 30–46.
45. MacCormick 1981: 170–1, noting how even their number was 'symbolic of the order of the universe, the four seasons, the four elements ...'. More widely, Williams 1985; Rees 2004.
46. Fitz and Fedak 1993; discussed in Chapter 5 of this book.
47. Kulikowski 2004: 69–84.
48. Price edict: translation in Maas 2010: 21–2. Lactantius is one cited Christian author who appears wholly unimpressed by all Tetrarchic reforms.

49. Money, circulation and inflation in the late Empire: Kent and Painter (eds) 1977; Whittaker 1980; Greene 1986: 45–66; Howgego 1996; Reece 1999: 129–45.
50. Coarelli 1999; Rinaldi Tufi 2005.
51. Paris (ed.) 2000. On wider Tetrarchic works, see Rinaldi Tufi 2005.
52. Mulvin 2002, with ownerships discussed on pp. 56–9.
53. Wilkes 1993.
54. Wilkes 1993: 77–82; Mulvin 2002: 81–3, 258–69.
55. Wilkes 1993: 46–52; Rinaldi Tufi 2005: 97, 104. The issue of related court ritual is not covered here, but see Ripoll and Gurt (eds) 2000 for wide coverage of palaces from late Roman to early medieval times.
56. *Hist. of Church* 9.9; see MacCormack 1981: 181–3. Overview of Constantine's reign: Cameron 1993a: 47–65. Two major exhibition catalogues are Donati and Gentili (eds) 2005 and Hartley *et al.* (eds) 2006.
57. Imperial regalia, displayed in the Palazzo Massimo alle Terme Museum, Rome: Panella 2008.
58. Cameron 1993a: 55–9.
59. Giuliano 1956; Pensabene and Panella (eds) 1999; recent discussion summarised in Liverani 2005a.
60. MacCormack 1981: 37–8 notes also how 'while the images of Sol [on the Arch] could be translated into Christian terms, Iuppiter and Hercules remained until the end gods of the pagans' – hence their clear absence.
61. Zosimus, *Nea Historia*, II, 22–8.
62. Cameron 1993a: 63–4, 170–2; Mango (ed.) 2002; Gregory 2005. Statuary and reuse: Ward-Perkins 2000a; Bassett 2004.
63. Rinaldi Tufi 2005: 97–9. See Chapters 4 and 5 of this book.
64. Zosimus, *Nea Historia*, II, 34. Cameron 1993a: 49–53. Licinius may have encouraged a Gothic incursion across the Danube – Heather 1998: 497.
65. MacCormack 1981: 185–8, 192; Williams 1985: 205, 209; Cameron 1993a: 57, 85–6; Hunt 1998a: 3–4.
66. For these complex events in Rome and in the north, see Hunt 1998a: 10–22.
67. Ammianus Marcellinus, Book 16.10. See Chapter 5 of this book.
68. Hunt 1998a: 28, 1998b: 54–9.
69. Chadwick 1998; Leadbetter 2000.
70. Ammianus Marcellinus, 29.6; Pitts 1989: 52–3; Carroll-Spillecke 1997.
71. Heather 1996: *The Goths*. Oxford: Basil Blackwell 98–103.
72. Lenski 2002: 331. Lenski analyses the Gothic appearance, revolt and subsequent movements and Roman responses and failures: 320–67. Summaries in Cameron 1993a: 132–7; Heather 1996: 130–5; Wolfram 1988: 117–134.
73. 31.10 – the historian reports the enemy's 'armed force numbered 40,000, though some to magnify the triumph of the emperor, put them at 70,000'. Lenski 2002: 366.
74. Cameron 1993a: 138; Heather 1996: 135, 137. See Chapter 3 of this book on the archaeology of Pannonia's fourth-century *limes*.
75. Cameron 1993a: 145–7.
76. Eunapius, *Breviarum*, IX: 60. Bishop Ambrose of Milan's account of the Theodosius–Eugenius conflict: Moorhead 1999: 197–203.
77. On such generals and 'barbarisation', noted by Gibbon as a significant determinant in Rome's decline, see Chapter 3 of this book, plus Cameron 1993a: 148–50; Elton 1996b: 134–52.
78. The influential E.A. Thompson 1982: 17 determines this as 'the beginning of the end for the Western Roman Empire itself'.

Notes

79. Olympiodorus, fr. 7. An excellent modern analysis is Burns 1994; summaries in Ferrill 1986: 86–116; Wolfram 1988: 139–71; Collins 1991: 51–7; Blockley 1998: 113–2, focusing on the military aspects. The invaders and some of their material culture are considered in Todd 2001: 97–127. Claudian: Cameron 1970.
80. On perceptions of Stilicho, compare Olympiodorus, frs 1 and 3.
81. Cavada 2002: 140–8, 150–4. Župančič 2002 associates a belt buckle with relocated Rhenish forces used at the battle between Roman and Visigothic armies on the Timavo river in AD 401. On military dress, see Swift 2000.
82. Blockley 1998: 121–2, contra Heather 1996: 146 who sees the confusing alliance as happening in 404/5 – but the failure of Alaric, if an ally of Stilicho, to aid him against Radagaisus should argue against this earlier date.
83. Olympiodorus, fr. 7. Heather 1996: 148 argues that many of these 'barbarian' slaves came from Radagaisus' failed forces.
84. Heather 1996: 148; Olympiodorus, frs 8 and 10.
85. Jerome, *Letters*, cxxvii; *Preface to Commentary on Ezekial*, I. See Moorhead 2001: 39–40 and Ward-Perkins 2005: 28–9, comparing the literary descriptions of both Jerome and Augustine; cf. Olympiodorus, fr. 11. On the archaeology of 410, see Chapter 5 of this book.
86. Gasparri 2004: 49–51.
87. Olympiodorus, fr. 24.
88. Ethnic groupings: Pohl 2004: 31–6. Jerome includes also Alamanni, Marcomanni, Quadi and Heruls – thus peoples from the upper Rhine and Danube now grouped under the broader (and older) label of Sueves. On the incursions, see Heather 2009.
89. Olympiodorus fr. 13. Knight 1999: 47–50, noting hints in the archaeology along the Rhine of disruption, plus new cemeteries with Frankish military grave goods. A small hoard of gold coins and silvered military belt set from the river Loire at Chécy belongs to 406–7; as the buckle probably derives from Richborough in Kent, this could have been lost by a soldier brought over from Britain with Constantine III: p. 40.
90. Olympiodorus, fr. 29 reports that damage to lands led to severe famine, prompting cannibalism in some besieged centres. See also Keay 1988: 202–17; Rodà 1997: 223–6; Kulikowski 2004: 151–75. Possible Vandal archaeology in Spain: Berndt and Steinacher (eds) 2008.
91. Kulikowski 2004: 154–6, noting that as Hydatius had calculated the world's end on 27 May 482, so 'his chronicle was consciously a history of the world's last days, and it is filled with signs and portents of the end'; and yet his words can be interpreted to show how 'Spain in the early fifth century is much less the scene of post-Roman apocalypse and much more a normal part of the gradually dissolving Western empire.'
92. Kulikowski 2004: 166–75; Olympiodorus, fr. 26.
93. Nixon 1992; Sivan 1992, arguing for a rapid assimilation, with Visigoths as new estate owners commissioning sarcophagi and mosaics.
94. Kulikowski 2004: 173–8.
95. Zosimus, *Nea Historia*, VI. 2. Gaillou and Jones 1991: 125–9 and Giot, Guigon and Merdrignac 2003: 58–64 identify signs from the mid-fourth century of some Romano-Britons migrating – marking the first stage of the process by which the region took the name Brittany.
96. Faulkner 2000b: 171–8, arguing for a 'peasant war', rejecting the name of Rome and its unhelpful emperors; Dark 1994: 50–64. On Hadrian's Wall few Roman forts see destructive ends: cf. Crow 2004: 108–14; see Chapter 8 of this book.
97. Bland and Johns 1993.
98. Mattingly 1996: 171–83. On Gildo, and his brothers Firmus and Mascezel, sons of a self-styled Moorish king, Nubel, a chief overseeing border lands for Rome in Mauretania

and Numidia and holding, like his sons, recognised Roman offices, see Blackhurst 2004. Claudian composed a panegyric about Gildo's uprising: Blackhurst 2004: 70–1.

99. Papers by Berndt and von Rummel in Berndt and Steinacher (eds) 2008, plus Mathisen 1999a.

100. Schwarcz 2004: 51–2 postulates Boniface's Goths were rivals to Visigoths who crossed with the Vandals.

101. See *Introduction* for quotes from Victor; Pohl 2004: 38–9 on numbers, which will have thinned as they took towns and established garrisons, but presumably they employed Berber/Moor and Gothic federates.

102. Mattingly 1996: 215; Cameron 2000: 552–5; Heather 2000: 5–12.

103. Schwarcz 2004: 55–7. Later Vandal activity and conflict: Courtois 1955; Cameron 2000; papers in Merrills (ed.) 2004. Pohl 2004: 41 highlights Geiseric's longevity.

104. Lewis and Runyan 1985: 10–11; whereas De Souza 1999: 233–4 notes instances of advance intelligence and ruses by the Vandals against both Western and Eastern Roman efforts.

105. De Souza 1999: 231–8. Not all raids will have been organised by the Vandal hierarchy, and undoubtedly much piratical activity occurred from North Africa and Sardinia as elsewhere. On shipwrecks, see Chapter 7 of this book.

106. Italian defensive responses: Christie and Rushworth 1988. Key edicts: *CT, Nov. Val.* 1.2 and 9.1.

107. Collins 1983: 83–5; Heather 2000: 21.

108. Priscus, fr. 38. De Souza 1999: 235.

109. Collins 1983: 20–5; Burgess 1992; cf. Heather 1992.

110. Burgess 1992: 22–7. For the confusing events in Gaul, see Heather 2000: 18–26. For these emergent kingdoms in Gaul and Spain, see Collins 2000: 112–24.

111. Collins 1983: 20–4, 49, noting minimal material or artistic trace of Sueves across 150 years of control here; Keay 1988: 205–9, identifying Suevic coin issues, initially with the imperial name on, commencing from the reign of Valentinian III; Kulikowski 2004: 199–203.

112. Collins 1983: 203–9. Kulikowski 2004 sees the archaeology of Mérida as a mirror of some of these late Roman period changes, noting traces of fifth-century destruction and loss of life: 209–14. Bierbrauer *et al.* (eds) (1994) Part IV, pp. 282–365, covers the archaeology, art and coinage of Visigothic Spain.

113. Priscus, fr. 43; Thompson 1948/96: 36–41 (with Heather's update, pp. 238–64); Maenchen-Helfen 1973; Collins 1983: 77–81; Heather 2000: 1–4. Military in Ferrill 1986: 140–51.

114. Burgundian defeat and resettlement: Todd 1992: 211–14. In the 450s they carved out new territory around Lyon and Vienne; their kingdom endured until 534 – Martin 1996: 52–5; Bonnet and Reynaud 2000; Wood 2008.

115. Thompson 1948/96: 98–103. Diplomatic missions to the Huns included the historian Priscus in 449, who provides many details on their court – 104–36.

116. Ferrill 1986: 148–50, noting the wild claims of Attila's army amassing up to 500,000 men. Thompson 1948/96: 148–56; Heather 2000: 17–18.

117. *Lib. Pont.*, Life of Leo I.

118. Thompson 1982: 151, 1996: 156–68. Collins 1983: 81 argues that 'had Aetius been murdered a good few years earlier the Western empire would have had a better chance of survival'.

119. Ostrogothic narrative and ethnogenesis: Heather 1996: 111–17, 151–8. Hunnic and post-Hunnic Pannonia and Hungary and evidence for Sueves, Gepids and Goths: Visy (ed.) 2003: 283–98. Bóna 1976, on the Gepids who claimed the old Hunnic heartland of the Carpathians. More broadly, Menghin, Springer and Wamers (eds) 1987.

120. Gothic conflict and unification: Heather 1996: 154–65.
121. Ferrill 1986: 155–8; Heather 2000: 21, 23–6; Innes 2007: 112–15. For all fifth-century Roman commanders, see entries in the *Prosopography of the Later Roman Empire*, Volumes I and II.
122. James 1988: 67–71, doubting a kingdom or territory of note; Vanderspoel, forthcoming (more positive on the kingdom), discussing other such possible Roman 'kings'. Rome and the fifth-century Franks: Perin 2008.
123. James 1988: 25–7; cf. Collins 1983: 88.
124. Malchus, fr. 14 – see Blockley 1981. Moorhead 2001: 42–3; Innes 2007: 121–3.

Chapter 2 Defending the Late Roman West: I. Armies, Commanders and Enemies

1. Ferrill 1986; Coulston 1990; Bishop and Coulston 1993; Elton 1996a,b; Southern and Dixon 1996; Tomlin 1989 and 2000; Lee 1998 and 2007; Whitby 2000 and 2007 (for Eastern Empire and Balkans).
2. *CT*, VII.17.1. Navy forces of the Danube and Black Sea: Bounegru and Zahariade 1996; on lake commands, see Christie 2007.
3. Seeck 1876; Goodburn and Bartholomew (eds) 1976; Hoffmann 1969 and 1970.
4. On non-Roman settlement and recruitment, see Elton 1996b: ch. 5; Cracco Ruggini 1984. Sarmatian *gentiles* and Frankish, Batavian and other *laeti* in Gaul: Knight 1999: 34–41.
5. James 1988: 44–51, with Halsall's (2007: 153–60) recent re-evaluation of the material.
6. Elton 1996b: 152–4 estimates an annual recruitment of about 30,000 to maintain an overall force of 500,000 soldiers. Also on recruitment and manpower, see Lee 2007: 74–85.
7. Bakker 1993; Schallmayer (ed.) 1995; summarised by Kuhnen 1997; Carroll 2001: 131–2; Roberto 2008.
8. O'Flynn 1983; Barnwell 1992.
9. Elton 1996b: 149, plus ch. 5.
10. Positive views on Stilicho's military and political skills: Heather 2005: 216–21; Halsall 2007: 199–214.
11. Painter 1991.
12. Cf. James 1988: 48–51, 56–7; Knight 1999: 37–9; Carroll 2001: 145–6; Waurick (ed.) 1980: 121ff, illustrating late Roman material (Gallo-Roman, Frankish, Burgundian) from burials associated with the frontier populations.
13. Soproni 1985; Visy 2001: 177–81 for Valeria province. See Heather 2007 on Gothic movements, settlement and Roman interactions in the Balkans in the late fourth century. Dichin: Poulter (ed.) 2007.
14. Haberl and Hawkes 1973; Alföldy 1974: ch. 12; *Severin* 1982 (exhibition catalogue with related essays, notably by Ubl); Christie 1992.
15. Wolfram 1988: 150–60; Pani Ermini 1999; Lançon 2000; Christie 2000a, 2006: 28–31.
16. Heather 1997, 2001; Pohl (ed.) 1997. Kiss 1986 discusses gold finds in the Carpathians, representing the massive flow of tribute to the various non-Roman groups and their frequent reworking of such coin into jewellery.
17. Burgundians: Todd 1992: 211–15. See Halsall 2007: ch. 11 for 'provincial society' in the fifth century and Visigothic and Frankish visibility in Spain and Gaul, respectively. Dress and identity: Swift 2000.
18. Wolfram 1988: 143, with note 145 (p. 433).
19. James 1988; Randsborg 1991: 94–102; Elton 1996b: 116–17; Lee 2007: 89–94.
20. Croce Da Villa and Di Filippo Balestrazzi (eds) 2001; nb. 245–9; Hoffmann 1963.
21. Ricci 1997; Arena *et al.* 2001: 60–70.

22. See Mackensen 1999 for Raetian supply bases, including fortified granaries; see Chapter 3 of this book for comparable bases in Pannonia. Army *annona* and campaign logistics: Lee 2007: 85–8, 95–8.
23. Elton 1996b: ch. 3 on organisation and weaponry, and chs 8 and 9 on strategy and operations. For equipment, see Note 1 above. Danish finds: Ilkjær 2002.
24. Swift 2000; Buora (ed.) 2002c.
25. Coulston 1991 and forthcoming.

Chapter 3 Defending the Late Roman West: II. Frontiers, Forts and Towns

1. Trade beyond Rome's frontiers: Cunliffe 1988. Frontiers in Britain: Breeze 1982.
2. Whittaker 1994; Elton 1996a; overview in Halsall 2007: 138–44. Graham 2006 offers an alternative view of frontiers and their contemporary perceptions and roles in communication. A useful tour (with historical commentary) of Rome's varied frontiers is Parker 2009.
3. Wells 1999 and Brather 2005 explore Roman contacts on both sides of the frontiers and assess materials from the 'barbarian' perspective.
4. Luttwak 1976 on the Empire's 'Grand Strategy'; see also Ferrill 1986. Mann, Elton and Whittaker, amongst others, have contributed much discussion; see papers in Pohl, Wood and Reimitz 2001.
5. Johnson 1979; Maxfield (ed.) 1989; Pearson 2002. Portchester: Cunliffe 1975 and 1976. Review of the Pannonian Danube frontier in Visy (ed.) 2003, notably pp. 204–21, sections by Fitz, Visy and Tóth; see Soproni 1985 and Visy 2001 for the later phases; Johnson 1983b; Parker 2009: 166–201. For the wider Danube in the late Roman and early Byzantine periods, see Poulter (ed.) 2007.
6. Breeze 1982; Breeze and Dobson 2000; summary in Jones and Mattingly 1990; Crow 2004; Parker 2009: ch. 1. See the various *Limes* volumes, notably Maxfield and Dobson (eds) 1991 and Groenman-van Waateringe *et al.* (eds) 1997.
7. Cf. Rushworth (ed.) 2009: 296–312, centred on Housesteads.
8. Collins and Allason-Jones (eds) 2010 on material aspects of the late Roman phases and people of Hadrian's Wall.
9. On ceramic supplies to Hadrian's Wall in the fourth century: Bidwell and Croom 2010. Brickstock 2010 considers coin supply.
10. Rushworth (ed.) 2009: ch. 11 discussion.
11. Bell 1998; Pearson 2002.
12. Hornsby and Laverick 1932.
13. Ulbert 1981; summarised in Christie 1991.
14. Brogiolo and Gelichi 1996; Christie 2006: 331–48. On rural change, see Arthur 2004.
15. Billeting, soldier–civilian interaction and disputes: Lee 2007: 163–76 and in general for the impact of war on the soldiers, population, land and economies of the late Empire.
16. Romer 1999: 474–5.
17. On these 'brigands', see Van Dam 1985: 25–56 (noting how later hagiographic sources equate them also as Christians resisting evil emperors: 53–6); Drinkwater 1992; Knight 1999: 54–7; Wickham 2006: 529–33.
18. Faulkner 2000b: 171–8 views peasant revolts as contributing much to the end of Roman rule in Britain.
19. For fifth-century Spain, see Kulikowski 2004: 182–3, preferring to see well-organised bands of bandits, swelled by ex-slaves and soldiers. More fully, see Bravo 2007.
20. Halsall 1992, 2007: 152–61.
21. Brown 1988; Halsall 1998b.
22. Harris (ed.) 1999; on shortages, see Garnsey 1990.

23. For example, *CT* 15.1.17 of AD 365; 15.1.37 from Milan in AD 398.
24. Johnson 1983b: ch. 3; Harries 1992: 81.
25. Johnson 1983b: ch. 5. For Italy, see Ward-Perkins 1984: 191–9; Christie 2006: ch. 4.
26. Pessoa 1991. For urban defences in Spain, see Fernández Ochoa and Morillo Cerdá 1997.
27. Overview in Lewin 1991. Thessaloniki and other eastern sites: Crow 2001, noting the Thessaloniki text as recording a prefect Hormisdas 'who completed this great city by unbreakable walls'. Amorium: Lightfoot and Lightfoot 2007.
28. Crickmore 1984; plus sections in Wacher 1995; Welsby 1982; Maloney and Hobley (eds) 1983. Summary in Mattingly 2006: 326–33 with tabulated listing. Colchester: Crummy 1997; London: Maloney 1983 and Lyon 2007.
29. Fulford 1983; Fulford 2006; website for the 'Town Life' excavations: www.silchester.rdg.ac.uk
30. Gallia Belgica: Johnson 1983b; Mertens 1983; Wightman 1985; overview in Knight 1999: ch. 2. Paris: Velay 1992; Autun: Young 2001; Tours: Galinié (ed.) 2007, 1988. Town walls in the south west: Garmy and Maurin (eds) 1996; Saint-Bertrand-de-Comminges: Esmonde Cleary, Jones and Wood 1998; Esmonde Cleary and Wood 2006. Valuable is the new analysis of Gallic defences by Dey 2010.
31. Galinié (ed.) 2007, particularly Seigne 2007a, b.
32. Garmy and Maurin 1996; for Bordeaux, see also Sivan 1992.
33. Town walls are also integral to Ausonius' praising of Toulouse: 'girt with a huge circuit of brick-built walls, along whose side flows the beautiful Garonne, home of uncounted people' (*Ordo*, 18).
34. Esmonde Cleary and Wood 2006. Their Chapter 2 evaluates the defences in terms of their build, facing, parapets, gates, towers, materials and techniques, enabling discussion on manpower and logistics: they estimate 23,500 man-hours, equating to 200 days for 120 men.
35. Bromwich 1993: 63–7. *Novempopulana*: Johnson 1983b: 107–13.

Chapter 4 Towns and Urban Society in the Late Empire

1. Celti: Keay, Creighton and Remesal Rodríguez 2000. Urbanism in Spain in general: Keay 1988; Díaz-Andreu and Keay (eds) 1997. Late Roman centres: Arce 1993; Kulikowski 2004; Bowes and Kulikowski (eds) 2005.
2. Tiermes website: http://www.tiermes.net/index.asp
3. Rich (ed.) 1992; Christie and Loseby (eds) 1996; Brogiolo *et al.* (eds) 2000; Slater (ed.) 2000; and for debates in Italy, see Christie 2006, ch. 3.
4. Braund (ed.) 1988; Barton (ed.) 1989. Ward-Perkins 1984: 3–13 is a neat overview of classical urban patronage.
5. Pliny, *Letters*, Book 10.37, 39, 49, 75, 76. Urban euergetism in Italy: Lomas and Cornell (eds) 2003. Yon 2001 discusses euergetism at Palmyra in Syria, showing emphasis on religious structures.
6. Mattingly 2006: ch. 9 for an overview of Romano-British towns; cf. Ottaway 1992: 46–81.
7. Roueché 1989; Whittow 2001.
8. Ward-Perkins 1984: 14–37 on declining 'secular munificence' after AD 300 – 'the established aristocracy no longer felt under such pressure publicly to display and confirm their positions of superiority' (p. 15).
9. Ward-Perkins 1984: 73–9; Christie 2006: 174–82 on Italy; Knight 1999: 85–111 on Gaul.
10. For example, Rich (ed.) 1992; Brogiolo 1996; Christie and Loseby (eds) 1996; Gelichi 1998; Brogiolo and Ward-Perkins (eds) 1999; Brogiolo *et al.* (eds) 2000; Ripoll and Gurt (eds) 2000; Burns and Eadie (eds) 2001; Lavan (ed.) 2001b; Liebeschuetz 2001a on the

capitals; Christie 2006 and Sami and Speed (eds) 2010 on Italian centres; Saradi 2006 for sixth-century cities of the Byzantine East.

11. For example, Ward-Perkins 1984 and Christie 2006 for Italy; Kulikowski 2004 for Spain; Bowden 2003 on Epirus; Leone 2007 on North Africa; Knight 1999 on Gaul; Faulkner 2000a, b, and White 2007.

12. Valencia: Ribera i Lacomba and Mesquida 1999. Tarraco: Keay 1996. Other cities: Olmo Enciso (ed.) 2008.

13. Beltrán de Heredia Bercero (ed.) 2002, with sections by Rodà de Llanza on Roman growth, Ripoll López on the early Christian city, and Bonnet and Beltrán de Heredia for church and Episcopal complex. See also Bonnet and Beltrán de Heredia 2000 and Ripoll 2000. Earlier views of the fifth- and sixth-century church form and liturgy: Godoy Fernández 1995: 202–7. Town walls: De Palol 1992.

14. Faulkner 2000b: 127–8.

15. For data on Roman to medieval London, see the MoLA (Museum of London Archaeology – formerly MoLAS) publications – for example, Bateman 2000; Rowsome 2000; Cowan 2003; Bateman, Cowan and Wroe-Brown 2008. See also Watson (ed.) 1998. On London's evolution into *Lundenwic*: Wells 2009: 88–120; cf. Ottaway 1992: 55–71, 101–3, 110; Milne 1985, 1995. On 'dark soils', see Macphail 2010.

16. Potter 1995. More widely for North African towns in late Roman contexts, see Leone 2007.

17. Fitz 1980; Fitz and Fedak 1993. On Székesfehérvár, see Visy (ed.) 2003: 350–1.

18. Wightman 1985; Arce 2000: 54–7. Merovingian royal works: Dierkens and Périn 2000: 277–80. Earlier trade role: Carroll 2001. Amphitheatre: Kuhnen 2009, noting for the third and fourth century the find of over 1,200 coins from the subterranean galleries and a set of about 50 burials (victims, gladiators?) at the rear of the amphitheatre.

19. Loseby 1996.

20. Keay *et al.* 2000; Patterson (ed.) 2004; previous work in Potter 1979: 98–100, 144, 165.

21. Gaffney, Patterson and Roberts 2001, 2004.

22. See papers in Lomas and Cornell (eds) 2003 (nb. by Holleran, Patterson, Harries). Dodge 1999; Coleman 2000.

23. DeLaine 2000 explores the materials and manpower to build the baths of Caracalla – pp. 129–36. Fuel needs: Blyth 1999.

24. For central Italy and the role of late Roman governors, see Ward-Perkins 1984: 23–7, 127–9. Samnium: entries in Capini and di Niro (eds) 1991.

25. For these sites, see Wightman 1985; Garmy and Maurin 1996; Halsall 1996; Keay 1996.

26. Canterbury: Blockley, Blockley, Blockley, Frere and Stow 1995: 17. Wroxeter: White and Barker 1998. Bath: Cunliffe 1995.

27. Leone 2007: 86–93, listing referenced baths, official buildings and other core repairs. Generally, new fourth-century bathing places were much smaller than early imperial establishments.

28. Coates Stephens 1998; Wilson 2000 on the Janiculum.

29. Zajac 1999.

30. Post-Roman bathing in Italy: Ward-Perkins 1984: 135–41; see Arthur 2002: 44–5 for Naples. On water use, more generally, see Squatriti 1998.

31. On royal towns and palaces with baths, see Ripoll and Gurt (eds) 2000.

32. Barton (ed.) 1989; Dodge 1999; Coleman 2000 on entertainment and related architectures in Rome especially. Rome's blood sports: Kyle 1998. Late Roman fates to these in Italy: Ward-Perkins 1984.

33. Romano-British amphitheatres: Fulford 1989 (Silchester); Bateman 2000 (London); Wilmott 2007 (Chester); Wilmott (ed.) 2009; Wilmott and Garner 2009. Colchester circus: Crummy 2006. On circuses generally, see Humphrey 1986.

Notes

34. Papers in Wilmot (ed.) 2009.
35. Panvini Rosati 1994.
36. Heintz 1998.
37. Ward-Perkins and Gibson 1987.
38. Bateman 2000; Bateman *et al.* 2008.
39. Fulford (ed.) 1989.
40. Niblett 2001.
41. Durán Cabello, Fernández Ochoa and Morillo Cerdan 2009. Valencia and Toledo: Ribera i Lacomba 1998. Tarraco: Godoy Fernández 1995: 191–202; Keay 1996.
42. Christie and Kipling 2000.
43. Loseby 1996.
44. Tours: Seigne 2007a, b; broader survey in Christie 2009.
45. Cuscito 1994. Maas 2010: 40–5 for a selection of relevant primary sources.
46. Changing construction modes in Rome: Santangeli Valenzani 2007.

Chapter 5 Three Capitals of the West: Rome, Milan, Ravenna

1. For imperial Rome, see Coulston and Dodge (eds) 2000. Population: Purcell 1999; Lo Cascio 2000. A well-crafted consideration of late antique Rome viewed from epigraphic data is Alföldy 2001.
2. Ammianus Marcellinus, Book 16.10. Fraschetti 1999; Curran 2000; Lançon 2000; Beard 2007 on triumphs and *adventus*.
3. La Follette 1994. Third-century building works: Coarelli 1999; Rinaldi Tufi 2005. For later works, see Pani Ermini 1999.
4. La Follette 1994: 16–22, 83–5.
5. Pani Ermini 1999: 50–1; Rea 2002: 126–34. Olympiodorus' fr. 26 on Rome's recovery.
6. Olympiodorus, fr. 41.1–2; he viewed some *domus* as virtual cities.
7. Pani Ermini 1992: 195–7; Lançon 2000: 73–5. Paulinus of Nola (see Chapter 6 in this book) records how he received Melania and Pinianus and, later, other wealthy refugees at the shrine of St Felix – Trout 1999: 119–20.
8. *Domus dei Valerii*: Brenk 1999, noting related Christian finds, notably a small hoard of silver vessels.
9. Aventine: La Follette 1994: 19–20, 81. Esquiline: Shelton 1981; Cameron 1985; Painter 2000.
10. Hostetter *et al.* 1994.
11. Augenti 1996; Delogu 2000: 93–5.
12. Meneghini 1993, 2000. Coates Stephens 2001 discusses recovery of materials reused in later contexts in Rome. An excellent overview is Meneghini and Santangeli Valenzani 2004.
13. Rea (ed.) 2002, nb. 170–227, 450–4.
14. *Crypta Balbi* 2000; Arena *et al.* (eds) 2001; Manacorda 2001.
15. *Crypta Balbi* 2000: 44–54; Manacorda 2001: 52–4.
16. Augenti 1996: 80–3.
17. Cassiodorus' Formula is for the appointment of an architect to assist the City prefect (*Var.* VII, 15), the implication being that it was an occasional post in State pay.
18. Pavolini 1986: 272; Pensabene 2000. Classic work on Ostia is by Meiggs 1973, with important updates in Gallina Zevi and Claridge (eds) 1996. Portus: Keay *et al.* 2005, observing shrinkage of warehouse usage in the late antique period. Key papers on late Roman and early medieval Rome and environs are in Paroli and Delogu (eds) 1993. On supply and population, see Harris (ed.) 1999.

19. Johnson 1983b: 69–76; Christie 2001, 2006: 319–24.

20. *Milano. Capitale* 1990; *La città e la sua memoria* 1997; Haug 2003: 65–85 summarises the archaeology. On milestones and roads, see Basso 1986; Laurence 1999: 82. On wider Tetrarchic works, see Rinaldi Tufi 2005.

21. Mori 1990; Mori and Sartori 1997.

22. Lusuardi Siena 1997; Lusuardi Siena *et al.* 1997; summarised in Christie 2006: 108–10.

23. Psalm 20: 7 of AD 386 – translation in Moorhead 1999: 151.

24. Rossignani, Sannazaro and Legrottaglie 2005. On finds tied to late Roman imperial dress, see Airoldi and Palumbo 2002; Sannazaro 2002.

25. Cf. Brogiolo and Olcese 1993: 677.

26. Key archaeological syntheses comprise Montanari (ed.) 1983; Maioli and Stoppioni 1987; *Storia di Ravenna* I and II.1 volumes (Susini (ed.) 1990; Carile (ed.)1991). Most recent is *Ravenna. Da capitale imperiale ...*, plus Augenti 2002, 2006a; Cirelli 2008; with an architectural analysis from Deliyannis 2010, building on and updating Deichmann 1976, 1989. Gillett 2001: 141 argues that Honorius' relocation to Ravenna became definitive only in AD 408.

27. Gelichi 2000 and Augenti 2006a.

28. Ward-Perkins 1984: 241–4. Other fifth century, pre-Ostrogothic churches, attested by textual references only, are the basilica Apostolorum, S. Agnese and S. Agata. Churches at Classe: Farioli Campanati in Montanari (ed.) 1983: 23–51.

29. Augenti 2002, 2006a.

30. Christie and Gibson 1988, determining a largely single-phase build, probably completed under Valentinian III; updates on the walls' archaeology in Cirelli 2008: 54–67.

31. Claudian, *On the Sixth Consulship of Honorius*, lines 531–6: see also lines 406–25 bemoaning Honorius' (and other emperors') extended absence from the Eternal City. Gillett 2001 argues that Rome rather than Ravenna was the seat of 'strategic and ceremonial functions' between the 440s and 470s.

32. Ward-Perkins 1984: 215, 241–4; Johnson 1988.

33. Classe finds illustrated in Montanari (ed.) 1983; updated overview in Augenti 2006a: 203–9. Sixth-century wealth and materials are illustrated in the catalogue *Santi Banchieri Re* (Augenti and Bertelli 2006).

34. Augenti 2006a: 196–200.

35. Rimini excavations discussed by Negrelli 2006, noting the decay of many fine houses by the end of the sixth century – potentially therefore earlier than at Ravenna itself – and subsequent burial activity and poorer houses on some of the sites. On rural productivity during the late antique peak, see Negrelli 2006: 238–43.

36. Brown 1998 draws on evidence recorded by the local ninth-century cleric Andreas Agnellus, who reported – for example, in his account of the episcopate of Damianus in c. AD 700 – that the long-established tradition of Sunday afternoon fights between citizens of all ages and backgrounds had seen, on one occasion, major spilling of blood between rival factions – these based on quarters associated with the town gates.

37. Gillett 2001: 141, 146, 161.

Chapter 6 Pagans and Christians in the Late Roman West

1. Janes 2002. A major author is Brown (1971, 1972, 1987, 1996 and 1998). See also Herrin 1987; Fowden 1998. Sourcebooks: Lee 2000a and Maas 2010.

2. Roman religion in Britain: Henig 1984; Jones and Mattingly 1990: 264–95. Bath: Cunliffe 1995. For Noricum, see Alföldy 1974: 135–40, 194–7; Šašel Kos and Scherrer (eds) 2002. Italy: Potter 1987. Spain: Keay 1988.

3. Meiggs 1973: 337–403; Bakker 1994.

Notes

4. Eunapius *Breviarum*, Book IX: 56, with Brown 1998: 646–7. Ammianus for AD 362 notes Julian the Apostate's anger when the temple of Apollo at Daphne was burnt down, viewed as an act of spite by local Christians: Book 22.13.
5. *CIL* 11.5265; *CT* 16.10.3; Lee 2000a: 92–3.
6. Knight 1999: 118.
7. Bloch 1963; Markus 1990: 28–9; Curran 2000. Regarding Praetextus' epitaph, Cameron 1999 views the priesthoods as inherited labels, not bold statements of paganism. Documentation in Lee 2000a: chs 5 and 6.
8. For example, *CT* 16.10.8 and 17; 15.6.1 and 2, 7.13. Lançon 2000: 92–6, 130–42.
9. Lim 1999: 269–74; Salzmann 1999: 124–6; Lançon 2000: 141–5.
10. Brown 1996: 35 argues some emperors colluded in assaults on major cult centres. Constantine's and his mother's acts of clearance of old shrines at sites of major early Christian significance in Jerusalem and Bethlehem are well documented: Caseau 2004: 120–5.
11. Knight 1999: 112–15 on comparable *vici* or market centres-cum-sanctuaries.
12. Fishwick 2002a: 81–91. Price 1986 on Roman Asia Minor. Colchester: Crummy 1997: 57–60.
13. Fishwick 2002a: 197 and ch. 5; on epigraphic loss, see 189–90.
14. Keay 1996: 28, 33, 36.
15. Lavan 2001a: 49–50 sees such palaces also as display points for imperial busts, effectively 'a quasi-religious continuation of the imperial cult'; if so, the statuary at Tarraco may belong to the *praetorium*, not the council offices.
16. Marin 2001; Marin and Vickers (eds) 2004. Cf. data from Eretria in Greece: Schmid 2001.
17. Some heads were recovered by antiquarians, notably Arthur Evans, who gave the heads of Livia and Mercury to the Ashmolean in Oxford in 1878; Vespasian's head was found a century later, the excavators describing how it must 'have rolled down the temple steps into the forum' after the temple's destruction.
18. Cameron 1999: 130; Sauer 2003: 139–42, plus 89–101.
19. Kyle 1998: 244.
20. Alföldy 1974: 194–7.
21. Meiggs 1973, stating that most are small and scattered and 'do not suggest great wealth' – p. 372. Sauer 2003: 18–19 notes that minimal data exist for their last phases. Oriental cults in Rome: Price 2000.
22. Nicholson 1995: 361; Sauer 1996: 7–9, 76–8; Cameron 1999: 109.
23. Nicholson 1995: 21–4.
24. Nicholson 1995: 30–2, noting the excavator's claim that some coin deposition by worshippers came after the mithraeum was abandoned. Gordon 1999 disputes some of Sauer's views.
25. Sauer 1996: 79–88.
26. Sauer 1996: 27.
27. Sauer 1996: 62–80.
28. Nicholson 1995: 361; Cameron 1999: 109. Sauer 2003: 135–6 argues for axe damage to the S. Prisca artwork.
29. Cameron 1999: 129.
30. Laurence 1999: 95–108. On the unreliability of early Christian sermons and hagiographies, see Clark 2001. See section 5.3 of Maas 2010 for the suppression of pagan cults.
31. Riggs 2001.
32. Mattingly 1995: 167–8, 211–13. In c. AD 400, letters between Augustine and Publicola showed late Roman landowners employing such tribal groups to guard crops and flocks and to help out at harvest time; they were allowed passage onto Roman lands after swearing pagan oaths to behave: Mattingly 1995: 186 with note 1 p. 231.

33. Riggs 2001: 294–6; Caseau 2004: 130.
34. Lizzi 1990: 169–72; Trout 1996: 176–8; Cantino Wataghin 2000: 211–19; Díaz 2000: 30.
35. Lizzi 1990: 167–8; Mennella 1998: 151, 156.
36. Van Dam 1993: 13–28; Knight 1999: 116–27; Bitel 2009: 42–5. Archaeologies of temple loss in Gaul: Goodman forthcoming, drawing especially on Fauduet 1993.
37. Caseau 2004: 106–13, noting reactions to pagan rural practice in fourth- to sixth-century Egypt and Syria.
38. Aquileia survey: Menis 1995. Other references: Christie 2006: 119–21.
39. Leadbetter 2000. On evolving later Roman historiography: Blockley 1981: 86–8; Croke and Emmett (eds) 1983; Rohrbacher 2002.
40. See Krautheimer 1980: 69–92; Pietri 1985–7: 362–3; Moorhead 1999; Salzman 2000: 355–60. Aristocratic asceticism: Curran 2000: 260–320.
41. 1985: ch. 7, 141–56. On conversions of Gallic elites, see Wes 1992.
42. Trout 1996, 1999.
43. Krautheimer 1980: 32–58; papers in Pani Ermini (ed.) (2000b), notably Pani Ermini, Guidobaldi, Pergola; for Italy see Ward-Perkins 1984: 65–84. Art and architecture: Milburn 1988; Elsner 1998.
44. Bowden 2001; on south Gaul, see Gauthier and Picard (eds) 1986; Harries 1992; Loseby 1992.
45. Notably Harries 1992, observing how Episcopal power varied from centre to centre dependent on urban status, saintly heritage, relics, congregations and so on. Overviews in Llewellyn 1993: 87–108; Liebeschuetz 2001a: 137–67.
46. Thompson 1982: 113–33.
47. Pietri 1985–7: 351–3; Campione and Nuzzo 1999: 17–21 and 25ff.
48. Italian examples: Christie 2006: ch. 3. Barcelona: Beltrán de Heredia Bercero (ed.) 2002. Geneva: Bonnet and Reynaud 2000. Ripoll and Gurt (eds) 2000 for late antique and early medieval capitals and churches.
49. Turin: Pejrani Baricco 1998. On church placements in Rome, see Lim 1999; Curran 2000; Fiocchi Nicolai 2000.
50. Key contributions: Harries 1992; Cantino Wataghin 1992 and 1995; Gauthier 1999; papers in Brogiolo and Ward-Perkins (eds) 1999; Pani Ermini 2000; Christie 2006: 91–112. On spolia: Alchermes 1994; Pensabene 2000.
51. Walmsley 1996: 131–41; Sauer 2001: 99; Saradi 2006: 398–400 (and ch. 13 generally). Anatolia: Harl 2001. Temple conversion in Cilicia: Bayliss 2004.
52. Spain: Arce forthcoming. Gaul: Goodman forthcoming.
53. On Carthage see Riggs 2001. Potter 1995: 64–79 surveys early Church spaces in North Africa, as at Bulla Regia, Hippo, Djemila and Tipasa.
54. Autun: Young 2001. Arles: Loseby 1996: 60–1. Loseby 1992 offers a wider survey of cathedrals in fifth-century Gaul. Cf. Knight 1999: 63–84.
55. 1999: 203–9.
56. Catacombs: Fiocchi Nicolai, Bisconti and Mazzoleni 1999, notably pp. 37–59. Art: Milburn 1988: 19–57. Cult of martyrs: Deichmann 1993: 51–69. Valuable contributions are in Pani Ermini (ed.) 2000b, including Fiocchi Nicolai 2000, discussing routes, guidebooks, pilgrim shelters, hostels. A law of 381 highlights the growing desire for burial close to the shrines of the apostles and martyrs – CT 9.17.6.
57. Harries 1992: 85–7.
58. Intramural burial: Brogiolo and Cantino Wataghin (eds) 1998; Cantino Wataghin and Lambert 1998; Cantino Wataghin 1999.
59. Arce 1997; Scott 2000, 2004; Dyson 2003: 90–2, highlighting Chiragan in south-west France, containing a vast collection of classical sculptures from its major, fourth-century phase.

60. Knight 1999: 126–7 for fifth- and sixth-century Gaul.
61. Ripoll and Arce 2000.
62. Maloney and Hale 1996. Cf. the *villa Fortunatus* at Fraga: Ripoll and Arce 2000: 75–7.
63. Volpe 1998; summarised in Francovich and Hodges 2003: 43–5; Christie 2006: 442–51.
64. Alföldy 1974. On Norican towns, see Šašel Kos and Scherrer (eds) 2002. On frontier zones, see Buora and Jobst (eds) 2002. For early Christianity, see Harreither 1999.
65. Eusebius, *Eccles. History*, V.5.1–7.
66. Images in Becatti 1957, nos 11, 12.
67. Harreither 1999: 19–23.
68. Jobst *et al.* 2002: 25, 27, with catalogue entries on pp. 56–62 and 81–5 with other finds from Melk, Tulln and Ernsthofen. The Christian designs on pots and lamps were, however, 'standard' on such products by the late fourth century and need not mean their owners were Christian. On chronological variations, see Petts 2003: 104–5.
69. Vipota: Lazar 2002: 96–7. Virunum: Glaser in Piccottini 2002: 129–32, 141–4.
70. Alföldy 1974: 210–11 argues for Christian destructions of these shrines.
71. Gáspár 2002: 7–9, 144, 153–6.
72. Gorsium: Fitz and Fedak 1993, contra Gáspár 2002: 129–34; Kekkut and Sopinae-Pécs: Gáspár 2002: 51–3, 66–91, plus Hudák and Nagy 2005.
73. Petts 2003: 41–8. A longer lasting heresy is Donatism which affected much of North Africa: Rives 1995; Shaw 2004.
74. Petts 2003: 41–8; Mawer 1995 analyses related small finds; Faulkner 2000b: 116–20, 127–8 offers a rather outspoken overview.
75. Arnold and Davies 2000: 132. Bede, *Eccles. Hist.* I, 7.
76. *Eusebius. History*, Book I, ch. 7. Niblett 2001: 137–9; Petts 2003: 33–5.
77. 2000: 127 and 123.
78. Jones and Mattingly 1990: 294–300. Caerwent: Arnold and Davies 2000: 129, 132. On villas: Scott 2000. Colchester and Gosbecks: Crummy 1997. Sauer 1996: 81 disputes such a late date for the Jupiter Column.
79. York: Roskams 1996. London: Petts 2003: 62–5.
80. Petts 2003: 57–9.
81. Jones 2002: 127–9. Jones 1994 for comparanda. Newest interpretation: Gilmour 2007. Petts 2003: 60–1 notes a larger church contender in the lower town at Flaxengate, but Jones 2002: 123 rejects this.
82. Scott 2000.
83. Meates 1979, 1987, arguing (1979: 18) that pagan and Christian practice ran together, implied by votive pots before the portrait busts of the Deep Room.
84. Petts 2003: 127–32; Plunkett 2005: 20–3. The Thetford hoard, interpreted as a safety cache by priests of a shrine of Faunus (see Johns and Potter 1983) might be reinterpreted as a Christian deposit.
85. Entries in Maxfield (ed.) 1989; Bell 1998; Pearson 2002: 169–70.
86. Birley, personal communication for Vindolanda with reports forthcoming; Bidwell and Speak 1994: 103–4 for South Shields; Crow 2004: 114–17 and Rushworth 2009: 321–2 for Housesteads.
87. Cameron 1993a: 66–80; Brown 1996: 41. Bishop Ambrose is a key source for the struggle against Arianism in Milan and Rome, often spilling out into open conflict – Moorhead 1999: 102–28.
88. Eunapius, Book IX: 48.2 for AD 378. Valens was posthumously blamed for imposing Arianism on the Goths by many sources – Lenski 2002: 262 notes a graffito from a south Anatolian church wall denouncing 'Emperor Valens you did wrong, for you surrendered the Church to the heretical Arians'. Ulfila and the Goths: Wolfram 1988: 75–85; Heather and Matthews 1991; Cusack 1999: 39–48.

89. Deliyannis 2010: ch. 5, nb. pp. 156–7, plus 184–5 on the Arian and Orthodox baptisteries.
90. Hunt 1992 on fifth-century Gallic pilgrims. Travelogues and travel: Wilkinson 1971: 3–30; Leyerle 2000, noting regular movements of bishops to synods, of letters, of embassies and so on.
91. Lawrence 1984: 45–53. For later contexts, see Foot 2006; De Rubeis and Marazzi (eds) 2008.
92. Moorhead 1999: 64, plus 51–4, 63–8. Lawrence 1984: 1–16 covers early monasticism. Boak 1995, discussing manpower shortages, underplays Church membership, monasticism or celibacy as contributory factors.
93. Van Dam 1985: 119–40.
94. Stewart 2000: 361–2. On Honoratus and his pupils, see Wes 1992: 255–8.
95. Roberts 1992.
96. Mathisen 1992.
97. Pergola 2000 and other papers in Pani Ermini (ed.) 2000b cover early pilgrims to Rome; later developments: Birch 1998.
98. Van Dam 1985, 1993 for saints, relics and leaders in late antique Gaul. New analysis of Genofeva by Bitel 2009. Velay 1992 describes Paris' ecclesiastical complexes.

Chapter 7 Communications, Trade and Land

1. McCormick 2001 and Wickham 2006 (nb. ch. 11) are essential reading and offer far more data than I supply here on the late Roman economy.
2. Laurence 1999; Kolb 2001; plus papers (nb. Broderson, Kolb, Salway) in Adams and Laurence (eds) 2001.
3. McCormick 2001: chs 5–7.
4. Basso 1986.
5. Ostia: Meiggs 1973; Pavolini 1986; Gallina Zevi and Claridge (eds) 1996. Portus: Coccia 1996; Keay et al. 2005, on the major surveys here and on canal systems linking the port to Rome. Shipping personnel: Aldrete and Mattingly 1999; McCormick 2001: chs 4 and 13.
6. Greene 1986: ch. 2; Throckmorton (ed.) 1987; Parker 1992. Varied wrecked river boats and barges with related merchandise, personal goods and so on covering c. 300 BC–AD 400 have been excavated at Pisa: Bruni (ed.) 2000; http://www.cantierenavipisa.it/
7. Greene 1986: 98–140 offers a valuable overview of regional trade and agricultural outputs.
8. Monte Testaccio: Panella 1999: 196–7. On the Tiber ports and warehouses and other, later, possible amphora dumps in the city, see De Caprariis 1999. Spanish trade data: Reynolds 2010.
9. McCann and Freed 1994. On Roman ship construction, see Throckmorton (ed.) 1987.
10. D'Oriano 2002.
11. See www2.rgzm.de/navis/Musea/Mainz/NavismusEngl.htm for the Mainz Ancient Shipping Museum.
12. For changes to the fabric of late Roman and late antique Portus, see Coccia 1996 and Keay et al. 2005.
13. Hurst 1992, 1994.
14. Luni's land, economy and port: Delano Smith et al. 1986. Archaeology: Frova (ed.) 1973–4, 1977. Bishop, church and late antique town: Durante 2003; Lusuardi Siena 2003.
15. Coastal surveys: Raban (ed.) 1988. Tel Dor excavations: http://dor.huji.ac.il/ Sebastos: Raban 2009. Cf. Kingsley 2001: 86–7.

16. For London's harbour/quay installations – showing use into the fourth century, but with diminishing continental imports – see Milne 1985. Marsden 1994: chs 4 and 5 discuss both boats and later Roman trade activities.

17. Ceramic supplies in Britain: Cooper 2000. Fourth-century ceramics on Hadrian's Wall: Bidwell and Croom 2010, noting a near total dominance of British wares from the early fourth century, becoming localised to east Yorkshire wares after 350; Mediterranean ceramic imports petered out by *c*. AD 300.

18. Southern Gaul: Hitchner 1992, drawing on Giardina (ed.) 1986. Vandal trade: Fulford 1980. Rome and grain supplies: Rickman 1980. For critical analyses of data for all western zones, see Wickham 2006: 720–59, plus McCormick 2001: 53–63. Piracy levels perhaps rose in the fourth and fifth centuries – thus Claudian's *On the Sixth Consulship of Honorius*, lines 132–40, calls pirates 'the terror of every sea, laden with the spoils of violence and the booty taken from many a captured merchantman' – De Souza 1999: 225–40.

19. Peacock, Bejaoui and Ben Lazreg 1990; Mackensen 1998; Bonifay 2004; Wickham 2006: 720–8. African Red Slip wares: Hayes 1972, who first showed how such industries and their long-distance trading continued fully into the seventh century.

20. South Etruria: Potter 1979. Tiber valley survey: Patterson (ed.) 2004. See also, for late Roman and early medieval contexts, Paroli and Delogu (eds) 1993.

21. See Note 7 for regional surveys. Ager Tarraconensis: Carreté, Keay and Millett 1995; North African olive oil production: Mattingly 1996; Mattingly, Barker, Gilbertson, and Jones 1996; Syrian productions: Decker 2001 and 2009.

22. Aldrete and Mattingly 1999: 193–200; Mattingly and Aldrete 2000.

23. Mackinnon 2004.

24. Supply shortages: Garnsey and Whittaker (eds) 1983; Garnsey 1990.

25. Whittaker 1993; Whittaker and Garnsey 1998: 281–5 provide a compact overview of the issue of *agri deserti*. See Christie 1996a for Italy. Tainter's 1988 model of collapse centred heavily on the vision of dramatic rural decay, over-exploitation of soils, labour shortages (nb. pp. 133–46).

26. *Milano. Capitale*, 233–304.

27. Arce 1997, Fig. 9; Berndt and Steinacher (eds) 2008, Fig. 4, p. 177. Arce 1997: 29 quotes Procopius (*Vandal War*, I.5.11) on how Gaiseric 'robbed them [Libyans/Roman elite] of their estates, which were both very numerous and excellent, and distributed them among the nation of the Vandals' – their former landowners either reduced to poverty or left as owners but heavily taxed. Innes 2007: 119 on cultural continuities. Mattingly 1989 on other documentary guides to 'no change'. Structural and artistic displays by rural elite: Scott 2004.

28. Christie 2004b. Key works (besides regional surveys noted in Notes 7 and 21): papers in Part II of Giardina (ed.) 1986; Barker and Lloyd (eds) 1991; van Ossel 1992; Favory and Fiches (eds) 1994; Barker (ed.) 1995; Van Ossel and Ouzoulias 2000; Burns and Eadie (eds) 2001; Mulvin 2002; Dyson 2003 (nb. ch. 5); Francovich and Hodges 2003 (nb. ch. 2); Bowden, Lavan and Machado 2004; Christie (ed.) 2004a; Lewit 2004; Volpe and Turchiano (eds) 2005 on southern Italy; Wickham 2006: ch. 8; Bowes 2010. For the East, see Decker 2010.

29. Dyson 2003: chs 1 and 2.

30. Chavarría 2007 (with a catalogue of 100 sites); 2004a, b.

31. Wickham 2006: 465–73, stressing villa display 'was firmly part of western Roman aris-tocratic identity', contrasting with the village order of the East (p. 478). Major Italian and Sicilian villas such as Piazza Armerina and Desenzano are discussed in Christie 2006 and Scott 2004.

32. For Torre de Palma, see also Maloney and Hale 1996. Cf. the group of opulent south-west Gallic/Pyrenean villas like Montmaurin and Lalonquette – Dyson 2003: 90–1.

33. De la Bédoyère 1993: ch. 4; Dark and Dark 1997: ch. 3; Scott 2000; Dark 2004, nb. 281–6, stressing industrial take-off in this period. Frocester Court: Price 2000.
34. Mulvin 2002, nb. chs 3 and 5.
35. Mulvin 2002, ch. 6; cf. Chavarría 2004b: 83–5. For Italy see Christie 2006: 442–51.
36. Schrunk and Begović 2000; Christie 2004b: 16–18.
37. Wickham 2006: 474–81, stressing variations depending on location; cf. Christie 2004b.
38. Lewit 2009. Britain: Dark and Dark 1997: 143–4; Rippon 2000. A south-west England case study is Fyfe and Rippon 2004. Cf. Christie 2006: 484–91 for rural environment changes in Italy.
39. See Lewit 2009: 89–90 for parts of Spain.
40. Nb. Francovich and Hodges 2003 for central Italy. Northern Gaul: Louis 2004.

Chapter 8 The Ends of Rome in the West

1. Snyder 1998: 17–25.
2. Dark 1994: 51–5; Petts 2003: 45–8.
3. Dark 1994; Snyder 1998: Part II on the sources; cf. James 2001; Fleming 2010: chs 2 and 3.
4. Cowie 2000; Burton 2007; plus Milne 1985, 1995. For London's late Roman archaeology, see Chapter 4 of this book.
5. Blockley et al. 1995; summarised in Ottaway 1992: 111–14; Loseby 2000a: 340, 350.
6. Niblett 2001. Reuse of Roman materials and spaces: Strickland 1988 on Chester. Recent work at Leicester reveals 'saxon' period intrusions and presences, and shows how in some areas, stumps at least of Roman structures were only fully robbed in the twelfth century: Speed 2010. Transitions to Anglo-Saxon control: Loveluck 1995.
7. Dark 1994: ch. 3, 2004: 286–94.
8. Dark 1994: 206–15; Snyder 1998: 176–98; Turner 2004 on trade and sites; wider discussion in Harris 2003. Gerrard 2004 on prolonged local ceramic supplies in the south west. Inscribed stones: Thomas 1994; Tedeschi 2005; Redknap and Lewis 2007.
9. White and Barker 1998; cf. Loseby 2000a: 332–6.
10. Bidwell and Speak 1994; Wilmott et al. 1997; Snyder 1998: 168–72. Collins and Allason-Jones (eds) 2010 review late and sub-Roman finds from the whole frontier region.
11. Higham 1986: 250–60; O'Brien 2010; Wilmott 2010. Latest Roman and sub-/post-Roman activities at Housesteads: Rushworth (ed.) 2009: 314–26. On the Northumbrian coast, excavations at Bamburgh are exploring the centre of Bernician power: www.bamburghresearchproject.co.uk/archaeology.html
12. Alföldy 1974: 213–20; updated for certain examples in Šašel Kos and Scherrer (eds) 2002; Glaser 2002 on Teurnia. On settlement here, see Bender 2001: 189–92; Parker 2009: 154–65.
13. Haberl and Hawkes 1973; Alföldy 1974: 220–7; Ubl 1982; Heather 2005: 407–15.
14. Curta 2001 for the sixth-century Balkans, highlighting farmers as soldiers and soldiers as farmers.
15. Heather 2005: 409, regarding troop numbers, set, through analysis of the Notitia Dignitatum, at about 10,000 for AD 400; perhaps only a quarter remained by the 460s, supplemented by federates.
16. Fischer and Geisler 1988; papers in Dannheimer and Dopsch (eds) 1988. Regensburg: Waldherr 1992; Codreanu-Windnauer 2004.
17. Courtois 1955; re-evaluations by Rushworth 2000, 2004.
18. Heather 1996: ch 8, with pp. 216–21 on Theoderic's manoeuvres with Zeno. Ostrogothic Italy: Wolfram 1988; Moorhead 1992; Bierbrauer et al. (eds) 1994; Amory 1997; sections in Christie 2006.

Notes

19. Rea 1999, 2002.
20. Cassiodorus, *Variae* III, 30. In AD 510 a 'Custodian of the Monuments' for Rome was indeed appointed (III, 31).
21. Gelichi 2000: 122–6; Augenti and Bertelli (eds) 2006; *Storia di Ravenna I, II* (Susini (ed.) 1990; Carile (ed.) 1991).
22. Palace: Gelichi 2000; Augenti (ed.) 2002; Cirelli 2008.
23. Deliyannis 2010: 115–18. Cf. Maioli and Stoppioni 1987. Gothic churches: Deichmann 1976: 325–30; Johnson 1988; Cirelli 2008: 92–100; Deliyannis 2010: ch. 5.
24. Rizzardi 1989, but with less conviction in Deliyannis 2010: 139–87; cf. Heather 1996: 245–6.
25. Moorhead 1992: 89–97; Llewellyn 1993: 42–4; Heather 1996: 248–76; Amory 1997: 227–34.
26. Augenti and Bertelli (ed.) 2007 (notably papers by Augenti and Cirelli).

Conclusions: An Empire Lost and Transformed

1. Nb. Heather 2000: 20–22.
2. For example, for Ostrogothic Italy and Lombard Italy: Arslan 1994, 1990. See also Hendy 1988.
3. Byzantine Italy: Zanini 1998; Christie 2006. Byzantine Africa: Pringle 1981.
4. Innes 2007: 182–94. New analyses on Byzantine centres: Saradi 2006; Zavagno 2009. Cf. papers in Christie and Loseby (eds) 1996 by Walmsley, Carver and Roskams; Decker 2009: 261–2 for Syria. On the positives and negatives of Arab takeover in Palestine, see Fiema 2001.
5. Classe: Augenti forthcoming.
6. Cf. Johnson 2010 on waste in late antique Italy and Rome, especially.
7. On dress and identity, see Buora (ed.) 2002; Swift 2000; Mattingly 2004. for Britain, see James and Millett (eds) 2001; Mattingly 2006: ch. 7.
8. Redfern and DeWitte 2010 consider health and mortality models for populations across the late Iron Age to Roman transition in Dorset, proposing a negative impact through Roman urbanisation. DNA and isotope analysis are meanwhile being used to question Viking roots and integrations – see Harding *et al.* 2010 – and a new interdisciplinary project at the University of Leicester is questioning migrations across the Roman to medieval periods in Britain: http://www2.le.ac.uk/projects/roots-of-the-british

Bibliography

Primary Sources

Ambrose, Letters – *Ambrose of Milan: Political Letters and Speeches*, translated by J.H.W.G. Liebeschuetz, with C. Hill (Translated Texts for Historians, Volume 43). Liverpool: Liverpool University Press, 2010.

Ammianus Marcellinus – *Ammianus Marcellinus, The Later Roman Empire (AD 354–378)*, selected and translated by W. Hamilton. Harmondsworth: Penguin, 1986.

Anon., *De Rebus Bell.* – Anonymous, *De Rebus Bellicis*, In: E. A. Thompson (ed), *A Roman Reformer and Inventor:* Oxford, 1952.

Augustine – St. Augustine, *Confessions*, Translated by R. S. Pine-Coffin, Harmondsworth: Penguin, 1979.

Aurelius Victor – Aurelius Victor, *De Caesaribus*, translated by H. Bird (Translated Texts for Historians, Volume 17). Liverpool: Liverpool University Press, 1994.

Ausonius – Ausonius, *Ordo Urbium Nobilium*, translated by H.G. Evelyn White, 2 vols. London: Loeb/Heinemann, 1919, 1921.

Bede, Eccles. Hist. – Bede, *Ecclesiastical History of the English People*, translated by L. Sherley-Price, London: Penguin, 1990.

Cassiodorus – Cassiodorus Senator, *Variae*, in T. Mommsen (ed.), *Monumenta Germaniae Historica, Auctores Antiquissimi, XII*, Berlin: Hiersmann, 1893–1894. Selected translations by S.J.B. Barnish in *The* Variae *of Magnus Aurelius Cassiodorus Senator* (Translated Texts for Historians, Volume 12). Liverpool: Liverpool University Press, 1992.

Cassius Dio – *Roman History. Epitomes of Books LXXI–LXXX*, translated by E. Cary (*Dio's Roman History*, Volume IX). London: Loeb/Heinemann, 1927.

CIL – *Corpus Inscriptionum Italicarum*, Berlin, 1863–.

Claudius Claudianus – *Claudian*, translated by M. Platnauer, 2 vols. New York & London: Loeb/Heinemann, 1922. See also *Panegyric*, translated by H. Isbell in *Last Poets of Imperial Rome*. London: Penguin, 1971.

CT – *Codex Theodosianus*, edited by T. Mommsen & P. Meyer. Berlin: Weidmann, 1905. Translated by C. Pharr, *The Theodosian Code and Novels and the Sirmondian Constitution*. Princeton: Princeton University Press, 1952 (reprinted in 1969).

Egeria – Egeria, *Travels. Egeria's Travels*, translated by J. Wilkinson. London: SPCK, 1971.

Eugippius, *Vita Severini* – Eugippius, *The Life of Saint Severinus*, translated by G. Robinson. London: Harvard, 1914.

Eunapius – Eunapius, *Fragments of the History by Eunapius*, translated by R.C. Blockley. Liverpool: Fancis Cairns, 1981, II, 1–150.

Eusebius – *History of the Church* – *Eusebius, The History of the Church from Christ to Constantine*, translated by G.A. Williamson. Harmondsworth & New York: Penguin Books, 1965 (revised by A. Louth, 1989).

Eutropius – *Eutropius: Breviarium*, translated by H. Bird (Translated Texts for Historians, Volume 14). Liverpool: Liverpool University Press, 1993.

Gildas – *De Excidio Britanniae*, in M. Winterbottom (ed. and trans.), *Gildas, The Ruin of Britain and Other Works*. London: Phillimore, 1978.

Gregory of Tours – *History of the Franks*, translated by L. Thorpe. Harmondsworth: Penguin Books, 1974.

Gregory of Tours *—Life of the Fathers*, translated by E. James (Translated Texts for Historians, Volume 1). Liverpool: Liverpool University Press, 1991 (2nd edition).

Greg. *Reg.* – Gregory the Great, *Registrum Epistolarum*, in P. Ewald & L.M. Hartmann (ed.), *Monumenta Germaniae Historica, Epistolae I and II*, Berlin: Hiersmann, 1887–1899.

Historia Augusta – Scriptores Historiae Augustae. Volume III, translated by D. Magie. Loeb Classical Library, London: Heinemann, 1932.

Hydatius – Hydatius, *Chronicle*, in T. Mommsen (ed.), *Monumenta Germaniae Historica, Auctores Antiquissimi, XI*. Berlin: Weidmann, 1894. See English translation and commentary in Muhlberger 1990.

Jerome – Jerome, *Letters*, edited by I. Hilberg, in *Corpus Scriptorum. Ecclesiasticorum Latinorum*, 54–56, Vienna: Ternpsky, 1910–18.

Lib. Pont. – Book of Pontiffs. *Liber Pontificalis*, edited by L. Duchesne, Paris, 1886–1892. Translated by R. Davis, *The Book of Pontiffs (Liber Pontificalis), The Lives of the Eighth-Century Popes* (Translated Texts for Historians, Volumes 5, 13). Liverpool: Liverpool University Press, 1989, 1992.

Libanius' *Speech – Libanius: Select Works*, Volume 2, edited and translated by A.F. Norman. Cambridge Mass & London: Harvard University Press and Loeb/Heinemann, 1977.

Magister Gregorius – J. Osborne, *Magister Gregorius. The Marvels of Rome*. Toronto: Pontifical Institute of Medieval Studies, 1987.

Malchus, Frags – Malchus *Fragments. The Fragmentary Classicising Historians of the Later Roman Empire. Eunapius, Olympiodorus, Priscus and Malchus*, translated by R.C. Blockley, 2 vols (ARCA: Classical and Medieval Texts, Papers and Monographs, 6), Liverpool: Fancis Cairns, 1981.

Not. Dign. – *Notitia Dignitatum*, edited by O. Seeck. Berlin: Weidmann, 1876 (reprinted Frankfurt: Minerva, 1962).

Nov. Marc., Nov. Th., Nov. Val. – Novels of Marcian, Novels of Theodosius and of Valentinian. See *CT – Codex Theodosianus.*

Olympiodorus – Olympiodorus, *Fragments of the History by Olympiodorus*, translated by R.C. Blockley. Liverpool: Fancis Cairns, 1981, II, 151–220.

Orosius – Paulus Orosius, *Seven Books of History against the Pagans*, translated by I.W. Raymond. New York: Columbia University Press, 1936.

Pacatus – Pacatus, *Panegyric of Theodosius*, translated by C.E.V. Nixon & B. Saylor Rodgers, in *In Praise of Later Roman Emperors. The Panegyrici Latini*, Berkeley & Oxford: University of California Press, 1994, 437–516.

Paulinus – Paulinus of Nola, *Epistulae et Carmines*, translated by R. Goldschmidt, in *Paulinus' Churches at Nola. Texts, Translations and Commentary*. Amsterdam: Uitgerers Maatschoppij, 1940.

Pliny, Letters – *The Letters of the Younger Pliny*, translated by B. Radice. Harmondsworth: Penguin, 1963.

Priscus – *Fragments of the History by Priscus*, translated by R.C. Blockley. Liverpool: Fancis Cairns, 1981, II, 221–400.

Procopius, *Gothic War* – Procopius of Caesarea, *The Gothic Wars*, translated by H.B. Dewing. New York & London: Loeb/Heinemann, 1914–35.

Prosper – Prosper of Aquitaine, *Epitoma Chronicon*, in T. Mommsen (ed.), *Monumenta Germaniae Historica, Auctores Antiquissimi, IX*. Berlin: Weidmann, 1892, 341–499. See English translation and commentary in Muhlberger 1990.

Rut. Nam. – Rutilius Claudius Namatianus, *De Reditu Suo*. English translation by H. Isbell, in *Last Poets of Imperial Rome*. London: Penguin, 1971.

SHA *–Scriptores Historiae Augustae.* Volume III, translated by D. Magie. London: Loeb Classical Library, Heinemann, 1932.

Symmachus, *Ep.* – Symacchus, *Epistulae*, in O. Seeck (ed.), *Monumenta Germaniae Historica, Auctores Antiquissimi, XII*. Berlin: Weidmann, 1883.

Symmachus, *Rel.* – Symmachus, *Relationes*. Translated by R.H. Barrow, *Prefect and Emperor. The Relationes of Symmachus, AD 384*. Oxford: Clarendon Press, 1973.

Tacitus, *Germania* – Tacitus, *The Agricola and the Germania*, translated by H. Mattingly (revised by S. Handford, 1970). Harmondsworth: Penguin Books, 1948. New edition and translation by J.B. Rives – *Tacitus. Germania*. Oxford: Clarendon Press, 1999.

Vegetius –*Vegetius: Epitome of Military Science*, translated by N.P. Milner (Translated Texts for Historians, Volume 16). Liverpool: Liverpool University Press, 1993.

Victor of Vita – *Victor of Vita: History of the Vandal Persecution*, translated by J. Moorhead (Translated Texts for Historians, Volume 10). Liverpool: Liverpool University Press:, 1992.

Zosimus, *Nea Historia* – Zosimus, *Nea Historia*, translated by J. Buchanan & H. Davies. London, 1967; also by R. Ridley, *Byzantina Australiensa 2*. Canberra, Australia: Australian Association for Byzantine Studies, 1982.

Sourcebooks

Baxter Wolf, K. (1991), *Conquerors and Chroniclers of Early Medieval Spain* (Translated Texts for Historians, Volume 9), Liverpool: Liverpool University Press.

Blockley, R. (1981), *The Fragmentary Classicising Historians of the Later Roman Empire. Eunapius, Olympiodorus, Priscus and Malchus*, 2 vols (ARCA: Classical and Medieval Texts, Papers and Monographs, 6), Liverpool: Francis Cairns.

Hekster, O. (2008), *Rome and Its Empire, AD 193–284* (Debates and Documents in Ancient History), Edinburgh: Edinburgh University Press.

Lee, A.D. (2000), *Pagans and Christians in Late Antiquity. A Sourcebook*, London: Routledge.

Maas, M. (2010), *Readings in Late Antiquity. A Sourcebook* (2nd edition), London: Routledge.

Muhlberger, S. (1990), *The Fifth-Century Chroniclers. Prosper, Hydatius and the Gallic Chronicler of 452* (ARCA Classical and Medieval Texts, Papers and Monographs, 27), Leeds: Carins.

Secondary Sources

Adams, C. & Laurence, R. (eds) (2001), *Travel and Geography in the Roman Empire*, London: Routledge.

Abed, A.B. & Duval, N. (2000), 'Carthage. La capitale du royaume et les villes de Tunisie à l'époque vandale', in G. Ripoll & J.M. Gurt (eds), *Sedes regiae (ann. 400–800)*, Barcelona: Reial Acadèmia de Bones Lletres, 163–218.

Aillagon, J.-J. (ed.) (2008), *Rome and the Barbarians. The Birth of a New World* (Exhibition Catalogue – Venice-Bonn-Rome), Milan: Palazzo Grassi/Skira Editore.

Airoldi, F. & Palumbo, A. (2002), '*Militaria* dalla necropoli rinvenuta nei cortili dell'Università Cattolica di Milano', in M. Buora (ed.), *Miles Romanus dal Po al Danubio nel Tardoantico (Atti del Convegno Internazionale, Pordenone – Concordia Sagittaria, 17–19 Marzo 2000)*, Pordenone: Sage Print, 81–98.

Alchermes, J. (1994), '*Spolia* in Roman Cities of the Late Empire: Legislative Rationales and Architectural Reuse', *Dumbarton Oaks Papers*, 48: 167–78.

Aldrete, G. & Mattingly, D. (1999), 'Feeding the City: The Organisation, Operation, and Scale of the Supply System for Rome', in D.S. Potter & D.J. Mattingly (eds), *Life, Death and Entertainment in the Roman Empire*, Ann Arbor: University of Michigan Press, 171–203.

Alföldy, G. (1974), *Noricum*, London & Boston: Routledge & Kegan Paul.

Alföldy, G. (2001), '*Difficillima tempora*: Urban Life, Inscriptions and Mentality in Late Antique Rome', in T.S. Burns & J.W. Eadie (eds), *Urban Centers and Rural Contexts in Late Antiquity*, East Lansing: Michigan State University Press, 3–24.

Amory, P. (1997), *People and Identity in Ostrogothic Italy, 489–554*, Cambridge: Cambridge University Press.

Ando, C. (2008), 'Decline, Fall, and Transformation', *Journal of Late Antiquity*, 1(1): 31–60.

Arce, J. (1993), 'La ciudad en la España tardoromana: ¿continuidad o discontinuidad?', in *Ciudad y comunidad cívica en Hispania, siglos II y III d.C.* (Collection de la Casa de Velázquez, 40), Madrid: Casa Velazquez, 177–84.

Arce, J. (1997), '*Otium et negotium*: The Great Estates, 4th–7th Century', in L. Webster & M. Brown (eds), *The Transformation of the Roman World, AD 400–900*, London: European Science Foundation/British Museum Press, 19–32.

Arce, J. (2000), 'La fundacíon de nuevas ciudades en el Imperio romano tardío: de Diocleciano a Justiniano (s. IV–VI)', in G. Ripoll & J.M. Gurt (eds), *Sedes regiae (ann. 400–800)*, Barcelona: Reial Acadèmia de Bones Lletres, 31–62.

Arce, J. (forthcoming), '*Fana, templa, delubra destrui praecipimus*: The End of the Temples in Roman Spain', in M. Mulryan & L. Lavan (eds), *Late Antique Paganism*, Leiden: Brill.

Arce, J., Ensoli, S. & La Rocca, E. (eds) (1997), *Hispania Romana. Da terra di conquista a provincia dell'impero*, Milan: Electa.

Arena, M.S., Delogu, P., Paroli, L., Ricci, M., Sagui, L. & Venditelli, L. (eds) (2001), *Roma dall'antichità al medioevo. Archeologia e storia nel Museo Nazionale Romano Crypta Balbi* (Ministero per i Beni e le Attività Culturali/Soprintendenza Archeologica di Roma), Milan: Electa.

Arnold, C.J. & Davies, J.L. (2000), *Roman and Early Medieval Wales*, Stroud: Sutton Publishing.

Arslan, E.A. (1990), 'Le monete', in G.C. Menis (ed.), *I Longobardi* (exhibition catalogue), Milan: Electa, 164–77.

Arslan, E.A. (1994), 'La moneta dei Goti in Italia', in V. Bierbrauer, O. von Hessen & E.A. Arslan (eds), *I Goti* (exhibition catalogue, Milan, Palazzo Reale, 28 gennaio–8 maggio 1994), Milan: Electa Lombardia, 252–65.

Arthur, P. (2002), *Naples. From Roman Town to City-State* (Archaeological Monographs of the British School at Rome 12), London: British School at Rome.

Arthur, P. (2004), 'From *Vicus* to Village: Italian Landscapes, AD 400–1000', in N. Christie (ed.), *Landscapes of Change: Rural Evolutions in Late Antiquity and the Early Middle Ages*, Aldershot: Ashgate, 103–33.

Augenti, A. (1996), *Il Palatino nel Medioevo. Archeologia e topografia (secoli VI–XIII)*, Rome: 'L'Erma' di Bretschneider.

Augenti, A. (ed.) (2002), *Palatia. Palazzi imperiali tra Ravenna e Bisanzio* (exhibition catalogue, October 2002–January 2003, Ravenna), Ferrara: Biblioteca Classense.

Augenti, A. (2003), 'Le sedi del potere a Roma tra tarda Antichità e alto Medioevo: archeologia e topografia', in A. Monciatti (ed.), *Domus et splendida palatia. Residenze papali e cardinalizie a Roma fra XII e XV secolo*, Pisa: Scuola Normale, 1–16.

Augenti, A. (2006a), 'Ravenna e Classe: archeologia di due città tra la tarda Antichità e l'alto Medioevo', in A. Augenti (ed.), *Le città italiane tra la tarda Antichità e l'alto Medioevo, Atti del Convegno (Ravenna, 26–28 Febbraio, 2004)* (Biblioteca di Archeologia Medievale, 20), Florence: All'Insegna del Giglio, 185–217.

Augenti, A. (ed.) (2006b), *Le città italiane tra la tarda Antichità e l'alto Medioevo, Atti del Convegno (Ravenna, 26–28 Febbraio, 2004)* (Biblioteca di Archeologia Medievale, 20), Florence: All'Insegna del Giglio.

Augenti, A. (forthcoming), 'Classe: Archaeologies of a Lost City', in N. Christie & A. Augenti (eds), *Vrbes Extinctae: Archaeologies of Abandoned Classical Towns*, Farnham & Burlington: Ashgate.

Augenti, A. & Bertelli, C. (eds) (2006), *Santi, banchieri, re. Ravenna e Classe nel VI secolo. San Severo il tempio ritrovato* (exhibition catalogue, 4 Marzo–8 Ottobre, 2006, San Nicolò, Ravenna), Milan: Skira.

Augenti, A. & Bertelli, C. (ed.) (2007), *Felix Ravenna. La croce, la spada, la vela: l'alto Adriatico fra V e VI secolo*, Milan: Skira.

Bachrach, B.S. (2000), 'Imperial Walled Cities in the West: An Examination of their Early Medieval *Nachleben*', in J. Tracy (ed.), *City Walls. The Urban Enceinte in Global Perspective*, Cambridge & New York: Cambridge University Press, 192–218.

Bakker, J. (1993), 'Raetien unter Postumus – Das Siegesdenkmal einer Juthungernschlacht im Jahre 260 n.Chr. aus Augsburg', *Germania*, 71: 369–86.

Bakker, J. (1994), *Living and Working with the Gods. Studies of Evidence for Private Religion and Its Material Environment in the City of Ostia (100–500 AD)*, Amsterdam: J.C. Gieben.

Barber, B. & Hall, J. (2000), 'Digging up the People of Roman London: Interpreting Evidence from Roman London's Cemeteries', in I. Haynes, H. Sheldon & L. Hannigan (eds), *London under Ground. The Archaeology of a City*, Oxford: Oxbow, 102–20.

Barker, G. (ed.) (1995), *A Mediterranean Valley. Landscape Archaeology and Annales History in the Biferno Valley*, London & New York: Leicester University Press.

Barker, G. & Lloyd, J. (eds) (1991), *Roman Landscapes. Archaeological Survey in the Mediterranean Region* (Archaeological Monographs of the British School at Rome, 2), London: British School at Rome.

Barnish, S. (1986), 'Taxation, Land and Barbarian Settlement in the Western Empire', *Papers of the British School at Rome*, liv: 170–95.

Barnish, S. (1987), 'Pigs, Plebeians and Potentes: Rome's Economic Hinterland, *c*.350–600 AD', *Papers of the British School at Rome*, lv: 157–85.

Barnish, S. (1988), 'Transformation and Survival in the Western Senatorial Aristocracy, *c*. AD 400–700', *Papers of the British School at Rome*, lvi: 119–55.

Barnish, S. (2000), 'Government and Administration', in A. Cameron, B. Ward-Perkins & M. Whitby (eds), *The Cambridge Ancient History. Volume XIV. Late Antiquity: Empire and Successors, AD 425–600*, Cambridge & New York: Cambridge University Press, 164–206.

Barnwell, P. (1992), *Emperor, Prefects and Kings: The Roman West, 395–565*, London: Duckworth.

Barton, I. (ed.) (1989), *Roman Public Buildings* (Exeter Studies in History, No. 20), Exeter: University of Exeter Press.

Bassett, S. (2004), *The Urban Image of Late Antique Constantinople*, Cambridge: Cambridge University Press.

Basso, P. (1986), 'I miliari della Venetia romana', *Archeologia Veneta*, 9: 11–228.

Bateman, N. (2000), *Gladiators at the Guildhall. The Story of London's Roman Amphitheatre and Medieval Guildhall*, London: Museum of London Archaeology Service.

Bateman, N., Cowan, C. & Wroe-Brown, R. (2008), *London's Roman Amphitheatre: Guildhall Yard, City of London* (MoLAS Monograph 35), London: Museum of London Archaeology Service.

Bauer, F.A. & Heinzelmann, M. (1999), 'The Constantinian Bishop's Church at Ostia: Preliminary Report on the 1998 Season', *Journal of Roman Archaeology*, 12: 342–53.

Bauer, F.A., Heinzelmann, M. & Martin, A. (2000), 'Untersuchungen in den unausgegrabenen Bereichen Ostias. Vorbericht zur zweiten Grabungskampagne in der Regio V', *Römische Mitteilungen*, 107: 375–415.

Bayliss, R. (2004), *Provincial Cilicia and the Archaeology of Temple Conversion* (British Archaeological Reports, International Series 1281), Oxford: Archaeopress.

Beard, M. (2007), *The Roman Triumph*, Cambridge, MA & London: Harvard University Press.

Becatti, G. (1957), *Colonna di Marco Aurelio*, Milan: Editoriale Domus.

Bell, T. (1998), 'Churches on Roman Buildings: Christian Associations and Roman Masonry in Anglo-Saxon England', *Medieval Archaeology*, 42: 1–18.

Beltrán de Heredia Bercero, J. (ed.) (2002), *From Barcino to Barcinona (1st to 7th Centuries). The Archaeological Remains of Plaça del Rei in Barcelona*, Institut de cultura, Barcelona: Museu d'Història de la Ciutat.

Bender, H. (2001), 'Archaeological Perspectives on Rural Settlement in Late Antiquity in the Rhine and Danube Area', in T.S. Burns & J.W. Eadie (eds), *Urban Centers and Rural Contexts in Late Antiquity*, East Lansing: Michigan State University Press, 185–98.

Berndt, G.M. & Steinacher, R. (eds) (2008), *Das Reich der Vandalen und seine (Vor-) Geschichten* (Forschungen zur Geschichte des Mittelalters, 13), Vienna: Österreichischen Akademie der Wissenschaften.

Bertók, G. (1997), '*Ripa Sarmatica*: Late Roman Counterfortifications on the Left Bank of the Danube', in W. Groenman-van Waateringe, B.L. Van Beek, W.J.H. Willems & S. Wynia (eds), *Roman Frontier Studies 1995. Proceedings of the XVIth International Congress of Roman Frontier Studies* (Oxbow Monograph 91), Oxford: Oxbow, 165–72.

Bidwell, P. & Croom, A. (2010), 'The Supply and Use of Pottery on Hadrian's Wall in the 4th Century AD', in R. Collins & L. Allason-Jones (eds), *Finds from the Frontier. Material Culture in the 4th–5th Centuries* (CBA Research Report 162), York: Council for British Archaeology, 20–36.

Bidwell, P. & Speak, S. (1994), *Excavations at South Shields Roman Fort, Volume 1* (Monograph Series No. 4), Newcastle upon Tyne: Society of Antiquaries of Newcastle upon Tyne with Tyne and Wear Museums.

Bierbrauer, V. (1994), 'Tracce archeologiche dei Visigoti fra il 376 e il 496–507', in V. Bierbrauer, O. von Hessen & E.A. Arslan (eds), *I Goti* (exhibition catalogue, Milan, Palazzo Reale, 28 gennaio–8 maggio 1994), Milan: Electa, 298–327.

Bierbrauer, V., von Hessen, O. & Arslan, E.A. (eds) (1994), *I Goti* (exhibition catalogue, Milan, Palazzo Reale, 28 gennaio–8 maggio 1994), Milan: Electa Lombardia.

Bintliff, J. & Hamerow, H. (eds) (1995), *Europe between Late Antiquity and the Middle Ages. Recent Archaeological and Historical Research in Western and Southern Europe* (British Archaeological Reports, International Series 617), Oxford: Tempus Reparatum.

Birch, D. (1998), *Pilgrimage to Rome in the Middle Ages. Continuity and Change*, Woodbridge: The Boydell Press.

Birley, A. (1987), *Marcus Aurelius: A Biography*, London: Batsford.

Birley, A. (1988), *The African Emperor: Septimius Severus* (2nd edition), London: Batsford.

Bishop, M. & Coulston, J.C. (1993), *Roman Military Equipment from the Punic Wars to the Fall of Rome*, London: Batsford.

Bitel, L.M. (2009), *Landscape with Two Saints. How Genofeva of Paris and Brigit of Kildare Built Christianity in Barbarian Europe*, Oxford & New York: Oxford University Press.

Blackhurst, A. (2004), 'The House of Nubel: Rebels or Players?', in A. Merrills (ed.), *Vandals, Romans and Berbers. New Perspectives on Late Antique North Africa*, Aldershot: Ashgate, 59–75.

Bland, R. & Johns, C. (1993), *The Hoxne Treasure. An Illustrated Introduction*, London: British Museum Press.

Bloch, H. (1963), 'The Pagan Revival in the West at the End of the Fourth Century', in A. Momigliano (ed.), *The Conflict between Paganism and Christianity in the Fourth Century*, Oxford: Clarendon Press, 193–218.

Blockley, R.C. (1981), *The Fragmentary Classicising Historians of the Later Roman Empire. Eunapius, Olympiodorus, Priscus and Malchus*, 2 vols (ARCA: Classical and Medieval Texts, Papers and Monographs, 6), Liverpool: Fancis Cairns.

Blockley, R.C. (1998), 'The Dynasty of Theodosius', in A. Cameron & P. Garnsey (eds), *The Cambridge Ancient History. Volume XIII. The Late Empire, AD 337–425*, Cambridge & New York: Cambridge University Press, 111–37.

Blockley, K., Blockley, M., Blockley, P., Frere, S. & Stow, S. (1995), *Excavations in the Marlowe Car Park and Surrounding Areas. Part I: The Excavated Sites* (The Archaeology of Canterbury, Volume 5), Whitstable: Canterbury Archaeological Trust.

Blyth, P. (1999), 'The Consumption and Cost of Fuel in Hypocaust Baths', in J. DeLaine & D.E. Johnston (eds), *Roman Baths and Bathing. Proceedings of the First International Conference on Roman Baths (Bath, 30 March–4 April 1992)* (Journal of Roman Archaeology Supplementary Series No. 37), Portsmouth, RI: Journal of Roman Archaeology, 87–98.

Boak, A. (1955), *Manpower Shortage and the Fall of the Roman Empire in the West* (Jerome Lectures, third series), Westport: Greenwood Press.

Bogdan Cătăniciu, I. (1981), *Evolution of the System of Defence Works in Roman Dacia* (British Archaeological Reports, International Series 116), Oxford: Tempus.

Bóna, I. (1976), *The Dawn of the Dark Ages. The Gepids and the Lombards in the Carpathian Basin*, Budapest: Corvina Press.

Bonifay, M. (2004), *Etudes sur la céramique romaine tardive d'Afrique* (British Archaeological Reports, International Series 1301), Oxford: Archaeopress.

Bonnet, C. & Beltrán de Heredia, J. (2000), 'El primer grupo Episcopal de Barcelona', in G. Ripoll & J.M. Gurt (eds), *Sedes regiae (ann. 400–800)*, Barcelona: Reial Acadèmia de Bones Lletres, 467–90.

Bonnet, C. & Reynaud, J.-F. (2000), 'Genève et Lyon, capitals burgondes', in G. Ripoll & J.M. Gurt (eds), *Sedes regiae (ann. 400–800)*, Barcelona: Reial Acadèmia de Bones Lletres, 241–66.

Bounegru, O. & Zahariade, M. (1996), *Les Forces Navales du Bas Danube et de la Mer Noire aux Ier–VIe Siècles* (Colloquia Pontica 2), Oxford: Oxbow Books.

Bowden, D. (1978), *The Age of Constantine and Julian*, London: Paul Elek.

Bowden, W. (2001), 'A New Urban Elite? Church Builders and Church Building in Late-Antique Epirus', in L. Lavan (ed.), *Recent Research in Late-Antique Urbanism* (Journal of Roman Archaeology Supplementary Series No. 42), Ann Arbor: Journal of Roman Archaeology, 57–68.

Bowden, W. (2003), *Epirus Vetus: The Archaeology of a Late Antique Province*, London: Duckworth.

Bowden, W., Lavan, L. & Machado, C. (eds) (2004), *Recent Research on the Late Antique Countryside* (Late Antique Archaeology 2), Leiden & Boston: Brill.

Bowes, K. (2006), 'Beyond Pirenne's Shadow? Late Antique San Vincenzo Reconsidered', in K. Bowes, K. Francis & R. Hodges (eds), *Between Text and Territory. Survey and Excavations in the Terra of San Vincenzo al Volturno* (Archaeological Monographs of the British School at Rome, 16), London: British School at Rome, 287–305.

Bowes, K. (2010), *Houses and Society in the Later Roman Empire*, London: Duckworth.

Bowes, K., Francis, K. & Hodges, R. (eds) (2006), *Between Text and Territory. Survey and Excavations in the Terra of San Vincenzo al Volturno* (Archaeological Monographs of the British School at Rome, 16), London: British School at Rome.

Bowes, K. & Kulikowski, M. (eds) (2005), *Hispania in Late Antiquity: Current Approaches*, Leiden & Boston: Brill.

Branigan, K. (1976), 'Villa Settlement in the West Country', in K. Branigan & P. Fowler (eds), *The Roman West Country. Classical Culture and Celtic Society*, Newton Abbot & Vermont: David & Charles, 120–41.

Brather, S. (2005), 'Acculturation and Ethnogenesis along the Frontier: Rome and the Ancient Germans in an Archaeological Perspective', in F. Curta (ed.), *Borders, Barriers, and Ethnogenesis. Frontiers in Late Antiquity and the Middle Ages* (Studies in the Early Middle Ages, Volume 12), Turnhout: Brepols, 139–71.

Braund, D. (ed.) (1988), *The Administration of the Roman Empire, 241 BC–AD 193* (Exeter Studies in History, No. 18), Exeter: University of Exeter Press.

Bravo, G. (2007), 'Ejército, agitacion social y conflict armado en Occidente tardorromano: un balance', *POLIS. Revista de ideas y formas políticas de la Antigüedad Clásica*, 19, 7–34.

Breeze, D. (1982), *The Northern Frontiers of Roman Britain*, London: Batsford.

Breeze, D. & Dobson, B. (2000), *Hadrian's Wall* (4th edition), Harmondsworth: Penguin.

Brenk, B. (1999), 'La cristianizzazione della Domus dei Valerii sul Celio', in W.V. Harris (ed.), *The Transformations of* Vrbs Roma *in Late Antiquity* (Journal of Roman Archaeology Supplementary Series No. 33), Ann Arbor: Journal of Roman Archaeology, 69–84.

Brickstock, R.J. (2010), 'Coins and the Frontier Troops in the 4th Century', in R. Collins & L. Allason-Jones (eds), *Finds from the Frontier. Material Culture in the 4th–5th Centuries* (CBA Research Report 162), York: Council for British Archaeology, 86–91.

Broderson, K. (2001), 'The Presentation of Geographical Knowledge for Travel and Transport in the Roman World', in C. Adams & R. Laurence (eds), *Travel and Geography in the Roman Empire*, London: Routledge, 7–21.

Brogiolo, G.P. (ed.) (1996), *Early Medieval Towns in the Western Mediterranean* (Atti del Convegno, Ravello, 22–24 Sett. 1994), (Documenti di Archeologia, 10), Mantua: Padus.

Brogiolo, G.P. (1999a), 'Ideas of the Town in Italy during the Transition from Antiquity to the Middle Ages', in G.P. Brogiolo & B. Ward-Perkins (eds), *The Idea and Ideal of the Town between Late Antiquity and the Early Middle Ages* (ESF Transformation of the Roman World, 4), Leiden & New York: Brill, 99–126.

Brogiolo, G.P. (ed.) (1999b), *S. Giulia di Brescia. Gli scavi dal 1980 al 1992. Reperti preromani, romani e alto medievali*, Florence: All'Insegna del Giglio.

Brogiolo, G.P. & Arnau, A. (eds) (2007), *Archeologia e società tra tardo antichità e alto medioevo (12° Seminario sul Tardo Antico e l'Alto Medioevo, Padova, 29 Sett.–1 Ott. 2005)*, (Documenti di Archeologia 44), Mantua: SAP Società Archeologica srl.

Brogiolo, G.P. & Cantino Wataghin, G. (eds) (1998), *Sepolture tra IV e VIII secolo (7° Seminario sul tardo antico e l'alto medioevo in Italia centro-settentrionale. Gardome Riviera, 24–26 Ottobre, 1996)*, (Documenti di Archeologia, 13), Mantua: Società Archeologica Padana srl.

Brogiolo, G.P. & Chavarria Arnau, A. (2005), *Aristocrazie e campagne nell'Occidente da Costantino a Carlo Magno* (Metodi e temi dell'archeologia medievale, 1), Florence: All'Insegna del Giglio.

Brogiolo, G.P. & Gelichi, S. (1996), *Nuove ricerche sui castelli altomedievali in Italia settentrionale*, Florence: All'Insegna del Giglio.

Brogiolo, G.P. & Olcese, G. (1993), 'Review of Scavi MM3', *Archeologia Medievale*, xx: 676–83.

Brogiolo, G.P. & Ward-Perkins, B. (eds) (1999), *The Idea and Ideal of the Town between Late Antiquity and the Early Middle Ages* (ESF Transformation of the Roman World, 4), Leiden & New York: Brill.

Brogiolo, G.P., Gauthier, N. & Christie, N. (eds) (2000), *Towns and their Territories between Late Antiquity and the Early Middle Ages* (ESF Transformation of the Roman World, 9), Leiden & New York: Brill.

Broise, H., Dewailly, M. & Jolivet, V. (2000), '*Horti Luculliani*: un palazzo tardoantico a Villa Medici', in S. Ensoli & E. La Rocca (eds), *Aurea Roma. Dalla città pagana alla città cristiana* (exhibition catalogue, 22 December 2000–20 April 2001), Rome: 'L'Erma' di Bretschneider, 113–16.

Bromwich, J. (1993), *The Roman Remains of Southern France*, London & New York: Routledge.

Brown, P. (1971), *The World of Late Antiquity. From Marcus Aurelius to Muhammad*, London: Thames and Hudson.

Brown, P. (1972), *Religion and Society in the Age of Saint Augustine*, London: Faber and Faber.

Brown, P. (1987), 'Late Antiquity', in P. Veyne (ed.), *A History of Private Life. I. From Pagan Rome to Byzantium*, Cambridge, MA & London: Belknap Press/Harvard University Press, 235–311.

Brown, P. (1996), *The Rise of Western Christendom. Triumph and Diversity, AD 200–1000*, Oxford & Malden: Blackwell Publishers.

Brown, P. (1998), 'Christianization and Religious Conflict', in A. Cameron & P. Garnsey (eds), *The Cambridge Ancient History. Volume XIII. The Late Empire, AD 337–425*, Cambridge & New York: Cambridge University Press, 632–64.

Brown, T.S. (1984), *Gentlemen and Officers. Imperial Administration and Aristocratic Power in Byzantine Italy, AD 554–800*, London: British School at Rome.

Brown, T.S. (1998), 'Urban Violence in Early Medieval Italy: The Cases of Rome and Ravenna', in G. Halsall (ed.), *Violence and Society in the Early Medieval West*, Woodbridge: Boydell Press, 76–89.

Brulet, R. (1989), 'The Continental *Litus Saxonicum*', in V. Maxfield (ed.), *The Saxon Shore. A Handbook* (Exeter Studies in History, No. 25), Exeter: University of Exeter, 45–77.

Bruni, S. (ed.) (2000), *Le navi antiche di Pisa. Ad un anno dall'inizio delle ricerche*, Florence: Edizioni Polistampa.

Buora, M. (2002a), 'La peste antonina in Aquileia e nel territorio circostante', in M. Buora & W. Jobst (eds), *Roma sul Danubio. Da Aquileia a* Carnuntum *lungo la via dell'ambra* (Cataloghi e monografie archeologiche dei Civici Musei di Udine, VI), Rome: 'L'Erma' di Bretschneider, 93–7.

Buora, M. (2002b), 'Militari e *militaria* ad Aquileia e nell'attuale Friuli', in M. Buora (ed.), *Miles Romanus dal Po al Danubio nel Tardoantico (Atti del Convegno Internazionale, Pordenone – Concordia Sagittaria, 17–19 Marzo 2000)*, Pordenone: Sage Print, 183–206.

Buora, M. (ed.) (2002c), *Miles Romanus dal Po al Danubio nel Tardoantico (Atti del Convegno Internazionale, Pordenone – Concordia Sagittaria, 17–19 Marzo 2000)*, Pordenone: Sage Print.

Buora, M. & Jobst, W. (eds) (2002), *Roma sul Danubio. Da Aquileia a* Carnuntum *lungo la via dell'ambra* (Cataloghi e monografie archeologiche dei Civici Musei di Udine, VI), Rome: 'L'Erma' di Bretschneider.

Burgess, R.W. (1992), 'From *Gallia Romana* to *Gallia Gothica*: The View from Spain', in J. Drinkwater & H. Elton (eds), *Fifth-Century Gaul: A Crisis of Identity?* Cambridge: Cambridge University Press, 19–27.

Burns, T.S. (1994), *Barbarians within the Gates of Rome. A Study of Roman Military Policy and the Barbarians, ca. 375–425 AD*, Bloomington & Indianapolis: Indiana University Press.

Burns, T.S. & Eadie, J.W. (eds) (2001), *Urban Centers and Rural Contexts in Late Antiquity*, East Lansing: Michigan State University Press.

Bursone, A. (2008), 'Trade Relations between Rome and the Barbarians', in J.-J. Aillagon (ed.), *Rome and the Barbarians. The Birth of a New World* (exhibition catalogue – Venice-Bonn-Rome), Milan: Palazzo Grassi/Skira Editore, 153–55.

Burton, E. (2007), 'From Roman to Saxon London: Saxon Burials at St Martin-in-the-Fields', *Medieval Archaeology*, 51: 255–8.

Cameron, A. (1970), *Claudian. Poetry and Propaganda at the Court of Honorius*, Oxford: Clarendon Press.

Cameron, A. (1976), *Circus Factions: Blues and Greens at Rome and Byzantium*, Oxford: Clarendon Press.

Cameron, A. (1985), 'The Date and Owners of the Esquiline Treasure', *American Journal of Archaeology*, 89: 135–45.

Cameron, A. (1993a), *The Later Roman Empire, AD 284–430*, London: Fontana.

Cameron, A. (1993b), *The Mediterranean World in Late Antiquity, AD 395–600*, London & New York: Routledge.

Cameron, A. (1998), 'Consular Diptychs in their Social Context: New Eastern Evidence', *Journal of Roman Archaeology*, 11: 384–403.

Cameron, A. (1999), 'The Last Pagans of Rome', in W.V. Harris (ed.), *The Transformations of* Vrbs Roma *in Late Antiquity* (Journal of Roman Archaeology Supplementary Series No. 33), Ann Arbor: Journal of Roman Archaeology, 109–22.

Cameron, A. (2000), 'Vandal and Byzantine Africa', in A. Cameron, B. Ward-Perkins & M. Whitby (eds), *The Cambridge Ancient History. Volume XIV. Late Antiquity: Empire and Successors, AD 425–600*, Cambridge & New York: Cambridge University Press, 552–68.

Cameron, A. & Garnsey, P. (eds) (1998), *The Cambridge Ancient History. Volume XIII. The Late Empire, AD 337–425*, Cambridge & New York: Cambridge University Press.

Cameron, A., Ward-Perkins, B. & Whitby, M. (eds) (2000), *The Cambridge Ancient History. Volume XIV. Late Antiquity: Empire and Successors, AD 425–600*, Cambridge & New York: Cambridge University Press.

Campione, A. & Nuzzo, D. (1999), *La Daunia alle origini cristiane* (Scavi e ricerche 10), Bari: Edipuglia.

Cantino Wataghin, G. (1992), 'Urbanistica tardoantica e topografia cristiana: termini di un problema', in G. Sena Chiesa & E. Arslan (eds), *Felix Temporis Reparatio (Atti del Convegno archeologico internazionale 'Milano capitale dell'impero romano', 8–11 Marzo 1990, Milan)*, Milan: Edizioni ET, 171–92.

Cantino Wataghin, G. (1995), 'Spazio cristiano e "civitates": status quaestionis', in P. Spanu (ed.), *Materiali per una topografia urbana. Status quaestionis e nuove acquisizioni* (V Convegno sull'archeologia tardoromana e medievale in Sardegna, Cagliari, 24–26 Giugno, 1988), Oristano: Editrice S'Alvure, 201–37.

Cantino Wataghin, G. (1999), 'The Ideology of Urban Burials', in G.P. Brogiolo & B. Ward-Perkins (eds), *The Idea and Ideal of the Town between Late Antiquity and the Early Middle Ages* (ESF Transformation of the Roman World, 4), Leiden & New York: Brill, 147–80.

Cantino Wataghin, G. (2000), 'Christianisation et organisation ecclésiastique des campagnes: l'Italie du Nord aux IVe–VIIIe siècles', in G.P. Brogiolo, N. Gauthier & N. Christie (eds), *Towns and Their Territories between Late Antiquity and the Early Middle Ages* (ESF Transformation of the Roman World, 9), Leiden & New York: Brill, 209–34.

Cantino Wataghin, G. & Lambert, C. (1998), 'Sepolture e città. L'Italia settentrionale tra IV e VIII secolo', in G.P. Brogiolo & G. Cantino Wataghin (eds), *Sepolture tra IV e VIII secolo (7° Seminario sul tardo antico e l'alto medioevo in Italia centro-settentrionale. Gardome Riviera, 24–26 Ottobre, 1996)*, (Documenti di Archeologia, 13), Mantua: Società Archeologica Padana srl, 89–114.

Capini, S. & di Niro, A. (eds) (1991), *Samnium. Archeologia del Molise*, Rome: Quasa.

Caporusso, D. (ed.) (1991), *Scavi MM3. Ricerche di archeologia urbana a Milano durante la costruzione della linea 3 della Metropolitana, 1982–1990*, 5 vols, Milan: Ministero per i Beni Culturali e Ambientali/Soprintendenza Archeologica della Lombardia, Edizioni ET.

Carandini, A., Cracco Ruggini, L. & Giardina, A. (eds) (1993), *Storia di Roma III: L'età tardoantica. II: I luoghi e le culture*, Turin: Giulio Einaudi.

Carile, A. (ed.) (1991), *Storia di Ravenna II. Dall'età bizantina all'età ottoniana*, Venice: Marsilio Editori.

Carreté, J.-M., Keay, S. & Millett, M. (1995), *A Roman Provincial Capital and its Hinterland. The Survey of the Territory of Tarragona, Spain, 1985–1990* (Journal of Roman Archaeology, Supplementary Series No. 15), Ann Arbor: Journal of Roman Archaeology.

Carroll, M. (2001), *Romans, Celts and Germans. The German Provinces of Rome*, Stroud: Tempus.

Carroll-Spillecke, M. (1997), 'The Late Roman Frontier Fort Divitia in Köln-Deutz and Its Garrisons', in W. Groenman-van Waateringe, B.L. Van Beek, W.J.H. Willems & S. Wynia (eds), *Roman Frontier Studies 1995. Proceedings of the XVIth International Congress of Roman Frontier Studies* (Oxbow Monograph 91), Oxford: Oxbow, 143–49.

Carver, M.O.H. (1993), *Arguments in Stone. Archaeological Research and the European Town in the First Millennium* (Oxbow Monograph 29), Oxford: Oxbow.

Caseau, B. (2004), 'The Fate of Rural Temples in Late Antiquity and the Christianisation of the Countryside', in W. Bowden, L. Lavan & C. Machado (eds), *Recent Research on the Late Antique Countryside* (Late Antique Archaeology 2), Leiden & Boston: Brill, 105–44.

Cau, M.A. (forthcoming), 'Urban Change on the Balearics in Late Antiquity', in
N. Christie & A. Augenti (eds), *Vrbes Extinctae: Archaeologies of Abandoned Classical Towns*, Farnham & Burlington: Ashgate.

Cavada, E. (2002), '*Militaria* tardoantichi (fine IV–V secolo) dalla valle dell'Adige e dalle aree limitrofe. L'informazione archeologica', in M. Buora (ed.), *Miles Romanus dal Po al Danubio nel Tardoantico (Atti del Convegno Internazionale, Pordenone – Concordia Sagittaria, 17–19 Marzo 2000)*, Pordenone: Sage Print, 139–62.

Ravenna. Da capitale imperiale (2005), *Ravenna. Da capitale imperiale a capitale esarcale. Atti del XVII Congresso Internazionale di Studio sull'Alto Medioevo (Ravenna, 6–12 Giugno, 2004)*, Spoleto: Centro Italiano di Studi sull'Alto Medioevo.

Chadwick, H. (1998), 'Orthodoxy and Heresy from the Death of Constantine to the Eve of the First Council of Ephesus', in A. Cameron & P. Garnsey (eds), *The Cambridge Ancient History. Volume XIII. The Late Empire, AD 337–425*, Cambridge & New York: Cambridge University Press, 561–600.

Chavarría Arnau, A. (2004a), 'Considerazioni sulla fine delle ville in Occidente', *Archeologia Medievale*, xxxi: 7–19.

Chavarría Arnau, A. (2004b), 'Interpreting the Transformation of Late Roman Villas: The Case of *Hispania*', in N. Christie (ed.), *Landscapes of Change: Rural Evolutions in Late Antiquity and the Early Middle Ages*, Aldershot: Ashgate, 67–102.

Chavarría, A. (2007), *El final de las 'villae' en 'Hispania' (siglos IV–VII d.C.)* (Bibliothèque de l'Antiquité Tardive 7), Brepols: Turnhout.

Christie, N. (1991), 'The Alps as a Frontier (AD 168–774)', *Journal of Roman Archaeology*, 4: 410–30.

Christie, N. (1992), 'The Survival of Roman Settlement along the Middle Danube: Pannonia from the Fourth to the Tenth Century AD', *Oxford Journal of Archaeology*, 11(3): 317–39.

Christie, N. (1996a), 'Barren Fields? Landscapes and Settlements in Late Roman and Post-Roman Italy', in G. Shipley & J. Salmon (eds), *Human Landscapes in Classical Antiquity. Environment and Culture*, London & New York: Routledge, 254–83.

Christie, N. (1996b), 'Towns and Peoples on the Middle Danube in Late Antiquity and the Early Middle Ages', in N. Christie & S.T. Loseby (eds), *Towns in Transition. Urban Evolution in Late Antiquity and the Early Middle Ages*, Aldershot: Scolar, 71–98.

Christie, N. (2000a), 'Lost Glories? Rome at the End of Empire', in J.C.N. Coulston & H. Dodge (eds), *Ancient Rome: The Archaeology of the Eternal City* (Oxford University School of Archaeology Monograph 54), Oxford: Alden Press, 306–31.

Christie, N. (2000b), 'Towns, Land and Power: German–Roman Survivals and Interactions in Fifth- and Sixth-Century Pannonia', in G.P. Brogiolo, N. Gauthier & N. Christie (eds), *Towns and their Territories between Late Antiquity and the Early Middle Ages* (ESF Transformation of the Roman World, 9), Leiden & New York: Brill, 275–97.

Christie, N. (2001), 'War and Order: Urban Remodelling and Defensive Strategy in Late Roman Italy', in L. Lavan (ed.), *Recent Research in Late-Antique Urbanism* (Journal of Roman Archaeology Supplementary Series No. 42), Ann Arbor: Journal of Roman Archaeology, 106–22.

Christie, N. (ed.) (2004a), *Landscapes of Change: Rural Evolutions in Late Antiquity and the Early Middle Ages*, Aldershot: Ashgate.

Christie, N. (2004b), 'Landscapes of Change in Late Antiquity and the Early Middle Ages: Themes, Directions and Problems', in N. Christie (ed.), *Landscapes of Change: Rural Evolutions in Late Antiquity and the Early Middle Ages*, Aldershot: Ashgate, 1–37.

Christie, N. (2006), *From Constantine to Charlemagne: An Archaeology of Italy, AD 300–800*, Aldershot: Ashgate.

Christie, N. (2007), 'From the Danube to the Po: The Defence of Pannonia and Italy in the Fourth and Fifth Centuries AD', in A. Poulter (ed.), *The Transition to Late Antiquity on* the Danube and Beyond (Proceedings of the British Academy, Volume 141), London: British Academy, 547–78.

Christie, N. (2009), 'No More Fun? The End of Amphitheatres and Games in the Late Roman West', in T. Wilmott (ed.), Roman Amphitheatres and Spectacula. A 21st Century Perspective (British Archeological Reports International Series 1946), Oxford: English Heritage/Chester Museum/Archaeopress, 221–32.

Christie, N. & Augenti, A. (eds) (forthcoming), Vrbes Extinctae: Archaeologies of Abandoned Classical Towns, Farnham & Burlington: Ashgate.

Christie, N. & Gibson, S. (1988), 'The City Walls of Ravenna', Papers of the British School at Rome, lvi: 156–97.

Christie, N. & Kipling, R. (2000), 'Structures of Power or Structures of Convenience? Exploiting the Material Past in Late Antiquity and the Early Middle Ages', in S. Pearce (ed.), Researching Material Culture (Leicester Archaeology Monographs 8, Material Culture Study Group Occasional Paper No. 1), Leicester: University of Leicester, 21–35.

Christie, N. & Loseby, S.T. (eds) (1996), Towns in Transition. Urban Evolution in Late Antiquity and the Early Middle Ages, Aldershot: Scolar.

Christie, N. & Rushworth, A. (1988), 'Urban Fortification and Defensive Strategy in Fifth and Sixth Century Italy: The Case of Terracina', Journal of Roman Archaeology, 1: 73–88.

Christlein, R. (1978), Die Alamannen. Archäologie eines lebendigen Volkes, Stuttgart: Konrad Theiss.

Chrysos, E. (2001), 'Ripa Gothica and Litus Saxonicum', in W. Pohl, I. Wood & H. Reimitz (eds), The Transformation of Frontiers. From Late Antiquity to the Carolingians (The Transformation of the Roman World, Volume 10), Leiden, Boston & Cologne: European Science Foundation/Brill, 69–72.

Chrysos, E. & Wood, I. (eds) (1999), East and West: Modes of Communication (ESF Transformation of the Roman World, 5), Leiden & New York: Brill.

Cirelli, E. (2008), Ravenna: archeologia di una città, Florence: All'Insegna del Giglio.

Clark, E.G. (2001), 'Pastoral Care: Town and Country in Late-Antique Preaching', in T.S. Burns & J.W. Eadie (eds), Urban Centers and Rural Contexts in Late Antiquity, East Lansing: Michigan State University Press, 265–84.

Coarelli, F. (1999), 'L'edilizia pubblica a Roma in età tetrarchica', in W.V. Harris (ed.), The Transformations of Vrbs Roma in Late Antiquity (Journal of Roman Archaeology Supplementary Series No. 33), Ann Arbor: Journal of Roman Archaeology, 23–33.

Coates Stephens, R. (1998), 'The Walls and Aqueducts of Rome in the Early Middle Ages, AD 500–1000', Journal of Roman Studies, 88: 166–78.

Coates Stephens, R. (2001), 'Muri dei bassi secoli in Rome: Observations on the Re-Use of Statuary in Walls Found on the Esquiline and Caelian After 1870', Journal of Roman Archaeology, 14: 217–38.

Coccia, S. (1996), 'Il Portus Romae alla fine dell'antichità nel quadro del sistema di approvvigionamento della città di Roma', in A. Gallina Zevi & A. Claridge (eds), "Roman Ostia" Revisited. Archaeological and Historical Papers in Memory of Russell Meiggs, Rome: British School at Rome/STI, 293–307.

Codreanu-Windnauer, S. (2004), 'Auf dem Spuren der Bajuwaren in Burgweinting', in Von der Steinzeit bis zum Mittelalter. 10 Jahre Flächengrabung in Regensburg-Burgweinting, Regensburg: Museen der Stadt, 70–9.

Coleman, K. (2000), 'Entertaining Rome', in J.C.N. Coulston & H. Dodge (eds), Ancient Rome: The Archaeology of the Eternal City (Oxford University School of Archaeology Monograph 54), Oxford: Alden Press, 210–58.

Collins, R. (1983), Early Medieval Spain. Unity in Diversity, 400–1000, London: MacMillan.

Collins, R. (1991), Early Medieval Europe, 300–1000, Basingstoke: MacMillan.

Collins, R. (2000), 'The Western Kingdoms', in A. Cameron, B. Ward-Perkins & M. Whitby (eds), *The Cambridge Ancient History. Volume XIV. Late Antiquity: Empire and Successors, AD 425–600*, Cambridge & New York: Cambridge University Press, 112–34.

Collins, R. & Allason-Jones, L. (eds) (2010), *Finds from the Frontier. Material Culture in the 4th–5th Centuries* (CBA Research Report 162), York: Council for British Archaeology.

Collins, R. & Gerrard, J. (eds) (2004), *Debating Late Antiquity in Britain AD 300–700* (British Archaeological Reports British Series 365), Oxford: Archaeopress.

Connor, A. & Buckley, R. (1999), *Roman and Medieval Occupation in Causeway Lane, Leicester. Excavations 1980 and 1991* (Leicester Archaeology Monographs, No. 5), Leicester: University of Leicester.

Cooper, N. (2000), 'Rubbish Counts: Quantifying Portable Material Culture in Roman Britain', in S. Pearce (ed.), *Researching Material Culture* (Leicester Archaeology Monographs 8, Material Culture Study Group Occasional Paper No. 1), Leicester: University of Leicester, 75–86.

Costambeys, M. (2001), 'Burial Topography and the Power of the Church in Fifth- and Sixth-Century Rome', *Papers of the British School at Rome*, lxix: 169–89.

Coster, C.H. (1968), *Late Roman Studies*, Cambridge, MA: Harvard University Press.

Coulston, J.C.N. (1990), 'Late Roman Armour, 3rd–6th Centuries AD', *Journal of Roman Military Equipment Studies*, 1: 139–60.

Coulston, J.C.N. (1991), 'The "Draco" Standard', *Journal of Roman Military Equipment Studies*, 2: 101–14.

Coulston, J.C.N. (forthcoming), 'Late Roman Military Equipment Culture', in A. Sarantis & N. Christie, *New Approaches to Warfare in Late Antiquity*, Leiden: Brill.

Coulston, J.C.N. & Dodge, H. (eds) (2000), *Ancient Rome: The Archaeology of the Eternal City* (Oxford University School of Archaeology Monograph 54), Oxford: Alden Press.

Courtois, C. (1955), *Les Vandals et l'Afrique*, Paris: Arts et Metiers Graphiques.

Cowan, C. (ed.) (2003), *Urban Development in North-West Roman Southwark. Excavations 1974–90* (MoLAS Monograph 16), London: Museum of London Archaeological Service.

Cowie, R. (2000), '*Londinium* to *Lundenwic*: Early and Middle Saxon Archaeology in the London Region', in I. Haynes, H. Sheldon & L. Hannigan (eds), *London under Ground. The Archaeology of a City*, Oxford: Oxbow, 175–205.

Coyler, C., Gilmour, B. & Jones, M. (1999), *The Defences of the Lower City: Excavations at the Park and West Parade, 1970–2, and a Discussion of Other Sites Excavated Up to 1994 (The Archaeology of Lincoln, Volume VII-2)* (Council for British Archaeology Reports 114), London: Council for British Archaeology.

Cracco Ruggini, L. (1984), 'I barbari in Italia nei secoli dell'impero', in G. Pugliese Carratelli (ed.), *Magistra Barbaritas. I Barbari in Italia*, Milan: Libri Scheiwiller, 3–51.

Cracco Ruggini, L. (2008), 'Rome and the Barbarians in Late Antiquity', in J.-J. Aillagon (ed.), *Rome and the Barbarians. The Birth of a New World* (exhibition catalogue – Venice-Bonn-Rome), Milan: Palazzo Grassi/Skira Editore, 204–15.

Creighton, J.D. & Wilson, R.J.A. (eds) (1999), *Roman Germany. Studies in Cultural Interaction* (Journal of Roman Archaeology Supplementary Series No. 32), Portsmouth, RI: Journal of Roman Archaeology.

Crickmore, J. (1984), *Romano–British Urban Defences* (British Archaeological Reports, British Series 126), Oxford: Tempus Reparatum.

Croce Da Villa, P. & Di Filippo Balestrazzi, E. (eds) (2001), *Concordia. Tremila anni di storia*, Rubano: Esedra.

Croke, B. & Emmett, A.M. (eds) (1983), *History and Historians in Late Antiquity*, Sydney, Oxford & Ontario: Pergamon Press.

Crow, J. (2001), 'Fortifications and Urbanism in Late Antiquity: Thessaloniki and Other Eastern Cities', in L. Lavan (ed.), *Recent Research in Late-Antique Urbanism* (Journal of Roman Archaeology Supplementary Series No. 42), Ann Arbor: Journal of Roman Archaeology, 89–105.

Crow, J. (2004), *Housesteads. A Fort and Garrison on Hadrian's Wall*, Stroud: Tempus.

Crummy, P. (1997), *City of Victory. The Story of Colchester – Britain's First Roman Town*, Colchester: Colchester Archaeological Trust.

Crummy, P. (2006), 'The Circus Comes to Britannia', *Current Archaeology*, 201: 468–75.

Crypta Balbi (2000), *Crypta Balbi, Museo Nazionale Romano*, Milan: Soprintendenza Archeologica di Roma, Electa.

Cunliffe, B.W. (1975), *Excavations at Portchester Castle. Volume I: Roman* (Society of Antiquaries Research Reports, No. 32), London: Society of Antiquaries.

Cunliffe, B.W. (1976), *Excavations at Portchester Castle. Volume II: Saxon* (Society of Antiquaries Research Reports, No. 33), London: Society of Antiquaries.

Cunliffe, B. (1988), *Greeks, Romans and Barbarians. Spheres of Interaction*, London: Batsford.

Cunliffe, B. (ed.) (1994), *The Oxford Illustrated Prehistory of Europe*, Oxford: Oxford University Press.

Cunliffe, B. (1995), *Roman Bath*, London: Batsford/English Heritage.

Curran, J. (1998), 'From Jovian to Theodosius', in A. Cameron & P. Garnsey (eds), *The Cambridge Ancient History. Volume XIII. The Late Empire, AD 337–425*, Cambridge & New York: Cambridge University Press, 78–110.

Curran, J. (2000), *Pagan City and Christian Capital. Rome in the Fourth Century*, Oxford: Clarendon Press.

Curta, F. (2001), 'Peasants as "Makeshift Soldiers for the Occasion": Sixth-Century Settlement Patterns in the Balkans', in T.S. Burns & J.W. Eadie (eds), *Urban Centers and Rural Contexts in Late Antiquity*, East Lansing: Michigan State University Press, 199–217.

Curta, F. (2005a), 'Frontier Ethnogenesis in Late Antiquity: The Danube, the Tervingi, and the Slavs', in F. Curta (ed.), *Borders, Barriers, and Ethnogenesis. Frontiers in Late Antiquity and the Middle Ages* (Studies in the Early Middle Ages, Volume 12), Turnhout: Brepols, 173–204.

Curta, F. (ed.) (2005b), *Borders, Barriers, and Ethnogenesis. Frontiers in Late Antiquity and the Middle Ages* (Studies in the Early Middle Ages, Volume 12), Turnhout: Brepols.

Cusack, C.M. (1999), *The Rise of Christianity in Northern Europe, 300–1000*, London & New York: Cassell.

Cuscito, G. (1994), 'Giochi e spettacoli nel pensiero dei Padri della Chiesa', in *Spettacolo in Aquileia e nella Cisalpina romana* (Antichità Altoadriatiche, xli), Udine: Arti Grafiche Friulane, 107–28.

Daniels, C.M. (1983), 'Town Defences in Roman Africa: A Tentative Historical Survey', in J. Maloney & B. Hobley (eds), *Roman Urban Defences in the West* (CBA Research Report No. 51), London: Council for British Archaeology, 5–19.

Dannheimer, H. & Dopsch, H. (eds) (1988), *Die Bajuwaren. Von Severin bis Tassilo, 488–788* (exhibition catalogue, Rosenheim-Bayern-Mattsee-Salzburg, 19 May–6 November 1988), Salzburg: Amt der Salzburger Landesregierung.

Dark, K. (1994), *Civitas to Kingdom. British Political Continuity, 300–800*, London & New York: Leicester University Press.

Dark, K. (2004), 'The Late Antique Landscape of Britain, AD 300–700', in N. Christie (ed.), *Landscapes of Change: Rural Evolutions in Late Antiquity and the Early Middle Ages*, Aldershot: Ashgate, 279–99.

Dark, K. & Dark, P. (1997), *The Landscape of Roman Britain*, Stroud: Sutton.

De Caprariis, F. (1999), 'I porti di Roma nel IV secolo', in W.V. Harris (ed.), *The Transformations of Vrbs Roma in Late Antiquity* (Journal of Roman Archaeology Supplementary Series No. 33), Ann Arbor: Journal of Roman Archaeology, 216–34.

Decker, M. (2001), 'Food for an Empire: Wine and Oil Production in North Syria', in
S. Kingsley & K. Decker (eds), *Economy and Exchange in the East Mediterranean during
Late Antiquity. Proceedings of a Conference at Somerville College, Oxford, 29th May, 1999*,
Oxford: Oxbow, 69–86.

Decker, M. (2009), *Tilling the Hateful Earth. Agricultural Production and Trade in the Late
Antique East*, Oxford: Oxford University Press.

Deichmann, F.W. (1976), *Ravenna. Hauptstadt des spätantiken Abendlandes. Kommentar
II.2*, Wiesbaden: F Steiner.

Deichmann, F.W. (1989), *Ravenna. Hauptstadt des spätantiken Abendlandes. Kommentar
II.3. Geschichte, Topografie, Kunst und Kultur*, Wiesbaden: Franz Steiner.

Deichmann, F.W. (1993), *Archeologia Cristiana* (Studia Archaeologica 63), Rome: 'L'Erma'
di Bretschneider (Italian translation of German original, *Einführung in di Christliche
Archäologie*, 1983.)

De la Bédoyère, G. (1993), *Roman Villas and the Countryside*, London: English Heritage.

DeLaine, J. (2000), 'Building the Eternal City: The Construction Industry of Imperial
Rome', in J.C.N. Coulston & H. Dodge (eds), *Ancient Rome: The Archaeology of the
Eternal City* (Oxford University School of Archaeology Monograph 54), Oxford: Alden
Press, 119–41.

DeLaine, J. & Johnston, D.E. (eds) (1999), *Roman Baths and Bathing. Proceedings of the
First International Conference on Roman Baths (Bath, 30 March–4 April 1992)* (Journal of
Roman Archaeology Supplementary Series No. 37), Portsmouth, RI: Journal of Roman
Archaeology.

Delano Smith, C., Mills, N., Gadd, D. & Ward-Perkins, B. (1986), 'Luni and the Ager
Lunensis: The Rise and Fall of a Roman Town and Its Territory', *Papers of the British
School at Rome*, liv: 81–146.

Deliyannis, D.M. (2010), *Ravenna in Late Antiquity*, Cambridge, New York & Melbourne:
Cambridge University Press.

Delogu, P. (2000), '*Solium Imperii – Vrbs ecclesiae*. Roma fra la tarda antichità e l'alto
medioevo', in G. Ripoll & J.M. Gurt (eds), *Sedes regiae (ann. 400–800)*, Barcelona: Reial
Acadèmia de Bones Lletres, 83–108.

De Palol, P. (1992), 'Transformaciones urbanas en Hispania durante el Bajo Imperio: los
ejemplos de Barcino, Tarraco y Clunia', in G. Sena Chiesa & E. Arslan (eds), *Felix
Temporis Reparatio (Atti del Convegno archeologico internazionale 'Milano capitale
dell'impero romano', 8–11 Marzo 1990, Milan)*, Milan: Edizioni ET, 381–94.

De Rubeis, F. & Marazzi, F. (eds) (2008), *Monasteri in Europa occidentale (secoli VIII–XI):
topografia e strutture*, Rome: Viella.

De Souza, P. (1999), *Piracy in the Graeco-Roman World*, Cambridge, New York &
Melbourne: Cambridge University Press.

Dey, H.W. (2010), 'Art, Ceremony, and City Walls: The Aesthetics of Imperial Resurgence
in the Late Roman West', *Journal of Late Antiquity*, 3(1): 3–37.

Dey, H.W. (2011), *The Aurelian Wall and the Refashioning of Imperial Rome, AD 271–855*,
Cambridge and New York: Cambridge University Press.

Diaconescu, A. (2004), 'The Towns of Roman Dacia: An Overview of Recent Research', in
W.S. Hanson & I. Haynes (eds), *Roman Dacia. The Making of a Provincial Society*
(Journal of Roman Archaeology Supplementary Series No. 56), Portsmouth, RI: Journal
of Roman Archaeology, 87–142.

Díaz, P.C. (2000), 'City and Territory in Hispania in Late Antiquity', in G.P. Brogiolo, N. Gauthier
& N. Christie (eds), *Towns and Their Territories between Late Antiquity and the Early Middle
Ages* (ESF Transformation of the Roman World, 9), Leiden & New York: Brill, 3–35.

Díaz-Andreu, M. & Keay, S. (eds) (1997), *The Archaeology of Iberia: The Dynamics of
Change*, London: Routledge.

Dierkens, A. & Périn, P. (2000), 'Les *sedes regiae* mérovingiennes entre Seine et Rhin', in
G. Ripoll & J.M. Gurt (eds), *Sedes regiae (ann. 400–800)*, Barcelona: Reial Acadèmia de
Bones Lletres, 267–304.

Dixon, P. (1992), 'The Cities Are Not Populated as Once They Were', in J. Rich (ed.), *The
City in Late Antiquity* (Leicester-Nottingham Studies in Ancient Society, Volume 3),
London: Routledge, 145–60.

Dodge, H. (1999), 'Amusing the Masses: Buildings for Entertainment and Leisure in the
Roman World', in D.S Potter & D.J. Mattingly (eds), *Life, Death and Entertainment in the
Roman Empire*, Ann Arbor: University of Michigan Press, 205–55.

Dodge, H. (2000), '"Greater than the Pyramids": The Water Supply of Ancient Rome', in
J.C.N. Coulston & H. Dodge (eds), *Ancient Rome: The Archaeology of the Eternal City*
(Oxford University School of Archaeology Monograph 54), Oxford: Alden Press,
166–209.

Donati, A. & Gentili, G. (eds) (2005), *Costantino il Grande. La civiltà antica al bivio tra
Occidente e Oriente* (exhibition catalogue, Rimini, Castel Sismondo, 13 Marzo–4 Sett.,
2005), Milan: Silvana Editoriale.

D'Oriano, R. (2002), 'Relitti di storia: lo scavo del porto di Olbia', in M. Khanoussi,
P. Ruggeri & C. Vismara (eds), *L'Africa Romana, Atti del XIV Congresso di Studi (Sassari,
2000)*, Rome: Carocci, 1247–60.

Drinkwater, J.F. (1987), *The Gallic Empire: Separatism and Continuity in the North-Western
Provinces of the Roman Empire, AD 260–274*, Stuttgart: F Steiner.

Drinkwater, J.F. (1992), 'The Bacaudae of Fifth-Century Gaul', in J. Drinkwater &
H. Elton (eds), *Fifth-Century Gaul: A Crisis of Identity?* Cambridge: Cambridge
University Press, 208–17.

Drinkwater, J.F. (1996), 'The "Germanic Threat on the Rhine Frontier": A Romano-Gallic
Artefact?', in R. Mathisen & H. Sivan (eds), *Shifting Frontiers in Late Antiquity*,
Aldershot: Variorum, 31–44.

Drinkwater, J.F. (2007), *The Alamanni and Rome, 213–496 (Caracalla to Clovis)*, Oxford:
Oxford University Press.

Drinkwater, J. & Elton, H. (eds) (1992), *Fifth-Century Gaul: A Crisis of Identity?* Cambridge:
Cambridge University Press.

Duncan-Jones, R.P. (1996), 'The Impact of the Antonine Plague', *Journal of Roman Archaeology*,
9: 108–36.

Durán Cabello, R., Fernández Ochoa, C. & Morillo Cerdan, Á. (2009), 'The Amphitheatres
in Hispania: Recent Investigations', in T. Wilmott (ed.), *Roman Amphitheatres and
Spectacula. A 21st Century Perspective* (British Archeological Reports, International
Series 1946), Oxford: English Heritage/Chester Museum/Archaeopress, 15–28.

Durante, A.M. (2003), 'La città vescovile di *Luna* nell'alto medioevo', in M. Marcenaro
(ed.), *Roma e la Liguria Maritima: secoli IV–X. La capitale cristiana e una regione di confine
(Istituto Internazionale di Studi Liguri. Atti dei Convegni, XI)*, Genoa-Bordighera: Istituto
Internazionale di Studi Liguri, 203–14.

Dyson, S. (2003), *The Roman Countryside*, London: Duckworth.

Elsner, J. (1998), 'Art and Architecture', in A. Cameron & P. Garnsey (eds), *The Cambridge
Ancient History. Volume XIII. The Late Empire, AD 337–425*, Cambridge & New York:
Cambridge University Press, 736–61.

Elton, H. (1992), 'Defence in Fifth-Century Gaul', in J. Drinkwater & H. Elton (eds), *Fifth-
Century Gaul: A Crisis of Identity?* Cambridge: Cambridge University Press, 166–76.

Elton, H. (1996a), *Frontiers of the Roman Empire*, London: Batsford.

Elton, H. (1996b), *Warfare in Roman Europe, AD 350–425*, Oxford: Clarendon Press.

Ennabli, A. (ed.) (1992), *Pour Sauver Carthage. Exploration et Conservation de la Cité
Punique, Romaine et Byzantine*, Tunis & Paris: INAA/UNESCO.

Ensoli, S. & La Rocca, E. (eds) (2000), *Aurea Roma. Dalla città pagana alla città cristiana* (exhibition catalogue, 22 December 2000–20 April 2001), Rome: 'L'Erma' di Bretschneider.

Esler, P.F. (ed.) (2000), *The Early Christian World*, 2 vols, London & New York: Routledge.

Esmonde Cleary, S. (2000), *The Ending of Roman Britain* (2nd edition; original 1989), London & New York: Routledge.

Esmonde Cleary, S. & Wood, J. (2006), *Saint-Bertrand-de-Comminges. III, Le rempart de l'antiquité tardive de la ville haute (Études d'archéologie urbaine)*, Pessac: Éditions de la Fédération Aquitainia.

Esmonde Cleary, S., Jones, M. & Wood, J. (1998), 'The Late Roman Defences at Saint-Bertrand-de-Comminges (Haute Garonne): Interim Report', *Journal of Roman Archaeology*, 11: 343–54.

Fauduet, I. (1993), *Atlas des Sanctuaires Romano-Celtiques de Gaule*, Errance: Paris.

Faulkner, N. (2000a), 'Change and Decline in Late Romano-British Towns', in T.R. Slater (ed.), *Towns in Decline, AD 100–1600*, Aldershot: Ashgate, 25–50.

Faulkner, N. (2000b), *The Decline and Fall of Roman Britain*, Stroud: Tempus.

Favory, F. & Fiches, J.-L. (eds) (1994), *Les campagnes de la France méditerranéenne dans l'Antiquité et le haut Moyen-Âge. Études micro-régionales* (Documents d'Archéologie Française, 42), Paris: MSH.

Fernández Ochoa, C. & Morillo Cerdá, A. (1997), 'Urban Fortifications and Land Defence in Later Roman Spain', in W. Groenman-van Waateringe, B.L. Van Beek, W.J.H. Willems & S. Wynia (eds), *Roman Frontier Studies 1995. Proceedings of the XVIth International Congress of Roman Frontier Studies* (Oxbow Monograph 91), Oxford: Oxbow, 343–6.

Ferrill, A. (1986), *The Fall of the Roman Empire. The Military Explanation*, London: Thames and Hudson.

Fiema, Z.T. (2001), 'Byzantine Petra – A Reassessment', in T.S. Burns & J.W. Eadie (eds), *Urban Centers and Rural Contexts in Late Antiquity*, East Lansing: Michigan State University Press, 111–31.

Finn, T.M. (2000), 'Mission and Expansion', in P.F. Esler (ed.), *The Early Christian World*, 2 vols, London & New York: Routledge, 295–315.

Fiocchi Nicolai, V. (2000), '*Sacra martyrium loca circuire*: percorsi di visita del pellegrini nei santuari martiriali del suburbio romano', in L. Pani Ermini (ed.), *Christiana Loca. Lo spazio cristiano nella Roma del primo millennio*, Rome: Fratelli Palombi Editori, 221–30.

Fiocchi Nicolai, V. (2004), 'Cimiteri paleocristiani e insediamenti nel territorio meridionale della Sabina Tiberina', in H. Patterson (ed.), *Bridging the Tiber. Approaches to Regional Archaeology in the Middle Tiber Valley* (Archaeological Monographs of the British School at Rome, 13), London: British School at Rome, 111–24.

Fiocchi Nicolai, V., Bisconti, F. & Mazzoleni, D. (1999), *The Christian Catacombs of Rome, History, Decoration, Inscriptions*, Regensburg: Schnell & Steiner.

Fischer, T. (1988), 'Römer und Germanen an der Donau', in H. Dannheimer & H. Dopsch (eds), *Die Bajuwaren. Von Severin bis Tassilo, 488–788* (exhibition catalogue, Rosenheim-Bayern-Mattsee-Salzburg, 19 May–6 November 1988), Salzburg: Amt der Salzburger Landesregierung, 39–46.

Fischer, T. & Geisler, H. (1988), 'Herkunft und Stammesbildung der Baiern aus archäologischer Sicht', in H. Dannheimer & H. Dopsch (eds), *Die Bajuwaren. Von Severin bis Tassilo, 488–788* (exhibition catalogue, Rosenheim-Bayern-Mattsee-Salzburg, 19 May–6 November 1988), Salzburg: Amt der Salzburger Landesregierung, 61–9.

Fishwick, D. (2002a), *The Imperial Cult in the Latin West. Studies in the Ruler Cult of the Western Provinces of the Roman Empire. Vol. III: Provincial Cult. Part 1: Institution and Evolution* (Religions in the Graeco-Roman World, Volume 145), Leiden, Boston & Köln: Brill.

Fishwick, D. (2002b), *The Imperial Cult in the Latin West. Studies in the Ruler Cult of the Western Provinces of the Roman Empire. Vol. III: Provincial Cult. Part 2: The Provincial Priesthood* (Religions in the Graeco-Roman World, Volume 146), Leiden, Boston & Köln: Brill.

Fitz, J. (1980), *Gorsium-Herculia-Tác*, Budapest: Corvina Kiadó.

Fitz, J. (1991), 'Neue Ergebnisse in der Limesforschung des Donaugebiets', in V. Maxfield & M. Dobson (eds), *Roman Frontier Studies 1989. Proceedings of the XVth International Congress of Roman Frontier Studies*, Exeter: University of Exeter Press, 219–24.

Fitz, J. & Fedak, J. (1993), 'From Roman Gorsium to Late-Antique Herculia: A Summary of Recent Work at Tác (NE Pannonia)', *Journal of Roman Archaeology*, 6: 261–73.

Fleming, R. (2010), *Britain after Rome. The Fall and Rise, 400 to 1070*, London: Allen Lane.

Foot, S. (2004), *Monastic Life in Anglo-Saxon England, c. 600–900*, Cambridge & New York: Cambridge University Press.

Fouracre, P. (ed.) (2005), *The New Cambridge Medieval History. Volume I: c. 500–c. 700*, Cambridge: Cambridge University Press.

Fowden, G. (1998), 'Polytheist Religion and Philosophy', in A. Cameron & P. Garnsey (eds), *The Cambridge Ancient History. Volume XIII. The Late Empire, AD 337–425*, Cambridge & New York: Cambridge University Press, 538–60.

Francovich, R. & Hodges, R. (2003), *Villa to Village. The Transformation of the Roman Countryside in Italy, c. 400–1000*, London: Duckworth.

Fraschetti, A. (1999), 'Veniunt modo reges Romam', in W.V. Harris (ed.), *The Transformations of Vrbs Roma in Late Antiquity* (Journal of Roman Archaeology Supplementary Series No. 33), Ann Arbor: Journal of Roman Archaeology, 235–48.

Frend, W.H.C. (2004), 'From Donatist Opposition to Byzantine Loyalism: The Cult of Martyrs in North Africa, 350–650', in A. Merrills (ed.), *Vandals, Romans and Berbers. New Perspectives on Late Antique North Africa*, Aldershot: Ashgate, 259–69.

Frova, A. (ed.) (1973–74), *Scavi di Luni I*, Rome: 'L'Erma' di Bretschneider.

Frova, A. (ed.) (1977), *Scavi di Luni II. Relazione delle campagne di scavo 1972–74*, Rome: 'L'Erma' di Bretschneider.

Fulford, M. (1980), 'Carthage, Overseas Trade, and the Political Economy,c. AD 400–700', *Reading Medieval Studies*, 6: 68–80.

Fulford, M. (1983), 'The Defensive Sequence at Silchester', in J. Maloney & B. Hobley (eds), *Roman Urban Defences in the West* (CBA Research Report No. 51), London: Council for British Archaeology, 85–9.

Fulford, M. (ed.) (1989), *The Silchester Amphitheatre. Excavations of 1979–85* (Britannia Monograph Series No. 10), London: Society for the Promotion of Roman Studies.

Fulford, M. (1996), 'Economic Hotspots and Provincial Backwaters: Modelling the Late Roman Economy', in C.E. King & D.G. Wigg (eds), *Coin Finds and Coin Use in the Roman World*, Berlin: Mann Verlag, 153–77.

Fulford, M. (2006), *Life and Labour in Late Roman Silchester: Excavations in Insula IX Since 1997* (Britannia Monograph 22), London: Society for the Promotion of Roman Studies.

Fulford, M. & Timby, J. (2000), *Late Iron Age and Roman Silchester. Excavations on the Site of the Forum-Basilica 1977, 1980–86* (Britannia Monograph Series No. 15), London: Society for the Promotion of Roman Studies.

Fulford, M. & Tyers, I. (1995), 'The Date of Pevensey and the Defence of an *Imperium Britanniarum*', *Antiquity*, 69: 1009–14.

Furger, A., Jäggi, C., Martin, M. & Windler, R. (1996), *Die Schweiz zwischen Antike und Mittelalter. Archäologie und Geschichte des 4. bis 9. Jahrhunderts*, Zürich: Verlag Neue Zürcher Zeitung.

Fyfe, R. & Rippon, S. (2004), 'A Landscape in Transition? Palaeoenvironmental Evidence for the End of the "Romano-British" Period in Southwest England', in R. Collins &

J. Gerrard (eds), *Debating Late Antiquity in Britain AD 300–700* (British Archaeological Reports British Series 365), Oxford: Archaeopress, 33–42.

Gabler, D. (2002), 'Tracce delle distruzioni dei Marcomanni in Pannonia', in M. Buora & W. Jobst (eds), *Roma sul Danubio. Da Aquileia a* Carnuntum *lungo la via dell'ambra* (Cataloghi e monografie archeologiche dei Civici Museu di Udine, VI), Rome: 'L'Erma' di Bretschneider, 69–74.

Gaffney, V., Patterson, H. & Roberts, P. (2001), 'Forum Novum-Vescovio: Studying Urbanism in the Tiber Valley', *Journal of Roman Archaeology*, 14: 59–79.

Gaffney, V., Patterson, H. & Roberts, P. (2004), '*Forum Novum* (Vescovio): A New Study of the Town and Bishopric', in H. Patterson (ed.), *Bridging the Tiber. Approaches to Regional Archaeology in the Middle Tiber Valley* (Archaeological Monographs of the British School at Rome, 13), London: British School at Rome, 237–51.

Gailliou, P. & Jones, M. (1991), *The Bretons*, Oxford: Blackwell.

Galinié, H. (1988), 'Reflections on Early Medieval Tours', in R. Hodges & B. Hobley (eds), *The Rebirth of Towns in the West, AD 700–1050* (CBA Research Report 68), London: Council for British Archaeology, 57–62.

Galinié, H. (ed.) (2007), *Tours antique et médiéval. Lieux de vie, temps de la ville. 40 ans d'archéologie urbaine* (30ᵉ Supplément, Revue Archéologique du Centre de la France), Tours: Fédération pour l'Edition de la Revue Archéologique du Centre de la France.

Gallien in der Späta (1980), *Gallien in der Spätantike. Von Kaiser Constantin zu Frankenkönig Childerich* (exhibition catalogue, Römisch-Germanisches Zentralmuseum, 1980–1981), Mainz: Philipp von Zabern.

Gallina Zevi, A. & Claridge, A. (eds) (1996), '*Roman Ostia*' *Revisited. Archaeological and Historical Papers in Memory of Russell Meiggs*, Rome: British School at Rome/STI.

Garmy, P. & Maurin, L. (eds) (1996), *Enceintes Romaines d'Aquitaine: Bordeaux, Dax, Périgueux, Bazas* (Documents d'Archéologie Française, No. 53), Paris: CNRS.

Garnsey, P. (1990), 'Responses to Food Crisis in the Ancient Mediterranean World', in L.F. Newman (ed.), *Hunger in History. Food Shortage, Poverty and Deprivation*, Oxford, UK & Cambridge, MA: Basil Blackwell, 126–46.

Garnsey, P. & Whittaker, C.R. (eds) (1983), *Trade and Famine in the Graeco-Roman World*, Cambridge: Cambridge Philological Society.

Garnsey, P. & Whittaker, C.R. (1998), 'Trade, Industry and the Urban Economy', in A. Cameron & P. Garnsey (eds), *The Cambridge Ancient History. Volume XIII. The Late Empire, AD 337–425*, Cambridge & New York: Cambridge University Press, 312–37.

Gáspár, D. (2002), *Christianity in Roman Pannonia. An Evaluation of Early Christian Finds and Sites from Hungary* (British Archaeological Reports, International Series 1010), Oxford: Archaeopress.

Gasparri, S. (2004), 'Il tesoro del re', in S. Gelichi & C. La Rocca (eds), *Tesori. Forme di accumulazione della ricchezza nell'alto medioevo (secoli V–XI)*, Rome: Viella, 47–67.

Gauthier, N. (1999), 'La topographie chrétienne entre idéologie et pragmatisme', in G.P. Brogiolo & B. Ward-Perkins (eds), *The Idea and Ideal of the Town between Late Antiquity and the Early Middle Ages* (ESF Transformation of the Roman World, 4), Leiden & New York: Brill, 195–209.

Gauthier, N. & Picard, J.-C. (eds) (1986), *Topographie chrétienne des cités de la Gaule, iii: Provinces ecclésiastiques de Vienne et d'Arles*, Paris: De Boccard.

Gelichi, S. (ed.) (1998), *Archeologia urbana in Toscana. La città altomedievale* (Documenti di Archeologia 17), Mantua: Società Archeologica Padana.

Gelichi, S. (2000), 'Ravenna, ascesa e declino di una capitale', in G. Ripoll & J.M. Gurt (eds), *Sedes regiae (ann. 400–800)*, Barcelona: Reial Acadèmia de Bones Lletres, 109–34.

Gelichi, S. & La Rocca, C. (eds) (2004), *Tesori. Forme di accumulazione della ricchezza nell'alto medioevo (secoli V–XI)*, Rome: Viella.

Gerrard, J. (2004), 'How Late Is Late? Pottery and the Fifth Century in Southwest Britain', in R. Collins & J. Gerrard (eds), *Debating Late Antiquity in Britain AD 300–700* (British Archaeological Reports, British Series 365), Oxford: Archaeopress, 65–75.

Giardina, A. (ed.) (1986), *Società Romana e Impero Tardoantico, Vol. III: le merci, gli insediamenti*, Rome-Bari: Laterza.

Gillett, A. (2001), 'Rome, Ravenna and the Last Western Emperors', *Papers of the British School at Rome*, lxix: 131–67.

Gilmour, B. (2007), 'Sub-Roman or Saxon, Pagan or Christian: Who Was Buried in the Early Cemetery at St Paul-in-the-Bail, Lincoln?', in L. Gilmour (ed.), *Pagans and Christians – from Antiquity to the Middle Ages. Papers in Honour of Martin Henig* (British Archaeological Reports, International Series 1610), Oxford: Archaeopress, 229–56.

Giot, P.-R., Guigon, P. & Merdrignac, B. (2003), *The British Settlement of Brittany. The First Bretons in Armorica*, Stroud: Tempus.

Giuliano, A. (1956), *Arco di Costantino*, Milan: Istituto editoriale domus.

Glaser, F. (2002), 'Teurnia', in M. Šašel Kos & P. Scherrer (eds), *The Autonomous Towns of Noricum and Pannonia – Die Autonomen Städte in Noricum und Pannonien* (Dissertationes Musei Nationalis Sloveniae, Situla 40), Narodni Muzej Slovenije: Ljubljana, 135–47.

Glick, T. (1995), *From Muslim Fortress to Christian Castle. Social and Cultural Change in Medieval Spain*, Manchester & New York: Manchester University Press.

Godman, P. (1985), *Poetry of the Carolingian Renaissance*, London: Duckworth.

Godoy Fernández, C. (1995), *Arqueología y liturgia. Iglesias Hispánicas (siglos IV al VIII)* (Biblioteca de la Universitat de Barcelona, 12), Barcelona: Universitat de Barcelona.

Goodburn, R. & Bartholomew, P. (eds) (1976), *Aspects of the Notitia Dignitatum* (British Archaeological Reports, International Series, 15), Oxford: Tempus Reparatum.

Goodman, P.J. (forthcoming), 'Temples in Late Antique Gaul', in M. Mulryan & L. Lavan (eds), *Late Antique Paganism*, Leiden: Brill.

Gordon, R. (1999), 'The End of Mithraism in the Northwest Provinces', *Journal of Roman Archaeology*, 12: 682–8.

Gorini, G. (1996), 'Currency in Italy in the Fifth Century AD', in C.E. King & D.G. Wigg (eds), *Coin Finds and Coin Use in the Roman World*, Berlin: Mann Verlag, 185–202.

Graham, M.W. (2006), *News and Frontier Consciousness in the Late Roman Empire*, Ann Arbor: University of Michigan Press.

Grant, M. (1967), *Gladiators*, Harmondsworth: Pelican.

Greene, K. (1986), *The Archaeology of the Roman Economy*, London: Batsford.

Greenhalgh, M. (1989), *The Survival of Roman Antiquities in the Middle Ages*, London: Duckworth.

Gregory, T. (2005), *A History of Byzantium*, Oxford: Blackwell.

Grierson, P. & Blackburn, M. (1986), *Medieval European Coinage. I. The Early Middle Ages (5th–10th Centuries)*, Cambridge & New York: Cambridge University Press.

Groenman-van Waateringe, W., Van Beek, B.L., Willems, W.J.H. & Wynia, S. (eds) (1997), *Roman Frontier Studies 1995. Proceedings of the XVIth International Congress of Roman Frontier Studies* (Oxbow Monograph 91), Oxford: Oxbow.

Guidobaldi, F. (1999), 'Le *domus* tardoantiche di Roma come "sensori" delle trasformazioni culturali e sociali', in W.V. Harris (ed.), *The Transformations of* Vrbs Roma *in Late Antiquity* (Journal of Roman Archaeology Supplementary Series No. 33), Ann Arbor: Journal of Roman Archaeology, 53–68.

Guidobaldi, F. (2000a), 'Distribuzione topografica, architettura e arredo delle *domus* tardoantiche', in S. Ensoli & E. La Rocca (eds), *Aurea Roma. Dalla città pagana alla città cristiana* (exhibition catalogue, 22 December 2000–20 April 2001), Rome: 'L'Erma' di Bretschneider, 134–36.

Guidobaldi, F. (2000b), 'L'organizzazione dei *tituli* nello spazio urbano', in L. Pani Ermini (ed.), *Christiana Loca. Lo spazio cristiano nella Roma del primo millennio*, Rome: Fratelli Palombi Editori, 123–30.

Gutiérrez Lloret, S. (1998), 'Eastern Spain in the Sixth Century in the Light of Archaeology', in R. Hodges & W. Bowden (eds), *The Sixth Century. Production, Distribution and Demand* (ESF Transformation of the Roman World, 3), Leiden & New York: Brill, 161–84.

Haberl, J. & Hawkes, C. (1973), 'The Last of Roman Noricum: St. Severin on the Danube', in C. Hawkes (ed.), *Greeks, Celts and Romans. Studies in Venture and Resistance*, London: Dent, 97–156.

Halsall, G. (1996), 'Towns, Societies and Ideas: The Not-So-Strange Case of Late Roman and Early Merovingian Metz', in N. Christie & S.T. Loseby (eds), *Towns in Transition. Urban Evolution in Late Antiquity and the Early Middle Ages*, Aldershot: Scolar, 235–61.

Halsall, G. (ed.) (1998a), *Violence and Society in the Early Medieval West*, Woodbridge: Boydell Press.

Halsall, G. (1998b), 'Violence and Society in the Early Medieval West: An Introductory Survey', in G. Halsall (ed.), *Violence and Society in the Early Medieval West*. Woodbridge: Boydell Press, 1–45.

Halsall, G. (2003), *Warfare and Society in the Barbarian West, 450–900*, London & New York: Routledge.

Halsall, G. (2007), *Barbarian Migrations and the Roman West, 376–568*, Cambridge: Cambridge University Press.

Hamerow, H. (2002), *Early Medieval Settlements. The Archaeology of Rural Communities in North-West Europe 400–900*, Oxford & New York: Oxford University Press.

Hanson, W.S. & Haynes, I. (eds) (2004), *Roman Dacia. The Making of a Provincial Society* (Journal of Roman Archaeology Supplementary Series No. 56), Portsmouth, RI: Journal of Roman Archaeology.

Harding, S., Jobling, M. & King, T. (2010), *Viking DNA: The Wirral and West Lancashire Project*, Nottingham: Nottingham University Press.

Harl, K. (2001), 'From Pagan to Christian in Cities of Roman Anatolia during the Fourth and Fifth Centuries', in T.S. Burns & J.W. Eadie (eds), *Urban Centers and Rural Contexts in Late Antiquity*, East Lansing: Michigan State University Press, 301–22.

Harreither, R. (1999), 'Das frühe Christentum im Limesgebiet. Von den Anfängen bis zum Ende der römischen Herrschaft', in R. Harreither & R. Pillinger (eds), *Frühes Christentum am Österreichischen Donaulimes* (exhibition catalogue, Traismauer, 8 Mai–1 Nov. 1999), Vienna: Druckerei Janetschek, 6–45.

Harries, J. (1992), 'Christianity and the City in Late Roman Gaul', in J. Rich (ed.), *The City in Late Antiquity* (Leicester-Nottingham Studies in Ancient Society, Volume 3), London: Routledge, 77–98.

Harries, J. (2003), '*Favor Populi:* Pagans, Christians and Public Entertainment in Late Antique Italy', in K. Lomas & T. Cornell (eds), '*Bread and Circuses'. Euergetism and Municipal Patronage in Roman Italy*, London & New York: Routledge, 125–41.

Harris, A. (2003), *Byzantium, Britain and the West: The Archaeology of Cultural Identity, 400–650*, Stroud: Tempus.

Harris, W.V. (ed.) (1999), *The Transformations of* Vrbs Roma *in Late Antiquity* (Journal of Roman Archaeology Supplementary Series No. 33), Ann Arbor: Journal of Roman Archaeology.

Hartley, E., Hawkes, J., Henig, M. & Mee, F. (eds) (2006), *Constantine the Great. York's Roman Emperor*, London & New York: York Museums Trust/Lund Humphries.

Haug, A. (2003), *Die Stadt als Lebensraum. Eine kulturhistorische Analyse zum spätantiken Stadtleben in Norditalien* (Internationale Archäologie 85), Rahden: Marie Leidorf.

Haverfield, F. (1912), 'Notes on the Roman Coast Defences of Britain, Especially in Yorkshire', *Journal of Roman Studies*, 2: 201–14.

Hayes, J. (1972), *Late Roman Pottery*, London: British School at Rome.

Haynes, I. & Hanson, W.S. (2004), 'An Introduction to Roman Dacia', in W.S. Hanson & I. Haynes (eds), *Roman Dacia. The Making of a Provincial Society* (Journal of Roman Archaeology Supplementary Series No. 56), Portsmouth, RI: Journal of Roman Archaeology, 11–31.

Haynes, I., Sheldon, H. & Hannigan, L. (eds) (2000), *London under Ground. The Archaeology of a City*, Oxford: Oxbow.

Haywood, R.M. (1958), *The Myth of Rome's Fall*, Westport: Greenwood (reprinted in 1979).

Heather, P. (1992), 'The Emergence of the Visigothic Kingdom', in J. Drinkwater & H. Elton (eds), *Fifth-Century Gaul: A Crisis of Identity?* Cambridge: Cambridge University Press, 84–94.

Heather, P. (1994), 'Literacy and Power in the Migration Period', in A. Bowman & G. Woolf (eds), *Literacy and Power in the Ancient World*, Cambridge: Cambridge University Press, 177–97.

Heather, P. (1996), *The Goths*, Oxford: Blackwell.

Heather, P. (1997), '*Foedera* and *Foederati* of the Fourth Century', in W. Pohl (ed.), *Kingdoms of the Empire. The Integration of Barbarians in Late Antiquity* (The Transformation of the Roman World, Volume 1), Leiden, Boston & Cologne: European Science Foundation/Brill, 57–73.

Heather, P. (1998), 'Goths and Huns, c. 320–425', in A. Cameron & P. Garnsey (eds), *The Cambridge Ancient History. Volume XIII. The Late Empire, AD 337–425*, Cambridge & New York: Cambridge University Press, 487–515.

Heather, P. (2000), 'The Western Empire, 425–76', in A. Cameron, B. Ward-Perkins & M. Whitby (eds), *The Cambridge Ancient History. Volume XIV. Late Antiquity: Empire and Successors, AD 425–600*, Cambridge & New York: Cambridge University Press, 1–32.

Heather, P. (2001), 'The Late Roman Art of Client Management: Imperial Defence in the Fourth-Century West', in W. Pohl, I. Wood & H. Reimitz (eds), *The Transformation of Frontiers. From Late Antiquity to the Carolingians* (The Transformation of the Roman World, Volume 10), Leiden, Boston & Cologne: European Science Foundation/Brill, 15–68.

Heather, P. (2005), *The Fall of the Roman Empire. A New History*, London: Macmillan.

Heather, P. (2007), 'Goths in the Roman Balkans c. 350–500', in A. Poulter (ed.), *The Transition to Late Antiquity on the Danube and Beyond* (Proceedings of the British Academy, Volume 141), London: British Academy, 163–90.

Heather, P. (2009), 'Why Did the Barbarian Cross the Rhine?' *Journal of Late Antiquity*, 2(1): 3–29.

Heather, P. & Matthews, J. (1991), *The Goths in the Fourth Century*, Liverpool: Liverpool University Press.

Heijmans, M. (1999), 'La topographie de la ville d'Arles durant l'Antiquité tardive', *Journal of Roman Archaeology*, 12: 143–67.

Heintz, F. (1998), 'Circus Curses and their Archaeological Contexts', *Journal of Roman Archaeology*, 11: 337–42.

Hekster, O. (2008), *Rome and Its Empire, AD 193–284*, Edinburgh: Edinburgh University Press.

Hendy, M.F. (1988), 'From Public to Private: The Western Barbarian Coinage as a Mirror of the Disintegration of Late Roman State Structure', *Viator*, 19: 29–78.

Henig, M. (1984), *Religion in Roman Britain*, London: Batsford.

Henig, M. (2006), 'Religious Diversity in Constantine's Empire', in E. Hartley, J. Hawkes, M. Henig & F. Mee (eds), *Constantine the Great. York's Roman Emperor*, London & New York: York Museums Trust/Lund Humphries, 85–95.

Higham, N. (1986), *The Northern Counties to AD 1000*, London & New York: Longman.

Hitchner, R. (1992), 'Meridional Gaul, Trade and the Mediterranean Economy in Late Antiquity', in J. Drinkwater & H. Elton (eds), *Fifth-Century Gaul: A Crisis of Identity?* Cambridge: Cambridge University Press, 122–31.

Hobley, B. (1983), 'Roman Urban Defences: A Review of Research in Britain', in J. Maloney & B. Hobley (eds), *Roman Urban Defences in the West* (CBA Research Report No. 51), London: Council for British Archaeology, 78–84.

Hodges, R. (ed.) (1993), *San Vincenzo al Volturno 1: The 1980–86 Excavations, Part I* (British School at Rome Archaeological Monograph 7), London: British School at Rome.

Hodges, R. (ed.) (1995), *San Vincenzo al Volturno 2: The 1980–86 Excavations, Part II* (British School at Rome Archaeological Monograph 9), London: British School at Rome.

Hodges, R. & Bowden, W. (eds) (1998), *The Sixth Century. Production, Distribution and Demand* (ESF Transformation of the Roman World, 3), Leiden & New York: Brill.

Hodges, R. & Hobley, B. (eds) (1988), *The Rebirth of Towns in the West, AD 700–1050* (CBA Research Report 68), London: Council for British Archaeology.

Hodges, R., Bowden, W. & Lako, K. (2004), *Byzantine Butrint: Excavations and Surveys, 1994–99*, Oxford: Oxbow/Butrint Foundation.

Hodgson, N. & Bidwell, P.T. (2004), 'Auxiliary Barracks in a New Light: Recent Discoveries on Hadrian's Wall', *Britannia*, xxxv: 121–57.

Hoffmann, D. (1963), 'Die spätrömischen Soldateninschriften von Concordia', *Museum Helveticum*, 20: 22–57.

Hoffmann, D. (1969), *Das spätrömische Bewegungsheer und die Notitia Dignitatum*, vols 1, 2, Munich: Rheinland Verlag.

Hoffmann, D. (1970), *Das spätrömische Bewegungsheer und die Notitia Dignitatum*, vols. 1, 2., Munich: Rheinland Verlag: Munich.

Hornsby, W. & Laverick, J.D. (1932), 'The Roman Signal Station at Goldsborough, Near Whitby', *The Archaeological Journal*, lxxxix: 203–19/53.

Hostetter, E., Howe, T.N., Brandt, J.R., St Clair, A., Peña, J.T., Parca, M., Gleason, K. & Miller, N.F. (1994), 'A Late-Roman *Domus* with Apsidal Hall on the NE Slope of the Palatine: 1989–1991 Seasons', in L. La Follette, C. Pavolini, M.-A. Tomei, E. Hostetter *et al.* & L. Ball (eds), *Rome Papers: The Baths of Trajan Decius, Iside e Serapide nel Palazzo, A Late Roman Domus on the Palatine, and Nero's Golden House* (Journal of Roman Archaeology Supplementary Series No. 11), Ann Arbor: Journal of Roman Archaeology, 131–81.

Howgego, C. (1996), 'The Circulation of Silver Coins, Models of the Roman Economy, and Crisis in the Third Century AD: Some Numismatic Evidence', in C.E. King & D.G. Wigg (eds), *Coin Finds and Coin Use in the Roman World*, Berlin: Mann Verlag, 219–36.

Hudák, K. & Nagy, L. (2005), *A Fine and Private Place. Discovering the Early Christian Cemetery of Sopianae-Pécs* (Heritage Booklets 4), Pécs: NKA.

Humphrey, J. (1986), *Roman Circuses. Arenas for Chariot Racing*, London: Batsford.

Humphries, M. (2000), 'Italy, AD 425–605', in A. Cameron, B. Ward-Perkins & M. Whitby (eds), *The Cambridge Ancient History. Volume XIV. Late Antiquity: Empire and Successors, AD 425–600*, Cambridge & New York: Cambridge University Press, 525–51.

Hunt, D. (1998a), 'The Successors of Constantine', in A. Cameron & P. Garnsey (eds), *The Cambridge Ancient History. Volume XIII. The Late Empire, AD 337–425*, Cambridge & New York: Cambridge University Press, 1–43.

Hunt, D. (1998b), 'Julian', in A. Cameron & P. Garnsey (eds), *The Cambridge Ancient History. Volume XIII. The Late Empire, AD 337–425*, Cambridge & New York: Cambridge University Press, 44–77.

Hunt, E.D. (1992), 'Gaul and the Holy Land in the Early Fifth Century', in J. Drinkwater & H. Elton (eds), *Fifth-Century Gaul: A Crisis of Identity?* Cambridge: Cambridge University Press, 264–74.

Hurst, J. (1992), 'L'Ilot de l'Amirauté, le port circulaire et l'Avenue Bourguiba', in Ennabli (ed.), *Pour Sauver Carthage. Exploration et conservation de la cité punique, romaine et byzantine*, Paris: UNESCO/INAA, 79–94.

Hurst, H. (1994), *Excavations at Carthage. The British Mission. Vol. II, 1, The Circular Harbour, North Side. The Site and Finds Other than Pottery* (British Academy Monographs in Archaeology, No. 4), Oxford: Oxford University Press.

Ilkjær, J. (2002), *Illerup Ådal. Archaeology as a Magic Mirror*, Moesgård: Moesgård Museum.

Innes, M. (2007), *Introduction to Early Medieval Western Europe, 300–900. The Sword, the Plough and the Book*, Abingdon & New York: Routledge.

James, E. (1988), *The Franks*, Oxford: Basil Blackwell.

James, E. (2001), *Britain in the First Millennium*, London: Arnold.

James, S. (1988), 'The *Fabricae*: State Arms Factories of the Later Roman Empire', in J.C. Coulston (ed.), *Military Equipment and the Identity of Roman Soldiers (Proceedings of the 4th Roman Military Equipment Conference)* (British Archaeological Reports, International Series 394), Oxford: British Archaeological Reports, 257–332.

James, S. (2005), 'Large-Scale Recruitment of Auxiliaries from Free Germany?', in Zs. Visy (ed.), *Limes XIX. Proceedings of the XIXth International Congress of Roman Frontier Studies (Pécs, Hungary, September 2003)*, Pécs: University of Pécs, 273–79.

James, S. & Millett, M. (eds) (2001), *Britons and Romans: Advancing an Archaeological Agenda*, York: Council for British Archaeology.

Janes, D. (2002), *Romans and Christians*, Stroud: Tempus.

Jobst, W., Kremer, G. & Piso, I. (2002), '*Iupiter optimus maximus k (arnuntus)*. Il signore dell'area sacra sul Pfaffenberg', in M. Buora & W. Jobst (eds), *Roma sul Danubio. Da Aquileia a Carnuntum lungo la via dell'ambra* (Cataloghi e monografie archeologiche dei Civici Musei di Udine, VI), Rome: 'L'Erma' di Bretschneider, 81–97.

Johns, C. & Potter, T.W. (1983), *The Thetford Treasure: Roman Jewellery and Silver*, London: British Museum Publications.

Johnson, M. (1988), 'Toward a History of Theoderic's Building Program', *Dumbarton Oaks Papers*, 42: 73–96.

Johnson, P.S. (2010), 'Investigating Urban Change in Late Antique Italy through Waste Disposal Practices', in D. Sami & G. Speed (eds), *Debating Urbanism. Within and Beyond the Walls, AD 300–700 (Proceedings of a Conference Held at the University of Leicester, 15th November 2008)* (Leicester Archaeology Monograph 17), Leicester: University of Leicester School of Archaeology and Ancient History, 167–93.

Johnson, S. (1979), *The Roman Forts of the Saxon Shore* (2nd edition), London: BCA.

Johnson, S. (1983a), *Burgh Castle: Excavations by Charles Green, 1958–61* (East Anglian Archaeology, Report No. 20), Gressenhall: Norfolk Archaeological Unit.

Johnson, S. (1983b), *Late Roman Fortifications*, London: Batsford.

Jones, B. & Mattingly, D. (1990), *An Atlas of Roman Britain*, Oxford: Blackwell.

Jones, A.H.M. (1964), *The Later Roman Empire, 284–602: A Social, Economic and Administrative Survey*, Oxford: Basil Blackwell.

Jones, M.J. (1994), 'St. Paul in the Bail, Lincoln. Britain in Europe?', in K. Painter (ed.), *'Churches Built in Ancient Times': Recent Studies in Early Christian Archaeology* (Society of Antiquaries, Occasional Paper 16), London: Society of Antiquaries of London, 325–47.

Jones, M.J. (2002), *Roman Lincoln. Conquest, Colony & Capital*, Stroud: Tempus.

Jørgensen, L. (2001), 'The "Warriors, Soldiers and Conscripts" of the Anthropology in Late Roman and Migration Period Archaeology', in B. Storgaard (ed.), *Military Aspects of the Aristocracy in Barbaricum in the Roman and Early Migration Periods. Papers from an International Research Seminar at the Danish National Museum, Copenhagen, 10–11*

December 1999 (Publications from the National Museum, Studies in Archaeology & History, Volume 5), Copenhagen: National Museum, 9–19.

Karagiorgou, O. (2001), 'Demetrias and Thebes: The Fortunes and Misfortunes of Two Thessalian Port Cities', in L. Lavan (ed.), *Recent Research in Late-Antique Urbanism* (Journal of Roman Archaeology Supplementary Series No. 42), Ann Arbor: Journal of Roman Archaeology, 182–215.

Keay, S. (1988), *Roman Spain*, London: British Museum Press.

Keay, S. (1996), 'Tarraco in Late Antiquity', in N. Christie & S.T. Loseby (eds), *Towns in Transition. Urban Evolution in Late Antiquity and the Early Middle Ages*, Aldershot: Scolar, 18–44.

Keay, S., Creighton, J. & Remesal Rodríguez, J. (2000), *Celti (Peñaflor). The Archaeology of a Hispano-Roman Town in Baetica: Survey and Excavations, 1987–1992* (University of Southampton, Department of Archaeology Monographs No. 2), Oxford: Oxbow Books.

Keay, S., Millett, M., Poppy, S., Robinson, J., Taylor, J. & Terrrenato, N. (2000), 'Falerii Novi: A New Survey of the Walled Area', *Papers of the British School at Rome*, lxviii: 1–93.

Keay, S., Millett, M., Paroli, L. & Strutt, K. (2005), *Portus. An Archaeological Survey of the Port of Imperial Rome* (Archaeological Monographs of the British School at Rome 15), London: British School at Rome.

Kent, J. & Painter, K. (eds) (1977), *Wealth of the Roman World. Gold and Silver, AD 300–700*, London: British Museum Press.

Kerr, W.G. (1997), 'The *Praetentura Italiae et Alpium* (ILS 8977): New Numismatic Perspectives', in W. Groenman-van Waateringe, B.L. Van Beek, W.J.H. Willems & S. Wynia (eds), *Roman Frontier Studies 1995. Proceedings of the XVIth International Congress of Roman Frontier Studies* (Oxbow Monograph 91), Oxford: Oxbow, 405–9.

King, A. (1990), *Roman Gaul and Germany*, London: British Museum Press.

King, C. (1996), 'Roman Copies', in C.E. King & D.G. Wigg (eds), *Coin Finds and Coin Use in the Roman World*, Berlin: Mann Verlag, 237–53.

Kingsley, S. (2001), 'Decline' in the Ports of Palestine in Late Antiquity', in L. Lavan (ed.), *Recent Research in Late-Antique Urbanism* (Journal of Roman Archaeology Supplementary Series No. 42), Ann Arbor: Journal of Roman Archaeology, 69–87.

Kingsley, S. & Decker, M. (eds) (2001), *Economy and Exchange in the East Mediterranean during Late Antiquity. Proceedings of a Conference at Somerville College, Oxford, 29th May, 1999*, Oxford: Oxbow.

Kiss, A. (1986), 'Die Goldfunde des Karpatenbeckens vom 5–10. Jahrhundert', *Acta Archaeologica Academiae Scientiarum Hungaricae*, xxxviii: 105–45.

Kiss, A. (1994), 'Archeologia degli Ostrogoti in Pannonia (456–473)', in V. Bierbrauer, O. von Hessen & E.A. Arslan (eds), *I Goti* (exhibition catalogue, Milan, Palazzo Reale, 28 gennaio–8 maggio 1994), Milan: Electa, 164–9.

Knight, J.K. (1999), *The End of Antiquity. Archaeology, Society and Religion, AD 235–700*, Stroud: Tempus.

Kolb, A. (2001), 'Transport and Communication in the Roman State: The *Cursus Publicus*', in C. Adams & R. Laurence (eds), *Travel and Geography in the Roman Empire*, London: Routledge, 95–105.

Krautheimer, R. (1980), *Rome. Profile of a City, 312–1308*, Princeton: Princeton University Press.

Krekovič, E. (1997), 'The Structure of Roman Import in Slovakia', in W. Groenman-van Waateringe, B.L. Van Beek, W.J.H. Willems & S. Wynia (eds), *Roman Frontier Studies 1995. Proceedings of the XVIth International Congress of Roman Frontier Studies* (Oxbow Monograph 91), Oxford: Oxbow, 233–6.

Kuhnen, H.-P. (1997), 'Wirtschaftliche Probleme und das Ende des römischen Limes in Deutschland', in W. Groenman-van Waateringe, B.L. Van Beek, W.J.H. Willems &

S. Wynia (eds), *Roman Frontier Studies 1995. Proceedings of the XVIth International Congress of Roman Frontier Studies* (Oxbow Monograph 91), Oxford: Oxbow, 429–34.

Kuhnen, H.-P. (2009), 'The Trier Amphitheatre: An Ancient Monument in the Light of New Research', in T. Wilmott (ed.), *Roman Amphitheatres and Spectacula. A 21st Century Perspective* (British Archeological Reports, International Series 1946), Oxford: English Heritage/Chester Museum/Archaeopress, 95–104.

Kulikowski, M. (2001), 'The Interdependence of Town and Country in Late Antique Spain', in T.S. Burns & J.W. Eadie (eds), *Urban Centers and Rural Contexts in Late Antiquity*, East Lansing: Michigan State University Press, 147–61.

Kulikowski, M. (2004), *Late Roman Spain and Its Cities*, Baltimore & London: John Hopkins University Press.

Kulikowski, M. (2007), *Rome's Gothic Wars from the Third Century to Alaric*, Cambridge & New York: Cambridge University Press.

Kuzmová, K. (1997), 'Die Verbreitung der Sigillaten im Vorfeld des nordpannonischen Limes und ihre sozial-ökonomischen Aspekte', in W. Groenman-van Waateringe, B.L. Van Beek, W.J.H. Willems & S. Wynia (eds), *Roman Frontier Studies 1995. Proceedings of the XVIth International Congress of Roman Frontier Studies* (Oxbow Monograph 91), Oxford: Oxbow, 237–9.

Kuzmová, K. (2002), 'La *terra sigillata* presso i Marcomanni e i Quadi e le relazioni tra l'area antistante il *limes* della Pannonia settentrionale e l'Italia', in M. Buora & W. Jobst (eds), *Roma sul Danubio. Da Aquileia a* Carnuntum *lungo la via dell'ambra* (Cataloghi e monografie archeologiche dei Civici Musei di Udine, VI), Rome: 'L'Erma' di Bretschneider, 153–8.

Kyle, D.G. (1998), *Spectacles of Death in Ancient Rome*, London & New York: Routledge.

La città e la sua memoria (1997), *La città e la sua memoria. Milano e la tradizione di sant'Ambrogio* (exhibition catalogue, 3 April–8 June 1997, Milan), Milan: Electa.

La Follette, L. (1994), 'The Baths of Trajan Decius on the Aventine', in L. La Follette, C. Pavolini, M.-A. Tomei, E. Hostetter *et al.* & L. Ball (eds), *Rome Papers: The Baths of Trajan Decius, Iside e Serapide nel Palazzo, A Late Roman Domus on the Palatine, and Nero's Golden House* (Journal of Roman Archaeology Supplementary Series No. 11), Ann Arbor: Journal of Roman Archaeology, 6–88.

La Follette, L., Pavolini, C. Tomei, M.-A., Hostetter, E. *et al.* & Ball, L. (1994), *Rome Papers: The Baths of Trajan Decius, Iside e Serapide nel Palazzo, a Late Roman Domus on the Palatine, and Nero's Golden House* (Journal of Roman Archaeology Supplementary Series No. 11), Ann Arbor: Journal of Roman Archaeology.

Lançon, B. (2000), *Rome in Late Antiquity. Everyday Life and Urban Change, AD 312–609* (original French edition 1995), Edinburgh: Edinburgh University Press.

Laurence, R. (1999), *The Roads of Roman Italy. Mobility and Cultural Change*, London & New York: Routledge.

Lavan, L. (2001a), 'The *Praetoria* of Civil Governors in Late Antiquity', in L. Lavan (ed.), *Recent Research in Late-Antique Urbanism* (Journal of Roman Archaeology Supplementary Series No. 42), Ann Arbor: Journal of Roman Archaeology, 39–56.

Lavan, L. (ed.) (2001b), *Recent Research in Late-Antique Urbanism* (Journal of Roman Archaeology Supplementary Series No. 42), Ann Arbor: Journal of Roman Archaeology.

Lavan, L. & Bowden, W. (eds) (2003), *Theory and Method in Late Antique Archaeology* (Late Antique Archaeology, Volume 1), Leiden & Boston: Brill.

Lavan, L., Özgenel, L. & Sarantis, A. (eds) (2007a), *Housing in Late Antiquity. From Palaces to Shops* (Late Antique Archaeology, Volume 3.2), Leiden & Boston: Brill.

Lavan, L., Zanini, E. & Sarantis, A. (eds) (2007b), *Technology in Transition AD 300–650* (Late Antique Archaeology, Volume 4), Leiden & Boston: Brill.

Lawrence, C.H. (1984), *Medieval Monasticism. Forms of Religious Life in Western Europe in the Middle Ages*, London: Longman.

Lazar, I. (2002), 'Celeia', in M. Šašel Kos & P. Scherrer (eds), *The Autonomous Towns of Noricum and Pannonia – Die Autonomen Städte in Noricum und Pannonien* (Dissertationes Musei Nationalis Sloveniae, Situla 40), Ljubljana: Narodni Muzej Slovenije, 71–101.

Leadbetter, B. (2000), 'From Constantine to Theodosius (and Beyond)', in P.F. Esler (ed.), *The Early Christian World*, 2 vols, London & New York: Routledge, 258–92.

Lee, A.D. (1993), *Information and Frontiers. Roman Foreign Relations in Late Antiquity*, Cambridge: Cambridge University Press.

Lee, A.D. (1998), 'The Army', in A. Cameron & P. Garnsey (eds), *The Cambridge Ancient History. Volume XIII. The Late Empire, AD 337–425*, Cambridge & New York: Cambridge University Press, 211–37.

Lee, A.D. (2000a), *Pagans and Christians in Late Antiquity. A Sourcebook*, London: Routledge.

Lee, A.D. (2000b), 'The Eastern Empire: Theodosius to Anastasius', in A. Cameron, B. Ward-Perkins & M. Whitby (eds), *The Cambridge Ancient History. Volume XIV. Late Antiquity: Empire and Successors, AD 425–600*, Cambridge & New York: Cambridge University Press, 33–62.

Lee, A.D. (2007), *War in Late Antiquity. A Social History*, Oxford: Blackwell Publishing.

Lenski, N. (2002), *Failure of Empire. Valens and the Roman State in the Fourth Century AD*, Berkeley, Los Angeles & London: University of California Press.

Leone, A. (2007), *Changing Townscapes in North Africa from Late Antiquity to the Arab Conquest*, Bari: Edipuglia.

Lewin, A. (1991), *Studi sulla città imperiale romana nell'Oriente tardoantico*, Como: New Press.

Lewin, A. (2001), 'Urban Public Building from Constantine to Julian: The Epigraphic Evidence', in L. Lavan (ed.), *Recent Research in Late-Antique Urbanism* (Journal of Roman Archaeology Supplementary Series No. 42), Ann Arbor: Journal of Roman Archaeology, 27–36.

Lewis, A. & Runyan, T. (1985), *European Naval and Maritime History, 300–1500*, Bloomington: Indiana University Press.

Lewit, T. (2004), *Villas, Farms and the Late Roman Rural Economy (Third to Fifth Centuries AD)* (British Archaeological Reports, International Series 568), Oxford: Archaeopress.

Lewit, T. (2009), 'Pigs, Presses and Pastoralism: Farming in the Fifth to Sixth Centuries AD', *Early Medieval Europe*, 17(1): 77–91.

Leyerle, B. (2000), 'Communication and Travel', in P.F. Esler (ed.), *The Early Christian World*, 2 vols, London & New York: Routledge, 452–74.

Liebeschuetz, J.H.W.G. (1979), *Continuity and Change in Roman Religion*, Oxford: Clarendon Press.

Liebeschuetz, J.H.W.G. (1992a), 'Alaric's Goths: Nation or Army?', in J. Drinkwater & H. Elton (eds), *Fifth-Century Gaul: A Crisis of Identity?* Cambridge: Cambridge University Press, 75–83.

Liebeschuetz, J.H.W.G. (1992b), 'The End of the Ancient City', in J. Rich (ed.), *The City in Late Antiquity* (Leicester-Nottingham Studies in Ancient Society, Volume 3), London: Routledge, 1–49.

Liebeschuetz, J.H.W.G. (2001a), *The Decline and Fall of the Roman City*, Oxford & New York: Oxford University Press.

Liebeschuetz, J.H.W.G. (2001b), 'The Uses and Abuses of the Concept of "Decline" in Late Roman History, or Was Gibbon Politically Incorrect?', in L. Lavan (ed.), *Recent Research in Late-Antique Urbanism* (Journal of Roman Archaeology Supplementary Series No. 42), Ann Arbor: Journal of Roman Archaeology, 233–7.

Lieu, S. & Montserrat, D. (eds) (1999), *Constantine. History, Historiography and Legend*, London & New York: Routledge.

Lightfoot, C. & Lightfoot, M. (2007), *A Byzantine City in Anatolia. Amorium. An Archaeological Guide*, Galatasaray: Homer Kitabevi.

Lim, R. (1999), 'People as Power: Games, Munificence and Contested Topography', in W.V. Harris (ed.), *The Transformations of Vrbs Roma in Late Antiquity* (Journal of Roman Archaeology Supplementary Series No. 33), Ann Arbor: Journal of Roman Archaeology, 265–81.

Liverani, P. (2005a), 'L'arco di Costantino', in A. Donati & G. Gentili (ed.), *Costantino il Grande. La civiltà antica al bivio tra Occidente e Oriente* (exhibition catalogue, Rimini, Castel Sismondo, 13 Marzo–4 Sett. 2005), Milan: Silvana Editoriale, 64–9.

Liverani, P. (2005b), 'Un nuovo stile di corte', in A. Donati & G. Gentili (ed.), *Costantino il Grande. La civiltà antica al bivio tra Occidente e Oriente* (exhibition catalogue, Rimini, Castel Sismondo, 13 Marzo–4 Sett. 2005), Milan: Silvana Editoriale, 70–3.

Lizzi, R. (1990), 'Ambrose's Contemporaries and the Christianisation of Northern Italy', *Journal of Roman Studies*, 80: 156–73.

Llewellyn, P. (1993), *Rome in the Dark Ages*, London: Constable (reprinted in 1971).

Lo Cascio, E. (1999a), 'The Population of Roman Italy in Town and Country', in J. Bintliff & K. Sbonias (eds), *Reconstructing Past Population Trends in Mediterranean Europe (3000 BC–AD 1800)* (The Archaeology of Mediterranean Landscapes, 1), Oxford: POPULUS/Oxbow, 161–72.

Lo Cascio, E. (1999b), '*Canon frumentarius, suarius, vinarius*: stato e privati nell'approvigionamento dell'*Vrbs*', in W.V. Harris (ed.), *The Transformations of Vrbs Roma in Late Antiquity* (Journal of Roman Archaeology Supplementary Series No. 33), Ann Arbor: Journal of Roman Archaeology, 163–82.

Lo Cascio, E. (2000), 'Il popolamento', in S. Ensoli & E. La Rocca (eds), *Aurea Roma. Dalla città pagana alla cittàc cristiana*, Rome: 'L'Erma' di Bretschneider, 52–4.

Lomas, K. & Cornell, T. (eds) (2003), *'Bread and Circuses'. Euergetism and Municipal Patronage in Roman Italy*, London & New York: Routledge.

Loseby, S.T. (1992), 'Bishops and Cathedrals: Order and Diversity in the Fifth-Century Urban Landscape of Southern Gaul', in J. Drinkwater & H. Elton (eds), *Fifth-Century Gaul: A Crisis of Identity?* Cambridge: Cambridge University Press, 144–55.

Loseby, S.T. (1996), 'Arles in Late Antiquity: *Gallula Roma Arelas* and *Urbs Genesii*', in N. Christie & S.T. Loseby (eds), *Towns in Transition. Urban Evolution in Late Antiquity and the Early Middle Ages*, Aldershot: Scolar, 45–70.

Loseby, S.T. (2000a), 'Power and Towns in Late Roman Britain and Early Anglo-Saxon England', in G. Ripoll & J.M. Gurt (eds), *Sedes Regiae (ann. 400–800)*, Barcelona: Reial Acadèmia de Bones Lletres, 319–70.

Loseby, S.T. (2000b), 'Urban Failures in Late-Antique Gaul', in T.R. Slater (ed.), *Towns in Decline, AD 100–1600*, Aldershot: Ashgate, 72–95.

Louis, E. (2004), 'A De-Romanised Landscape in Northern Gaul: The Scarpe Valley from the 4th to the 9th Century AD', in W. Bowden, L. Lavan & C. Machado (eds), *Recent Research on the Late Antique Countryside* (Late Antique Archaeology 2), Leiden & Boston: Brill, 479–503.

Loveluck, C. (1995), 'Acculturation, Migration and Exchange: The Formation of an Anglo-Saxon Society in the English Peak District, 400–700 AD', in J. Bintliff & H. Hamerow (eds), *Europe between Late Antiquity and the Middle Ages. Recent Archaeological and Historical Research in Western and Southern Europe* (British Archaeological Reports International Series 617), Oxford: Tempus Reparatum, 84–98.

Lusuardi Siena, S. (1997), 'Il complesso episcopale. Il gruppo cattedrale', in *La città e la sua memoria. Milano e la tradizione di sant'Ambrogio* (exhibition catalogue, 3 April–8 June 1997, Milan), Milan: Electa, 36–9.

Lusuardi Siena, S. (2003), 'Gli scavi nella cattedrale di Luni nel quadro della topografia cittadina tra tarda antichità e medioevo', in M. Marcenaro (ed.), *Roma e la Liguria Maritima: secoli IV–X. La capitale cristiana e una regione di confine (Istituto Internazionale di Studi Liguri. Att dei Convegni, XI)*, Genoa-Bordighera: Istituto Internazionale di Studi Liguri, 195–202.

Lusuardi Siena, S., Bruno, B., Villa, L., Fien, L., Giozza, G., Sacchi, F. & Arslan, E. (1997), 'Le nuove indagini archeologiche nell'area del Duomo', in *La città e la sua memoria. Milano e la tradizione di sant'Ambrogio* (exhibition catalogue, 3 April–8 June 1997, Milan), Milan: Electa, 40–67.

Luttwak, E.N. (1976), *The Grand Strategy of the Roman Empire, From the First Century* AD *to the Third*, Baltimore: John Hopkins Press.

Lyon, J. (2007), *Within These Walls. Roman and Medieval Defences North of Newgate at the Merrill Lynch Financial Centre, City of London* (Museum of London Archaeology Service Monograph 33), MOLAS: Museum of London.

MacCormack, S.G. (1981), *Art and Ceremony in Late Antiquity*, Berkeley, Los Angeles & London: University of California Press.

Mackensen, M. (1998), 'New Evidence for Central Tunisian Red Slip Ware with Stamped Decoration (ARS style D)', *Journal of Roman Archaeology*, 11: 355–70.

Mackensen, M. (1999), 'Late Roman Fortifications and Building Programmes in the Province of *Raetia*: The Evidence of Recent Excavations and Some New Reflections', in J.D. Creighton & R.J.A. Wilson (eds), *Roman Germany. Studies in Cultural Interaction* (Journal of Roman Archaeology Supplementary Series No. 32), Portsmouth, RI: Journal of Roman Archaeology, 199–244.

MacKinnon, M. (2004), *Production and Consumption of Animals in Roman Italy: Integrating the Zooarchaeological and Textual Evidence* (Journal of Roman Archaeology Supplementary Series No. 54), Ann Arbor: Journal of Roman Archaeology.

MacMullen, R. (1990), *Changes in the Roman Empire. Essays in the Ordinary*, Princeton: Princeton University Press.

Macphail, R.I. (2010), 'Dark Earth and Insights into Changing Land Use of Urban Areas', in D. Sami & G. Speed (eds), *Debating Urbanism. Within and Beyond the Walls,* AD *300– 700 (Proceedings of a Conference Held at the University of Leicester, 15th November 2008)* (Leicester Archaeology Monograph 17), Leicester: University of Leicester, 145–65.

Maenchen-Helfen, O.J. (1973), *The World of the Huns. Studies in their History and Culture*, Berkeley: University of California Press.

Maioli, M.G. & Stoppioni, M.L. (1987), *Classe e Ravenna tra terra e mare. Città, necropoli, monumenti*, Milan: Edizioni Sirri.

Maloney, J. (1983), 'Recent Work on London's Defences', in J. Maloney & B. Hobley (eds), *Roman Urban Defences in the West* (CBA Research Report No. 51), London: Council for British Archaeology, 96–117.

Maloney, J. & Hobley, B. (eds) (1983), *Roman Urban Defences in the West* (CBA Research Report No. 51), London: Council for British Archaeology.

Maloney, S. & Hale, J. (1996), 'The Villa of Torre de Palma (Alto Alentejo)', *Journal of Roman Archaeology*, 9: 275–94.

Manacorda, D. (2001), *Crypta Balbi. Archeologia e storia di un paesaggio urbano*, Milan: Electa.

Manacorda, D. & Zanini, E. (1989), 'The First Millennium AD in Rome: From the *Porticus Minucia* to the Via delle Botteghe Oscure', in K. Randsborg (ed.), *The Birth of Europe. Archaeology and Social Development in the First Millennium AD* (Analecta Romana Instituti Danici, Suppl. XVI), Rome: 'L'Erma' di Bretschneider, 25–32.

Mango, C. (ed.) (2002), *The Oxford History of Byzantium*, 'L'Erma' di Bretschneider: Oxford University Press.

Marcone, A. (1998), 'Late Roman Social Relations', in A. Cameron & P. Garnsey (eds), *The Cambridge Ancient History. Volume XIII. The Late Empire, AD 337–425*, Cambridge & New York: Cambridge University Press, 338–70.

Marin, E. (2001), 'The Temple of the Imperial Cult (Augusteum) at Narona and Its Statues: Interim Report', *Journal of Roman Archaeology*, 14: 80–112.

Marin, E. & Vickers, M. (eds) (2004), *The Rise and Fall of an Imperial Shrine: Roman Sculpture from the Augusteum at Narona*, Split: Archaeological Museum.

Markus, R. (1990), *The End of Ancient Christianity*, Cambridge: Cambridge University Press.

Marsden, P. (1994), *Ships of the Port of London. First to Eleventh Centuries AD* (English Heritage Archaeological Report 3), London: English Heritage.

Martin, M. (1996), 'Von der römischen Randprovinz zu einer zentralen Region des Abendlandes', in A. Furger, C. Jäggi, M. Martin, & R. Windler, *Die Schweiz zwischen Antike und Mittelalter*, Zürich: Verlag Neue Zürcher Zeitung, 41–59.

Martin-Kilcher, S., with Amrein, H. & Horisberger, B. (eds) (2008), *Der Römische Goldschmuck aus Lunnern (Zh). Ein Hortfund des 3. Jahrhunderts und seine Geschichte* (Collectio Archæologica 6), Zürich: Chronos Verlag/Schweizerische Landesmuseen.

Mathisen, R. (1992), 'Fifth-Century Visitors to Italy: Business of Pleasure?', in J. Drinkwater & H. Elton (eds), *Fifth-Century Gaul: A Crisis of Identity?* Cambridge: Cambridge University Press, 228–38.

Mathisen, R. (1999a), 'Sigisvult the Patrician, Maximinus the Arian, and Political Stratagems in the Western Roman Empire, c. 425–50', *Early Medieval Europe*, 8: 173–96.

Mathisen, R. (1999b), *Ruricius of Limoges and Friends. A Collection of Letters from Visigothic Gaul* (Translated Texts for Historians 30), Liverpool: Liverpool University Press.

Mathisen, R. & Sivan, H. (eds) (1996), *Shifting Frontiers in Late Antiquity*, Aldershot: Variorum.

Mattingly, D. (1989), 'Olive Cultivation and the Albertini Tablets', *L'Africa romana*, 6: 403–15.

Mattingly, D. (1995), *Tripolitania*, London: Batsford.

Mattingly, D. (1996), 'First Fruit? The Olive in the Roman World', in G. Shipley & J. Salmon (eds), *Human Landscapes in Classicial Antiquity. Environment and Culture*, London & New York: Routledge, 213–53.

Mattingly, D. (2004), 'Being Roman: Expressing Identity in a Provincial Setting', *Journal of Roman Archaeology*, 17: 5–25.

Mattingly, D. (2006), *An Imperial Possession. Britain in the Roman Empire, 54 BC–AD 409*, London: Allen Lane/Penguin Books.

Mattingly, D. & Aldrete, G. (2000), 'The Feeding of Imperial Rome: The Mechanics of the Food Supply System', in J.C.N. Coulston & H. Dodge (eds), *Ancient Rome: The Archaeology of the Eternal City* (Oxford University School of Archaeology Monograph 54), Oxford: Alden Press, 142–65.

Mattingly, D., Barker, G., Gilbertson, D. & Jones, G.D.B. (1996), *Farming the Desert: The UNESCO Libyan Valleys Archaeological Survey in Tripolitania*, 2 vols, Paris, London & Tripoli: UNESCO, Society of Libyan Studies, Department of Antiquities.

Mawer, F. (1995), *Evidence for Christianity in Roman Britain: The Small Finds* (British Archaeological Reports, British Series 243), Oxford: Tempus Reparatum.

Maxfield, V. (ed.) (1989), *The Saxon Shore. A Handbook* (Exeter Studies in History, No. 25), Exeter: University of Exeter.

Maxfield, V. & Dobson, M.J. (eds.) (1991), *Roman Frontier Studies 1989: 15th International Congress of Roman Frontier Studies*, Exeter: Exeter University Press.

Mazor, G. (1999), 'Public Baths in Roman and Byzantine Nysa-Scythopolis (Bet She'an)', in J. DeLaine & D.E. Johnston (eds), *Roman Baths and Bathing. Proceedings of the First*

International Conference on Roman Baths (Bath, 30 March–4 April 1992) (Journal of Roman Archaeology Supplementary Series No. 37), Portsmouth, RI: Journal of Roman Archaeology, 292–302.

Mazzolani, L.S. (1970), *The Idea of the City in Roman Thought. From Walled City to Spiritual Commonwealth* (translated from 1967 *L'idea di città nel mondo romano* by S. O'Donnell), London: Hollis & Carter.

McCann, A.M. & Freed, J. (1994), *Deep Water Archaeology. A Late-Roman Ship from Carthage and an Ancient Trade Route Near Skerki Bank Off Northwest Sicily* (Journal of Roman Archaeology Supplementary Series No. 13), Ann Arbor: Journal of Roman Archaeology.

McCormick, M. (2001), *Origins of the European Economy. Communciations and Commerce AD 300–900*, Cambridge & New York: Cambridge University Press.

Meates, G.W. (1979), *The Roman Villa at Lullingstone, Kent. Volume I: The Site* (Monograph Series of the Kent Archaeological Society No. I), London & Tonbridge: Kent Archaeological Society/Whitefriars Press.

Meates, G.W. (ed.) (1987), *The Roman Villa at Lullingstone, Kent. Volume II: The Wall Paintings and Finds* (Monograph Series of the Kent Archaeological Society No. III), London & Tonbridge: Kent Archaeological Society/Whitefriars Press.

Meiggs, R. (1973), *Roman Ostia* (2nd edition), Oxford: Clarendon Press.

Meneghini, R. (1989), 'Roma. Ricerche nel Foro di Traiano – Basilica Ulpia: un esempio di sopravvivenza di strutture antiche in età medievale', *Archeologia Medievale*, xvi: 541–59.

Meneghini, R. (1993), 'Il foro ed i mercati di Traiano nel medioevo attraverso le fonti storiche e d'archivio', *Archeologia Medievale*, xx: 79–120.

Meneghini, R. (2000), 'Roma – Strutture alto medievali e assetto urbano tra le regioni VII e VIII', *Archeologia Medievale*, xxvii: 303–10.

Meneghini, R. & Santangeli Valenzani, R. (1993), 'Sepolture intramuranee e paesaggio urbano a Roma tra V e VII secolo', in L. Paroli & P. Delogu (eds), *La storia economica di Roma nell'alto medioevo alla luce dei recenti scavi archeologici* (Atti del Seminario, Roma, 2–3 Aprile 1992) (Biblioteca di Archeologia Medievale, 10), Florence: Insegna del Giglio, 89–112.

Meneghini, R. & Santangeli Valenzani, R. (1995), 'Sepolture intramuranee a Roma tra V e VII secolo d.C. – Aggiornamenti e considerazioni', *Archeologia Medievale*, xxii: 283–90.

Meneghini, R. & Santangeli Valenzani, R. (2004), *Roma nell'altomedioevo: topografia e urbanistica della città dal V al X secolo*, Rome: Libreria dello Stato.

Menghin, W., Springer, T. & Wamers, E. (eds) (1987), *Germanen, Hunnen und Awaren. Schätze der Völkerwanderungszeit. Die Archäologie des 5. und 6. Jahrhunderts an der mittleren Donau und der östlich-merowingische Reihengräberkreis*, Nurnberg: Germanisches Nationalmuseum.

Menis, G.C. (1995), 'Antichi santuari cristiani dell'area aquileiese in luoghi sacri pagani', in *Akten des XII. Internationalen Kongresses für Christliche Archäologie (Bonn, 22–28 Sept. 1991)* (Studi di Antichità Classica LII – Jahrbuch für Antike und Christentum, Ergänzungsband, 20), Città del Vaticano/Münster: Pontificio Istituto di Archeologia Cristiana/Aschendorffsche Verlagsbuchhandlung, 1033–6.

Mennella, G. (1998), 'La cristianizzazione rurale in Piemonte: il contributo dell'epigrafia', in L. Mercando & E. Micheletto (eds), *Archeologia in Piemonte. Vol. III: Il Medioevo*, Turin: Soprintendenza Archeologica del Piemonte, 151–60.

Mercando, L. & Micheletto, E. (eds) (1998), *Archeologia in Piemonte. Vol. III: Il Medioevo*, Turin: Soprintendenza Archeologica del Piemonte.

Merrills, A. (ed.) (2004), *Vandals, Romans and Berbers. New Perspectives on Late Antique North Africa*, Aldershot: Ashgate.

Mertens, J. (1983), 'Urban Wall Circuits in Gallia Belgica in the Roman Period', in J. Maloney & B. Hobley (eds), *Roman Urban Defences in the West* (CBA Research Report No. 51), London: Council for British Archaeology, 42–57.

Milano. Capitale (1990), *Milano. Capitale dell'Impero Romano, 286–402 d.C.* (exhibition catalogue, Milano – Palazzo Reale), Milan: Electa.

Milburn, R. (1988), *Early Christian Art and Architecture*, Berkeley & Los Angeles: University of California Press.

Millett, M. (1990), *The Romanization of Britain: An Essay in Archaeological Interpretation*, Cambridge: Cambridge University Press.

Milne, G. (1985), *The Port of Roman London*, London: English Heritage/Batsford.

Milne, G. (1995), *Roman London*, London: English Heritage/Batsford.

Mitchell, J. & Hansen, I.L. (eds) (2001), *San Vincenzo al Volturno 3: The Finds from the 1980–86 Excavations* (Studi e ricerche di archeologia e storia d'arte, 3), 2 vols, Spoleto: Centro Italiano di Studi sull'Alto Medioevo.

Mócsy, A. (1974), *Pannonia and Upper Moesia. A History of the Middle Danube Provinces of the Roman Empire*, London & Boston: Routledge & Kegan Paul.

Montanari, G.B. (ed.) (1983), *Ravenna e il porto di Classe. Venti anni di ricerche archeologiche tra Ravenna e Classe* (Fonti e Studi, 7), Bologna: University Press.

Moorhead, J. (1992), *Theoderic in Italy*, Oxford: Clarendon Press.

Moorhead, J. (1999), *Ambrose. Church and Society in the Late Roman World*, London: Longman.

Moorhead, J. (2001), *The Roman Empire Divided, 400–700*, London: Longman.

Morandini, F. (2008), 'The Late Classical Bronzes of Brescia', in J.-J. Aillagon (ed.), *Rome and the Barbarians. The Birth of a New World* (exhibition catalogue – Venice-Bonn-Rome), Milan: Palazzo Grassi/Skira Editore, 182–3.

Moreland, J. (1994), 'Wilderness, Wasteland, Depopulation and the End of the Roman Empire?' *Accordia Research Papers*, 4: 89–110.

Mori, A.C. (1990), 'Le mura', in *Milano. Capitale dell'Impero Romano, 286–402 d.C.* (exhibition catalogue, Milano – Palazzo Reale), Milan: Electa, 98.

Mori, A.C. & Sartori, A. (1997), 'Le mura e le terme', in *La città e la sua memoria. Milano e la tradizione di sant'Ambrogio* (exhibition catalogue, 3 April–8 June 1997, Milan), Milan: Electa, 28–32.

Muhlberger, S. (1992), 'Looking Back from Mid-Century: The Gallic Chronicler of 452 and the Crisis of Honorius' Reign', in J. Drinkwater & H. Elton (eds), *Fifth-Century Gaul: A Crisis of Identity?* Cambridge: Cambridge University Press, 28–37.

Mulvin, L. (2002), *Late Roman Villas in the Danube-Balkan Region* (British Archaeological Reports, International Series 1064), Oxford: Archaeopress.

Naumann-Steckner, F. (1997), 'Death on the Rhine: Changing Burial Customs in Cologne, 3rd–7th Century', in L. Webster & M. Brown (eds), *The Transformation of the Roman World, AD 400–900*, London: European Science Foundation/British Museum Press, 143–79.

Negrelli, C. (2006), 'Rimini tra V ed VIII secolo: topografia e cultura materiale', in A. Augenti (ed.), *Le città italiane tra la tarda Antichità e l'alto Medioevo, Atti del Convegno (Ravenna, 26–28 Febbraio 2004)* (Biblioteca di Archeologia Medievale, 20), Florence: All'Insegna del Giglio, 219–71.

Niblett, R. (2001), *Verulamium. The Roman City of St. Albans*, Stroud: Tempus.

Nicholson, O. (1995), 'The End of Mithraism', *Antiquity*, 69: 358–62.

Nixon, C.E.V. (1992), 'Relations between Visigoths and Romans in Fifth-Century Gaul', in J. Drinkwater & H. Elton (eds), *Fifth-Century Gaul: A Crisis of Identity?* Cambridge: Cambridge University Press, 64–74.

Noble, T.F.X. (ed.) (2006), *From Roman Provinces to Medieval Kingdoms*, New York & Abingdon: Routledge.

Norwich, J.J. (1990), *Byzantium. The Early Centuries*, Harmondsworth: Penguin Books.

O'Brien, C. (2010), 'The Emergence of Northumbria: Artefacts, Archaeology, and Models', in R. Collins & L. Allason-Jones (eds), *Finds from the Frontier. Material Culture in the 4th–5th Centuries* (CBA Research Report 162), York: Council for British Archaeology, 110–19.

O'Flynn, J.M. (1983), *Generalissimos of the Western Roman Empire*, Alberta: University of Alberta Press.

Olmo Enciso, L. (ed.) (2008), *Recópolis y la ciudad en la época visigoda* (Zona Arqueológica, 9), Alcalá de Henares: Museo Arqueológico Regional.

Orlandi, S. (1999), 'Il Colosseo nel V secolo', in W.V. Harris (ed.), *The Transformations of* Vrbs Roma *in Late Antiquity* (Journal of Roman Archaeology Supplementary Series No. 33), Ann Arbor: Journal of Roman Archaeology, 249–63.

Osborne, R. (1985), 'The Roman Catacombs in the Middle Ages', *Papers of the British School at Rome*, liii: 278–328.

Ottaway, P. (1992), *Archaeology in British Towns. From the Emperor Claudius to the Black Death*, London: Routledge.

Ottaway, P. (1997), 'Recent Excavations of the Late Roman Signal Station at Filey, North Yorkshire', in W. Groenman-van Waateringe, B.L. Van Beek, W.J.H. Willems & S. Wynia (eds), *Roman Frontier Studies 1995. Proceedings of the XVIth International Congress of Roman Frontier Studies* (Oxbow Monograph 91), Oxford: Oxbow, 135–41.

Painter, K. (1991), 'The Silver Dish of Ardabur Aspar', in E. Herring, R. Whitehouse & J. Wilkins (eds), *Papers of the Fourth Conference of Italian Archaeology, 2. The Archaeology of Power, Part 2*, London: Accordia Research Centre, 73–9.

Painter, K. (2000), 'Il tesoro dell'Esquilino', in S. Ensoli & E. La Rocca (eds), *Aurea Roma. Dalla città pagana alla città cristiana* (exhibition catalogue, 22 December 2000–20 April 2001), Rome: 'L'Erma' di Bretschneider, 140–6.

Panella, C. (1986), 'Le merci: produzioni, itinerari e destini', in A. Giardina (ed.), *Società Romana e Impero Tardoantico, Vol. III: le merci, gli insediamenti*, Rome-Bari: Laterza, 431–59.

Panella, C. (1999), 'Rifornimenti urbani e cultura materiale tra Aureliano e Alarico', in W.V. Harris (ed.), *The Transformations of* Vrbs Roma *in Late Antiquity* (Journal of Roman Archaeology Supplementary Series No. 33), Ann Arbor: Journal of Roman Archaeology, 183–215.

Panella, C. (2008), 'Imperial Insignia from the Palatine Hill', in J.-J. Aillagon (ed.), *Rome and the Barbarians. The Birth of a New World* (exhibition catalogue – Venice-Bonn-Rome), Milan: Palazzo Grassi/Skira Editore, 86–91.

Pani Ermini, L. (1992), 'Roma tra la fine del IV e gli inizi del V secolo', in G. Sena Chiesa & E. Arslan (eds), *Felix Temporis Reparatio (Atti del Convegno archeologico internazionale 'Milano capitale dell'impero romano', 8–11 Marzo 1990, Milan)*, Milan: Edizioni ET, 193–202.

Pani Ermini, L. (1993–94), 'Città fortificate e fortificazione delle città fra V e VI secolo', *Rivista di Studi Liguri*, lix–lx: 193–206.

Pani Ermini, L. (1999), 'Roma da Alarico a Teoderico', in W.V. Harris (ed.), *The Transformations of* Vrbs Roma *in Late Antiquity* (Journal of Roman Archaeology Supplementary Series No. 33), Ann Arbor: Journal of Roman Archaeology, 35–52.

Pani Ermini, L. (2000a), 'Lo "spazio cristiano" nella Roma del primo millennio', in L. Pani Ermini (ed.), *Christiana Loca. Lo spazio cristiano nella Roma del primo millennio*, Rome: Fratelli Palombi Editori, 15–37.

Pani Ermini, L. (ed.) (2000b), *Lo spazio cristiano nella Roma del primo millennio*, Rome: Fratelli Palombi Editori.

Panvini Rosati, F. (1994), 'Anfiteatri, circhi, stadi nelle monete romane', in *Spettacolo in Aquileia e nella Cisalpina romana* (Antichità Altoadriatiche, XLI), Udine: Arti Grafiche Friulane, 99–105.

Paris, R. (ed.) (2000), *Via Appia. The Villa of the Quintili*, Milan: Soprintendenza Archeologica di Roma Electa.

Parker, A.J. (1992), *Ancient Shipwrecks of the Mediterranean and the Roman Provinces* (British Archaeological Reports, International Series 580), Oxford: Tempus Reparatum.

Parker, P. (2009), *The Empire Stops Here*, London: Jonathan Cape.

Paroli, L. & Delogu, P. (eds) (1993), *La storia economica di Roma nell'alto medioevo alla luce dei recenti scavi archeologici* (Atti del Seminario, Roma, 2–3 Aprile 1992) (Biblioteca di Archeologia Medievale, 10), Florence: All'Insegna del Giglio.

Patterson, H. (ed.) (2004), *Bridging the Tiber. Approaches to Regional Archaeology in the Middle Tiber Valley* (Archaeological Monographs of the British School at Rome, 13), London: British School at Rome.

Pauli, L. (1984), *The Alps. Archaeology and Early History* (translation of *Die Alpen in Frühzeit und Mittelalter*, Munich, 1980), London: Thames and Hudson.

Pavolini, C. (1986), 'L'edilizia commerciale e l'edilizia abitativa nel contesto di Ostia tardoantica', in A. Giardina (ed.), *Società Romana e Impero Tardoantico, Vol. III: le merci, gli insediamenti*, Rome-Bari: Laterza, 239–97.

Peacock, D., Bejaoui, F. & Ben Lazreg, N. (1990), 'Roman Pottery Production in Central Tunisia', *Journal of Roman Archaeology*, 3: 59–84.

Pearson, A. (2002), *The Roman Shore Forts. Coastal Defences of Southern Britain*, Stroud: Tempus.

Pejrani Barrico, L. (1998), 'La basilica del Salvatore e la cattedrale di Torino: considerazioni su uno scavo in corso', in L. Mercando & E. Micheletto (eds), *Archeologia in Piemonte. Vol. III: Il Medioevo*, Turin: Soprintendenza Archeologica del Piemonte, 133–51.

Pensabene, P. (2000), 'Reimpiego e depositi di marmo a Roma e a Ostia', in S. Ensoli & E. La Rocca (eds), *Aurea Roma. Dalla città pagana alla città cristiana* (exhibition catalogue, 22 December 2000–20 April 2001), Rome: 'L'Erma' di Bretschneider, 341–50.

Pensabene, P. & Panella, C. (eds) (1999), *Arco di Costantino. Tra archeologia e archeometria*, Rome: 'L'Erma' di Bretschneider.

Percival, J. (1976), *The Roman Villa*, London: Batsford.

Pergola, P. (2000), 'Dai cimiteri ai santuari martiriali (IV–VIII secolo)', in L. Pani Ermini (ed.), *Christiana Loca. Lo spazio cristiano nella Roma del primo millennio*, Rome: Fratelli Palombi Editori, 99–106.

Perin, P. (2008), 'The Franks and Rome', in J.-J. Aillagon (ed.), *Rome and the Barbarians. The Birth of a New World* (exhibition catalogue – Venice-Bonn-Rome), Milan: Palazzo Grassi/Skira Editore, 342–5.

Pessoa, M. (1991), *The Augustan Wall of Conímbriga*, Condeixa-a-Nova: IPPC.

Petts, D. (2003), *Christianity in Roman Britain*, Stroud: Tempus.

Piccottini, G. (2002), 'Virunum', in M. Šašel Kos & P. Scherrer (eds), *The Autonomous Towns of Noricum and Pannonia – Die Autonomen Städte in Noricum und Pannonien* (Dissertationes Musei Nationalis Sloveniae, Situla 40), Ljubljana: Narodni Muzej Slovenije, 103–34.

Pietri, C. (1985–87), 'Note sur la Christianisation de la "Ligurie"', *Quaderni del Centro Studi Lunensi*, 10–12: 351–80.

Pietri, C. (1992), 'Aristocratie milanaise: païens et chrétiens au IVe siècle', in G. Sena Chiesa & E. Arslan (eds), *Felix Temporis Reparatio (Atti del Convegno archeologico internazionale 'Milano capitale dell'impero romano', 8–11 Marzo 1990, Milan)*, Milan: Edizioni ET, 157–70.

Pitts, L.F. (1989), 'Relations between Rome and the German "Kings" on the Middle Danube in the First to Fourth Centuries AD', *Journal of Roman Studies*, 79: 45–58.

Plunkett, S. (2005), *Suffolk in Anglo-Saxon Times*, Stroud: Tempus.

Pohl, W. (ed.) (1997), *Kingdoms of the Empire. The Integration of Barbarians in Late Antiquity* (The Transformation of the Roman World, Volume 1), Leiden, Boston & Cologne: European Science Foundation/Brill.

Pohl, W. (ed.) (1998), *Strategies of Distinction. The Construction of Ethnic Communities, 300–800* (ESF Transformation of the Roman World, 2), Leiden & New York: Brill.

Pohl, W. (2004), 'The Vandals: Fragments of a Narrative', in A. Merrills (ed.), *Vandals, Romans and Berbers. New Perspectives on Late Antique North Africa*, Aldershot: Ashgate, 31–47.

Pohl, W., Wood, I. & Reimitz, H. (eds) (2001), *The Transformation of Frontiers. From Late Antiquity to the Carolingians* (The Transformation of the Roman World, Volume 10), Leiden, Boston & Cologne: European Science Foundation/Brill.

Potter, D.S. (1999), 'Entertainers in the Roman Empire', in D.S Potter & D.J. Mattingly (eds), *Life, Death and Entertainment in the Roman Empire*, Ann Arbor: University of Michigan Press, 256–325.

Potter, D.S. & Mattingly, D.J. (eds) (1999), *Life, Death and Entertainment in the Roman Empire*, Ann Arbor: University of Michigan Press.

Potter, T.W. (1979), *The Changing Landscape of South Etruria*, London: Elek.

Potter, T.W. (1987), *Roman Italy*, London: British Museum Press.

Potter, T.W. (1995), *Towns in Late Antiquity: Iol Caesarea and Its Context* (Ian Sanders Memorial Fund, Occasional Publication 2), Exeter: Short Run Press.

Potter, T.W. & King, A. (eds) (1997), *Excavations at La Mola di Monte Gelato. A Roman and Medieval Settlement in South Etruria* (Archaeological Monographs of the British School at Rome, 11), London: British School at Rome/British Museum.

Poulter, A. (2000), 'The Roman to Byzantine Transition in the Balkans: Preliminary Results on Nicopolis and Its Hinterland', *Journal of Roman Archaeology*, 13: 346–58.

Poulter, A. (ed.) (2007), *The Transition to Late Antiquity on the Danube and Beyond* (Proceedings of the British Academy, Volume 141), London: British Academy.

Price, E. (2000), *Frocester. A Romano-British Settlement, Its Antecedents and Successors. Volume 1. The Sites*, Stonehouse: Gloucester and District Archaeological Research Group.

Price, S. (1986), *Rituals and Power: The Roman Imperial Cult in Asia Minor*, Cambridge: Cambridge University Press.

Price, S. (2000), 'Religions of Rome', in J.C.N. Coulston & H. Dodge (eds), *Ancient Rome: The Archaeology of the Eternal City* (Oxford University School of Archaeology Monograph 54), Oxford: Alden Press, 290–305.

Pringle, D. (1981), *The Defence of Africa from Justinian to the Arab Conquest* (British Archaeological Reports, International Series 99), Oxford: Tempus Reparatum.

Provost, S. (2001), 'City Walls and Urban Area in Late-Antique Macedonia: The Case of Philippi', in L. Lavan (ed.), *Recent Research in Late-Antique Urbanism* (Journal of Roman Archaeology Supplementary Series No. 42), Ann Arbor: Journal of Roman Archaeology, 123–35.

Purcell, N. (1999), 'The Populace of Rome in Late Antiquity: Problems of Classification and Historical Description', in W.V. Harris (ed.), *The Transformations of Vrbs Roma in Late Antiquity* (Journal of Roman Archaeology Supplementary Series No. 33), Ann Arbor: Journal of Roman Archaeology, 135–61.

Raban, A. (ed.) (1988), *Archaeology of Coastal Changes* (British Archaeological Reports, International Series 404), Oxford: Tempus Reparatum.

Raban, A. (2009), *The Harbour of Sebastos (Caesarea Maritima) in Its Roman Mediterranean Context* (British Archaeological Reports, International Series 1930), Oxford: Archaeopress.

Rajtár, J. (2002), 'Nuove testimonianze archeologiche delle guerre dei Marcomanni a nord del medio Danubio', in M. Buora & W. Jobst (eds), *Roma sul Danubio. Da Aquileia a*

Carnuntum *lungo la via dell'ambra* (Cataloghi e monografie archeologiche dei Civici Musei di Udine, VI), Rome: 'L'Erma' di Bretschneider, 99–120.

Rambaldi, S. (2009), *L'edilizia pubblica nell'impero romano all'epoca dell'anarchia militare (235–284 d.C.)* (Studi e Scavi 22), Bologna: Ante Quem.

Randsborg, K. (1991), *The First Millennium AD in Europe and the Mediterranean: An Archaeological Essay*, Cambridge: Cambridge University Press.

Raven, S. (1993), *Rome in Africa* (3rd edition), London & New York: Routledge.

Rea, R. (1993), 'Roma: l'uso funerario della valle del Colosseo tra tardo antico e alto medioevo', *Archeologia Medievale*, 20: 645–56.

Rea, R. (1999), 'Il Colosseo. Destrutturazione e riuso tra IV e VIII secolo', *Melanges de l'Ecole Française de Rome. Moyen Age*, 111: 183–95.

Rea, R. (ed.) (2002), *Rota Colisei. La valle del Colosseo attraverso i secoli*, Milan: Electa.

Redfern, R.C. & DeWitte, S.N. (2010), 'A New Approach to the Study of Romanization in Britain: A Regional Perspective of Cultural Change in Late Iron Age and Roman Dorset Using the Siler and Gompertz-Makeham Models of Mortality', *Amercian Journal of Physical Anthropology*, 144(2): 269–85.

Redknap, M. & Lewis, J.M. (2007), *A Corpus of Early Medieval Inscribed Stones and Stone Sculpture in Wales. Volume 1: South-East Wales and the English Border*, Cardiff: University of Wales Press.

Reece, R. (1992), 'The End of the City in Roman Britain', in J. Rich (ed.), *The City in Late Antiquity* (Leicester-Nottingham Studies in Ancient Society, Volume 3), London: Routledge, 136–44.

Reece, R. (1999), *The Later Roman Empire. An Archaeology, AD 150–600*, Stroud: Tempus.

Rees, R. (2004), *Diocletian and the Tetrarchy*, Edinburgh: Edinburgh University Press.

Reynolds, J. (1988), 'Cities', in D. Braund (ed.), *The Administration of the Roman Empire, 241 BC–AD 193* (Exeter Studies in History, No. 18), Exeter: University of Exeter Press, 15–51.

Reynolds, P. (1995), *Trade in the Western Mediterranean, AD 400–700: The Ceramic Evidence* (British Archaeological Reports International Series 604), Oxford: Tempus Reparatum.

Reynolds, P. (2010), *Hispania and the Roman Mediterranean, AD 100–700. Ceramics and Trade*, London: Duckworth.

Ribera i Lacomba, A. (1998), 'The Discovery of a Monumental Circus at *Valentia* (Hispania Tarraconensis)', *Journal of Roman Archaeology*, 11: 318–37.

Ribera i Lacomba, A. & Mesquida, M.R. (1999), *L'Almoina: el nacimento de la Valentia Cristiana (Quaderns de Difusió Arqueològica, 5)*, Valencia: Ajuntament de Valencia.

Ricci, M. (1997), 'Relazioni culturali e scambi commerciali nell'Italia centrale romano-longobarda alla luce della Crypta Balbi in Roma', in L. Paroli (ed.), *L'Italia centro-settentrionale in età longobarda* (Atti del Convegno, Ascoli Piceno, 6–7 Ott. 1995), Florence: All'Insegna del Giglio, 239–71.

Rich, J. (ed.) (1992), *The City in Late Antiquity* (Leicester-Nottingham Studies in Ancient Society, Volume 3), London: Routledge.

Richmond, I. (1930), *The City Walls of Imperial Rome*, Oxford: Clarendon Press.

Rickman, G. (1980), *The Grain Supply of Ancient Rome*, Oxford: Oxford University Press.

Riggs, D. (2001), 'The Continuity of Paganism between the Cities and Countryside of Late Roman Africa', in T.S. Burns & J.W. Eadie (eds), *Urban Centers and Rural Contexts in Late Antiquity*, East Lansing: Michigan State University Press, 285–300.

Rinaldi Tufi, S. (2005), 'La grande architettura fra Diocleziano e Costantino a Roma e nel mondo romano', in A. Donati & G. Gentili (ed.), *Costantino il Grande. La civiltà antica al bivio tra Occidente e Oriente* (exhibition catalogue, Rimini, Castel Sismondo, 13 Marzo–4 Sett. 2005), Milan: Silvana Editoriale, 92–105.

Ripoll, G. (2000), 'Sedes regiae en la Hispania de la antigüedad tardía', in G. Ripoll & J.M. Gurt (eds), Sedes regiae (ann. 400–800), Barcelona: Reial Acadèmia de Bones Lletres, 371–401.

Ripoll, G. & Arce, J. (2000), 'The Transformation and End of Roman Villae in the West (Fourth–Seventh Centuries): Problems and Perspectives', in G.P. Brogiolo, N. Gauthier & N. Christie (eds), Towns and their Territories between Late Antiquity and the Early Middle Ages (ESF Transformation of the Roman World, 9), Leiden & New York: Brill, 63–114.

Ripoll, G. & Gurt, J.M. (eds) (2000), Sedes regiae (ann. 400–800), Barcelona: Reial Acadèmia de Bones Lletres.

Rippon, S. (2000), 'Landscapes in Transition: The Later Roman and Early Medieval Periods', in D. Hooke (ed.), Landscape: The Richest Historical Record (Supplementary Series 1), Amesbury: Society for Landscape Studies, 47–61.

Rives, J.B. (1995), Religion and Authority in Roman Carthage from Augustus to Constantine, Oxford: Clarendon Press.

Rives, J.B. (1999), Tacitus. Germania (Clarendon Ancient History Series), Oxford: Clarendon Press.

Rizzardi, C. (1989), 'L'arte dei Goti a Ravenna: motivi ideologici, aspetti iconografici e formali nella decorazione musiva', XXXVI Corso di Cultura sull'Arte Ravennate e Bizantina: Ravenna e l'Italia fra Goti e Longobardi, Ravenna: Edizioni del Girasole, 365–88.

Roberto, U. (2008), 'The Altar to the Goddess Victory in Augsburg (Germany)', in J.-J. Aillagon (ed.), Rome and the Barbarians. The Birth of a New World (exhibition catalogue – Venice-Bonn-Rome), Milan: Palazzo Grassi/Skira Editore, 1801–81.

Roberts, M. (1992), 'Barbarians in Gaul: The Response of the Poets', in J. Drinkwater & H. Elton (eds), Fifth-Century Gaul: A Crisis of Identity? Cambridge: Cambridge University Press, 97–106.

Rodà, I. (1997), 'Hispania. From the Second Century AD to Late Antiquity', in M. Díaz-Andreu & S. Keay (eds), The Archaeology of Iberia: The Dynamics of Change, London: Routledge, 211–34.

Rogers, A. (2010), 'Late Roman Towns as Meaningful Places: Re-Conceptualising Decline in the Towns of Late Roman Britain', in D. Sami & G. Speed (eds), Debating Urbanism. Within and Beyond the Walls, AD 300–700 (Proceedings of a Conference Held at the University of Leicester, 15th November 2008) (Leicester Archaeology Monograph 17), Leicester: University of Leicester, 57–81.

Rohrbacher, D. (2002), The Historians of Late Antiquity, London & New York: Routledge.

Romer, F. (1999), 'Famine, Pestilence and Brigandage in Italy in the Fifth Century AD', in D. Soren & N. Soren (eds), A Roman Villa and a Late Roman Infant Cemetery. Excavation at Poggio Gramignano Lugnano in Teverina (Biblioteca Archaeologica 23), Rome: 'L'Erma' di Bretschneider, 465–75.

Roskams, S. (1996), 'Urban Transition in Early Medieval Britain: The Case of York', in N. Christie & S.T. Loseby (eds), Towns in Transition. Urban Evolution in Late Antiquity and the Early Middle Ages, Aldershot: Scolar, 262–88.

Rossignani, M.P., Sannazaro, M. & Legrottaglie, G. (eds) (2005), La signora del sarcofago. Una sepoltura di rango nella necropoli dell'Università Cattolica (Contributi di archeologia, 4: Ricerche archeologiche nei cortili dell'Università Cattolica), Milan: Vita & Pensiero.

Roueché, C. (1989), Aphrodisias in Late Antiquity. The Late Roman and Byzantine Inscriptions Including Texts from the Excavations at Aphrodisias Conducted by Kenan T. Erim (Journal of Roman Studies Monograph, 5), London: Society for the Promotion of Roman Studies.

Rowsome, P. (2000), Heart of the City. Roman, Medieval and Modern London Revealed by Archaeology at 1 Poultry, London: MoLAS.

Rushworth, A. (2000), 'From Periphery to Core in Late Antique Mauretania', in
G. Fincham, G. Harrison, R. Holland & L. Revell (eds), *TRAC 99: Proceedings of the Ninth Annual Theoretical Roman Archaeology Conference, Durham 1999*, Oxford: Oxbow, 90–103.

Rushworth, A. (2004), 'From Arzuges to Rustamids: State Formation and Regional Identity in the Pre-Saharan Zone', in A. Merrills (ed.), *Vandals, Romans and Berbers. New Perspectives on Late Antique North Africa*, Aldershot: Ashgate, 77–98.

Ruscu, D. (2004), 'The Supposed Extermination of the Dacians: The Literary Tradition', in W.S. Hanson & I. Haynes (eds), *Roman Dacia. The Making of a Provincial Society* (Journal of Roman Archaeology Supplementary Series No. 56), Portsmouth, RI: Journal of Roman Archaeology, 75–85.

Rushworth, A. (ed.) (2009), *Housesteads Roman Fort – The Grandest Station*, 2 vols, London: English Heritage.

Sabrié, R. & Sabrié, M. (2002), *Le Clos de la Lombarde. Un Quartier de Naronne dans l'Antiquité*, Narbonne: CNRS.

Saguì, L. (ed.) (1998), *Ceramica in Italia: VI–VII secolo. Atti del Convegno in onore di John W. Hayes (Roma, 11–13 Maggio 1995)* (Biblioteca di Archeologia Medievale, 14), 2 vols, Florence: All'Insegna del Giglio.

Salway, B. (2001), 'Travel, *itineraria* and *tabellaria*', in C. Adams & R. Laurence (eds), *Travel and Geography in the Roman Empire*, London: Routledge, 22–66.

Salzman, M. (1999), 'The Christianisation of Sacred Time and Sacred Space', in W.V. Harris (ed.), *The Transformations of* Vrbs Roma *in Late Antiquity* (Journal of Roman Archaeology Supplementary Series No. 33), Ann Arbor: Journal of Roman Archaeology, 123–34.

Salzman, M. (2000), 'Elite Realities and Mentalités: The Making of a Western Christian Aristocracy', *Arethusa*, 33: 347–62.

Sami, D. & Speed, G. (eds) (2010), *Debating Urbanism. Within and Beyond the Walls*, AD 300–700 *(Proceedings of a Conference Held at the University of Leicester, 15th November 2008)* (Leicester Archaeology Monograph 17), Leicester: University of Leicester.

Sannazaro, M. (2002), 'Attestazioni di militari e *militaria* a Milano', in M. Buora (ed.), *Miles Romanus dal Po al Danubio nel Tardoantico (Atti del Convegno Internazionale, Pordenone – Concordia Sagittaria, 17–19 Marzo 2000)*, Pordenone: Sage Print, 65–80.

Santangeli Valenzani, R. (2007), 'Public and Private Building Activity in Late Antique Rome', in L. Lavan, E. Zanini & A. Sarantis (eds), *Technology in Transition AD 300–650* (Late Antique Archaeology, Volume 4), Leiden & Boston: Brill, 435–49.

Saradi, H.G. (2006), *The Byzantine City in the Sixth Century. Literary Images and Historical Reality*, Athens: Society of Messenian Archaeological Studies.

Šašel Kos, M. & Scherrer, P. (eds) (2002), *The Autonomous Towns of Noricum and Pannonia – Die Autonomen Städte in Noricum und Pannonien* (Dissertationes Musei Nationalis Sloveniae, Situla 40), Ljubljana: Narodni Muzej Slovenije.

Sauer, E. (1996), *The End of Paganism in the North-Western Provinces of the Roman Empire. The Example of the Mithras Cult* (British Archaeological Reports, International Series 634), Oxford: Tempus Reparatum.

Sauer, E. (2003), *The Archaeology of Religious Hatred in the Roman and Early Medieval World*, Stroud: Tempus.

Schallmayer, E. (ed.) (1995), *Der Augsburger Siegesaltar. Zeugnis einer unruhigen Zeit* (Saalburg-Schriften 2), Bad Homburg: Saalburgmuseum.

Schmid, S.G. (2001), 'Worshipping the Emperor(s): A New Temple of the Imperial Cult at Eretria and the Ancient Destruction of Its Statues', *Journal of Roman Archaeology*, 14: 113–41.

Schrunk, I. & Begović, V. (2000), 'Roman Estates on the Island of Brioni, Istria', *Journal of Roman Archaeology*, 13: 252–76.

Schwarcz, A. (2004), 'The Settlement of the Vandals in North Africa', in A. Merrills (ed.), *Vandals, Romans and Berbers. New Perspectives on Late Antique North Africa*, Aldershot: Ashgate, 49–57.

Scott, S. (2000), *Art and Society in Fourth-Century Roman Britain*, Oxford: Oxford University Committee for Archaeology.

Scott, S. (2004), 'Elites, Exhibitionism and the Society of the Late Roman Villa', in N. Christie (ed.), *Landscapes of Change: Rural Evolutions in Late Antiquity and the Early Middle Ages*, Aldershot: Ashgate, 39–65.

Scull, C. (1995), 'Approaches to Material Culture and Social Dynamics of the Migration Period in Eastern England', in J. Bintliff & H. Hamerow (eds), *Europe between Late Antiquity and the Middle Ages. Recent Archaeological and Historical Research in Western and Southern Europe* (British Archaeological Reports, International Series 617), Oxford: Tempus Reparatum, 71–83.

Seigne, J. (2007a), 'Les trios temps de l'amphithéâtre antique', in H. Galinié (ed.), *Tours antique et médiéval. Lieux de vie, temps de la ville. 40 ans d'archéologie urbaine* (30ᵉ Supplément, Revue Archéologique du Centre de la France), Tours: Fédération pour l'Edition de la Revue Archéologique du Centre de la France, 238–46.

Seigne, J. (2007b), 'La fortification de la ville au Bas Empire, de l' amphitheatre-fortresse au *castrum*', in H. Galinié (ed.), *Tours antique et médiéval. Lieux de vie, temps de la ville. 40 ans d'archéologie urbaine* (30ᵉ Supplément, Revue Archéologique du Centre de la France), Tours: Fédération pour l'Edition de la Revue Archéologique du Centre de la France, 247–55.

Sena Chiesa, G. & Arslan, E. (eds) (1992), *Felix Temporis Reparatio (Atti del Convegno archeologico internazionale 'Milano capitale dell'impero romano', 8–11 Marzo 1990, Milan)*, Milan: Edizioni ET.

Severin (1982), *Severin. Zwischen Römerzeit und Völkerwanderung* (exhibition catalogue), Linz.

Shaw, B.D. (2004), 'Who Were the Circumcellions?', in A. Merrills (ed.), *Vandals, Romans and Berbers. New Perspectives on Late Antique North Africa*, Aldershot: Ashgate, 227–58.

Shelton, K. (1981), *The Esquiline Treasure*, London: British Museum.

Shipley, G. & Salmon, J. (eds) (1996), *Human Landscapes in Classicial Antiquity. Environment and Culture*, London & New York: Routledge.

Shipley, G., Vanderspoel, J., Mattingly, D. & Foxhall, L. (eds) (2006), *The Cambridge Dictionary of Classical Civilization*, Cambridge & New York: Cambridge University Press.

Siker, J.S. (2000), 'Christianity in the Second and Third Centuries', in P.F. Esler (ed.), *The Early Christian World*, 2 vols, London & New York: Routledge, 231–57.

Simpson, C.J. (1995), *Excavations at San Giovanni di Ruoti, Volume II: The Small Finds*, Toronto: University of Toronto Press.

Sivan, H. (1992), 'Town and Country in Late Antique Gaul: The Example of Bordeaux', in J. Drinkwater & H. Elton (eds), *Fifth-Century Gaul: A Crisis of Identity?* Cambridge: Cambridge University Press, 132–43.

Slater, T.R. (ed.) (2000), *Towns in Decline, AD 100–1600*, Aldershot: Ashgate.

Snyder, C.A. (1998), *An Age of Tyrants. Britain and the Britons, AD 400–600*, Stroud: Sutton.

Sommer, C.S. (1999), 'From Conquered Territory to Roman Province: Recent Discoveries and Debate on the Roman Occupation of SW Germany', in J.D. Creighton & R.J.A. Wilson (eds), *Roman Germany. Studies in Cultural Interaction* (Journal of Roman Archaeology Supplementary Series No. 32), Portsmouth, RI: Journal of Roman Archaeology, 160–98.

Soproni, S. (1985), *Die letzten Jahrzehnte des Pannonischen Limes* (Münchner Beiträge zur Vor- und Frühgeschichte, Band 38), Munich: C.H. Beck'sche.

Sordi, M. (1983), *The Christians and the Roman Empire*, translated by A. Bedini. London & Sydney: Editoriale Jaca Book/Croom Helm.

Soren, D. & Soren, N. (eds) (1999), *A Roman Villa and a Late Roman Infant Cemetery. Excavation at Poggio Gramignano Lugnano in Teverina* (Biblioteca Archaeologica 23), Rome: 'L'Erma' di Bretschneider.

Southern, P. & Dixon, K.R. (1996), *The Late Roman Army*, London: Batsford.

Speed, G. (2010), 'Mind the (Archaeological) Gap: Tracing Life in Early Post-Roman Towns', in D. Sami & G. Speed (eds), *Debating Urbanism. Within and Beyond the Walls, AD 300–700 (Proceedings of a Conference Held at the University of Leicester, 15th November 2008)* (Leicester Archaeology Monograph 17), Leicester: University of Leicester, 83–109.

Spettacolo in Aquileia (1994), *Spettacolo in Aquileia e nella Cisalpina romana* (Antichità Altoadriatiche, XLI), Udine: Arti Grafiche Friulane.

Squatriti, P. (1998), *Water and Society in Early Medieval Italy, AD 400–1000*, Cambridge & New York: Cambridge University Press.

Stevens, S.T. (1996), 'Transitional Neighborhoods and Suburban Frontiers in Late- and Post-Roman Carthage', in R. Mathisen & H. Sivan (eds), *Shifting Frontiers in Late Antiquity*, Brookfield: Variorum, 187–200.

Stevens, S.T., Kalinowski, A. & van der Leest, H. (1998), 'The Early Christian Pilgrimage Complex at Bir Ftouha, Carthage: Interim Report', *Journal of Roman Archaeology*, 11: 371–83.

Stewart, C. (2000), 'Monasticism', in P.F. Esler (ed.), *The Early Christian World*, 2 vols, London & New York: Routledge, 344–66.

Storgaard, B. (2001a), 'Himlingøje – Barbarian Empire or Roman Implantation?', in B. Storgaard (ed.), *Military Aspects of the Aristocracy in Barbaricum in the Roman and Early Migration Periods. Papers from an International Research Seminar at the Danish National Museum, Copenhagen, 10–11 December 1999* (Publications from the National Museum, Studies in Archaeology & History, Volume 5), Copenhagen: National Museum, 95–111.

Storgaard, B. (ed.) (2001b), *Military Aspects of the Aristocracy in Barbaricum in the Roman and Early Migration Periods. Papers from an International Research Seminar at the Danish National Museum, Copenhagen, 10–11 December 1999* (Publications from the National Museum, Studies in Archaeology & History, Volume 5), Copenhagen: National Museum.

Storia di Roma III.1 (1993), *Storia di Roma III: L'età tardoantica. I: Crisi e trasformazioni*, Turin: Giulio Einaudi.

Strickland, T.J. (1988), 'The Roman Heritage of Chester: The Survival of the Buildings of Deva After the Roman Period', in R. Hodges & B. Hobley (eds), *The Rebirth of Towns in the West, AD 700–1050* (CBA Research Report 68), London: Council for British Archaeology, 109–18.

Stuppner, A. (2002), 'Rinvenimenti germanici a nord di Carnuntum', in M. Buora & W. Jobst (eds), *Roma sul Danubio. Da Aquileia a Carnuntum lungo la via dell'ambra* (Cataloghi e monografie archeologiche dei Civici Musei di Udine, VI), Rome: 'L'Erma' di Bretschneider, 21–32.

Susini, G. (ed.) (1990), *Storia di Ravenna I. L'evo antico*, Venice: Marsilio Editori.

Swan, V. (2007), 'Dichin (Bulgaria): Interpreting the Ceramic Evidence in Its Wider Context', in A. Poulter (ed.), *The Transition to Late Antiquity on the Danube and Beyond* (Proceedings of the British Academy, Volume 141), London: British Academy, 251–80.

Swift, E. (2000), *The End of the Western Roman Empire. An Archaeological Investigation*, Stroud: Tempus.

Tainter, J.A. (1988), *The Collapse of Complex Societies*, Cambridge & New York: Cambridge University Press.

Tedeschi, C. (2005), Congeries Lapidum. *Iscrizioni britanniche dei secoli V–VII. Vol. 1: Introduzione, edizione e commento; Vol. 2: Tavole*, Florence: Tipografia Latini/Scuola Normale Superiore di Pisa.

Tejral, J. (1997), 'The Amber Route and the Roman Military Campaigns North of the Middle Danube Area during the First Two Centuries AD', in *Peregrinatio Gothica* (Supplementum AD Acta Musei Moraviae, Scientiae Sociales, 82), 111–36.

The Engraved Word (2005), *The Engraved Word. The Bible at the Beginning of Christian Art* (Vatican Museums, Pio Christian Museum, 29 September 2005–7 January 2006), Rome: Società Biblica Britannica & Forestiera/Musei Vaticani.

Thomas, C. (1981), *Christianity in Roman Britain to AD 500*, London: Batsford.

Thomas, C. (1994), *And Shall These Mute Stones Speak? Post-Roman Inscriptions in Western Britain*, Cardiff: University of Wales Press.

Thomas, C. (1998), *Christian Celts. Messages and Images*, Stroud: Tempus.

Thompson, E.A. (1948/1996), *The Huns* (revised and with Afterword by P. Heather), Oxford: Blackwell.

Thompson, E.A. (1982), *Romans and Barbarians. The Decline of the Western Empire*, Wisconsin & London: University of Wisconsin Press.

Throckmorton, P. (ed.) (1987), *History from the Sea. Shipwrecks and Archaeology. From Homer's Odyssey to the Titanic*, London: Mitchell Beazley.

Todd, M. (1987), *The Northern Barbarians, 100 BC–AD 300* (rev. ed. of 1975 text), Oxford: Basil Blackwell.

Todd, M. (1992), *The Early Germans*, Oxford & Cambridge: Blackwell.

Todd, M. (2001), *Migrants and Invaders. The Movement of Peoples in the Ancient World*, Stroud: Tempus.

Tomlin, R.S.O. (1989), 'The Late-Roman Empire', in J. Hackett (ed.), *Warfare in the Ancient World*, London: Guild, 222–49.

Tomlin, R.S.O. (2000), 'The Legions in the Late Empire', in R. Brewer (ed.), *Roman Fortresses and Their Legions*, London: Society of Antiquaries/National Museums & Galleries of Wales, 159–79.

Tomlinson, R. (1992), *From Mycenae to Constantinople. The Evolution of the Ancient City*, London: Routledge.

Topál, J. (1997), 'Ethnic Components in the Cemeteries Along the *Limes* of Pannonia Inferior', in W. Groenman-van Waateringe, B.L. Van Beek, W.J.H. Willems & S. Wynia (eds), *Roman Frontier Studies 1995. Proceedings of the XVIth International Congress of Roman Frontier Studies* (Oxbow Monograph 91), Oxford: Oxbow, 537–45.

Toynbee, J. & Painter, K. (1986), 'Silver Picture Plates of Late Antiquity', *Archaeologia*, 108: 15–65.

Tracy, J. (ed.) (2000), *City Walls. The Urban Enceinte in Global Perspective*, Cambridge & New York: Cambridge University Press.

Trout, D. (1996), 'Town, Countryside and Christianisation at Paulinus' Nola', in R. Mathisen & H. Sivan (eds), *Shifting Frontiers in Late Antiquity*, Aldershot: Variorum, 175–86.

Trout, D. (1999), *Paulinus of Nola: Life, Letters, and Poems*, Berkeley, Los Angeles & London: University of California Press.

Turner, S. (2004), 'Coast and Countryside in "Late Antique" Southwest England, c. AD 400–600', in R. Collins & J. Gerrard (eds), *Debating Late Antiquity in Britain, AD 300–700* (British Archaeological Reports, British Series 365), Oxford: Archaeopress, 25–32.

Ubl, H. (1982), 'Die archäologische Erforschung der Severinsorte und das Ende der Römerzeit im Donau-Alpenraum', in *Severin. Zwischen Römerzeit und Völkerwanderung* (exhibition catalogue), Linz, 71–97.

Ulbert, Th. (ed.) (1981), *Ad Pirum (Hrušica). Spätrömische Passbefestigung in den Julischen Alpen*, (Münchner Beiträge zur Vor- und Frühgeschichte, 31), Munich: C.H. Beck'sche.

Van Dam, R. (1985), *Leadership and Community in Late Antique Gaul*, Berkeley & Los Angeles: University of California Press.

Van Dam, R. (1992), 'The Pirenne Thesis and Fifth-Century Gaul', in J. Drinkwater & H. Elton (eds), *Fifth-Century Gaul: A Crisis of Identity?* Cambridge: Cambridge University Press, 321–33.

Van Dam, R. (1993), *Saints and Their Miracles in Late Antique Gaul*, Princeton: Princeton University Press.

Van Ossel, P. (1992), *Etablissements ruraux de l'Antiquité tardive dans le nord de la Gaule* (Gallia Suppl. 51), Paris: CNRS.

Van Ossel, P. & Ouzoulias, P. (2000), 'Rural Settlement Economy in Northern Gaul in the Late Empire: An Overview and Assessment', *Journal of Roman Archaeology*, 13: 133–60.

Velay, P. (1992), *From Lutetia to Paris. The Island and the Two Banks*, Paris: CNRS.

Visy, Zs. (2001), 'Towns, Vici and Villae: Late Roman Military Society on the Frontiers of the Province Valeria', in T.S. Burns & J.W. Eadie (eds), *Urban Centers and Rural Contexts in Late Antiquity*, East Lansing: Michigan State University Press, 163–84.

Visy, Zs. (ed.) (2003), *Hungarian Archaeology at the Turn of the Millennium*, Budapest: Department of Monuments of the Ministry of National Cultural Heritage.

Visy, Zs. (ed.) (2005), *Limes XIX. Proceedings of the XIXth International Congress of Roman Frontier Studies (Pécs, Hungary, September 2003)*, Pécs: University of Pécs.

Volpe, G. (ed.) (1998), *San Giusto. La villa, le ecclesiae. Primi risultati dagli scavi nel sito rurale di San Giusto. (Lucera): 1995–1997*, Bari: Edipuglia.

Volpe, G. & Turchiano, M. (eds) (2005), *Paesaggi e insediamenti rurali in Italia meridionale fra Tardoantico e Altomedievo (Atti del Primo Seminario sul Tardoantico e l'Altomedievo in Italia meridionale, Foggia 12–14 Febbraio 2004)*, Bari: Edipuglia.

Von Carnap-Bornheim, C. & Ilkjær, J. (2000), 'Römische Militaria aus der jüngere römischen Kaiserzeit in Norwegen – "Export" römischer *negotiatores* oder "Import" germanischer *principes*?' *Münstersche Beiträge zur antiken Handelsgeschichte*, xix(2): 40–61.

Wacher, J. (1995), *The Towns of Roman Britain* (2nd edition), London: Batsford.

Waldherr, G. (1992), *Castra Regina – Regensburg. From Roman Legionary Fortress to the Seat of the Dukes of Bavaria*. Leicester: Department of History, University of Leicester.

Walmsley, A. (1996), 'Byzantine Palestine and Arabia: Urban Prosperity in Late Antiquity', in N. Christie & S.T. Loseby (eds), *Towns in Transition. Urban Evolution in Late Antiquity and the Early Middle Ages*, Aldershot: Scolar, 126–58.

Ward-Perkins, B. (1984), *From Classical Antiquity to the Middle Ages. Urban Public Building in Northern and Central Italy, AD 300–850*, Oxford: Clarendon Press.

Ward-Perkins, B. (1988), 'The Towns of Northern Italy: Rebirth or Renewal?', in R. Hodges & B. Hobley (eds), *The Rebirth of Towns in the West, AD 700–1050* (CBA Research Report 68), London: Council for British Archaeology, 16–27.

Ward-Perkins, B. (1996), 'Urban Continuity?', in N. Christie & S.T. Loseby (eds), *Towns in Transition. Urban Evolution in Late Antiquity and the Early Middle Ages*, Aldershot: Scolar, 4–17.

Ward-Perkins, B. (1997), 'Continuists, Catastrophists, and the Towns of Post-Roman Northern Italy?' *Papers of the British School at Rome*, lxv: 157–76.

Ward-Perkins, B. (1998), 'The Cities', in A. Cameron & P. Garnsey (eds), *The Cambridge Ancient History. Volume XIII. The Late Empire, AD 337–425*, Cambridge & New York: Cambridge University Press, 371–410.

Ward-Perkins, B. (2000a), 'Constantinople: A City and Its Ideological Territory', in G.P. Brogiolo, N. Gauthier & N. Christie (eds), *Towns and Their Territories between Late Antiquity and the Early Middle Ages* (ESF Transformation of the Roman World, 9), Leiden & New York: Brill, 325–45.

Ward-Perkins, B. (2000b), 'Land, Labour and Settlement', in A. Cameron, B. Ward-Perkins & M. Whitby (eds), *The Cambridge Ancient History. Volume XIV. Late Antiquity: Empire and Successors, AD 425–600*, Cambridge & New York: Cambridge University Press, 315–44.

Ward-Perkins, B. (2000c), 'Specialized Production and Exchange', in A. Cameron, B. Ward-Perkins & M. Whitby (eds), *The Cambridge Ancient History. Volume XIV. Late Antiquity: Empire and Successors, AD 425–600*, Cambridge & New York: Cambridge University Press, 346–91.

Ward-Perkins, B. (2001), 'Specialisation, Trade, and Prosperity: An Overview of the Economy of the Late Antique Eastern Mediterranean', in S. Kingsley & K. Decker (eds), *Economy and Exchange in the East Mediterranean during Late Antiquity. Proceedings of a Conference at Somerville College, Oxford, 29th May, 1999*, Oxford: Oxbow, 167–78.

Ward-Perkins, B. (2005), *The Fall of Rome and the End of Civilization*, Oxford & New York: Oxford University Press.

Ward-Perkins, J.B. & Gibson, S. (1987), 'The "Market Theatre" Complex and Associated Structures, Cyrene', *Libyan Studies*, 18: 43–72.

Watson, A. (1999), *Aurelian and the Third Century*, London & New York: Routledge.

Watson, B. (ed.) (1998), *Roman London. Recent Archaeological Work* (Journal of Roman Archaeology Supplementary Series Number 24), Portsmouth, RI: Journal of Roman Archaeology.

Gallien in der Spätantike. Von Kaiser Constantin zu Frankenkönig Childerich (exhibition catalogue, Römisch-Germanisches Zentralmuseum, 1980–1981), Mainz: Philipp von Zabern.

Webster, L. & Brown, M. (eds) (1997), *The Transformation of the Roman World, AD 400–900*, London: European Science Foundation/British Museum Press.

Wells, P.S. (1999), *The Barbarians Speak. How the Conquered Peoples Shaped Roman Europe*, Princeton & Oxford: Princeton University Press.

Wells, P.S. (2009), *Barbarians to Angels. The Dark Ages Reconsidered*, London: W.W. Norton.

Welsby, D.A. (1982), *The Roman Military Defence of the British Provinces in Its Later Phases*, Oxford: British Archaeological Reports.

Wes, M.A. (1992), 'Crisis and Conversion in Fifth-Century Gaul: Aristocrats and Ascetics between "Horizontality" and Verticality', in J. Drinkwater & H. Elton (eds), *Fifth-Century Gaul: A Crisis of Identity?* Cambridge: Cambridge University Press, 252–63.

Whitby, M. (2000), 'The Army, c. 420–602', in A. Cameron, B. Ward-Perkins & M. Whitby (eds), *The Cambridge Ancient History. Volume XIV. Late Antiquity: Empire and Successors, AD 425–600*, Cambridge & New York: Cambridge University Press, 288–313.

Whitby, M. (2007), 'The Late Roman Army and the Defence of the Balkans', in A. Poulter (ed.), *The Transition to Late Antiquity on the Danube and Beyond* (Proceedings of the British Academy, Volume 141), London: British Academy, 135–61.

White, R. (2007), *Britannia Prima: Britain's Last Roman Province*, Stroud: Tempus.

White, R. & Barker, P. (1998), *Wroxeter. Life and Death of a Roman City*, Stroud: Tempus.

Whittaker, C.R. (1980), 'Inflation and the Economy in the Fourth Century AD', in C. King (ed.), *Imperial Revenue, Expenditure and Monetary Policy in the Fourth Century AD (The 5th Oxford Symposium in Coinage and Monetary History)* (British Archaeological Reports, International Series 76), Oxford: Tempus Reparatum, 1–22.

Whittaker, C.R. (1993), *Land, City and Trade in the Roman Empire* (Variorum Collected Studies 408), Aldershot: Ashgate.

Whittaker, C.R. (1994), *Frontiers of the Roman Empire*, Baltimore: Johns Hopkins University Press.

Whittaker, C.R. & Garnsey, P. (1998), 'Rural Life in the Later Roman Empire', in A. Cameron & P. Garnsey (eds), *The Cambridge Ancient History. Volume XIII. The Late Empire, AD 337–425*, Cambridge & New York: Cambridge University Press, 277–310.

Whittow, M. (2001), 'Recent Research on the Late-Antique City in Asia Minor: The Second Half of the 6th *c*. Revisited', in L. Lavan (ed.), *Recent Research in Late-Antique Urbanism* (Journal of Roman Archaeology Supplementary Series No. 42), Ann Arbor: Journal of Roman Archaeology, 137–53.

Wickham, C. (1998), 'Overview: Production, Distribution and Demand', in R. Hodges & B. Hobley (eds), *The Rebirth of Towns in the West, AD 700–1050* (CBA Research Report 68), London: Council for British Archaeology, 279–92.

Wickham, C. (2006), *Framing the Early Middle Ages. Europe and the Mediterranean, 400–800*, Oxford & New York: Oxford University Press.

Wickham, C. & Hansen, I. (eds) (2000), *The Long Eighth Century* (ESF Transformation of the Roman World, 10), Leiden & New York: Brill.

Wiedemann, T. (1992), *Emperors and Gladiators*, London & New York: Routledge.

Wigg, A. (1999), 'Confrontation and Interaction: Celts, Germans and Romans in the Central German Highlands', in J.D. Creighton & R.J.A. Wilson (eds), *Roman Germany. Studies in Cultural Interaction* (Journal of Roman Archaeology Supplementary Series No. 32), Portsmouth, RI: Journal of Roman Archaeology, 35–53.

Wightman, E. (1985), *Gallia Belgica*, London: Batsford.

Wilkes, J. (1993), *Diocletian's Palace, Split: Residence of a Retired Roman Emperor* (Ian Sanders Memorial Fund, Occasional Publication 1), Exeter: Short Run Press.

Williams, S. (1985), *Diocletian and the Roman Recovery*, London: Batsford.

Williams, S. & Friell, G. (1994), *Theodosius. The Empire at Bay*, London: Batsford.

Wilmott, T. (2007), *The Roman Amphitheatre in Britain*, Stroud: The History Press.

Wilmott, T. (ed.) (2009), *Roman Amphitheatres and Spectacula. A 21st Century Perspective* (British Archeological Reports, International Series 1946), Oxford: English Heritage/Chester Museum/Archaeopress.

Wilmott, T. (2010), 'The Late Roman Frontier: A Structural Background', in R. Collins & L. Allason-Jones (eds), *Finds from the Frontier. Material Culture in the 4th–5th Centuries* (CBA Research Report 162), York: Council for British Archaeology, 10–16.

Wilmott, T. & Garner, D. (2009), 'Excavations on the Legionary Amphitheatres of Chester (Deva), Britain', in T. Wilmott (ed.), *Roman Amphitheatres and Spectacula. A 21st Century Perspective* (British Archeological Reports, International Series 1946), Oxford: English Heritage/Chester Museum/Archaeopress, 63–74.

Wilmott, T., with Hird, L., Izard, K. & Summerfield, J. (1997), *Birdoswald. Excavations of a Roman Fort on Hadrian's Wall and Its Successor Settlements: 1987–92* (English Heritage Archaeological Report 14), London: English Heritage.

Wilson, A. (2000), 'The Water-Mills on the Janiculum', *Memoirs of the American Academy in Rome*, 45: 219–46.

Wilson, P. (ed.) (2002), *Cataractonium: Roman Catterick and Its Hinterland. Parts I and II* (Council for British Archaeology Research Reports 128, 129), York: Council for British Archeology.

Winkler, M.M. (ed.) (2009), *The Fall of the Roman Empire. Film and History*, Bognor Regis: Wiley-Blackwell.

Wirth, G. (1997), 'Rome and its Germanic Partners in the Fourth Century', in W. Pohl (ed.), *Kingdoms of the Empire. The Integration of Barbarians in Late Antiquity* (The Transformation of the Roman World, Volume 1), Leiden, Boston & Cologne: European Science Foundation/Brill, 13–55.

Witschel, C. (2004), 'Re-evaluating the Roman West in the 3rd *c*. AD', *Journal of Roman Archaeology*, 17: 251–77.

Wolfram, H. (1988), *History of the Goths* (rev. ed., translated by T. Dunlap from German original of 1979). Berkeley, Los Angeles & London: University of California Press.

Wood, I.N. (1992), 'Continuity or Calamity: The Constraints of Literary Models', in
J. Drinkwater & H. Elton (eds), *Fifth-Century Gaul: A Crisis of Identity?* Cambridge:
Cambridge University Press, 9–18.

Wood, I.N. (1998), 'The Barbarian Invasions and First Settlements', in A. Cameron &
P. Garnsey (eds), *The Cambridge Ancient History. Volume XIII. The Late Empire,* AD
337–425, Cambridge & New York: Cambridge University Press, 516–37.

Wood, I.N. (2000), 'The North-Western Provinces', in A. Cameron, B. Ward-Perkins &
M. Whitby (eds), *The Cambridge Ancient History. Volume XIV. Late Antiquity: Empire and
Successors,* AD *425–600*, Cambridge & New York: Cambridge University Press, 497–523.

Wood, I.N. (2008), 'The Burgundians', in J.-J. Aillagon (ed.), *Rome and the Barbarians. The
Birth of a New World* (exhibition catalogue – Venice-Bonn-Rome), Milan: Palazzo
Grassi/Skira Editore, 337–9.

Woolf, G. (1998), *Becoming Roman: The Origins of Provincial Administration in Gaul,*
Cambridge & New York: Cambridge University Press.

Yon, Y.-B. (2001), 'Euergetism and Urbanism in Palmyra', in L. Lavan (ed.), *Recent Research
in Late-Antique Urbanism* (Journal of Roman Archaeology Supplementary Series
No. 42), Ann Arbor: Journal of Roman Archaeology, 173–81.

Young, B.K. (2001), 'Autun and the Civitas Aeduorum: Maintaining and Transforming a
Regional Identity in Late Antiquity', in T.S. Burns & J.W. Eadie (eds), *Urban Centers and
Rural Contexts in Late Antiquity*, East Lansing: Michigan State University Press, 25–46.

Zahariade, M. (1997), 'Strategy and Tactic in Roman Dacia', in W. Groenman-van
Waateringe, B.L. Van Beek, W.J.H. Willems & S. Wynia (eds), *Roman Frontier Studies
1995. Proceedings of the XVIth International Congress of Roman Frontier Studies* (Oxbow
Monograph 91), Oxford: Oxbow, 603–8.

Zajac, N. (1999), 'The *Thermae*: A Policy of Public Health or Personal Legitimation?', in
J. DeLaine & D.E. Johnston (eds), *Roman Baths and Bathing. Proceedings of the First
International Conference on Roman Baths (Bath, 30 March–4 April 1992)* (Journal of
Roman Archaeology Supplementary Series No. 37), Portsmouth, RI: Journal of Roman
Archaeology, 99–105.

Zanini, E. (1994), *Introduzione all'archeologia bizantina*, Rome: Nuova Italia Scientifica.

Zanini, E. (1998), *Le Italie bizantine. Territorio, insediamenti ed economia nella provincia
bizantina d'Italia (VI–VIII secolo)*, Bari: Edipuglia.

Zanker, P. (1988), *The Power of Images in the Age of Augustus*, Ann Arbor: University of
Michigan Press.

Zavagno, L. (2009), *Cities in Transition: Urbanism in Byzantium between Late Antiquity and
the Early Middle Ages (*AD *500–900)* (British Archaeological Reports, International Series
S2030), Oxford: Archaeopress.

Župančič, M. (2002), 'Kann die Verschiebung der römischen Truppen vom Rheinland nach
Norditalien in den Jahren 401/402 archäologisch bezeugt werden?', in M. Buora (ed.),
*Miles Romanus dal Po al Danubio nel Tardoantico (Atti del Convegno Internazionale,
Pordenone – Concordia Sagittaria, 17–19 Marzo 2000)*, Pordenone: Sage Print, 231–42.

Index

Index

Index

Index

Lightning Source UK Ltd.
Milton Keynes UK
UKHW020141300321
381228UK00004B/44